MW00772307

ARMS AND THE WOMAN

Classical Tradition and Women Writers in the Venetian Renaissance

FRANCESCA D'ALESSANDRO BEHR

THE OHIO STATE UNIVERSITY PRESS

COLUMBUS

Copyright © 2018 by The Ohio State University.
All rights reserved.

Library of Congress Cataloging-in-Publication Data
Names: D'Alessandro Behr, Francesca, author.
Title: Arms and the woman : classical tradition and women writers in the Venetian
    Renaissance / Francesca D'Alessandro Behr.
Other titles: Classical memories/modern identities.
Description: Columbus : The Ohio State University Press, [2018] | Series: Classical
    memories/modern identities | Includes bibliographical references and index.
Identifiers: LCCN 2017058977| ISBN 9780814213711 (cloth ; alk. paper) | ISBN 0814213715
    (cloth ; alk. paper)
Subjects: LCSH: Italian literature—Women authors—History and criticism. | Women and
    literature—Italy—History—16th century. | Women and literature—Italy—History—17th
    century. | Women—Italy—Venice—History—16th century. | Women—Italy—Venice—
    History—17th century. | Women—Italy—Venice—Social conditions—16th century. |
    Women—Italy—Venice—Social conditions—17th century. | Fonte, Moderata, 1555–
    1592—Criticism and interpretation. | Marinella, Lucrezia, 1571–1653—Criticism and
    interpretation.
Classification: LCC PQ4063 .D35 2018 | DDC 850.9/9287094531—dc23
LC record available at https://lccn.loc.gov/2017058977

Cover design by Janna Thompson-Chordas
Text design by Juliet Williams
Type set in Adobe Minion Pro

♾ The paper used in this publication meets the minimum requirements of the American
National Standard for Information Sciences—Permanence of Paper for Printed Library
Materials. ANSI Z39.48-1992.

A Chiara, pars alia mei

CONTENTS

~

ACKNOWLEDGMENTS

IF MY ATTRACTION to ancient epic was kindled from the very early years of my life when my mom and dad gave me a narrative version of the *Aeneid* as a gift, my interest in Renaissance romance epics written by women was sparked by Valeria Finucci's article on Moderata Fonte dating back to 1994. Eventually my interest in women's production of epic was nourished during a 2003 NEH Summer Institute titled "A Literature of Their Own? Women Writing: Venice, London, Paris, 1550–1700" (Chapel Hill, NC), organized by Dr. Albert Rabil and lead, for the Italian section, by Virginia Cox and Anne J. Schutte. The writing of this book allowed me to join these two passions together.

My research for this monograph has been made possible thanks to several grants obtained from my institution, the University of Houston, including a Faculty Development Grant (2001), a Women Studies Summer Grant (2004), a Small Grant (2012), and a Sabbatical Leave (Spring 2013). I am very grateful to all of those in my college who have believed in this project and supported me with the means to make it possible. I would also like to express my gratitude to the Giorgio Cini Foundation for the Residential Scholarship during the Summer of 2012 that enabled my serene sojourn at the Centro Vittore Branca on the island of San Giorgio Maggiore in Venice.

During the many years spent working on this book, I have also enjoyed the intellectual support, advice, and encouragement of many colleagues, relatives, and friends. They know who they are, and I owe a lot to all of them.

A heartfelt thanks goes to Series Editors Richard Armstrong and Paul Allen Miller, as well as to OSUP Editors, Tara Cyphers, Lindsay Martin, and Eugene O'Connor; above all, to Eugene, who demonstrated enthusiasm for the topic at an early stage and later on chose excellent blind readers to review my manuscript. Gratitude is also owed to Wolfgang Haase, former editor of the *International Journal of the Classical Tradition,* who read my reflections on the ending of the *Floridoro* and encouraged me to develop them.

Of course, the present volume could not have become a reality without the constant support of my family both in the United States (my treasured Tom, Gervin, and John-Paul) and in Italy (all my beloved Italian relatives).

Since this book has been written to be accessible to experts as well as nonexperts, it contains English translations of Italian, Latin, and Greek. For *Enrico, Nobiltà,* and *Merito*—the texts that I explore in more detail together with the *Floridoro*—I acknowledge that I have employed published translations (Marinella 2009; Marinella 1999; Fonte 1997); however, my use of them is minimal enough in proportion to the whole in order to count as fair use.

INTRODUCTION

AS A WOMAN of the late Renaissance, the Venetian Moderata Fonte was not allowed to attend school, but Niccolò Doglioni, her principal biographer, recounts how she demanded that her brother share his grammar books and explain what he learned at school.[1] His lectures made a strong impression on the girl, who eventually began to study independently. Soon she could read and even compose in Latin.

This anecdote inspired my research, whose goal is to reveal the intellectual empowerment that knowledge of the classical tradition (Greek and Roman literature) granted women during the Early Modern Age.[2] A good education,

---

1. "When her brother came home from school (he was at grammar school by this stage), little Modesta would come up and pester him to show her and explain to her what he had been taught that day; and she would so fervently impress what he said on her memory that she retained a great deal more of what he had learned than he himself did. And she threw herself into the study of letters that with the help of the grammar books she read and committed to memory and Saraceni's arpicordo (harpsichord), she could soon read any Latin book very fluently and could even write fairly well in Latin" (Fonte 1997: 34–35). Moderata Fonte is the self-chosen pseudonym of Modesta da Pozzo. In her edition of *Il merito,* Virginia Cox observes about the harpsichord that although generally considered an instrument, it is here a kind of language-learning aid; what this *arpicordo* really is and how it works remains obscure. Another instance of secondhand learning (through that of her brothers) is documented by Stevenson 2005: 309 for Martha Marchina (1600–42).

2. I use the term *Renaissance* with reference to the period of time between 1300 and 1650 in Europe that was typified by a cultural rebirth related to the rediscovery of the classics and that fostered ideals of human excellence in several fields (e.g. fine arts, literature, philosophy,

which in those days coincided with reading the classics, gave women a con-textualized and relativist perspective about their society, its configuration, and agendas. These women employed canonical texts normally used to reinforce their inferiority and the status quo to opposite ends, namely, the establishment of their own worth as women. They envisioned societies structured according to ethics different from those of their societies.

Women's lives in Renaissance Italy were predictable: they were expected to produce and raise children (preferably males). Few were offered the chance to study, and those who were would be schooled at home with their broth-ers' tutors. In his famous study of the Italian Renaissance, Jacob Burckhardt was struck by the seeming abundance of brilliant women during the period, in which he believed that the Italian intellectual arena was open to women on the same terms as to men.[3] Recent scholars have been more careful in assessing the situation, noting that this phenomenon was more apparent than real. New studies on women and education during the Early Modern Age emphasize the general decline in opportunities for women as compared to men; the greater effect of family, class, and city on women's education; the small number of women who actually received an education along humanist lines; and the obstacles such women encountered.[4] For instance, in the Quat-trocento, the female humanists Isotta Nogarola, Cassandra Fedele, and Laura Cereta devoted their lives to study, but despite their intellect—or because of it—they were criticized and pressured to marry or enter convents. Marriage and motherhood were considered antithetical to scholarly pursuits, proper only for men. Nogarola and Fedele could choose this latter option only when

---

civic humanism). I also refer to aspects of the age and of the thinking of the subjects of this study, relative to political, social, economical, technological, scientific, and religious phenom-ena that reveal less obvious patterns of progressive transformation, and that are distinct from, if not entirely disconnected from, humanist inspiration. These aspects of the study are properly considered phenomena in the development of Early Modern Europe. Therefore in this book I use both terms (Renaissance and Early Modern), given that the nature of my argument is poised between historicist and presentist interests. On the one hand, I highlight texts and ideas which anticipate modernity and postmodernity; on the other, I focus on the reception of Classi-cal learning as the cultural matrix underlying developments of human discovery, self-discovery, and empowerment. For this problematic issue, see Dubrow 1994: 1025–26; Marcus 1992; Muir 1995, esp. 1090–110; King 2003: viii–xiii; Starn 2007. Concerning *presentism*, see *Past and Pres-ent* 234.1 (2017), which is dedicated to the topic in general.

3. "To understand the higher forms of social intercourse at this period, we must keep before our minds the fact that women stood on a footing of perfect equality with men" (Bur-khardt 1878: 396). *Die Kultur der Renaissance in Italien* appeared in 1860 and was translated into English in 1878.

4. The trend began with Joan Kelly's famous article "Did Women Have a Renaissance?" (Kelly 1977: 137–64) and scholars still debate the issue of women's status during the Renaissance. The scholarship on the topic is vast: see King 1991; Cox 2008: xiff.; Gibson 1989; Herlihy 1995: 33–57; Hurlburt 2007.

widowed and free to return to their studies. Even the Venetian Elena Lucrezia Cornaro Piscopia, who lived two centuries later and acquired a university
degree in philosophy, became a Benedictine oblate and lived her life at home
as if she were in a monastery.[5] Venetian society was basically misogynistic,
and no matter how much power women gained from conspicuous dowries,
the institutional and political framework of Venice did not allow them positions of authority or any real power.[6] Even their ability to study and learn was
limited. The Venetian Arcangela Tarabotti (1604–52) decries women's inability
to attain university degrees. Women's erudition was generally viewed by men
at the time with some skepticism.

Renaissance treatises about instruction show a strongly gendered understanding of education as they attempt to reconcile women's education with
conventional norms of stereotypical sexual behavior, emphasizing chastity,
silence, and obedience for women, and courageous and active virtue for men.
While most authors agreed about the innate inferiority of girls' minds, they
usually concluded that at least some girls were as intelligent and capable as
boys; all the same, gender bias occurred in almost every aspect of Renaissance education. Silvio Antoniano, whose pedagogical treatise *De Christi-
ana puerorum educatione* (*On the Christian Education of Children*, 1583) was
often reprinted, objected to women knowing "how to 'orate or write poetry'
or learning languages, not seeing the advantage that would be derived from
this for the common good or for the girls themselves."[7] Learning for girls was
not deemed important and was accepted primarily as a way to stabilize their
characters.[8] Because of this, the range of authors recommended for girls was
narrow, regularly excluding the pagan classics.

During the Renaissance, key disciplines of humanistic studies such as
rhetoric, history, poetry, and moral philosophy were considered fundamental for boys destined to become lawyers, politicians, clerks, or physicians, all
needing to be persuasive in the public sphere. For them, education was still
largely conceived of as the study of classical authors, essential for developing dialectical skills and eloquence. After learning basic grammar, students
were exposed to rhetoric through Cicero; to history through Caesar, Valerius
Maximus, or Sallust; and to poetry through Virgil.[9] The humanistic curricu-

---

5. See Maschietto 2007: 109; Stevenson 2005: 159–65.

6. For the economy of Venice during the Late Renaissance and the anthropological repercussions of the substantial dowries required for women, see Chojnacki 2000: 169–85.

7. Maschietto 2007: 45.

8. In line with biblical teaching as well as Aristotelian and Galenic conceptions of the
body and the mind, women were understood as more irrational and physically and morally
weaker than men: see Allen 2002: 65–103; Jordan 1990: 2934; Maclean 1980: 28–46.

9. Kallendorf 1999: 24–25.

lum was founded on the *studia humanitatis,* or "grammar, rhetoric, history, poetry, and moral philosophy, based on the reading and interpretation of their standard ancient authors in Latin and, to a lesser extent, in Greek."[10] Attention was given to the style and moral content of the texts under study. The *studia humanitatis* fostered "humanity" conceived of as understanding, benevolence, or the capability to make proper moral choices, and as a more assertive faculty to shape the world through fortitude, prudence, eloquence, and love of honor. The stress on virtuous and effective action as the principal goal of learning remained a founding principle of humanism. In adherence to Greco-Roman *vir-tus* ("manliness")—a distinctively male attitude essential for the battlefield or in court—Renaissance virtue was primarily connected to men operating in the public field. Consequently, women, destined to remain at home, were excluded from this curriculum.[11] Virtue for them was posited mainly as chastity, marital obedience, care of the family, and religious piety. Leonardo Bruni in his *De studiis et litteris (On Studies and Letters,* 1412–15) seems to have disapproved of women studying rhetoric, because he saw it as transgressing the social-ethical norms that reserved the public virtue of eloquence for men.[12] In his book *De institutione feminae Christianae (On the Education of a Christian Woman,* 1523) Juan Luis Vives, an influential educational theorist of the sixteenth century, recommended the study of Latin grammar and style for girls, but he also made clear that rhetoric was to be omitted because women should not be allowed to work outside the home.[13] Even the enlightened Erasmus, although impressed by the erudition of Thomas More's daughters, could not

---

10. Kristeller 1961: 10; in general, see also Garin 1958: 306–433, 473–503. For the importance of Latin in higher education, see Grendler 2002.

11. Gray 1963: 497–514. Allen 2002: 761–1037 explores the topic of women's education.

12. Gibson 1989: 12 and contra Cox 2009: 47–75. Sider 2005: 272 notes that, although discouraging the study of rhetoric for women, Bruni does outline a comprehensive program of classical readings for them. But classical authors had to remain subordinate to their philosophical and religious training. Holt Parker points out how challenging the act of writing was for Early Modern women: "while the role of reading poetry is at best problematic for women, writing poetry has no role at all. As a public act, it is unsuitable; as a private act, unnecessary" (quoted in Gold et al. 1997: 250). For the schooling of boys and girls in Venice, see Martelli 2011: 159–60. A good introduction to the topic of women humanists and the difficulties they encountered in publishing is that of Robin in Cereta 1997: 7–8.

13. Friedman 1985: 63, quoting Vives's text: "For it neither becometh a woman to rule a school, nor to live amongst men, nor speak abroad, and shake off her demureness and honesty, either all together, or else a great part; which if she be good, it were better to be at home within and unknown to other folks, and in company to hold her tongue demurely, and let few see her, and none at all hear her."

see any practical reason "to construct a system of education for women when no purpose for it existed."[14]

Greek and Latin were essential for approaching the classics, but the practical way in which boys acquired knowledge of such languages made women's access to them improbable, since it entailed detachment from the family and a kind of resocialization. Aristocratic boys at first spoke the vernacular (the language spoken by their mothers and wet-nurses), but eventually they were encouraged, perhaps even forced, to abandon their mother tongue in favor of Latin, the language of educated men. Early in their lives, boys transitioned from tutors to formal schooling, and they were forbidden to speak in the vernacular while at school.[15] In his 1971 book *Rhetoric, Romance and Technology: Studies in the Interaction of Expression and Culture*, Walter J. Ong notes how formalized language education during the Renaissance bore strong resemblances to puberty rites in other cultures.[16] He reflects on how such rites provided a special marginal environment in which the initiate broke with his past, often by undergoing an ordeal or accomplishing difficult tasks. Special sets of rules might be in force while other excesses were tolerated; in this peculiar atmosphere, the initiate became receptive to the imparted message. Ong believes that these conditions were at work in the gender- and language-based segregation of the schools of the Renaissance, where boys were brought up basically outside the family. The male child "came to adult stature seeing himself as a member of a linguistic, intellectual and social elite dedicated to preserving the heritage of Antiquity, guarding it from corruption and entrusting it to the future."[17] Higher education, anthropologically speaking, ensured that members of the elite shared the same cultural background. Within this rigidly dichotomized social, educational, and linguistic order, there was no place for

---

14. Jordan 1990: 56–64, outlining Erasmus's complex position toward women, considered the spiritual equal of men but also a husband's political subordinate and natural inferior. See also Sowards 1982: 87; Woodward 1904: 150. There were exceptions to the general rule of women's exclusion from education (e.g., men's wish to showcase them, their improved ability to teach their children, etc.), but the decision squarely belonged to their fathers: see Stevenson 2005: 152–53.

15. For women's education in the Renaissance, see Gibson 1989, and, about education in general in the Renaissance, see Grendler 1991. For the situation in Venice, see especially Grendler 1991: 42–71 and 2013: 675–99.

16. Ong 2012: 13–141. The book gathers Ong's essays written over twenty-one years, including "Latin Language Study as Renaissance Puberty Rite," first published in *Studies in Philology* 56 (1959): 103–24. On the influence of Ong on current scholarship, see Harteley's introduction "Before Ongism" in Ong 2002. Harteley states: "Ong popularised the idea that knowledge is a product of language, and that the medium in which language is communicated by—voice, writing, print—makes us think along certain path-dependent lines . . . thus Ongism is the place where mind is determined by medium" (xiv).

17. Gibson 1989: 16; Stevenson 2005: 410–28.

women who were schooled at home and in the vernacular. The few women skilled in classical languages were viewed with suspicion even when praised; they were not fully accepted but rather tolerated, deemed intruders in a field considered unpractical and dangerous to their souls.[18] If a cultural accommodation for learned women ultimately occurred in Europe, it was controlled by men and favored men's interests.[19]

Although humanism was socially conservative, it was essential to the development of critical thinking and the reassessment of all given assumptions, even its own. *Litterae* (learning and education) provided the means to broaden the individual's personality beyond the distinctiveness of a situation; through learning, self-experience was related to the most significant experiences of the history of humankind.[20] The study of the classics became a powerful tool for men and women searching for alternative ways to frame the social order. Humanistic training was not an empty study of classical authors and grammar; rather, it fostered the systematic analysis of history, society, and a realist view of phenomena based on careful observation. Humanistic education with its emphasis on practical decision-making appeared better suited to the human condition than training in theoretical and speculative matters. It also developed one's ability to persuade others and effectiveness in the public arena. Both scholastic and humanistic thought criticized authority, but while the scholastics did so through the logical analysis of individual statements, the humanists did it by trying to comprehend the individual circumstances of the author. To the humanist mind, truth appeared particular, conditioned, and limited.[21] For instance, the humanists' understanding of how languages and texts evolve over time made some of them profoundly aware of the contingency of history and the role of human intervention in cultural constructions.[22]

---

18. Bulckaert 2010: 19–20, quoting Ann Kingsmill's poem: "Did I my lines intend for public view / how many censures, wou'd their faults pursue . . . / Alas! A woman that attempts the pen / such an intruder on the rights of men." Sometimes women were accused of plagiarism: see Stevenson 2005: 159.

19. Stevenson 2005: 409–28 highlights what she calls "the principle of limitation," that women were dependent on the goodwill of men of the ruling elite and families who gave them the "essential tools of 'manhood,'" convinced that this held no revolutionary menace whatsoever" (411). Biagioli 1993: 84 points out how even modern universities were not neutral machines for the dispensation of knowledge but rather devices to reproduce social hierarchies; even when women demonstrated their intellectual faculties outside of universities, universities remained closed to them.

20. Zanardi 2011: 485.

21. Nauert 2006: 20. For the destabilizing force of humanism, see Bouwsma 2000; Fubini 2003; Hankins 2006: 118–41; Jurdjevic 2007: 246.

22. Waswo 1987.

This aspect of the humanistic training is essential for understanding the women authors analyzed in this book because intellectual relativism—the ability to evaluate circumstances and apply principles to specific contexts—characterizes their view of women. For example, Lucrezia Marinella's sensitivity to circumstances is evident in her treatise *La nobiltà et eccellenza delle donne, co' difetti e mancamenti de gli uomini* (*The Nobility and Excellence of Women with the Defects and Vices of Men*, 1600), where Aristotle, a classical author who exhibited cultural bias against women, is first criticized and then employed to bolster and prove women's worth.[23] Marinella made ample use of intellectual resources from her classical training. In 1599, the controversy about the worth of women was rekindled by the publication of Giuseppe Passi's *I donneschi difetti* (*The Defects of Women*). Passi used classical and religious texts to undermine women's value, intelligence, and ability.[24] Marinella defended women, realizing that ancient sources did not agree about their worth. While Aristotle blamed women, Plato, Lycurgus, and many honored writers "praised them to the skies, putting the malicious to shame."[25] She also noticed that women were regarded in different ways in different countries,[26] capitalizing on observed discrepancies and redeploying some of the texts used by Passi to prove him wrong.

Marinella displayed extraordinary scholarship by the standards of her day, particularly with respect to the many sources cited, often with greater accuracy than her contemporaries. The philological precision she demonstrates in the *Nobiltà* proves not only that she had access to the texts but also that she understood the importance of an accurate and careful presentation of an author's claims. She criticizes issues through extensive citations, which she eventually reinterprets for her own purposes. Marinella often quotes the same author as both an authority in support of her arguments and a target. The effect of this technique is to undermine or relativize the authority of that source. This aspect of her methodology distinguishes her from other pro-woman writers of her century and can be defined as inherently humanistic.[27] Fonte, although probably reading the classical canon in translation, was similarly a formidable interpreter of it. Ultimately, their exposure to the classics

23. Conti Odorisio 1979: 63 links Venice's bias toward women to Aristotle.
24. Kolsky 2001: 973–89.
25. Marinella 1999: 74. Marinella's *Nobiltà* was a response to *The Defects of Women*. In it Passi revealed contempt for all women, considered inferior beings in absolute need of men's control. He also ridiculed eloquent women, repeating Pericles's famous dictum (*Thuc.* 2.45.2) that silence is a woman's best ornament (Passi 1618: 204).
26. Marinella 1999: 74.
27. Ross 2009: 289*ff.*; Deslauriers 2012.

was an essential tool to criticize Renaissance society's shortcomings in general and prejudices against women in particular.

VIRGIL AND THE VENETO

The role of Virgil's work—especially his *Aeneid*—in Venice is central to this study. Judging from its many reprints and copies present in Italy during the Renaissance, we can assess that the *Aeneid* was a key text in the peninsula and particularly in the Venetian environment. Craig Kallendorf has examined 251 copies of Virgil's poetry (including commentaries and translations) published in the region between 1469 and 1600 and has discussed how a specifically Venetian community of readers received Virgilian themes.[28] As Kallendorf points out, Virgil was the most studied classical author in the Veneto, and Venice was responsible for one-third to one-half of all books published in Italy during this period, making a good case for the centrality of the Virgilian text to Venetian culture. The moral values epitomized by Virgil's hero Aeneas were of special interest to the Venetians, who shared with the Romans the idea of creating a just social order and viewed themselves as true descendants of the Romans. Kallendorf compellingly argues that Virgilian themes reinforced Venetian moral and religious values, and Venetians welcomed Virgil as a positive ideological influence supporting "the myth of Venice," centered on the notion of the allegedly unique social and political stability of that "most serene" city ("La Serenissima").

Over the course of several centuries, Venice crafted a portrait of itself that responded to and capitalized on specific historical circumstances, such as its victory over Constantinople (1204) during the Fourth Crusade, its triumph over its main maritime antagonist Genoa in 1380, its resilience against the League of Cambrai (a compact of European powers formed in 1508 and committed to the weakening of the expanding Republic), and even its resistance to papal power (culminating in the interdicts of 1508 and 1606).[29] Venice attributed its success to internal political stability based on a balanced constitution and a ruling patriciate selflessly devoted to the commonwealth. This idealized image presented Venetians as the true inheritors of the Roman Republic. They liked to believe that, thanks to their civic virtue, God continuously granted them his favor. Already in the twelfth-century *Origo civitatum Italiae seu*

---

28. Kallendorf 1999. Renaissance material culture confirms the popularity of the *Aeneid*, whose characters and themes are used in the decoration of *cassoni*, chests built in pairs commissioned by parents for their betrothed children: see Franklin 2014.

29. Rosand 2001: 1–3.

Venetiarum (also known as *Chronicon Altinate et Chronicon Gradense*), the unidentified author explained that the name of Veneti or Eneti was derived from Aeneas since Venice was founded by Trojan exiles.[30] According to the myth, Venice "was the inheritor to ancient Rome, the culmination of a long historical process that led from the fall of Troy to the emergence of the Serenissima: the return of Ulysses to his homeland and Aeneas' marriage to Lavinia were interpreted as steps to the founding of the city."[31] Renaissance teachers, readers, and commentators unceasingly pointed out that Venice was the new Rome, and Aeneas's behavior (in the *Aeneid*) was deemed exemplary for the shaping of good Venetian citizens. In the Veneto area as well as the rest of Italy, through the study of rhetoric, dialectic, and texts like the *Aeneid,* boys were encouraged to become assertive, competitive, persuasive, and good civil servants.[32]

But it soon became evident that classical texts could lend themselves to more than one interpretation. Renaissance readers became aware of conflicting views characterizing seminal classical works. Early on they noticed the modern phenomenon that Mikhail Bakhtin has called *heteroglossia,* the presence of competing perspectives within the same text.[33] As Kallendorf explains in *The Other Virgil*—a revisionist account of how some European and Transatlantic authors perceived, imitated, and used the *Aeneid* from the fourteenth through nineteenth centuries—this same *Aeneid* could also be read pessimistically and employed as a significant precedent for writers who wanted to express doubts and anxieties about the exercise of power, which utilizes violence and single-mindedly promotes certain values, views, and groups.[34] Each of the dissenting authors featured in Kallendorf's book interpreted or appropriated the *Aeneid* without flattering rulers or defending their imperial projects and pretensions; instead, they countered dominant paradigms with

---

30. Fortini-Brown 1996: 12–13.

31. Fortini-Brown 1996: esp. 30–33, 70–74; Kallendorf 1999: 26–27; Muir 1981: 65–74; Rosand 2007: 13.

32. Although at times the importance of classical literature has been exaggerated (e.g., Garin 1965), Hankins's 1990 reductionist approach is extreme. Gouwens 1998 is an excellent survey of scholarship on the importance of humanism.

33. The term *heteroglossia* (Russian *raznorecie*) was coined by Bakhtin 1981: 261 in the essay "Discourse in the Novel." Heteroglossia "represents the co-existence of socio-ideological contradictions between the present and the past, between differing epochs of the past, between different socio-ideological groups in the present, between tendencies, schools, circles, and so forth, all given a bodily form (DN 291)" (quoted in Vice 1997: 291). Heteroglossia can characterize all genres and types of oral or written discourse. Dialogism and polyphony are essential applications of *heteroglossia.* For bibliography on these separate but related topics, see Adlam and Shepherd 2000.

34. Kallendorf 2007: 35–50.

alternative ones. They used the *Aeneid* "as a way to envision a society that was different."[35]

Lucrezia Marinella and Moderata Fonte did the same: they employed the *Aeneid* and other canonical classical texts—normally used to reinforce women's inferiority and the status quo—to advertise their excellence and promote values not always appreciated by their societies. They recognized the intricate polyphony of the classics and pulled out of them the voices that best fit their agenda and sensibility. Negotiation with classical epics already visible in male-authored texts (e.g., those highlighted by Kallendorf) is also a hallmark of female-penned poems. Unfortunately, so far, Marinella and Fonte's literary production has been mostly analyzed within the Italian canon, ignoring the import of classical sources. Current criticism of the twenty-first century has not yet deemed their texts worthy of the type of *archeology* to which male-penned works have long been exposed. My study remedies this gap by unearthing in Marinelli and Fonte's epics echoes from Antiquity and references to seminal books from Greece and Rome. By reading the classics (particularly Virgil's *Aeneid* and Ovid's elegies), they gained a contextualized perspective about their society and its configuration, and by writing their own books, they intimated alternative values, ultimately striving to persuade their contemporaries to see the world in a different way. If on the one hand Marinella and Fonte were constrained by the Italian environment and the limitations described above, they on the other hand benefited from the rich Venetian cultural climate of the end of the Cinquecento, their connections to the Venetian literary circles (academies), and the knowledge of the classical works on the shelves of their fathers and brothers. The presence of writers like them allows us to understand that women in Venice fared better than in other cities because they profited from the open and varied cultural environment of a society characterized by the circulation of ancient texts, proud of its independence from the Holy See, and widely exposed to Northern influences and Eastern erudition. Venice was a large port city opened to foreign influence, where the printing industry thrived and certain groups and individuals fostered women's literary production, learning, and exposure to current cultural debates.[36] Although women's acquaintance with ancient sources was in large part dependent on the availability of translations (not many women could read in the original language), some acquired an excellent education, including familiarity with the classics.

---

35. Ibid., 14. See also Robin 1991.
36. Benedetti's introduction in Marinella 2012: 3–4. For a general overview of the Renaissance printing industry and Venetian monopoly, see Richardson 1999.

Like their male peers living in Venice, Marinella and Fonte read the *Aeneid*. Through a close textual engagement, I point out how much their romance epics—the *Floridoro* and the *Enrico*—utilized Virgil's masterpiece. There are at least three sections of the *Aeneid* that represent fundamental starting points for these writers' epic elaborations. They are the final duel between Turnus and Aeneas in Book 12, Aeneas's abandonment of Dido in Book 4, and his journey to the underworld in Book 6. While Fonte notices Aeneas's shortcomings in his final duel and criticizes them by developing a heroine who spares her antagonist, Marinella condemns her society and its systematic undermining of the woman's point of view by exploiting the power of the abandoned woman, whose archetype can be found in Virgil's Dido. Careful analysis of the many classical echoes of the abandoned Clelia and Areta in the *Enrico* reveals the importance of private desire in an epic whose stated purpose is to celebrate Venetian collective polity. As devout wives, Clelia and Areta's only choice is the acceptance of their husbands' decision to depart for war. But their lamenting of that decision suggests not only independent volition but also criticism of ethics prioritizing battle honor over family welfare. Marinella carefully elaborates Aeneas's conundrum during his dalliance with Dido: fulfillment of private desire versus completion of a political career. Besides paying close attention to the moral and literary dynamics in *Aeneid* 4, Marinella seems also particularly attuned to Virgil's pessimistic voice and tragic style in Book 6, which she employs to undercut military triumphalism. In several passages, Marinella's subtle pessimism highlights the fragility of earthly accomplishments, especially those with human costs. Her decision to echo some of the gloomiest episodes of the *Aeneid* (e.g., Anchises's direct address to Marcellus in *Aeneid* 6 and Aeneas's lamentation over Pallas's dead body in *Aeneid* 11) or to glorify characters (e.g., Erina) who are devoted to peace and pastoral ideals can be framed as a strategy well suited to a pacifist agenda.

Often ancient epic tales are narratives about the naturalization of force or violence, described in such a way that they appear as natural phenomena.[37] This kind of operation is typical of epic, and yet our best specimens (e.g., the *Aeneid* or the *Iliad*) also contain their counter-song, minor tales woven into the macronarrative that resist the genre's glorification of war and patriarchal society.[38] The episodes I pursue in this analysis of Fonte and Marinella's heroic poems—as the epic genre is designated in the late Renaissance—reveal *truths* about their worlds that differ from those naturalized by their societies and the epic genre. These truths (such as women's ability to make valid ethical choices or the importance of peace) most of the time could only be alluded to by cit-

---

37. Wofford 1999: 244.
38. Ibid., 257. On laments as "anti-epic" components of epic poems, see Perkell 2008.

ing other texts. These softly spoken realizations, difficult to hear in the epic uproar, are essential clues of the complexity and innovative charge of their writings. Furthermore, in dealing with female writers of romance epics we must remember that they are interacting with a genre dominated by men, that their writings (and to a degree their entire existence as independent thinkers) are tied to benevolent men or open-minded cities ruled by men. Keeping this fact in mind, my reading will often be against the grain: it must be sensitive to what can be only indirectly expressed and assess "the rhetorical status of elliptic phenomena," or the meaning of silence.[39] A rhetoric built on silence is essential for writers like Fonte and Marinella, who cannot simply state what they think, but must have recourse to alternative, indirect means. Because women's "drama of rebellion" proceeds through engagement of the kind of ideological negotiation described above, often it must be modulated in compromises or silences apparent only to the perceptive reader.[40]

SEVENTEENTH-CENTURY VENICE AND WOMEN

Fonte and Marinella's literary output must be viewed in light of the complex cultural dynamics characterizing Venice during their lives. In the sixteenth century, Venice was still the scene for intense political, philosophical, and religious dialogue, although this debate may have only minimally contributed to the practical emancipation of women. At the beginning of the Cinquecento, the city's cultural vigor fostered the publication of many books, especially classical texts in the original Greek and Latin, while at the same time promoting vernacular translations. Interest in *volgare* (i.e., Italian) peaked in Venice and Padua, as we can tell from Pietro Bembo's *Prose della volgar lingua* (Venice, 1525), in which Bembo recognizes the urgent need to improve *volgare* in the light of the perfection of the Latin language.[41] Looking for publishers, scholars and writers went to Venice. They were attracted by the quality of the local typography as well as by the city's liberal atmosphere. In contrast to other cities where censorship and state regulations protected the nascent trade, in Venice the printing industry was basically unregulated in the first years of its development. Aldo Manuzio, probably the most influential printer of the

---

39. Saccone 1992: 37, quoting Franchi's 1987 "Le figure del silenzio: Statuto retorico dei fenomeni ellittici"; Glenn 1997: 1–18.

40. "Drama of rebellion" is from Jones 1990: 5. For silence in texts authored by women, see Zanini-Cordi 2008: 152.

41. Sgarbi 2014: 16. For the advance of the *volgare* and its relationship to the *questione della lingua*, see Dionisotti 1968; Di Silvio 1979; Mazzacurati 1965; Migliorini 1961: 321–42; Sanson 2010; Vitale 1978.

Italian Renaissance, began printing at the end of the fifteenth century and worked in Venice until his death, joining the second wave of printers who established that city as the center of the European printing industry in the sixteenth century. Manuzio focused on publishing Greek books, but he also published numerous others in Latin, Italian, and Hebrew. While Greek poetry, oratory, historiography, theology, and non-Aristotelian philosophy were translated for the first time, the medieval translations of Aristotle and of Greek scientific writers were replaced by new humanist translations into Latin. These Latin translations were read much more widely than the original Greek texts. In fact, despite its remarkable increase, the study of Greek in the Renaissance never attained the importance of the study of Latin.[42] Finally, if early and middle fifteenth-century humanists had concentrated on new translations from Greek into Latin, rather neglecting the vernacular, the sixteenth century saw a proliferation of vernacular works in all fields and, especially from the 1530s on, intense activity in translating classical works into Italian.[43]

Even if in the seventeenth century Venice's economic vitality dwindled, its wealth was increasingly invested in safer enterprises (such as the acquisition of land), and its monopoly of the printing industry was in part undercut by Rome, intellectually Venice continued to be an essential point of reference. As Virginia Cox notes, women's writings peaked between the end of the sixteenth century and the beginning of the seventeenth.[44] Religious debate was particularly energetic with the leadership of the "young" (*i giovani*) in Venice's politics. A decade after the war of Cyprus (1570–73), while Venice had lost some of its political hegemony, the Hapsburgs controlled Europe, and the pope found new force through the Counter-Reformation, the young rose up in the Serenissima. The presence of this new faction in the Venetian government fostered a renewal of ideas, freedom, and relative tolerance. The *giovani* were a radical party inside the patrician political class, which while promoting artistic activities in 1582 broke the power of the Council of Ten and forced the Venetian oligarchy to return political control to the senate. They were influential for the establishment of opera and the theatre.[45] They had little tolerance

---

42. Kristeller 2004: 121; Garin 1949–50: 55–104. Some famous Aristotelian scholars of the Renaissance (e.g., Pomponazzi) could not read Greek. During the early Renaissance, we also find the Latin translations of the Greek commentators on Aristotle, e.g., the work of Alexander of Aphrodisias and Themistius Simplicius, authors unknown to the Middle Ages and now finally available to all of those who could read Latin. Kristeller 1996: 97.

43. Bernstein 1998: 11–29; Kallendorf 2010; Maclean 2012; Merisalo 2015; Richardson 2004; Taylor 2014.

44. Cox 2008: introduction, xi–xxviii.

45. Muir 2011. About this moment in Venetian history, Calcagno 2006: 356 writes, "The Interdict of 1606 and the Jesuit order's expulsion from Venice were followed by a period of unprecedented freedom in the publishing domain, which lasted until the end of the 1640s,

for the pope's intrusion into state affairs and defended Venetian rights during the Interdetto, a *cause célèbre* engaging much of Europe in a debate over
Church interference in the life of the state and fostering intellectual, political,
and religious examination.[46]

During this time, women profited greatly from the animated discussion
about women and their potential (*querelle des femmes*), the Europe-wide
debate that began two centuries earlier and that in Venice in the late sixteenth
century was fostered by the publication of many books on the topic as well
as by members of literary circles called *accademie* (e.g., the Accademia della
Fama, Veneziana, and degli Incogniti) that dominated Venetian literary life.[47]
In fact, it is in Venice that for the first time the debate engaged female writers in a significant way. Distinguished members of the academies encouraged
women's printed rebuttals (such as those produced by Tarabotti, Fonte, and
Marinella) to men's derogatory works (e.g., the abovementioned *Defects of
Women*).[48] The members of these academies (especially the Incogniti) were
linked to publishers and the University of Padua. They also played an important role in the political life of Venice. They were committed to the preservation

---

when the new political reality of the War of Candia imposed the re-establishment of a closer
relationship between Venice and Rome." Members of the Accademia degli Incogniti produced
several opera librettos.

46. Pope Paul V had warned Venice that its prosecution of two clergy members would
lead to excommunication of its leaders and the prohibition of all sacramental life except in life-
or-death emergencies. But the Venetian leadership did not obey, and in April 1606 the papal
threat went into effect. A clash for the obedience of the clergy and the laity within the republic
followed: in its midst, most churches were kept functioning by the government, but especially
pro-papal forces like the Jesuits were expelled: see Bowsma 1968: 97–109, 162–232; Lane 1973:
393–96; Tarpley 2009: 165–92. Even in the two centuries preceding the crisis of the Interdetto,
Venice and Rome at times were openly hostile to each other: see Cozzi 1979; De Vivo 2007:
157–99; Pin 2006; Viggiano 2013.

47. *Querelle*'s themes appear already in the work of Christine de Pisan; see Kelly 1982: 4*ff*.
For the Italian academies and women, see Benzoni 1977, 1988; Fahy 2000; Stevenson 2005: 312–
23; Graziosi 1992; Heller 2003: chaps. 1 and 2; Bolzoni 1995; Fenlon 1995; Miato 1998. McClure
2013: 119–59 studies Italy's first all-female academy, Academy of the Assicurate in Siena.

48. Many books tied to the *querelle* and discussed by Jordan were published in Venice, e.g.,
Ortensio Landi, *Lettere di molte valorose donne, nelle quali chiaramente appare non esser ne di
eloquentia ne di dottrina alli huomini inferiori* (1549); Niccolò Gozze, *Governo della famiglia*
(1589); Paolo Caggio, *Iconomica* (1552); Alessandro Piccolomini, *Della institutione di tutta la vita
dell'huomo nato nobile e in città libera* (1552); Torquato Tasso, *Discorso della virtù feminile e donnesca* (1582); Fausto da Longiano, *Delle nozze* (1554); Giacomo Lanteri, *Della economica* (1560);
Stefano Guazzo, *La civil conversatione* (1575); Sperone Speroni, *Dialoghi* (1596); and Luigi Dardano, *La bella e dotta difesa delle donne in verso e prosa* (1554). See Jordan 1990: 134–72; Cox
2008: 91–99 for more on the "'feminized' literary landscape." For the defense of women as men's
way to defend their own civilized and elitist masculinity, see Dialeti 2011.

of the Serenissima and its myth.[49] Their interests were wide-ranging, eclectic, and often unorthodox, including magic, eroticism with overt homosexuality, and criticism of Christian values. But so long as the Incogniti refrained from criticizing the Venetian government, they remained relatively free of government denigration, even when many of them encountered the disapproval of the Holy Office.[50] Many of the Incogniti studied at the University of Padua and were tied to Cesare Cremonini (1550–1631), a famous professor of Aristotelian philosophy. Cremonini proposed views of women's inferiority that were even more adverse than those of Aristotle.[51] In the *Nobiltà*, Marinella displays her philosophical assertiveness and is not afraid to criticize Aristotle and those who, like Cremonini, followed him.

Although the Incogniti were progressive thinkers in several areas, their attitude toward women is not easy to define. They both supported and opposed women's intellectual endeavors; while for the publication of several of her works Arcangela Tarabotti received the patronage of Giovanni Francesco Loredan, founder of the Accademia, she was left to her own devices for the publication of her treatise, which harshly criticized fathers for forcing their daughters into convents for familial financial gain.[52] It seems that women were only marginally and certainly informally part of the academies, whose regulations did not provide a place or specific functions for women. Texts such as Tasso's *Discorso della virtù feminile e donnesca* (*Discourse on Feminine and Womanly Virtue*, 1582) and Passi's *I donneschi difetti* (1599) remind women of their place and reveal, especially for the Veneto area, an ideologically contested arena. If it is true that the multiple defenses of the female gender authored by women responding to men's treatises expose an expansion of women's involvement in areas from which they had been previously excluded and reflect the emergence of the female author, it is not clear that

---

49. Barbierato 2012: 167–72; Heller 2003: 48ff. For the Accademia Veneziana, see Bolzoni 1981.

50. Muir 2006: 338–39. See also Dooley 1999.

51. Westwater 2008: 11–12; Spini 1983.

52. Carroll 2014: 637; Robin 2007: 47: "Tightly connected to the publishing industry, whose capital was Venice, the academies existed to perform, discuss, and distribute new literary works—and, ultimately, to establish a new canon of modern Italian writers . . . their members represented an array of social classes and professions . . . moving freely between academies, members shared information, works, and ideas across cities. Though the poet Laura Terracina was inducted in to the *Incogniti* in Naples, Gaspara Stampa joined the *Dubbiosi* in Venice, and Laura Battiferra was a Siena *Intronati* member, women were for the most part excluded from these clubs." A similar view appears in Fahy 2000 and, on the Venetian environment, in Heller 2003: 48–68; Cox 2016 is more optimistic. Even Marinella's literary activity seems to have been affected by the academy's members: see Lavocat in Marinella 1998: XIV.

this animated discussion is simply a "staged literary battle."[53] Instead, it may unmask deep-seated prejudices about women, biases that had *real* negative consequences for their lives. Overall, the emerging picture of women's integration into the cultural life of Venice and northern Italy between 1560 and 1630 remains problematic.

The involvement of women in this intellectual debate is illustrated through Ortensio Lando's *Lettere di molte valorose donne* (*Letters of Many Valiant Women*, 1549), a book purporting to be the collected correspondence of literate noblewomen from the Veneto area. Although Lando himself wrote some (perhaps all) of these letters, many of the women mentioned were historical characters, and, above all, Lando's fiction—of women writing letters on various themes—is credible. The book is a significant illustration of the Venetian environment because if on the one hand it is plausible to believe in the fiction of erudite women who, having seriously pondered the humanist representation of virtue and being familiar with the classical tradition "rewrite the humanist history from which they have been excluded" and "exploit the resources of their spiritual equality in fictions that express their own empowerment," on the other it magnifies the presence of a man who allows women to speak.[54] The women allegedly writing these letters are from the Veneto area, born and bred in Marinella's and Fonte's cultural milieu.

NEGOTIATION AND SUBVERSION

During the late Renaissance, restriction from public arenas of learning and debate reduced women's field of action, but those who wrote books were partially able to undermine this situation. By focusing on Fonte and Marinella's appropriation of classical literature in their romance epics, I highlight their contribution to the Western literary tradition, presented as a polyphonic cultural heritage. An interdisciplinary approach to the topic—one that considers the roles of classical and Renaissance authors within poems written by women and that is sensitive to gender and cultural dynamics—forms the core of my discussion. My exploration expands on such studies as Constance Jordan's *Renaissance Feminism* (1990) and Sarah Gwyneth Ross's *Birth of Feminism* (2009) by focusing on a genre (romance epic) that these scholars did not consider when analyzing Renaissance debates and reflections about sex and

---

53. The expression is from the seminal discussion in Cox 2008: 175, which documents the complexity of this environment while adding the misogyny of Baroque aesthetic.

54. Quotes are from Jordan 1990: 138. About Lando's *Lettere*, see Ray 2009: 45–81. In Lando's letters, women's relationship to classical texts is of paramount importance even if the author's ultimate point may be a criticism of humanism and theoretical knowledge.

gender. By concentrating on what and how women wrote, Jordan's and Ross's investigations highlight Renaissance women's growing self-conscience and potentials. They showcase Early Modern women's awareness of being writers belonging to a community of male *and* female writers. Their texts address those of their male predecessors but also those of other women. Ross and Jordan underline how learned women openly display a determination "to expose the disjuncture between women's capacities and their social roles."[55] In their epic texts, Fonte and Marinella likewise display an awareness of women's condition gained through their own life stories, as members of a larger community of women, and exposure to the classics.[56]

Engendering Renaissance epic—especially the epic works written by women and featuring memorable female characters—is what female authors are effecting and what I explore.[57] As scholars have begun to integrate the category of gender into their analyses of the seminal classical texts of Antiquity and of the Renaissance, the same paradigm must be applied to works by women in the Early Modern Age. Questioning women's access to and reshaping of the literary process helps us understand how female authors constructed sex and gender within a predominantly male literary tradition. This approach is particularly important to this genre, as classical epic is characterized by gender asymmetry: traditionally in epic the masculine is constructed as paradigmatically positive, victorious, and normative. Starting with the *Iliad,* the epics were composed by, primarily read by, and centrally concerned with men. The genre was also instrumental in the construction of Greek and Roman masculinity. According to Allison Keith, Latin epicists "scrutinize the conventions of Roman *virtus* ('manliness') in 'poetry that trains men' by inculcating 'the values, examples of behavior, [and] cultural models' by which Rome won and governed her Mediterranean empire."[58] In addition, the epic creation of mas-

---

55. Ross 2009: 275. Cf. Bulkaert 2005: 16, who notices that in female erudite networks recurring themes of discussion include the woman's condition and women's learning. For a definition of politics and critical inquiry that makes the epic accessible as a work of political thought, see Hammer 1998.

56. The works produced by Marinelli and Fonte can be compared to those by Tarabotti: see Paulicelli 2014: 185: "Tarabotti's writing is characterized by a sense of urgency and a need to assert herself and her intellectual persona, while taking pains to defend herself from the kind of misogynistic attacks that had been launched after her response to Buoninsegni's *Satira.* Tarabotti is always acutely aware that she is a writer who can advocate her position in the world through publishing, and by using writing as an act and platform for self-creation and therefore freedom."

57. The bibliography on the topic is large; for an overview, see Foley 2005: 105–18. For ancient Roman epic, see Keith 2000; Hinds 2000. For women's role in shaping the historical record and the need to broaden history writing to include genres and subgenres deemed suitable for women in certain centuries, see Spongberg 2002: esp. chaps. 1–3.

58. Keith 2000: 6.

culine identity entails the recognition and justification of hierarchies of group, gender, and nationality, often in narratives about foreign conquest and those featuring proper interactions among groups and sexes. Much of the power of Latin epic lies in its tendency toward what we could call universalization, the construction of a pervasive model by which Roman social relations are organized, understood, and replicated. In this model, women must submit to men's will, and they are obliterated or reduced to invisibility when they do not. This paradigm of female subjugation was of particular importance in Venetian society, an environment in which the control of women was seen as an essential precondition for the stability and maintenance of the state.[59] But these Renaissance female epicists refute this normative logic and create dissident female characters who are part of the plot and whose voices assert women's perspectives and contributions to the debate on the human condition.

If during the Renaissance male writers project their "horror of effeminacy" onto female figures and feature women mainly to talk about men, I follow Constance Furey's approach and explore "how women as textual characters and as living interlocutors, writers, and loci of praise, were implicated in the humanists' quest for meaning."[60] It is possible to assess women's views and perspectives by carefully analyzing how they construct their plots and characters (especially female characters), as well as by paying attention to the books to which they allude. Renaissance men are not the only gender trying to understand what it means to be fully human; women are engaged in the same exploration. If we wonder how ancient texts affected male humanists, the same question should be formulated about women who chose to read the classics: we should focus on the impact of texts on them, "in light of humanists' own emphasis on the persuasive force of eloquence and, therefore, on the transformative power of reading."[61] We will see how the study of the classics, read in the original or in translation, helped women to gain a historicist approach to evaluating *facts* and history. It is not essential to establish in what specific form women accessed the classics, if they read them in the original or in translation, as *cento* reductions, or in anthologies, compilations, and compendia. What it is crucial is that they read them and reflected on them. This book offers ample evidence that humanistic education (envisioned above

---

59. For the objectification of women and their subjugation to family and state in Venice, see Francesco Barbaro, *De re uxoria* (1416). The subjugation of wives and the absolute authority of the husband were considered essential for maintaining household order. A parallel between order in the family and in the state is also constructed by Erasmus, for whom a woman must obey her husband even when his behavior does not reflect his authority and righteousness; similarly, secular authority must be obeyed even if unjust. See Jordan 1990: 62.

60. The first quote comes from Correll 1990: 258, the second from Furey 2006: 173.

61. Gouwens 1998: 62.

all as knowledge of the classics) "provides an especially rich site for explor-
ing the power of the past to shape and transform its students,"[62] including
women. Although women's access to ancient sources was often dependent on
the availability of translations, the elaboration of classical texts was a meaningful heritage that they felt compelled to consider, question, and contextualize.[63] I clarify and interpret the multiple classical echoes heard in the romance
epics by Moderata Fonte and Lucrezia Marinella, whose texts retain a series
of competing discourses that challenge and interrogate each other, refusing to
be collapsed into a single master discourse.[64]

My inquiry was born not simply to establish that the reception of classical
texts by women occurred, but rather to determine what it meant for women
and their society. While the importance of classical reception is a well studied phenomenon for Renaissance male authors educated to read, appreciate,
and reinterpret ancient texts, the same phenomenon for women of that time
is typically overlooked or dismissed because of their linguistic deficiency in
Latin and Greek. Consequently, this book is dedicated to the exploration of
the topic of women as readers.[65] I show that poetry written in the imitation
of another text should be read as both a record of textual interpretation and
as an implicit instance of criticism. Despite the aid from men to these women
authors and their difficulty in treating fundamental issues with a basically
male readership, their act of reading is presented as "an assertion of individu-
ality, a separation from societal restriction and expectations, or, to use Janice
Radway's words, 'a declaration of independence.'"[66] Radway has demonstrated

---

62. Ibid., 55. For the importance of education in empowering women, see Spence et al.
2010.

63. At the end of the 1990s, Barbara Gold, Paul Allen Miller, and Charles Platter lamented
how scholarship on medieval and early Renaissance literature produced by women largely
ignored the influence of classical culture. Their 1997 volume tried to correct this deficiency,
which I believe persists. See Stevens 2005; Bulckaert 2010.

64. Martindale's 1993 approach to intertextuality has been crucial to mine. Excellent discussion about the limits of intertextuality, allusion, and reference is in Hinds 1998 with good
bibliography on the topic. I endorse Hind's approach when he writes, "As philologists, we need
not cease to offer tidy and controlled descriptions of allusions which poets themselves will often
have tried to make tidy and controlled, provided that we do not confuse this aspiration to tidi-
ness with an absoluteness of philological rigour. We need not cease to reify topoi, provided that
we understand the provisionality of any such reification, for author and reader alike. We may
even continue to use the deadpan 'cf.' when needed, provided that we treat it as an invitation to
interpret rather than as the end of interpretation. The critic, like the poet, can bring only finite
resources to the infinity of discourse" (51). More recently, about reception studies, see Brockliss
et al. 2012: 4–19 and Harrison 2001.

65. The subject is gaining importance in reception studies; the pioneering study is Radway
1984. For a survey of different approaches, see Goldstein and Machor 2008.

66. Badia and Phegley 2005: 5. For a survey of books typically read by women, see Richardson 1999: 145–51.

how even romance novels produced in the 1970s, assumed to be framed by patriarchal views and agendas, were read by American women as a means to escape the demands of motherly and spousal duties. Ultimately, Radway interprets their act of reading as a pursuit of freedom, getting in touch with a part of their selves ignored by society. Similarly, Fonte and Marinella's appropriation of ancient texts (even those supposedly upholding traditional patriarchal views) enabled them to explore their selfhood and to react to a society that recognized them only as wives and mothers.

Finally, from a theoretical point of view, I follow Ann Rosalind Jones and stress that women's works must be read alongside those of their male contemporaries.[67] In her investigation of Renaissance love lyric written by women, Jones uses the Marxist term "negotiation" to explore early modern women's engagement with and manipulation of literary conventions occurring in love poems written by men. Once women decided to enter the world of scholarly pursuits, they encountered great obstacles. These difficulties had profound repercussions on their writings and lives; however, Jones's approach allows us "to resist interpretative frameworks that doom the women of the past—or the present—to a relentlessly disempowered relation to political and cultural practices" and to see women poets as subjects and agents who, although always caught up in the politics of gender ideology and dominant signifying systems, are nonetheless able to move within those systems.[68]

Women's appropriation of men's books is a significant phenomenon, because when a member of the sex systematically excluded from a certain cultural activity or performance actively recreates it, she is destabilizing the very system that prohibits her claim to that activity and to public language.[69] Therefore Fonte and Marinella's adoption and reinterpretation of the literary and linguistic codes of their male peers must be carefully evaluated because subordinate groups tend to respond to the cultural assumptions encoded into hegemonic forms and systems of representation in an original way. One of the most interesting aspects of women's reception of classical texts appears to be their "countercultural" charge. Because women read independently, they were much less conditioned by the views and filters inherited by those edu-

---

67. Jones 1990: 1–4. For the ongoing discussion about feminist approaches to literature, see Comensoli and Stevens 1998. Jones's 1990 methodological premises and the textual dynamics she analyzes in her introduction (1–10) have been useful to me in framing Fonte and Marinelli's interactions with ancient sources and male-dominated genres. Important observations on the intersubjective context in which women and men elaborate ideas and construct systems of meaning can be found in Bruner 1996.

68. Jones 1990: 9–10.

69. Ibid., 4.

cated in the institutional framework of the schools.[70] Women detected in the texts they read objectionable or problematic aspects that they unpacked and used to criticize current ideological preconceptions about their society. They often noticed the gap between authorial intentions and textual meaning and capitalized on it in their writings. Even when "modestly" reproducing stereotypes and discourses borrowed from men, they are changing them and astutely vocalizing a "master narrative" with different intentions.[71] Classical texts, however, represent an essential starting point for these female authors wanting to redeploy rather than reject them. By reading outside the homosocial order and being excluded from the body politic, Fonte and Marinella's interpretation of classical texts seems less subject to group dynamics, their views conditioned by a nascent female culture fostered by women's publication of books. Even if they ultimately abided by the sociopolitical system in which they were immersed, they display an awareness of the inequalities and problems inherent to that system and its patriarchal infrastructures.[72]

AN EXAMPLE OF CRITICISM FROM LUCREZIA MARINELLA

Leaving aside theoretical formulations, and before entering into an extended discussion of Moderata Fonte's *Tredici canti del Floridoro* (*Thirteen Cantos of Floridoro*) and Lucrezia Marinella's *L'Enrico, overo Bisantio acquistato* (*Henry, or Byzantium Gained*), I offer a practical example, from Marinella's oeuvre, of the rhetorical operation outlined above. Marinella was one of the most educated women of her day. She was born in 1571 in Venice, and her well-to-do family encouraged her intellectual pursuits. Her father and brother could read Greek and they could have taught it to her, since her writings display deep knowledge of a wide variety of Greek texts. A late marriage also facilitated her dedication to writing and linguistic knowledge. Her writing shows that she has read many ancient sources, and her poetic "self-fashioning" proceeds by alluding, at times almost verbatim, to specific lines of famous Greek and Latin

---

70. Aiston 2010: 4: "Women's educational agency is often practiced in informal and marginal circumstances, outside of mainstream, formal institutions."

71. Pender 2012: 1–15.

72. Jed 2011: 117–18 reflects on how Tarabotti understood tyranny and freedom in relation to the political status and body of daughters. While men openly condemned the depravity of the tyrant in their political discourses, they promoted a *ragion di stato* that legitimized fathers' tyranny over their daughters. Medioli 2012: 221–39 discusses evident "protofemminismo" in all the works of Tarabotti. Ross 2009: 198–210 underlines Marinella's adoption of a feminism acceptable to the men closest to her (e.g., her father as well as patron Lucio Scarano).

authors to project a peculiar image of herself.[73] In her treatise the *Nobiltà et eccellenza delle donne co' difetti e mancamenti degli uomini* (*Nobility and Excellence of Women with the Defects and Vices of Men,* 1601), we see her debt and challenge to classical Antiquity as well as her capacity to redeploy suggestions from classical texts when she apostrophizes women and their intellect in the following way:

> O che dono, che doti . . . poichè con la loro bellezza ponno alzar le menti degli uomini in Dio. Chi potrà mai a pieno lodarti ricchissimo thesoro del mondo tutto? Io confesso, che s'io hauessi tante lingue, quante foglie vestono gli arbori nella ridente primavera, ouero quanta arena è nella sterile e infeconda Libia, io non potrei incominciar a dar principio alle tue lodi; perciocchè non solamente la beltà innalza in Dio le fredde menti ma rende il più ostinato e crudo cuore humile e mansueto. (Marinella 1621: 31)[74]

> What a gift, what dowries . . . since with their beauty they can lift the minds of men towards God. Who will be able to praise you most rich treasure of the entire world? I confess that if I had so many tongues, as many leaves as cover the trees in spring, or as many grains of sand as are found in sterile and barren Libya, I could not begin to give them praise; since not only beauty lifts cool minds to God but makes the most obstinate and rough heart humble and meek.

This passage is a good example of Marinella's mode of citation. Aside from the Petrarchan and Neoplatonic content of this eulogy, according to which women with their beauty lead men toward God, and the idea that Orpheus-

---

73. Marinella's innumerable quotations of Greek sources reveal her familiarity with several Greek authors, whom, as was customary also for men, she read and quoted in Latin translation. In this study, when I consider main ideas and characters that Marinella borrows from Greek authors, I provide an English translation or close paraphrase of the original text to help readers recall the passage in question. I do not include the original Greek, which Marinella may not have even consulted. Readers should also keep in mind that my analysis does not focus on Marinella's treatise the *Nobiltà* but on her *Enrico,* a romance epic written in Italian, where by necessity Marinella does not quote ancient texts verbatim but alludes to them, i.e., by recalling their plots, characters, phrasing, and agenda. Different is the case with Latin, which I cite verbatim followed by English translation, especially when trying to establish a direct allusion in Marinella's Italian to specific Latin lines. Overall, in my exploration I invite the reader "to move freely within a web of texts, a web only loosely tethered to reality outside texts" (Wood 2012: 165). About the challenge of reception, see ibid., 163–74. For Renaissance self-fashioning, Greenblatt 1983.

74. There are three main editions of the *Nobiltà*: Marinella 1600 (ed. Ciotti), Marinella 1601 (ed. Ciotti), and Marinella 1621 (ed. Combi). The 1601 edition is an expanded version of that printed the year before. The edition of 1621 is identical to that of 1601.

like women can tame beast-like men, Marinella is indirectly criticizing the traditional Venetian custom of the dowry by speaking of women as a treasure in themselves. In Renaissance Venice, women could not marry without a dowry, which for aristocratic families had to be substantial. Often even a rich family could afford to pay only one dowry, obliging many girls to become nuns against their will. This problem, called *monacazione forzata*, is clear in the writings of Tarabotti (1604–52), especially her *Tirannia paterna* (*Paternal Tyranny*) and *Inferno Monacale* (*Monastic Hell*), in which she denounces the monstrosity of coercion into religious life.[75] Indirectly taking a stance in this debate, Marinella affirms that women's worth is intrinsic.

Of interest in this citation is Marinella's employment of the classical topos of the many tongues. In *Iliad* 2.488–93, at the beginning of the Catalogue of Ships, Homer shows awareness of the difficulty of enumerating in full the Greek forces and leaders participating in the Trojan expedition and asks for help:

> I could not tell over the multitude of them nor name them,
> Not if I had ten tongues and ten mouths, not if I had
> A voice never to be broken and a heart of bronze within me,
> Not unless the Muses of Olympia, daughters
> Of Zeus of the aegis, remembered all those who came beneath Ilion.
> I will tell the lords of the ships, and the ships' numbers. [trans. Lattimore][76]

In Latin poetry, the mention of "the many tongues" becomes traditional to the point that the satirist Persius stresses that "this is what poets or prophetesses always say asking for a hundred voices and mouths and tongues for their poems" ("Vatibus hic mos est, centum sibi poscere voces, / centum ora et linguas optare in carmina centum," *Sat.* 5.1–2). Several poets in Rome employ the Homeric topos; prominent among them Virgil in Book 6 of the *Aeneid* ("Non, mihi si linguae centum sint oraque centum, / ferrea vox, omnis scelerum com-

---

75. Sperling 1999 documents how female monasticism served the ruling male patriciate, whose members forced their daughters into convent life in order to pursue their political network agendas. See Weaver 2006; Tarabotti 2012.

76. In the early 1360s, Leontius Pilatus completed a line-by-line Latin translation of both the *Iliad* and the *Odyssey*; see Desmond 2012: 21–40. In 1537, the first printed Latin version of the *Odyssey* and *Iliad* was published in Venice by the translator Andreas Divus for the printer Jacob a Burgofrancho. It followed, more or less accurately, Pilatus's text. The Aldine edition of the *Odyssey* was published in 1504. About the history of the *Versio Latina* of Homer, see Sowerby 1996: 161–202. For a survey of Homeric translations in the Middle Ages and Renaissance, see Armstrong 2014, esp. 176–77, in which he notices that Latin translations of Homer are understudied, and the long history of Latin translations in the age of printing awaits full exploration (176). For Odysseus's myth in Italian opera, see Ronsard 2007.

prendere formas / omnias poenarum percurrere nomina possim," "Not if I had a hundred tongues, a hundred mouths, a voice of iron, could I tell all the forms of wickedness or spell out the names of every torment," *Aen.* 6.625–27), when the Sibyl is speaking to Aeneas and is about to enumerate the many punishments of the Underworld, but also in *Georgics* 2.42–44, when, addressing Maecenas, the poet explains that he would need "a hundred tongues and mouths and iron voice" (*centum sint oraque centum, ferrea vox*) to describe all the different branches of arboriculture.

In the passage quoted above, Marinella casts herself as a new Sibyl who does not announce the many retributions of Tartarus, but rather the countless qualities of women. She would like to have as many tongues as the trees have leaves in spring in order to perform her task exhaustively. Although in *Aeneid* 6 the Sibyl does not mention leaves and trees, it is well known how in the same book, lines 74–76, Aeneas had asked the prophetess to express her insights about the future aloud rather than entrusting them to the leaves. Virgil's use of the topos is original, because in it the Sibyl and not the poet himself is the chosen speaker of the cliché.[77] The Sibyl takes a central role in *Aeneid* 6 as prophetess and guide of a man who is initiated into the mysteries of the Underworld and, in the same way, in her *Nobiltà,* Marinella becomes the prophetess of unknown truths about women. In a society dominated by prejudices toward women, this praise is atypical, and yet Marinella is keen to voice it by utilizing a well known rhetorical turn of phrase from male poets.[78]

The reference to the trees and leaves "of the smiling spring" in the Italian text may have been facilitated by Marinella's memory of *Georgics* 2.42–44, while the grains of Libyan sand come from the elegiac context of Catullus 7, where the poet in love with Lesbia links them to her kisses ("Quaeris, quot mihi basationes . . . sint satis . . . quam magnus numerus Libyssae harenae," "You ask me how many kisses . . . should be enough . . . as big a number as the Libyan grains of sand," 7.1–3). A poetic cliché is almost never "inert" but infinitely malleable and expressive of the gathering momentum and proliferation of multiple poetic voices.[79] Marinella uses these fossilized poetic elements with creativity and an agenda: she begins by identifying with the Sibyl and the world of epic but immediately links it to the realm of love by tying the topos of "the many tongues" to Catullus's verses and a poem through which a man expresses his desire for a woman and, indirectly, his indifference toward

---

77. Gowers 2005: 174.

78. Marinella reuses the topos "of the many tongues" in her *Enrico* 26.86, when she deplores the many deaths caused by one of the Crusaders; she claims that not even if thousands of tongues and mouths were given to her by heaven, nor if her voices were more resonant and harder than steel, could she enumerate them. See Galli Stampino 2014: 79.

79. Hinds 1998: 45–47.

politics. The allusion to an elegiac poet is intrinsically meaningful. By using a powerful woman—the Sibyl—and a poet, Catullus, who rejects the world of epic to link his fame to a woman and private desire, Marinella is making precise editorial choices that allow her to extol women. She is saying that she is interested not in the epic enumeration of armies and war, but in a more productive enterprise: the understanding of women's worth, which in turn should facilitate their relationships with men. The image she uses to praise women is vivid and linked to fertility and wealth. Women are described as "the most rich treasure of the all world" ("ricchissimo thesoro del mondo tutto"), and the poetess's words are intended to unearth these gems, resulting in a better world and men more pliable. Though outwardly in contrast to imagery of fertility, even the bareness and aridity of Libya ("sterile e infeconda Libia") are meant to evoke Catullus's elegiac poetry with his cravings for Lesbia's kisses, and thus the importance of women.

In terms of classical allusions and strategic maneuvering, the citation above mirrors Marinella's entire oeuvre. This kind of rhetorical technique and the classical authors employed here will again appear in her heroic poem the *Enrico*. In it, Marinella engages in a sophisticated dialogue with a literary and philosophical tradition that stimulates and haunts her own writing. If she borrows specific wordings and key concepts from ancient texts, she also seems able to detect some contradictions at the heart of that tradition. Marinella is ready to muster them to subtly advance her antiwar and pro-woman agenda. L. Westwater has observed that while the Venetian writer in *Nobiltà* engages Antiquity and male ideas head-on, in later works she seems to reshape rather than reject several of these notions, and in this process to undermine them more thoroughly "by quietly creating a value system that privileges the feminine, not the masculine."[80] As we will see in the *Enrico*, the sheer juxtaposition of different ancient subtexts, especially the concomitant presence of epic and elegy (*Iliad, Aeneid, Metamorphoses, Heroides*, etc.), with their competing agendas and discourses, problematizes the unfolding action and alerts the reader to its complexity. Marinella does not openly indict the opinions of men; rather, in a nuanced way, she uses them to interweave an ingenious criticism of stereotypical Renaissance ideas. Although, superficially, she writes a work that follows male agendas and glorifies masculine accomplishments, she composes a discreet counter-song that challenges and complicates the male epic agenda.

---

80. Westwater 2003: 155. Similarly, Prosperi 2011: 31*ff.* underlines how Marinella's last poems, although superficially less abrasive than her *Nobiltà*, display a pro-woman agenda. An analogous rhetorical maneuver appears in some of Cereta's letters: see McCue Gill 2009: 146–47 (e.g., the letter to Pietro Zecchi); Jones 1990; more recently, Pender 2012: 10–12 (about "new formalism").

WORKS UNDER STUDY AND STRUCTURE
OF THE MONOGRAPH

Both texts examined in this book can be ascribed to the category of romance epic. While the humanist epic proper, written in Latin, was inaugurated by Petrarch with his *Africa,* which featured the labors of Scipio Africanus, Boccaccio's *Teseida* is the prototype for the romance epic (often also referred to as epic romance, romance, chivalric epic, or heroic poem), a hybrid form written in the vernacular, mixing traditional mythological and love themes. This newly created type of epic was destined to become popular during the Renaissance, especially when authors started to blend medieval chivalric romances (the *matière de France* originating from the Chanson de Roland and the *matière de Bretagne,* especially the Arthurian cycle) with epic themes and plots derived from the ancient classics. Following Boccaccio, from the mid-fourteenth century on, poets challenged themselves with this double task: appropriating popular chivalric poems with their emphasis on loyalty, magic, and courtly love while imitating classical authors such as Virgil, Ovid, Statius, and Lucan.[81] It is a mistake to separate the culture of humanism and its classical revival from the simultaneous development of the epic written in vernacular: both were undertaken by the same group of people and coexisted side by side.[82] Poems like Petrarch's *Africa* or Ariosto's *Orlando Furioso* as well as Vida's *Christiad* can be considered examples of humanistic epics. Some Renaissance critics such as Giraldi Cinthio and Pigna argued that romance epic and epic were distinct genres, but others, like Tasso, believed that ancient and modern epic poems were working within the same genre.[83] Fonte's *Floridoro* and Marinella's *Enrico* can be ascribed to this hybrid genre and confirm the image of a relatively widespread humanist culture able to influence vernacular texts.

This book is organized in three parts. Each part contains several chapters envisioned as articulations of a composite discourse. In chapter 1, I examine

---

81. Everson 2001; Burrow 1993; Murrin 1994.

82. Everson 2001: 327.

83. The debate, which pitted romance against epic, was widespread and generated numerous treatises, e.g., Giraldi Cinthio, *Discorso intorno al comporre dei romanzi* (1554), G. B. Pigna, *I Romanzi* (1554), G. G. Trissino, *La poetica* (1529), and Tasso's *Discorsi dell'Arte Poetica,* written in the 1560s but published later in 1587. In the broadest terms, Renaissance critics observed that while epic is built around the single action of one man, its subject matter based on *truth* and on characters of high birth, romances combined truth and falsehood and were structured around the deeds of many men, with the aim of eliciting pleasure and wonder (*meraviglia*) in the reader: see Everson 2001: 272–78; Norton and Cottino-Jones 1999: 322–39; Patterson 1984: 168–74; Weinberg 1961: 1:445–46.

the writing of the Venetian Moderata Fonte, who casts Risamante, the female protagonist of *Tredici canti del Floridoro* (1581), as a beautiful, chaste, and ethically competent amazon. By highlighting the virtues of a woman, the author addresses the equality of the genders and participates in the Renaissance *querelle des femmes*. The defense of the intellectual, moral, and practical capabilities of women, an issue that this writer considers at length in her dialogue *Il merito delle donne* (*The Worth of Women*, 1600), emerges as a crucial move in the creation of a female knight who exemplifies women's ability to excel in any field. In order to fully establish the caliber and range of Fonte's intellectual accomplishments, I compare her chivalric epic (one of the first written by a woman) to Renaissance epics such as Ariosto's *Orlando Furioso* (1532) and Virgil's *Aeneid*. Only through this analysis it is possible to understand how a genre ideologically connected to war and patriarchy has been reinterpreted through a woman's lens, and how through the ending of the *Floridoro* Fonte frames violence in the epic genre as a problem, not a solution. Fonte criticizes this epic agenda of domination when, in a climactic duel, her lady knight instead spares her antagonist. Some humanists like Petrarca, Filelfo, Vegio, and Pontano share Fonte's preoccupations with epic violent endings, in which Fonte reveals herself capable of reading Virgil's translated masterpiece on her own terms. My study also tries to determine how reading the *Aeneid* in translation may have influenced Fonte's interpretation of the original and, in turn, her views and literary production. Chapter 2 is devoted to the amazons portrayed in Lucrezia Marinella's *Enrico* and contextualizes her epic through the ideas about women's nature previously developed in her treatise *Nobiltà*, but also in the light of Fonte's Risamante and the amazons depicted by Virgil, Ariosto, and Tasso.

Further examination of Renaissance women's romance epic in relationship to the classical heritage is developed in Part II, where I consider in much more detail the *Enrico*, its author, and environment. Chapter 3 frames Marinella's poem as inspired by the doge Enrico Dandolo's participation in the Fourth Crusade (1202–4), the starting point of Venice's political and economic greatness. The expedition, originally organized to capture Jerusalem, was soon redirected against the Byzantine Empire and Constantinople. In this work, Marinella mixes echoes from chivalric poems (such as those of Ariosto and Tasso) with ideas and themes taken from Virgil and Ovid (especially *Heroides* and *Metamorphoses*). The focus of chapters 3 and 4 is on abandoned wives (Clelia and Areta) and the importance of love and family. Marinella wants to champion a Christian yet feminine view of morality, while at the same time she criticizes notions typical of late Renaissance Venice (i.e., the inferiority of women). A careful analysis of the many classical echoes in the stories of Clelia and Areta reveals the power of private desire in an epic allegedly written to celebrate Venice and collective enterprises. Marinella justifies love, affirming that private claims are as valid as concerns for the community. Once again, war seems to be a target. In this epic, Marinella promotes ideas developed in *Nobiltà* advocating a pacifist model of society built on women's ethical excellence and repudiating Aristotle's opinions in *Politics* and *Generation of Animals* about women's inferiority. In a truly historicist perspective, Marinella understands that the value and worth of objects and individuals are often tied to circumstances and that the classics, for centuries employed to foster a historically defined agenda that chastised and diminished the worth of women, can be subtly engaged to opposite ends. My analysis of the *Enrico* follows the trajectory from the first part of my study. By employing a close reading of the text, I monitor traces from important early modern and ancient works. Besides considering Marinella's conclusions in her *Nobiltà*, in Part II, I focus on (1) the process through which a genre normally chosen by men and structured to promote patriarchy and male agendas can be remapped by a female author; (2) the essential role of Ovid's *Metamorphoses* and *Heroides* in the Clelia and Areta narratives; (3) the function of the abandoned woman and lamentation within this epic and the wider epic tradition; and (4) how atypical interpretations of Virgil's *Aeneid* are preferred over those normally highlighted by Venetian humanists.

Part III is devoted to the exploration of the prophetess/enchantress in Marinella and Fonte's epics. Marinella rewrites this character normally constructed as ambiguous or negative by male authors (e.g., Homer and Virgil's Circe, Ariosto's Alcina, Tasso's Armida) and turns it into a completely positive figure. Already Fonte in her *Floridoro* had created a good enchantress in Circetta and reflected on the story of Circe in Homer's *Odyssey*, showing sympathy for Circe. Marinella continues to show a desire to comment on the *Odyssey* and to push further the metamorphosis of the enchantress. Her enchantress Erina reminds the hero Venier (one of the protagonists of the *Enrico*) and the city of Venice about the futility of war and earthly glory. Through Erina, Marinella restructures an important topos of epic—that of the encounter between a powerful female enchantress and a brave soldier in a beautiful and remote place. If in stories written by men the living embodiment of earthly paradise is stereotypically a beautiful woman who lures the hero away from his destiny and epic identity, in Marinella's poem, Erina, despite being beautiful and unbaptized, is not a symbol of temptation. On the contrary, she searches for God through the contemplation and study of nature.

She does not propose enticement of the senses, but philosophical inquiry of causes, solitude, and study as channels to reach God and happiness. In the encounter between Venier and Erina, the challenge to *kleos* is voiced in the name of humanistic ideals, which are also tied to the fulfillment of men as spiritual creatures.

Part III is also concerned with the implications of the *locus amoenus.* Through Erina's criticism of enterprises that are typically praised in epic, Marinella lets us perceive a polarization of the moral values associated with two literary traditions (epic and pastoral) and respective points of view that are explored and linked to this author's subtle pessimism. Erina's island is a turning point at which the hero Venier is offered a new paradigm of existence. Erina would like to persuade him to choose the benefits of this pastoral and peaceful existence. She reminds him, and therefore the city of Venice, about the dangers of war and empire. Cleverly, Marinella constructs a plot in which Erina's ancestors have grown wicked in Venice and are able to change, amend, and perfect themselves far away from that urban life, in the isolation of an island. In the poem, Erina becomes the symbol of peace and love of wisdom, ideals that are forgotten by Venier as well as by the society in which he lives. With Erina's island, Marinella displays an understanding of the ancient philosophical debate about the states of life (contemplation versus action) and links it to epic and to the pastoral world. Marinella uses the limitations of earthly accomplishments and the elusive but persistent pessimism of the *Aeneid* to undermine the active life in favor of the contemplative life. In this rhetorical maneuver, she summons Virgil's *Aeneid* as well as Cicero's *Somnium Scipionis* (*The Dream of Scipio*).

In the *Enrico,* Erina becomes a cipher of Marinella, a woman whose erudition, for better or worse, cannot be accommodated by the society in which she lives. Significantly, the interaction between Erina and Venier, himself a symbol of Venice, does not have consequences. The two remain isolated, unable to seriously consider the other's priorities. Marinella's deepest aspirations—to highlight human spiritual needs, women's worth, and the absurdity of war—in this historical moment and in Venice can only be uttered through a marginalized character. Erina inhabits a text deprived of a true political, familiar, and public existence; she fosters her excellence on an island described as a paradise of bounty, beauty, and freedom but ultimately fenced off from history and the real world. Perhaps it is in this segment of the epic where we can see most clearly the difficulties a female writer faced in contrasting the genre's assumptions and rebelling against the limitations imposed on women during the Early Modern Age. Although by the seventeenth century women's intellect had been recognized by men, and they were encouraged and empowered by the achievements of other women,[84] women remained unable to claim a true status for themselves in the public arena. This monograph is aimed at restoring their intellectual contributions to the history of ideas and our understanding of their role in the Venetian cultural milieu. It also frames classical Antiquity as an enduring force to be reckoned with, an enduring tool for human discovery and self-discovery.

84. Stevenson 2005: 4.

PART I

Female Fighters

On Women, War, and *Pietas*

CHAPTER 1

Lady Knights and *Pietas*

IN THIS CHAPTER I situate Moderata Fonte's *Il merito delle donne* (*The Worth of Women*), together with her epic *Tredici canti del Floridoro* (*Thirteen Cantos of Floridoro*), within the *querelle des femmes*—the centuries-long European debate over women's capabilities and nature.[1] Born Modesta da Pozzo in Venice in 1555, Fonte belonged to the citizens' class, which occupied a middle place between the nobles and the lower class. Despite the early death of her parents to the plague of 1556, she received a good education in the house of her maternal grandmother, whose second husband, Prospero Saraceni, gladly shared his knowledge and library with the gifted girl. When Niccolò Doglioni, an educated Venetian, married the daughter of Saraceni, Fonte was welcomed into his house and encouraged to study, compose, and publish. After she mar-

---

1. On the *querelle,* see Collina 1989: 145: "In the Sixteenth Century the 'discourse' on women witnesses a development never reached so far and, in the second half of the century, it becomes a sort of literary challenge in which every person capable of writing can engage. At the same time it undergoes profound modifications: it is not any longer approached from the margin, within texts devoted to other topics, but becomes the autonomous theme of monographic treatments." For basic bibliographical information on the *querelle,* see Hacke in Fonte 2002: 16–17; Kelso 1956; Zimmermann 1994; Malpezzi Price 1989: 165–81. For the *querelle* in the seventeenth century, see Campbell 2006: 1–14; 2011: 80. For the *Orlando Furioso* as a romance epic that (like the *Floridoro*) intervenes in the debate on women, see Cox 1997: 134–46; Shemek 1989; Benson 1992.

ried the man Doglioni chose for her, Filippo de' Zorzi, a respected and educated lawyer, she continued to write.[2]

Although Fonte was brought up among learned relatives and friends who
encouraged her literary interests, her dialogue *Il merito delle donne* depicts
a group of Venetian noblewomen in a secluded garden speaking about their
lives without the binding presence of their husbands.[3] Not accidentally, some
of these women take advantage of the playful frame and seclusion to lament
the yoke of marriage and to reveal wealthy widowhood as the most blessed of
all situations.[4] *Il merito* is not the first text in which Fonte reckons women as
protagonists of the story: the *Floridoro*[5] is not only one of the first romance
epics written by a woman,[6] but it is also unique for having as its protagonist
a woman, the amazon Risamante.[7] In the plot, while the other characters are
simply engaged in searching and fighting for women or in jousting tournaments to demonstrate their valor, Risamante is the warrior *en quête*; she is
fighting to recover a part of the kingdom that her twin sister, Biondaura, has
taken from her.

Valeria Finucci has noticed how difficult it must have been for a woman
to pursue in an original way a genre traditionally written by men and hav-

2. Cox in Fonte 1997: 2*ff.*, Malpezzi Price 2003: 27–39; Rosenthal 1992: 84–86.

3. Fonte 1997: 46. Besides an English translation, Cox provides background on Fonte's life
and women's status in the Early Modern Period (1–23). Likewise, Chemello, editor of the dialogue's primary modern edition, supplies an introduction (Fonte 1988: IX–LXIII) and basic bibliography for *Il merito delle donne*; cf. Kolsky 1993: 57–96; Guthmüller 1992: 258–79. Fonte 2002
is the German translation; it also includes D. Hacke's substantial introduction and bibliography.

4. Fonte 1997: 56; Rosenthal 1992: 107–8; Jones 1998: 164–75; an excellent bibliography on
women in Venice can be found in Ambrosini 2000: 442.

5. While Italian excerpts are from Valeria Finucci's 1995 edition, the English translations
are mine. I have included extensive quotations in Italian and English from Fonte's oeuvre for
the dual purpose of facilitating interpretation while giving a taste of this poorly known text. In
the interest of readers across disciplines, a bibliography on Fonte is provided along with syn-
thesizing overviews of scholarship on topics more widely studied.

6. Chronologically, the first known Italian Renaissance romance epic written by a woman
was D'Aragona's *Il meschino, altramente detto il guerrino* (*The Wretch Otherwise Known as Guerrino*, 1560), but its authorship is contested (see Cox 2008: 312n167). Julia Hairston is currently
preparing the introduction and notes for a translation by John C. McLucas of d'Aragona's *Il
meschino* that will appear in The Other Voice in Early Modern Europe series. On women as
writers of chivalric poetry in the Renaissance, see Cox 1997: 134–45.

7. Female warriors in literary works and prose epics of the late Middle Ages are studied by
Bendinelli Predelli 1994; Allaire 1994; Robinson 1985; and Tomalin 1982, who explore *guerriere*
in prescriptive and literary texts ranging from the 1400s to the 1600s, revealing the difficulty
for male authors to accommodate these women within their cultural paradigms. The presence
of amazons (approved or not) is nevertheless well established. On Bradamante's development
from warrior to wife, see Finucci 1992: 230–53; for a fine analysis of amazon figures in Ariosto,
see Stoppino 2011. On the artistic representation of powerful women, see Dixon 2002.

ing at its center male characters and patriarchy.[8] She wonders whether such a highly codified genre could allow for new positions and for an inversion of roles. Finucci answers these questions positively. Yet the difficulties of creating a new female hero while remaining attached, as Fonte does, to a classical epic plot and to an aesthetic *mise en scène* invariably reproduced according to the needs and agendas of a male main character cannot be underestimated. For these reasons, Finucci concludes that Fonte is unable to recreate, under the sign of difference, the tradition of which she strove to be a part.[9]

But did Fonte remained *trapped* in the male-defined paths and ideology of epic, as Finucci suggests? Did she fail to find positive and original solutions to the ideological problems of the genre? In answering these questions, I focus on stanzas 58–70 of Canto 13 of the *Floridoro*, describing the battle resulting in Risamante's victory over her sister, Biondaura. In this canto, Risamante has almost completed the conquest of Armenia, the kingdom that her sister refuses to share with her. Biondaura, as a final resort, has employed Clorida-bello, a king madly in love with her, to fight as her champion in the battle that will determine which of the two sisters will rule over Armenia. To assess Fonte's sophistication and the originality of the battle she crafts in Canto 13, I compare this battle scene to a similar episode, the *singolar tenzone* between Risamante and the Parthian giant Macandro, placed by Fonte at the beginning of the poem (Cantos 1–2), in diametrical opposition to Canto 13.[10] I also compare it with two famous final battles well known to a majority of Renaissance readers: the duel between Aeneas and Turnus in Book 12 of Virgil's *Aeneid* and Ruggiero's fight against Rodomonte in Canto 46 of Ariosto's *Orlando Furioso*.[11] In chapter 2, I broaden the scope by comparing Risamante's behavior to that of the amazons featured in *L'Enrico, overo Bisantio acquistato* (1635), another romance epic work penned by a woman from Venice and published about fifty years after the *Floridoro*.

---

8. Finucci 1994: 207: "What in the end a literary genre so tied to the male imaginary can offer to women, a genre so full of tournaments, battles, sea monsters, military parades, genealogies and encomiastic and selective readings of the most blood-soaked events?" (my translation).

9. Finucci 1994: 223–24, 231: "I would like to shift the emphasis on the cultural imagery because only in this way, I believe, is it possible to record the difference—the estrangement—that a female writer projects on the various literary genres, at a textual and thematic level. In the case of Fonte, as I believe to have demonstrated, such a difference must be recognized in her lack of desire, *or perhaps in her inability to rewrite, time after time, even if she wanted what tradition handed down*" (emphasis and trans. are mine). More optimistic is Kolsky 1999: 182, who believes that Fonte's reshaping of the genre successfully "undermines the patriarchal ideology central to epic. For the critique of male-dominated society is not sporadic in the poem."

10. These are the only two battles fought by Risamante against human adversaries. The third battle is against a snake at 3.1–17.

11. On Virgil's popularity in the Renaissance, see Zabughin 1923 and Wilson-Okamura 2010. On the literary canonization of the *Orlando Furioso*, see Javitch 1991.

Fonte implicitly criticizes the endings of these earlier epics by showing that in the climactic duel her lady knight does not follow the same pattern of unnecessary violence. Applying Quint's ideas[12] on repetition to the plot of the *Floridoro*, I illustrate how Risamante is described as a knight who at first repeats the stereotypical moves and mistakes of her previous enemy (Macandro) as well as those of her male epic predecessors (Aeneas/Rodomonte) but later in Canto 13 finds a way out of that archetype, accepting her femininity and a more humane victory that involves sparing her enemy. Humanists like Francesco Petrarca, Francesco Filelfo, Maffeo Vegio, Giovanni Pontano, Antonio Possevino, Lionardo Salviati, and Torquato Tasso share Fonte's preoccupations with violent epic endings. They argue that courage cannot be mixed with anger and criticize the ending of the *Aeneid*: Fonte, in the *Floridoro*, uses women's pity and ability to refrain from excessive violence as the indispensable traits of a better hero and the proof of female superiority. This conclusion is articulated more openly in Fonte's masterpiece *Il merito delle donne*.[15]

TRUNCATED STORIES

Stanza 70 of Canto 13 is the last stanza in the only printed edition, prepared by Doglioni for the printer Rampazetti in Venice and published in 1581. The book is visibly incomplete: not only does the title *Tredici canti* unusually describe the number of Cantos rather than the name of the protagonist with or without a qualifying adjective but also the story's two main narrative threads—one connected to Floridoro as ancestor of the founders of Venice, the other linked to Risamante as originator of the Medici family—have been set in motion but are far from being resolved, as neither character is yet married.[13] The unfinished nature of the work is also clearly revealed by the transitional character of the last lines:[14]

Quel che poi ne successe altrove io canto,
Ch'ora di Celsidea vuo' dirvi alquanto.
(*Fl.* 13.70.7–8)

What happened later I sing somewhere else,
Because now I want to tell you about Celsidea.[15]

---

12. Quint 1993: 3–18.
13. Kolsky 1999: 168.
14. Fonte 1995: XVIII, XLV: here Finucci clarifies that no manuscript has ever been found. For her modern edition, she uses only the 1581 edition.
15. Translations of *Floridoro* are mine unless stated otherwise.

Fonte usually marks the ending of a Canto by clearly expressing in the first person her will to stop and to continue in the next.[16] In the lines above, while the Risamante-Biondaura story is interrupted (13.70.7), the wish to reintroduce the tale of Celsidea is expressed in the authorial first person, without a clear allusion to a new Canto. Although, considering the quoted passage, we cannot tell whether Fonte will talk about Celsidea "now" in the next line or in the next Canto, it seems logical that at 13.70.7–8 we have two references to two continuations: one nearer in the future, marked by the word "now" and referring to the immediate renewal of the action connected to Celsidea in the present Canto, and another in the next Canto, marked by the adverb "elsewhere." Both meanings are possible, since in each Canto this writer typically introduces two or three episodes, and in 13 she has already related two (Circetta's prophecy of the Venetian glory and Risamante's victory over Cloridabello).

Doglioni's biography of Fonte provides further confirmation of the incompleteness of the poem, informing the reader that "compose ella in casa mia il Poema del Floridoro, non pur il stampato, ma altro ancora, che non è dato alle stampe," "during her stay in my household, she wrote the *Floridoro* (not just the Cantos that appeared in the published edition, but others that have not yet been published)."[17] Unfortunately, the *altro ancora* is lost, and Doglioni does not reveal why the book was published before being finished.

According to Finucci, *Il Floridoro*'s truncated ending is somewhat predictable and significant. The writer, a respectable Venetian citizen and subtle interpreter of Renaissance ideological strictures, is able to construct transgressive roles for her female characters only if she does not have to confirm or reject them through an ending.[18] This is an interesting possibility: Fonte would try to preserve her freedom and at the same time undercut the subversive power of her work by refusing to finish it, by withholding the crucial interpretation supplied in closure. While Risamante's future as a wife and mother is reassuringly predicted in the text, Fonte does not narrate her domestication. Fonte's powerlessness to shape the end of her work can be interpreted in line with Quint's pattern in *Epic and Empire,* and the *Floridoro* can be classified as an epic of the vanquished, one that, focusing on victims rather than victors, identifies the shortcomings of the epic and tries to resist them, often without a positive solution.[19] Quint explores the idea of *resistance* and identifies in the Neronian poet Lucan the originator of the *epic of the vanquished,* a rival,

---

16. E.g., she concludes Canto 1 by saying, "On the third [day] there arrives a knight / about whom I hope to narrate in the next Canto" (*Fl.* 1.100.7–8).

17. Fonte 1988: 9n28 = Fonte 1997: 36.

18. Fonte 1995: XXXVIII.

19. Quint 1993: 8–9, 133. On closure in post-Augustan epic, see Hardie 1993: 1–19.

anti-Virgilian tradition of epic whose major poems—the *Pharsalia, La Arau-
cana* of Alonso de Ercilla, and *Les Tragiques* of Agrippa d'Aubigné—embrace
the politically defeated. *Floridoro* would embrace the cause of women as the
socially disadvantaged.

Even if in the *Floridoro* the attempt to resist traditional epic orientation
produces stories without an ending, we do have in the Biondaura-Risamante
segment at least one important narrative thread with a positive conclusion.[20]
Undoubtedly, the battle between Risamante and Cloridabello constitutes a
meaningful ending not only in the lady knight's obtaining a kingdom but also
in the ideological contest that Fonte is fighting through her heroine. In this
preliminary closure, the excellence of women, a theme that Fonte considers at
length in *Il merito delle donne,* is manifested in the creation of a female knight
who exemplifies women's ability to shine in physical and intellectual matters:

> Sempre s'è visto e vede (pur ch'alcuna
> Donna v' abbia voluto il pensier porre)
> Nella milizia riuscir più d'una,
> E 'l pregio e 'l grido a molti uomini torre;
> E così nelle lettere e in ciascuna
> Impresa, che l'uom pratica e discorre,
> Le donne sì buon frutto han fatto e fanno,
> Che gli uomini a invidiar punto non hanno.
> (*Fl.* 4.2)

> Numerous women throughout history have attained success in military life,
> outstripping the achievements of many of their male comrades, and the
> same still occurs whenever a woman turns her energies to this kind of activ-
> ity. The same may be said of the profession of letters, and all other activities
> in which men engage: women's achievements have been and are such that
> they have no cause to envy men.[21]

Besides the narrator's remarks, as we will see, the duel between Risamante
and Cloridabello establishes once again the excellence of women and provides
a comment on one of the genre's traditional conclusions: the hero's victory
obtained through his enemy's slaughter.

---

20. Kolsky 1999: 169 agrees with this opinion.
21. Translation from Fonte 1997: 262.

FIGHTING LIKE A MAN: THE DUEL BETWEEN
RISAMANTE AND MACANDRO

In the first Canto of the *Floridoro*, Macandro, to prove that his queen Biond-aura is more beautiful than princess Celsidea of Athens, challenges the warriors of Athens and the surrounding territories to fight him. We find in these lines a narrative context that will be represented again at the end of the poem: a prince in love with the beautiful Biondaura, queen of Armenia, is anxious to establish in combat his beloved's supremacy.

Biondaura's portrait establishes her symbolic presence, hung on a tree by Macandro, who devotedly and proudly addresses it like the image of a goddess:

> Appeso a un ramo avea del Sacro Olivo
> Un'effigie di donna alma e gentile,
> D'un aspetto sì nobile e sì divo,
> Che raro alcun se gli trovò simile.
> A questo che parea, non finto, vivo,
> Sì lo ritrasse un diligente stile,
> Inchinossi l'altier divoto e fido,
> E roppe insieme il ciel con questo grido:
> (*Fl.* 1.32)

On a branch of the sacred olive tree he had hung the image of a woman magnificent and gentle with a look so noble and so divine that a similar one could scarcely be found. In front of this image which seemed to be alive, not artificial—in such a diligent manner had it been rendered—the devoted and faithful proud one [Macandro] knelt down while at the same time shattering heaven with this outcry:

> "Ben che degn'io non sia d'un favor tale,
> O de l'Armenia e del mio cor Regina,
> Ch'essendo un cavallier vile e mortale
> Esaltar cerchi una beltà divina;
> Pur accetta il voler pronto e leale,
> Che sol la tua grandezza adora e inchina,
> E degna, ch'io per te vinca or gli Achei,
> Che poi voglio anco in ciel vincer gli dèi."
> (*Fl.* 1.33)

"Even though I am not worthy of such a favor, queen of Armenia and of my heart, and even though being (only) a modest and mortal knight I try to exalt a divine beauty, still accept my ready and loyal will which adores and kneels only in front of your greatness, and grant that for you I may vanquish the Achaeans now, I who desire later even to vanquish the gods in heaven."

Macandro's pride and spite seem to originate with Biondaura. He plainly admits that he is nothing without the queen's inspiration and that he dares heroic deeds only in her name. He can "vanquish the Achaeans" (1.32.7) or challenge the gods (1.32.8) only under the sign of his beloved, and in fact the image (*effigie*, 1.32.8) of the woman is prominently located in the scene. A typical motif of medieval and Renaissance literature is at work here, that of men in love with idealized women who become trophies or, as Virginia Woolf noticed, "looking-glasses possessing the magic or delicious power of reflecting the figure of men at twice its natural size."[22] Macandro's exaltations of the queen are only pretenses to assert his strength and valor.

It is also remarkable that Macandro treats Biondaura exactly as Orlando treats Angelica in the *Orlando Furioso*. Neither couple has a sexual relationship, and the men idealize the objects of their desire as some sort of compensation. Macandro's unrequited and chaste love toward Biondaura is fashioned after Petrarchan love, in which the woman is silent and unreachable.[23] In her first portrayal of love, Fonte exaggerates Petrarchan clichés to criticize lovers who accept a fixed characterization of the beloved lady and a rigid allocation of both lovers' roles: on the one hand we have a woman who is beautiful and silent to the point where a picture can be substituted for her; on the other hand we have an arrogant, vocal, and manipulative man who fights in her name.[24]

Many valiant warriors are unseated by the giant who collects their shields as proof of victory. But at the beginning of Canto 2, when Macandro believes

---

22. Greene 1999: 35.

23. The link between love and sexual frustration has been thematized in courtly love. Whether self-imposed or forced, the restraint of the troubadours is adopted in Petrarch's lyric and becomes a hallmark of Renaissance Platonic love: see Scaglione 1997: 557; Wollock 2011. Finucci 1992: 129 connects courtly love with Freud's and Lacan's psychological model: "For Lacan, man's need to put woman on a pedestal, as evident in courtly love literature, reflects his own lack. 'For the man, whose lady was entirely, in the most servile sense of the term, his female subject,' he writes, 'courtly love is the only way of coming off elegantly from the absence of sexual relation' (God and the *Jouissance*, 141). To control this threat, Orlando makes an icon of Angelica. Overvaluation of women is, after all, in the Freudian scenario, what man does in regard to his chosen object when he overcomes his own adolescent narcissism ('On Narcissism,' p. 94). Beauty so satisfies Orlando that he is content to have Angelica fetishistically, by transforming her whole body, the signifier of his desire, into a fetish. In doing so he can entertain feelings of godly omnipotence without fear of failure."

24. For women as interchangeable objects of their desire for men, see Shemek 1998: 50*ff*.

that no other knight will challenge him, Risamante, wearing armor and believed by everyone to be a man, shows up to fight against the seemingly invincible foreigner. The fight proceeds in a calculated crescendo. With her lance, Risamante wounds her enemy, who tries in vain to strike her on the head. Macandro handles his sword and again turns his fury against Risamante's head:

> Sì forte lo percosse a mezza fronte,
> Che gli tolse ogni senso, e avrebbe reso
> L'alma smarrita al regno di Acheronte,
> *Se l'elmo fin non lo tenea difeso.*
> (*Fl.* 2.14.1–4)

So violently [Macandro] hit him [Risamante] in the middle of the forehead that he made him [Risamante] faint and would have sent the dazed soul to the kingdom of Acheron if the fine helmet had not defended him.

The description hides Risamante's gender: twice she is introduced with the male personal pronoun (*Lo percosse . . . gli tolse*). Fonte depicts the scene from the point of view of two audiences—the internal (the spectators of the fight) and external (the reader)—neither of which is aware of the disguise. She emphasizes the life-saving helmet, seemingly the heroine's greatest protection, through an allusion to Ruggiero's helmet in his battle against Rodomonte in the *Orlando Furioso*:

> Con quella estrema forza che percuote
> La machina ch'in Po sta su due navi,
> E levata con uomini e con ruote
> Cader si lascia su le aguzze travi;
> *Fere il pagan Ruggier, quanto più puote,*
> *Con ambe man sopra ogni peso gravi:*
> *Giova l'elmo incantato; che senza esso,*
> *Lui col cavallo avria in un colpo fesso.*
> (*OF* 46.122)

With that excessive force through which the pile-driver standing in the Po on twin pontoons, after being raised by men with winches, drops onto the pointed stakes, (with similar force) the pagan put all his weight (and no weight was heavier) behind his two-handed blow as he struck Ruggiero: the enchanted helmet saved Ruggiero—without it, the blow would have cleft rider and steed in two. (trans. Waldman, adapted)

The emphasis on the helmet and the head likely alludes to Bradamante's head
wound mentioned in Ariosto's *Orlando Furioso* at 25.26. Risamante, like Bradamante, achieves power and superiority "by cloaking her feminine identity
in armor" that "renders her invisible and disintegrates the materiality of her
female body."[25] In the *Orlando Furioso*, Bradamante's wound and haircut are
recalled at significant moments as a reference to woman's castration: they
demonstrate that she is not a man, "for she has literally inscribed on her body
the symbolic castration that makes her a woman."[26] A different logic seems to
be at work in a poem written by a woman: the female writer does not yield
to Ariosto's impulse to reveal the lady knight's female identity and presumed
weakness by enacting a symbolic castration. Risamante is not wounded, and
we do not discover that she is a woman. Her identity is hidden under Fonte's
language and a helmet.

At *Floridoro* 2.17 it is Risamante who wounds the giant on the thigh,
immediately after which she defends herself in a graphic scene:

> Macandro ancora il colpo all'elmo segna
> Del cavallier con tutto il suo potere,
> Alza ei lo scudo, e sulla vaga insegna
> Del giglio il brando impetuoso fere.
> Ben crede il cavallier, ch'in Parthia regna
> Farlo in due pezzi al pian morto cadere;
> Taglia lo scudo e taglia anco il cimiero,
> Ma resse l'elmo al colpo orrendo e fiero.
> (*Fl.* 2.17)

> Macandro again aims his hit at the helmet of the knight with all his power,
> he [the knight] lifts the shield and the impetuous sword strikes the beautiful
> emblem of the lily. The knight who rules in Parthia is sure he will make him
> fall dead on the plain in two pieces. He cuts the shield and even the plume
> but the helmet resisted the horrendous and fierce blow.

Risamante is again described grammatically as a man (*cavallier . . . ei*), yet in
the mention of the white lily that protects the woman, Fonte seems to yield to
a traditional view that makes virginity and chastity the most important qualities for women. White female attire symbolizes virginity, and as does the lily
in the medieval and Renaissance traditions. In paintings, the presence of a

---

25. Shemek 1989: 93–94. On armor as a symbol of wholeness in the *OF*, see Bellamy 1992:
94.

26. Finucci 1992: 243.

vase of lilies is typically associated with the Immaculate Conception of Mary.[27] This conservative emphasis on female purity is paired with a further comment on gender reversal, implied in the following *ottavas* when the sexual dimension of the battle becomes evident.[28]

In stanza 20, Macandro exploits his enemy's confusion by coming closer to try to give the fatal blow. The attempt is unsuccessful, and the contest proceeds with sexual innuendo, in the mention of one warrior's closed thighs and the other warrior's newly erected sword. The ambiguous connotations of the fighters' identities evoke a homosexual skirmish:

> Macandro disdegnoso che conosce,
> Ch'alcuno de suoi pensier non avea effetto,
> Poi che 'l guerrier [Risamante] tien strette ambe le cosce,
> E non lascia accostar petto con petto;
> Per dargli (se esser può) l'estreme angosce,
> E mandargli lo spirito al stigio tetto,
> Ripiglia il brando e drizza il colpo crudo
> In loco tal che nol difende scudo.
> (*Fl.* 2.20)

Upset Macandro who realizes that not one of his ideas is successful because the knight keeps his thighs closed and does not let [his] breast come near to [his] breast, in order to give him [Risamante] (if it can happen) extreme distresses and send his spirit to the house of Styx, takes again the sword and directs his cruel blow at the spot which the shield does not defend.

For a while legs remain closed and breasts apart; then Risamante's sword penetrates her enemy's flesh and kills him:

> E poi caccia la spada aspra e pungente
> Sopra la coscia all'alma empia e ribella;
> Passa la punta ria tra 'l ventre, e 'l fianco
> Due palmi, e 'l fa venir di vita manco.
> (*Fl.* 2.21.5–8)

---

27. Risamante's armor and attire are described at 2.5.1–2: "Her emblem was a white lily on a green background, and her dress was green and white." Fonte 1988: 164 underscores white as connoting simplicity and purity. It is also the color worn by Ariosto's Bradamante (*OF* 1.60.3).

28. Interesting observations on how "looking" becomes sexualized in the battles of the *OF* and the *Gerusalemme Liberata* in Günsberg 1987: 27–31.

Then [the warrior] thrusts [his] sharp and piercing sword above the thigh of
that impious and rebellious soul, the cruel point cuts through between the
belly and the flank two hand-widths wide, causing him to lose life.

The battle is described using the terms of an amorous encounter, and we learn
only when the winner takes off his helmet that he is in fact a woman. In Tasso's *Gerusalemme Liberata* and Ariosto's *Orlando Furioso,* the subordination of
the masculine traits in the female characters is achieved through the martial
defeat of Gildippe, Clorinda, and Bradamante by a male warrior.[29] Yet in Ariosto, neither Bradamante nor Marfisa suffers major overthrows at the hands
of a man, confirming Ariosto's "protofeminism." Many duels that make up so
much of Ariosto's war material employ sexual language that particularly resonates when one of the combatants is a female. The winner usually has a more
potent phallic apparatus than the loser, who is at least cast down, and often
penetrated, by the victor. Following this logic, Ariosto's resistance to showing
women losing in combat is a symptom "of his over-all reluctance to portray
women as humiliated, sexually or otherwise."[30] *Floridoro* 2.20–21 would confirm that Fonte read Ariosto and, following his lead, did not wish to victimize
her heroine by subjecting her to a major martial defeat. At the same time, in
Risamante's killing of Macandro, Fonte is also suggesting that a woman can
replace a man, and that this substitution comes with risks: fighting women can
be as brutal as fighting men. Yet the writer's pessimistic judgment about the
violent act (rape/murder) is implied and defused in the indeterminacy of the
warrior's identity and in the negative connotation (*ria*) qualifying the sword
rather than the person wielding it.

The Parthian king's death is a bit surprising if we recall the rules of the
tournament (1.18–19), which did not demand the killing of one's antagonist.
Irony is present in the term "fierce"[31] given to Macandro, who so far has
slaughtered none of his enemies, while it is Risamante, the "warrior who was
kind and courteous" (*guerrier che gentile era e cortese,* 2.25.1), who kills her
opponent.

The episode ends with the revelation of Risamante's female identity and
the audience's bewilderment at her similarity to the portrait Biondaura (2.27).
The unveiling of Risamante provokes amazement (*e si maravigliar,* 2.27.7) and
confusion. Risamante is believed to be Biondaura, and King Cleardo feels he
must question her motives. He asks why she has killed the valiant supporter of
her honor ("a dir, perch'avea tratto / di vita un che 'l suo onore chiaro e sereno

---

29. Günsberg 1987: 20*ff.*; Finucci 1992: 230–53.

30. McLucas 1988: 41–42. For Bradamante's originality as an amazon, see Roche 1988: 113–
33, esp. 114. Cf. Stoppino 2012: chaps. 1 and 2.

31. Macandro is called *feroce* at 2.18.4 and *rio* "bad" in the *argumentum* of Canto 2.

/ rendea," 2.29.5–7). The lady knight reveals herself to be Biondaura's twin and tells her story: how she was abducted by the wizard Celidante, who trained her as a warrior, and how her sister, once revealed as her twin, had denied her a share of the kingdom. For the first time the reader learns that Risamante's real enemy is her twin, a woman whose exterior is ironically similar to that of the lady knight but who does not seem to share anything else with her. Besides the similarity between the two sisters, Risamante's "manifest valor," her martial ability, most impresses the audience.

TWIN STORIES

We find a similar story in the last Canto of the *Floridoro*: Risamante must fight Cloridabello, another man in love with Biondaura, who makes him her champion, "either to save herself or to fall with him" ("o per salvarsi o per cader con ello," 13.57.8). The situation and development of the plot are remarkably similar to the Macandro episode. Yet there is one crucial difference: Risamante will not kill her antagonist.

At *Floridoro* 12.58–59, the duel between Risamante and Cloridabello, king of Babylonia, is qualified as the final fight, which will determine who will rule Armenia; likewise, in the *Aeneid* (12.75–80), the battle between Turnus and Aeneas is characterized as decisive for the outcome of the entire war. Enclosed by the city walls, Biondaura's and Risamante's armies as well as the citizens of Artemita watch the two knights' final struggle (13.48.1–4).[32] While the herald explains the conditions of the fight, Risamante grows impatient and starts the duel:

Ma non avea finito di dir questo
Anco l'alfier che l'inclita guerriera,
Sendole ormai 'l posar troppo molesto,
Ritornò ardita alla battaglia fiera.
Cloridabel non fu di lei men presto
E menò un colpo alla donzella altiera,
Ma scarso alquanto fu, che se cogliea
A pien la spalla destra le fendea.
(*Fl.* 13.60)

---

32. "The inhabitants of Artemita climbing on the wall / sadly look at the cruel duel; / the armies outside the field / admire which of the two (warriors) is more worthy" (*Fl.* 13.48.1–4); cf. *Aeneid* 12.122–24, where the Italian and Trojan armies gather by the doors while the people occupy the towers and the top of the gates to watch the duel between Aeneas and Turnus (*Aen.* 12.131–33); the scene is repeated at *Aen.* 12.704–9.

The herald had not yet finished saying this when the illustrious warrior, this pause being too bothersome [for her] to bear, boldly went back to the fierce battle. Cloridabel was not less quick than she and delivered a blow to the proud maiden, but it was too weak a blow; for if it had fully hit, it would have severed her right shoulder.

This time the gender of the opponents is clear. Risamante is called "glorious female warrior" and "proud maiden," characterized by feminine adjectives (*ardita, altiera*) as well as by female pronouns (*lei, le,* "she, her"). Cloridabello tries to cut into the girl's shoulder. When she sees that her enemy has succeeded, and blood is squirting out of the wound, she is ashamed. The shame on the maiden's cheek is depicted with a vivid simile:

> Risamante al gran colpo in viso venne
> Vermiglia più che in sul mattin la rosa,
> E fu lo sdegno tal che ne divenne
> Poco men che insensata e furiosa,
> Perché se tinta è ben di sangue tutta
> Non era ancora del suo macchiata e brutta.
> (*Fl.* 13.61.3–8)

Risamante at the great blow turned, on her face, redder than the rosy sky at dawn, and her disdain was such that she became almost insane and infuriated because even if she is all covered with blood, she was not yet spotted and polluted with his.

Here Risamante turns red like Ruggiero at the end of the *Orlando Furioso* (46.124–25). In that poem, the warrior, unseated from his horse by Rodomonte, turning toward his beloved and frightened Bradamante and feeling more shame than anger (*più che d'ira, di vergogna pieno,* 46.125.2),[33] craved a quick reprisal ("ad emendar presto quell'onta, / stringe la spada, e col pagan s'affronta," "in order to quickly amend that shame / he seizes his sword and faces the pagan," 46.125.78).

In stanza 62 of the *Floridoro*, driven by fury and desirous of vengeance, the woman wounds her enemy in the head:

> *Spinta da gran furor lo scudo getta,*
> *E con ambe le man la spada presa,*
> *Disegna far sul capo la vendetta*

---

33. Ariosto 1999.

Più debita alla man che l'avea offesa.
Cloridabello alza lo scudo in fretta,
Visto il colpo calar, per sua difesa,
Taglia in due parti il colpo altier lo scudo
E penetra nel capo il brando crudo.
(*Fl.* 13.62)

Incensed by a great fury she throws away her shield, and grabbing her sword
with both hands she plans to exact on the head the vengeance that was rather
due to the hand that had offended her. Cloridabello quickly lifts his shield,
having seen the blow falling (on him), for his defense; the haughty slash cuts
in two the shield, and the cruel sword penetrates his head.

Reenacting the maiden's actions during her previous duel, Cloridabello covers
his head with the shield, which is cut in two, while Risamante starts behaving like Macandro. It is a moment of great suspense and role reversal, as the
situation and language allude directly to Rodomonte's behavior in *Orlando
Furioso* 46.121:

Quando si vide in tante parti rosse
Il pagan l'arme, e non poter schivare
Che la più parte di quelle percosse
Non gli andasse la carne a ritrovare;
A maggior rabbia, a più furor si mosse,
Ch'a mezzo il verno il tempestoso mare;
Getta lo scudo, e a tutto suo potere
Su l'elmo di Ruggiero a due man fere.
(*OF* 46.121)[34]

Now the pagan, seeing his armor bloodied at so many points, and aware that
he could not prevent most of the sword-strokes from reaching his flesh, *was
goaded to a greater fury* than the sea in a winter storm. *He threw away his
shield and with all his might brought his sword down two-handed on Ruggiero's helmet.* (trans. Waldman, slightly adapted)

Both Risamante's and Rodomonte's anger is increased by the sight of blood on
their armor. They react by throwing down their shields, grasping their swords
with both hands, and directing them toward the head of the adversary.

---

34. For the Italian text of *Orlando Furioso* I am using Ariosto 1999.

Risamante's untempered reactions are not surprising: they are crafted to underscore her similarity to the *Furioso*'s antagonists. Ariosto in Canto 46 assimilates Ruggiero to Rodomonte, and compares the knights to enraged dogs engaged in deadly combat (46.138). Ruggiero's initial agreement to spare Rodomonte (*e di lasciarlo vivo gli fa patto*, 46.137.4) fades away, and the Este ancestor repeatedly plunges his knife into his opponent's forehead:[35]

> E due e tre volte ne l'orribil fronte,
> Alzando, più ch'alzar si possa, il braccio,
> Il ferro del pugnale a Rodomonte
> Tutto nascose, e si levò d'impaccio.
> Alle squalide ripe d'Acheronte,
> Sciolta dal corpo più freddo che giaccio,
> Bestemmiando fuggì l'alma sdegnosa,
> Che fu sì altiera al mondo e sì orgogliosa.
> (*OF* 46.140)

So two or three times he raised his arm to its full height and plunged the dagger to the hilt in Rodomont's horrible forehead, thus assuring his own safety. Released from its body, now ice-cold, the angry soul which, among the living, had been so proud and insolent, fled cursing down to the dismal shores of Acheron. (trans. Waldman, slightly adapted)

Similarly, with unsettling violence, Aeneas in the concluding lines of Virgil's *Aeneid* does not preserve that *pietas* which has motivated and qualified the hero's actions throughout his mission. In his final fight against Turnus, the Trojan hero after an initial hesitation and desire to comply with his enemy's plea for mercy ("Aeneas volvens oculos *dextramque repressit*; / et iam iamque magis *cunctantem flectere sermo coeperat*" "Rolling his eyes, *Aeneas repressed his hand* / and more and more *the speech started to affect the hesitating man*," 12.939–41), furious at the sight of Pallas's sword belt, sinks his blade into the Rutulian's chest:[36]

> Ille, oculis postquam saevi monumenta doloris
> Exuviasque hausit, *furiis accensus et ira*
> *Terribilis* (. . .)

---

35. For a comparison of the endings of the *Orlando Furioso* and the *Aeneid*, see Thomas 2001: 284–86; Burrow 1997: 83.

36. Virgil swerves from the Homeric model by making the spear wound not fatal. This feature is important for Ariosto and Fonte. On Aeneas's hesitation, see Hardie 1993: 146; Behr 2014: 197–212. Translations of Virgil's *Aeneid* are mine unless otherwise specified.

Ferrum adverso sub pectore condit
Fervidus; ast illi solvuntur frigore membra
Vitaque cum gemitu fugit indignata sub umbras.
(*Aen.* 12.945-7 . . . 950-52)

For when the sight came home to him,
Aeneas raged at the relic of his anguish
Worn by this man as a trophy. *Blazing up*
And terrible in his anger (. . .)
He sank his blade *in fury* in Turnus' chest.
Then all the body slackened in death's chill,
And with a groan for that indignity
His spirit fled into the gloom below. (trans. Fitzgerald)

Servius explains *indignata*, qualifying Turnus's soul, as a rejoinder to Aeneas's denial of mercy.[37] Unbridled violence characterizes this last meeting which, given the terms of the treaty between the Trojans and the Latins, should have been much more restrained.[38] Aeneas at the end of the poem fails to embrace the self-imposed standards that were supposed to bestow on him the right to rule in Italy.[39] He becomes the new Achilles. In *Aeneid* 12, the past returns with a dismaying difference; this time, the Trojans are the victors.

David Quint has brilliantly explored the purpose of repetition in the Augustan text. Quint distinguishes regressive repetition as "obsessive circular return to a traumatic past" from "repetition-as-reversal." The latter allows a crucial difference, thanks to which the past can be mastered. According to Quint, these two narrative patterns match two typical reactions of the victim of a trauma. The victim, as Freud describes in *Beyond the Pleasure Principle*, responds to trauma by repeatedly reenacting his victimization; sometimes, though, he reproduces the original dramatic situation to create a new version of it in which he is not the victim anymore.[40] According to the latter pattern, the Trojans would return to war, with a different adversary, to become the winners.

---

37. It is only one of the several interpretative possibilities given by Servius; see Paratore 1990: 271. On *Aen.* 12.951-52, see Thomas 2001: 150-53.

38. At *Aeneid* 12.187-94, Aeneas clarifies the outcome if he wins: he wants Trojans and Italians to be friends under identical laws and gods; he asks for no kingdom for himself, just a town.

39. On this controversial ending, see Thomas 2001: 278-96 (with useful bibliography) and below.

40. Quint's 1993: 50-51 analysis of the dialectic between the epic of the winners and that of the losers is compelling and argued with a wide variety of historiographical and literary evidence. For a review, see Farrell 1994.

In Quint's analysis, victory logically constitutes the positive pole. Progress and mastery of the past can only be connected to the kind of resolution
provided by the hero's or winner's adversaries because it is victory that grants
the plot sense and meaning, and, retrospectively, makes every action just and
justifiable. In other words, the "vindication and reciprocity of doing unto others what has been done to oneself"[41] in epic are codified and praiseworthy.
While in the confrontation between Risamante and Macandro Fonte gives a
stereotypical example of combat that endorses unnecessary violence, in the
concluding lines of Canto 13 of the *Floridoro* (the fight between Risamante and
Cloridabello), she revises this conception of epic as legitimization of triumph
through violence, and of violence through triumph.

BRUTAL ENDINGS AND THEIR CRITICS

To understand better Fonte's response to the epic tradition, it is necessary
to analyze more precisely the problems and critical discussion that focuses
on the ends of the *Aeneid* and the *Orlando Furioso*. In Virgil's and Ariosto's
poems, the fury characterizing the men at the origin of the Roman and the
Este dynasties, respectively, is not openly criticized by their narrators. In both
poems, the writers bring the curtains down suddenly, glossing over the brutal
endings. Critics in several ages have been perplexed at this silence and how it
should be interpreted. We cannot be sure of Virgil's endorsement of Aeneas's
anger, and, as Ralph Johnson has suggested, we may be inclined to think that
Virgil is underscoring in his epic Aeneas's moral failing and moral failing generally as the founding act of all empires.[42]

Some scholars have considered this position as fundamentally ahistorical,
imposing on the Augustan text modern preoccupations, particularly American intellectuals' antiimperialistic concerns.[43] Yet Craig Kallendorf has recently
pointed out that critics from late twentieth-century, post–Vietnam War America are not the only ones to see ambiguities complicating the Virgilian text.
The elements brought to relevance by the recent "pessimistic school" were

---

41. Quint 1993: 75.

42. This is the view maintained by the "Harvard," or "pessimistic" school: see Brooks 1953;
Clausen 1966; Dubois 1982: 28–51; Johnson 1976; Parry 1963; Putnam 1965; Wallace-Hadrill 1982.
E.g., Dubois 1982: 51: "The sorrow the reader feels at the end of the *Aeneid* serves to emphasize
the tenuousness of Vergil's harmony, the delicacy of the compromise, the fear that beneath the
surface of sovereignty, peace, and stasis, the age of iron has come, will come again." Recently
Putnam 2012. Contra: Galinsky 1988: 321–48; 1994: 191–201; 1997: 89–100; Otis 1963; Pöschl
1950; Stahl 1993: 174–211; Thomas 1990: 64–71. For an overview of the discussion, see Behr 2014;
Horsfall 1995: 192–16; Kallendorf 1989: 1–18; Putnam 1999: 210–30.

43. Galinsky 1988; Harrison 1990; Serpa 1987: 76–88; Wlosok 1990.

present not only in scholarship produced during the 1920s, 1930s, and 1940s[44] but also during the Italian Renaissance, when some intellectuals censured, more or less openly, Aeneas's behavior in the final conflict with Turnus.[45]

Francesco Petrarca (1304–74), for instance, in *De otio religioso* underscores the remoteness of the *Aeneid* from Christian standards, ultimately blaming Aeneas for his lack of piety. Likewise, Francesco Filelfo (1398–1481) in his philosophical work *De morali disciplina* rejects Aristotle's doctrine of just anger,[46] maintaining that true strength cannot be linked to anger. He illustrates the point by showing Aeneas's failing in the final lines of the *Aeneid* and by creating in his own epic poem, the *Sphortias,* a hero (Francesco Sforza) who, even on the battlefield, is able to control *ira.* In his description of the annihilation of Piacenza in the *Sphortias,* Filelfo does not obliterate its violence. At times he intrudes upon the narration and apostrophizes the gods, begging them to halt Sforza's men and the cruelty that their leader cannot restrict. Yet Sforza himself is depicted as a perfect master of his own emotions. He never attacks without having been provoked and strikes only in self-defense.[47]

Maffeo Vegio (1407–58) indirectly admits the moral ambiguity of the end of the *Aeneid* by adding to the Virgilian version a thirteenth book (known as the *Supplementum*), which picks up where Virgil left off and includes Turnus's funeral, Aeneas's marriage to Lavinia, the founding of the city of Lavinium, and Aeneas's apotheosis.[48] This book became famous during the sixteenth century and was normally printed alongside Virgil's poem.[49] Even Ludovico Dolce's translation of the *Aeneid,* without including a translation of Vegio's *Supplement,* emulates it, ending with Aeneas's marriage and the hero's apotheosis.

If on the one hand Vegio is trying to magnify the praise of Aeneas, who is assumed to heaven as a reward for his worthy deeds (*Supplementum,* 611–31) and characterized in Vegio's tract *De educatione liberorum et eorum claris moribus* as a "man endowed with every virtue" (*virum omni virtute praeditum*),[50]

---

44. Kallendorf 1999: 393 (discussing Horsfall).

45. Ibid., 394–403; Kallendorf 2015: 35–40.

46. Robin 1991: 75.

47. The portrait of Sforza's virtues on the battlefield is so exaggerated that, in this episode, he resembles a caricature; see Robin 1991: 76.

48. Michael Putnam is the editor and translator of the most recent edition of Vegio's *Supplementum,* which I have used for quotes. For a short summary of the plot recounted in Vegio's Book 13 of the *Aeneid,* see also Cox Brinton 2002: 52 (= argumentum).

49. E.g., Vegio's *Supplementum* was included in Adam de Ambergau's edition of the *Aeneid* (1471) and translated by Gavin Douglas as part of his Scottish version, completed in 1513 and published in 1553; see Putnam 2004: xxiii. Thomas 2001: 280 states that during the Renaissance Vegio's work "became an object of satire and emulation."

50. Kallendorf 1989: 104.

on the other hand the humanist's urge to draw an anger-free Aeneas and an obviously guilty Turnus implies that Virgil's handling of the topic is inadequate. Vegio indirectly compels the reader to compare his perfectly moderate hero and happy ending to Virgil's passionate protagonist and tragic conclusion.[51] If Aeneas in the *Supplement* is not made into a Christian hero, he is nevertheless improved; Vegio calls him *victor magnanimus* ("great-souled victor," *Supplementum* 2–3), differentiating him from the Virgilian hero described in *Aeneid* 12.946–47 as *furiis accensus et ira terribilis* ("fired with fury and terrible in his anger"). Free of wrath, Vegio's Aeneas is able "to put aside the final words of vendetta that Virgil's narrator allots him (12.947–49) immediately before he kills and to replace them with a reasoned, high-minded discussion of why Turnus deserved death."[52] Vegio was not the only one trying to rewrite the ending of the *Aeneid*. Several continuations appeared between the fifteenth and seventeenth centuries.[53]

Giovanni Pontano (1426–1503) is another humanist scholar and poet who, in a passage of his treatise *De fortitudine*, theorizes that courage as a virtue cannot be mingled with anger. In his opinion, in the *Aeneid* it is left to Turnus to show how *fortitudo* can be preserved by containing wrath. From the perspective of Christian chivalric codes of honor, even Antonio Possevino (1533–1611) in his *Dialogo d'honore* (1553) openly criticizes Aeneas's conduct in the battle against Turnus by establishing as the duel's goal not the death of one of the opponents, but the recuperation of lost honor.[54] Finally, Lionardo Salviati (1540–87), in an epistolary exchange with Giovanni de' Bardi da Vernio, raises moral objections against Aeneas's actions, suggesting that "the end of the *Aeneid* fails to propel him clearly into the new civilization he was supposed to establish."[55]

---

51. Putnam 2004: xix–xxi; Kallendorf 1989: 100–128; Cox Brinton 2002: 1–50; Thomas 2001: 284: "At 13.36–48 Vegio's Aeneas first grants return of the corpse of Turnus, so closing out the possibility that it could receive the treatment of a Hector. . . . He then brilliantly shifts the blame for his own actions to the Ausonians: 'driven by *your* rage' (47 *vestris actus furiis*)—thereby suppressing his *own furiae*, so prominent in *Aeneid* 12.946" (emphasis original). Although, as Putnam observes, Vegio's text reveals "inexorable classicizing" echoes (xviii) and his desire "not to have Aeneas, in however oblique a manner, suffer the change from paganism to Christianity" (ibid.), the text also discloses Vegio's impulse to compete with an imperfect ethical model and improve upon it. For a comparison of Vegio's ending with Virgil's, see Putnam 2004: vii–xxiii and McGill's review of Putnam's book.

52. Putnam 2004: xx.

53. E.g., Pier Candido Decembrio's *Aeneid* supplement, written around 1419. For more on this work, see Schneider 1985: 136–38; Cox Brinton 2002: 2.

54. Seem 1990: 117–18.

55. Kallendorf 1999: 397–400; Sitterson 1992: 13, who shows how even Landino, the *Aeneid*'s principal Renaissance allegorizer, indirectly demonstrates Aeneas's failure: "[Landino] does not go beyond book six not just because the first six books fit his Neoplatonism so (relatively)

With her characterization of the heroine Risamante, Moderata Fonte can be added to the list of critics who debate aspects of the *Aeneid*. The end of the *Aeneid* is echoed in Ariosto's *Orlando Furioso*, Fonte's most important generic matrix for the *Floridoro*'s ending in Canto 13.[56] If we cannot be sure about the meaning of Ariosto's "citation" of the most enigmatic moment of the *Aeneid* (Turnus's slaughter by Aeneas) in the duel between Ruggiero and Rodomonte—especially as Virgil's very ending could be the target of Ariosto's notorious irony[57]—Fonte deviates from what both endings have in common: the hero's escalating anger, culminating in the enemy's death.

While Virgil and Ariosto end their poems as many influential epics of the Western world do, with the hero's victory established through ambiguous violence that, as we have seen, was to be criticized by some Renaissance and modern critics, Moderata Fonte, in her heroine's climactic battle, offers a remedy to these epics' violent and problematic conclusions.[58] In her poem she reproduces all the topoi of final battles up to the crucial point of Risamante's pious pardon of her enemy. If in epic "the incessant quest for adventure is nothing but a quest for recognition through the establishment of one's superiority—that is to say, one's difference from the others,"[59] in forgiveness this Renaissance writer reconsiders the equation between superiority and violent victory. She seems to assert that the difference between losers and winners cannot really be marked simply by brute force.[60] What Quint, after Freud, has called progress from the point of view of the plot, or the psyche of a victim, does not seem to coincide with moral progress. Instead, it resembles the particular process that C. Bandera describes with regard to the *Aeneid*.

---

well—as an allegorical journey toward the contemplative life, with the last six books an allegory of the inferior active life—but because book twelve is disturbingly inimical to his purposes" (Sitterson 1992: 11).

56. Collina 1989: 148; Malpezzi Price 1994a: 206, adding Bernardo Tasso's *Amadigi* (published in 1560 and changed later into *Floridante*) and Tasso's *Gerusalemme Liberata*. On the popularity of the *Furioso* among female readers in the sixteenth century, see Cox 1997: 134–38.

57. Bellamy 1994; Javitch 1984: 1030–32; Kennedy 1973.

58. E.g., in Homer's *Iliad*, Achilles kills Hector (Book 22); in the *Odyssey*, Odysseus kills the suitors (Book 22); in Virgil's *Aeneid*, Aeneas kills Turnus (Book 12); in the *Chanson de Roland*, Thierry kills Pinabel (*Laisses* 284–86) with the consequent execution of Ganelon; in Ariosto's *Orlando Furioso*, Ruggiero kills Rodomonte (Canto 46); and in Tasso's *Gerusalemme Liberata*, Tancredi kills Aladino while Goffredo kills Emireno (Canto 20).

59. Donato 1986: 41.

60. Allusion is a key feature in the study of any text with strong generic attributes. For a study of allusion that goes beyond a traditional *Quellenforschung*, see Conte 1974: esp. 5–14 and 1996; Edmunds 2001; Greene 1982: esp. 28–53; Hardie 1993; Hinds 1998; Pucci 1987: esp. 236–46; Suzuki 1989: esp. 1–17.

Bandera uses Girard's theory as it is explicated in *Violence and the Sacred* and applies it to the end of the *Aeneid*.[61] According to Girard, sacrificial crisis is employed when human violence threatens the destruction of a community. In times of extreme hardship, as the ultimate means to stop violence and save the community, a victim is chosen and slaughtered as a scapegoat.[62] Bandera believes that in the *Aeneid* (Books 6–12), the community experiences threatening violence; Turnus's death is the sacrifice of the scapegoat.[63] Bandera's treatment is significant for my argument because it focuses on the violence that characterizes the conclusion of the process (the sacrifice) and the "fearful symmetry" between Aeneas and Turnus, the sacrificer and the sacrificed.[64] During their final duel in the *Aeneid,* these protagonists are caught up in the reciprocity of their roles: if in Italy the victorious Aeneas is a second Achilles, then Turnus inevitably becomes a Trojan Aeneas or Hector, so, as Bandera explains, "by deliberately suggesting the parallel between this part of his own poem and the *Iliad,* Virgil is making Aeneas fight his own double, his enemy twin."[65] This observation brings us back to the *Floridoro* and Risamante's similarity to the upset Ruggiero and angered Rodomonte. Engaging Cloridabello, she repeats almost programmatically the martial strategies previously employed by those characters (anger, abandonment of the shield, urge to hit the enemy on the head as a revenge). In Canto 2, Fonte features the amazon's similarity with Macandro by conveying a false impression about her gender. But why should Risamante try to repeat her enemy's moves? According to Quint's analysis, the loser attempts to replicate the past in search of a way out of it; Risamante was not the victim but the winner. I believe that Fonte was not happy with Risamante's behavior, as she lost something even though she was victorious. Fonte wishes to show that Risamante's previous victory came at the cost of her own identity. Risamante's killing of Cloridabello will risk

---

61. Bandera 1981: 220–21.

62. Ibid., 217–24.

63. Ibid., 223.

64. Ibid., 230*ff.*: "the social order rises originally out of the same thing that can also annihilate it." Bandera's reading about the end of the *Aeneid* has influenced Warren 2001, who analyzes the importance of the verb *immolare* in Turnus's death, and Putnam 2001: 104, who writes, "The epic's final line—*vitaque cum gemitu fugit indignata sub umbras* ("and his life flees, resentful, with a groan under the shades")—is repeated from Book 11, where the death in question is that of the warrior-maiden Camilla. So once more we are propelled not so much out into a grand future as back towards a world of repetitions, a world which has revealed to us an Aeneas transformed from suffering Trojan into brutal, raging actor." For criticism of Bandera, see Smith 1999. On the end of the *Aeneid,* see also Farron 1982; Hardie 1997a: 139–52.

65. Bandera 1981: 233. Similarly, Fichter 1982: 104 on Ruggiero and Rodomonte: "In one of his aspects Rodomonte is Ruggiero's old carnality; in another Rodomonte is Ruggiero's former adherence to justice in its Old Law formulation as righteousness without charity." For the compulsion to repeat, see also Bellamy 1992: 75–78.

confirming her brutalization, her similarity to the enemy Biondaura and to some problematic epic predecessors.

Also important is the twins' similarity. They not only look alike but "also want the same thing and only by fighting to obtain it does each of them narcissistically identify with the other and reconnect, so to speak symbiotically, the masculine side to the feminine side."[66] The sisters' desire is mimetic because it feeds actively on the other sister's desire. In this regard, they behave like typical male knights, whose eagerness to obtain a woman or sword is magnified by their peers' desire for the same objects. In the battle against Macandro and even in the conclusive clash (13.61–62), Risamante is cast as a traditional knight: yet, as we will see when looking closely at 13.63, 70ff., in the final segment of the duel against Cloridabello, she transcends that male model and proves that in *pietas* resides the difference between her and her epic predecessors. Generosity distinguishes her from her sister's male selfishness.

FONTE AND HER "SOURCES"

In the final characterization of Risamante in Canto 13, Fonte is certainly influenced by the gentle knight of the *Orlando Furioso*, Ariosto's Bradamante, whose human spoils of war, despite her valor, are scant. Bradamante kills only Pinabello in the *Furioso* and Martasino and Daniforte in the *Orlando Innamorato*. Generally, Bradamante does not like to kill her enemies.[67] This attitude is not confined to her character alone; there are other merciful characters in the poem. According to Colin Burrow, in the *Orlando Furioso* we see a "pitying instinct" and a reaction to Virgil's portrayal of the Aeneas/Turnus encounter in Book 12 in episodes in which the heroes, momentarily abandoning the war, rescue characters in distress or when, during an engagement in combat, they renounce the opportunity of striking the fatal blow. The primary role of pity is evident in Canto 19.10 when Zerbino spares the young Medoro:

---

66. Finucci 1994: 225. The symbiosis of "feminine" and "masculine," as described by Finucci, is realized only in Risamante.

67. Finucci 1992: 236. On Bradamante's meekness in dealing with her family, see Shemek 1998: 120–21. Lilian Robinson recognizes and interprets Bradamante's moderation in connection to early modern political necessities. According to Robinson (1985: 105), the theory and practice of the early modern state demanded a ruler who could manipulate all situations through compromise, balance, and control: "It was not woman the Renaissance state required, but a principle that the culture defined as female." Contra: Shemek 1998: 227. Cloridabello in the *Floridoro*, since he fights in place of Risamante's sister, represents her and therefore cannot be eliminated.

Stese la mano in quella chioma d'oro,
E strascinollo a sé con violenza:
Ma come gli occhi a quel bel volto mise,
Gli ne venne pietade, e non l'uccise.
(*OF* 19.10.5–8)

He reached out and grasped his golden curls and tugged him forward petu-
lantly—but when he laid eyes on the youth's handsome face he took pity on
him and did not slay him. (trans. Waldman)

Here pity in a duel is represented as a viable chivalric alternative, especially
when the duel is anticlimactic. Risamante follows the example of Bradamante
and Zerbino even during the ultimate struggle against Cloridabello.

Fonte's merciful female warrior implies that wars and battles are tests of
who we are, and suggests that victories are more complicated than the simple
destruction of the enemy. Confronting her predecessors' conclusions and the
epic code, she looks for a better way to shape a central narrative duel, one that
will mark the crucial difference between Risamante and her male predecessors as well as between the lady knight and her twin sister.[68] When Risamante
injures her adversary, she does not let her anger prevail. Without hesitation,
she decides to spare him:

Il re stordito cade e 'l verde piano
D'un corrente ruscel vermiglio irriga;
La guerriera, c'ha 'l cor molle e umano,
Vistosi il meglio aver di quella briga
Gli corre sopra e con pietosa mano
Dell'elmo sanguinoso il capo sbriga,
E dimostra a ciascun la sua vittoria
Nel volto smorto, ond'ha trionfo e gloria.
(*Fl.* 13.63)

The stunned king falls and wets the green plain with a streaming vermilion
rivulet; the lady knight, who has a soft and humane heart, realizing that she
has the upper hand in that matter, *runs over to him and with a compassion-*
ate hand removes the bloody helmet from his head and demonstrates to

---

68. The repetition of a topos is not an innocent maneuver: "Sheer repetition creates a
topos, resulting in the building up of an automatically receptive and conditioned response,
thereby reinforcing what have become received values, in a sort of ideological *fait accompli*."
Günsberg 1987: 12.

everyone her victory by showing his deadly pale face, from which she has triumph and glory.

In Fonte's description, the *corrente ruscel vermiglio*, or sign of Cloridabello's demise, is reminiscent of stanza 135 of the *Orlando Furioso*, where Rodomonte, seriously wounded, falls on the ground:

Del capo e de le schene Rodomonte
La terra impresse; e tal fu la percossa,
Che da le piaghe sue, come da fonte,
Lungi andò il sangue a far la terra rossa.
Ruggier, c'ha la fortuna per la fronte,
Perché levarsi il Saracin non possa,
L'una man col pugnale gli ha sopra gli occhi,
L'altra alla gola, al ventre gli ha i ginocchi.
(*OF* 46.135)

Rodomont dented the ground with his head and shoulders; such was the impact *that a gush of blood, as from a spring, from his wounds spurted high to color the earth red. To prevent the Saracen from rising again, Ruggiero, who had Fortune by the mane,* held a dagger over his eyes with one hand while the other clutched his throat as he knelt on his belly. (trans. Waldman, modified)

We would expect Risamante, exploiting the moment, to behave like Ruggiero, who used the opportunity to pin the enemy to the ground; as Risamante "rushes to the enemy," we think of Ruggiero and are alarmed about the outcome, but then, with a pointed contrast, the image of Ruggiero holding fortune by the mane is replaced by that of the female knight with her soft and humane heart.[69] Risamante's emotional route, unlike that of Aeneas and Ruggiero, is not from pity to anger but from anger to compassion: she does not try to overcome her opponent but, suddenly and without hesitation, interrupts the combat and frees her opponent from his helmet. The air inhaled by Cloridabello somehow preserves the life in him and allows his survival ("l'aer che prese il re dell'elmo privo / qualche spirito in lui serbò di vita, / onde rivenne e dimostrossi vivo," "the air which the king left without the helmet inhaled preserved in him some life for which he came back and demonstrated himself alive," 13.64.1–3). To the advantage of her lady knight, Fonte exploits and

69. Note the parallel construction.

supersedes the morally ambiguous endings of the *Furioso* and of the *Aeneid*,
Aeneas's and Ruggiero's hesitation, and their similarity.

While Fonte's familiarity with Ariosto's masterpiece is clear, it is much
harder to determine how well and in which form she knew the *Aeneid*. We
cannot rule out the possibility that she read Virgil in Latin, and certainly she
was familiar with the *Aeneid* in Italian translation. In Fonte's biography,[70]
Doglioni observes that she was extremely gifted and that she learned Latin. In
the introduction to her edition of *Il merito*, Chemello,[71] following Doglioni,
affirms that Fonte knew Latin, but we cannot be sure how well. Her high level
of education suggests a solid cultural background. In *Il merito*, not only does
she mention Virgil in connection with his birthplace Mantua,[72] but she also
alludes to several characters of the *Aeneid*: to Camilla as a woman skilled at
arms;[73] to Dido, who despite her chastity was treated unfairly by Aeneas;[74]
and to Nisus and Euryalus for their loyal friendship in times of hardship.[75] In
the *Floridoro* (11.55ff.), Acreonte and Marcane's nocturnal ambush of Celsidea
is also modeled on Nisus and Euryalus's night raid (*Aeneid* 9) as well as on
Ariosto's story of Cloridano and Medoro. While these friends in both works
reciprocate affection, Acreonte cares only about himself, and his demand for
posthumous vengeance contrasts with Euryalus's request that Ascanius care
for his bereaved mother (*Aeneid* 9.378–89).[76] Another echo of the *Aeneid*
might be in *Floridoro* 5.73–74: Nicobaldo's distress ("fiera cagion . . . sendomi
ritornata or nel pensiero / sforzommi a lagrimar come vedesti," "a bitter cause
. . . now coming back to my memory / made me cry, as you saw." 6.4.1 . . . 3–4)
in narrating his past fulfills Risamante's request and resembles Aeneas's disturbing recollections, summoned by Dido, of past experiences ("quamquam
animus meminisse horret luctuque refugit, / incipiam" "although my soul is
horrified at the memory and recoils in grief / I will begin," *Aen.* 2.12).

Fonte's masterpiece *Il merito* demonstrates further familiarity with other
Latin authors such as Cicero, Ovid, and Pliny the Elder,[77] but, as Virginia Cox

---

70. Fonte 1988: 3–9 = Fonte 1997: 31–42.

71. Fonte 1988: XVII.

72. Fonte 1988: 102 = Fonte 1997: 156.

73. Fonte 1988: 62 = Fonte 1997: 100.

74. Fonte 1988: 67 = Fonte 1997: 112.

75. Fonte 1988: 78 = Fonte 1997: 126.

76. Kisacky 2002 underscores this contrast. Not only is Acreonte cast according to the
model of false friends given in *Il merito* (Fonte 1988: 79), but he is also almost the archetype
for the negative and vengeful knight.

77. E.g., Fonte 1997: 104 alludes to the story of Erysichthon (*Metamorphoses* 8.738–878);
to Procne's myth and to Ceyx turned into a halcyon (Fonte 1988: 90 = Fonte 1997: 140, cf.
Met. 6.438ff. and 11.710–48); and to Lycaon turned into a wolf (in the story of Lioncorno, who
becomes a unicorn, Fonte 1988: 107–11 = Fonte 1997: 161–5, cf. *Met.* 1.232–390). She cites in

points out,[78] Fonte never quotes any author in Latin. If Fonte was familiar only with translations of Virgil's work and we consider the nature of these adaptations, her independent mind in evaluating some episodes derived from the *Aeneid* is particularly striking. The free adaptations of the *Aeneid* offered translators a chance not only to experiment with Italian but also to transform poetic texts into more explicit didactic tools.[79] If Italian renditions of the *Aeneid* turn it into a conservative text that praises the chastity of women and the blameless behavior of Aeneas, Fonte reads the *Aeneid* in a more original fashion.

In the sixteenth century, one of the most frequently reprinted translations of the *Aeneid* was the *Sei primi libri del Eneide di Virgilio, tradotti à piu illustre et honorate donne* (*First Six Books of the Aeneid, Translated for the Most Distinguished and Honored Women*), first published in Venice in 1540 by Comin da Trino at the prompting of Nicolò d'Aristotele, called Zoppino. The frontispiece explains that the work consists of the first six books of the *Aeneid,* each prepared by a different translator and each dedicated to a different woman. To advise the "distinguished" women reading the classical masterpiece, the edition contained dedicatory introductions offering, besides *aulici complimenti,*[80] conventional and even trite reflections on the poem, and suggestions for how women should read it.[81] For example, Aldobrando Cerretani, translator of *Aeneid* 5, praises his dedicatee Girolama Carli Piccolomini for her chastity and faithfulness to her late husband. He draws a parallel between her devotion and Aeneas's *pietas* toward Anchises.[82] Fonte certainly does not equate pity with

---

Italian *Tristia* 1.9.5–6 (Fonte 1988: 78 = Fonte 1997: 125). Furthermore, Fonte 1988: 111 = Fonte 1997: 166 mentions Pliny by name, and Pliny's *Naturalis Historia* seems to be the main source for several extraordinary anecdotes retold in the dialogue (e.g., Fonte 1988: 85 = Fonte 1997: 135 about talking magpies described by Pliny *NH* 10.59.118; Fonte 1988: 98*ff.* = Fonte 1997: 130*ff.* about extraordinary spring waters, cf. *NH* 2.106.230*ff.*; for more examples, see Cox's index in Fonte 1997: 270–90). Chemello (Fonte 1988: LVIII) mentions some Renaissance Italian translations of Pliny's work. For *rifacimenti* and the translation of the Greek and Latin classics in the Renaissance, see De Caprio 2012.

78. Fonte 1997: 35.

79. Borsetto 1989: 13: "At levels which cannot be immediately ascertained but without a doubt are more common, there is the modernization of the Latin text, the attempt to develop in these translations, 'secondary' discourses (on love, customs, behavior) traditionally found in other genres, the redefinition (based on current discussions on Aristotle's *Poetics*) of humanistic ideas of 'imitation,' 'model' and 'poetry'" (my translation).

80. Zabughin 1923: 360.

81. See Borsetto 1989: 26–32. Another translation targeting women is that of Aldobrando Cerretani, published by the ducal printer Lorenzo Torrentino in Florence in 1560. It has introductions and endings intended to flatter and instruct the female audience; e.g., Cerretani praises chaste married women and warns of love's omnipotent flame. See Zabughin 1923: 360–62; Borsetto 1989: 191.

82. Borsetto 1989: 30.

chastity. She also indirectly takes issue with some of the ideas about women contained in Ludovico Dolce's translation of the *Aeneid*. This paraphrase was published in 1572 by Gabriele Giolito de' Ferrari, includes fifty-four Cantos,[83] and provides the most extensive paratext among the Italian versions of the Virgilian text. There is no proper commentary in this edition, but it contains, besides textual allegories at the beginning of each Canto, a final *Tavola delle sententie*, or list of memorable phrases arranged by keywords followed by their corresponding page numbers. This thematic index includes the keyword *donna* ("woman") and a phrase explaining what about women appears in the plot: "Che donna spesso varia, e cangia uoglia, et è mutabil piú ch'al uento foglia, 351" ("That women often change their mind and desires, and that they are more fickle than a leaf in the wind, 351"). Thanks to the page number, we understand that Dolce is negatively commenting on Dido's infatuation with Aeneas and unfaithfulness to the memory of her husband Sychaeus. The episode might have been used to prove Aeneas's fickleness as he delays in Africa, forgetting about his mission to Italy, yet Dolce says nothing about Aeneas's behavior.[84] An interesting counterpoint to this comment indirectly appears in the *Floridoro*'s emphasis on male fickleness. In Fonte's treatment, men often wish to help women but are easily distracted by something else. In the plot, several knights embark on challenging enterprises, but they lack the steadfastness to pursue their goal to the end.[85]

Dolce also underlines women's need to be chaste. In the allegory preceding Canto 36, he explains:

> Per Didone, che disperata disegna d'ammazzarsi, e s'ammazza, si conosce, quanto possa in un'animo generoso il pentimento d'una cosa mal fatta, e quanto debbono esser caute le donne, e massime quelle, che sono in concetto d'honorate, e d'honeste, e in darsi in preda a uno lasciuo appetito, peroche spesso elle sono ingannate, e non resta appresso di loro senon infamia, pentimento, e rimordimento continuo della tormentata coscienza.[86]

---

83. Italian paraphrases of Virgil's *Aeneid* notoriously employ many more verses than the original Latin, and several translators and commentators are aware of this problem; see Borsetto 1989: 89–153.

84. On the reception of Dido, see Watkins 1995; Thomas 2002: 154–89.

85. E.g., Risardo (Canto 2) decides to help Raggidora, unjustly accused of killing her lover and the king of Egypt, but is twice distracted by other events (the tournament for Celsidea and Odoria's request to accompany her to Delphi, both narrated in Canto 4). On his way to fight for Celsidea, Silano is delayed by Circetta (Canto 8). Ultimately, we do not know if Silano will help Circetta. Ulisse, *ingrato e rio,* "ungrateful and bad" (Canto 5.41.4, etc.), does not remain with Circe; Finucci (Fonte 1995: XXV) describes all men in the poem, except perhaps Filardo, as *cavalieri antieroici e maschi falliti* (antiheroic knights and failed males). A similar observation is made by Malpezzi Price 1994a: 205–6.

86. Dolce 1527: 347.

Through Dido, who in desperation plans to kill herself and in fact kills herself, we can understand how much, in a noble soul, remorse for a bad action can accomplish and how cautious women must be, and most of all those who have the reputation to be honorable and honest, and in giving themselves prey to a lascivious appetite, because they often are mistaken, and nothing is left of them if not infamy, repentance and continuous regret of their tormented conscience.

Once chastity is abandoned, nothing else matters. This is what Dolce believes to be the lesson to draw from Dido's encounter with Aeneas. Fonte, at the beginning of Canto 5 in the *Floridoro,* discourages women from falling in love because of the nature of men:

> Fuggan le donne pur più che 'l peccato,
> Più che 'l morir l'officio dell'amare,
> C'han la più parte il cor gli uomini ingrato
> Per quel ch'io leggo e spesso odo contare.
> (*Fl.* 5.3.1–4)

Let women flee even more than sin, more than death, the business of love, since for the most part men have an ungrateful heart, (judging) from what I read and often hear in songs.

Men's "perfidious and betraying" mind (5.2.4) compromises the enterprise of love.[87] *Il merito* repeats and illustrates this evaluation in a list of chaste women like Lucretia, Polyxena, and Dido, who "suffered as a result of their love for some man and who have eventually been tricked by him, betrayed and abandoned."[88]

Finally and most importantly for my argument, throughout Dolce's version of the *Aeneid* the protagonist is singled out for his piety and virtue: even when Aeneas kills Turnus, in one of the allegories preceding Canto 54, Dolce suggests that the Trojan hero is rightly avenging Pallas, for "it is not possible to moderate just anger without vengeance" ("non potendosi temperar un giusto sdegno senza vendetta," 536). If Dolce interprets Aeneas's slaughter of Turnus as a sign of the hero's rightful indignation, in the last lines of her poem Fonte makes clear that anger must be curbed by compassion: Risamante successfully employs both courage and compassion to affirm her superiority.

---

87. Malpezzi Price 1989: 177.
88. Fonte 1997: 112.

After the insanity and fury displayed at 13.61, she shows her humanity by sparing Cloridabello (13.63) and, as Angelica had done with Medoro (*OF* 19.20–22), she treats the king's wound:

> Con gran pietà fé l'inclita guerriera
> Quel re condur nel regio padiglione
> E medicar, che forte piagato era,
> Trattandolo da re non da prigione.
> (*Fl.* 13.70.1–4)

> With great pity the distinguished female knight
> Had that king brought to the royal tent
> And cured, for he was seriously wounded,
> Treating him as a king not as a prisoner.

Risamante, recognizing Cloridabello's royal identity, gives him due respect: it is exactly the acknowledgment of Risamante's royalty that Biondaura rejects, denying her sister a share of Armenia. In a manner not different from that of some perceptive Renaissance readers of epic, Fonte in Canto 13 of the *Floridoro* becomes a proponent of mercy. Her rejection of violence as the typical hallmark of epic conclusions is vividly captured and opposed in the memorable image of an amazon who chooses to spare her worthy enemy.

CHAPTER 2

Women and Compassion

THE ADVENT OF the *giovani* who, emerging in the 1570s "tried to redefine the character of both internal and foreign policy in Venetian politics" and questioned Venetian traditional neutrality may have affected Fonte, whose criticism of violence is also consistent with an awareness of the importance of peace in a city tied to commerce with the East as much as Venice was.[1] Furthermore, the Catholic Reformation may also be a factor in the characterization of a conciliatory heroine. Fonte's solution certainly resonates with Tasso's attempt to end the *Gerusalemme Liberata* by emphasizing the compassion of Goffredo, who spares Altamoro:

> Segue i vinti Goffredo, e poi s'arresta,
> Ch'Altamor vede a piè di sangue tinto,
> Con mezza spada, e con mezzo elmo in testa
> Da cento lance ripercosso e cinto.
> Grida egli a' suoi: "Cessate; e tu, barone,

---

1. Viggiano 2013: 74; Meyer Setton 1991: 1; McNeill 1974: 139: "From a practical point of view, Venice had strong reasons to stand aloof from Spanish and papal efforts to recruit help against the Turks and the French. Particularly after the Ottomans took control of Egypt and the Syrian coast (1517), the Venetian economy could only prosper if merchants had access to ports under Ottoman control. War did not bring economic returns, as it had in earlier days when Venetian ships had been the terror of the Aegean. On the contrary, it brought only physical hardship and financial difficulties."

Renditi, io son Goffredo, a me prigione."
(*GL* 20.140.3–8)[2]

Godfrey pursues the beaten, then he stops
When he sees Altamor, blood-stained, at his feet,
With half a sword, half a helmet on his head,
Battered and surrounded by a hundred lances,
"Enough," the captain cries to his men.
"Baron, my name is Godfrey. Give yourself to me as prisoner"
(Trans. Esolen, modified)

In Book 20, Goffredo's compassion toward Altamoro concludes a series of duels, each culminating in the death of the pagan enemy (20.101–8, Rinaldo kills Adrasto and Solimano; 20.120, Rinaldo kills Tissaferne; 20.137, Goffredo slays Emireno). The sparing of Altamoro underlines Tasso's desire to distinguish his poem from traditional epic: Tasso's protagonist displays "Christian mercy rather than Vergilian vengeance."[3] In refusing to kill her enemy, Risamante leans toward the values that Tasso considers necessary for the Christian hero. But Fonte's desire to conclude her work pacifically does not seem particularly linked to religious preoccupations, even though her decision to situate the poem in a pre-Christian time might have been a way to avoid attacks motivated by religious anxieties originating in the Counter-Reformation.[4]

While in Tasso's *Liberata* and in its revisionist ending Christian concerns represent an essential factor, in her last canto Fonte prioritizes "feminist" con-

---

2. The Italian edition is Tasso 1961.

3. Seem 1990: 125, pointing out that a similar desire exists in the duel between Argante and Raimondo and in the final battle between Argante and Tancredi (Canto 19). Contra: Garrison 1992: 179–87. Garrison thinks that the duels in the final book of the *Liberata* do not clearly establish the new ethical credentials of the Christian camp. Proof of the failure would be Tasso's modification of those duels in the *Conquistata*. More generally, while the evolution of *pietas* toward *misericordia*, already developed by Augustine in the fifth century, can make violent endings difficult to integrate into a Christian epic environment, violence resulting from just anger, the desire to obtain justice, or the supremacy of the better party almost becomes an ethical necessity. For the merging of the heroic code with new Counter-Reformation exigencies, see Hampton 1990: 81–134; Gregory 2006.

4. In Venice, the Inquisition in 1547 and the Venetian Index of Prohibited Books in 1549 heightened some anxieties. Accusations of smuggling forbidden books, brought against booksellers, caused the migration of some printers to other cities and fostered the move toward publishing less controversial material (e.g., devotional and religious books). For an overview of the decline of the Venetian printing industry, see Burke 2000: esp. 404–6; Grendler 1977; Quondam 1980: 51–105; Richardson 1999: 45. On religious apprehension in epic, see Garrison 1987: esp. 161–205.

siderations.[5] Her reaction to a world that, while praising women's chastity and beauty, does not recognize their other qualities becomes clear at the end of Canto 13, when Risamante's gender is revealed and Cloridabello comments on her victory. Risamante's identity is disclosed in stanza 65, and the revelation creates confusion (as in Canto 2). Cloridabello thinks that his adversary is Biondaura and cannot understand why his beloved seems to have decided to defeat him:

> A Risamante i giudici donaro
> La palma e l'adornar di lauree fronde;
> Si tolse ella l'elmetto e mostrò chiaro
> Il suo bel viso e le sue chiome bionde.
> Ma come il re prigion, che sente amaro
> Duol per Biondaura e dentro si confonde,
> Costei mirò tanto simile ad ella,
> Pensò che fusse la sua donna bella.
> (Fl. 13.65)

To Risamante the judges gave the palm (of victory) and they adorned her with laurel fronds; she took off her helmet and showed her pure and beautiful face and her blond hair. But as the king, her prisoner, who feels bitter pain for Biondaura and is all confused inside, looked at her so similar to the other, he thought she was his beautiful mistress.

The scene reminds the reader of Canto 32.79 of *Orlando Furioso* where, in Tristano's castle, Bradamante, after defeating her male adversaries, taking off her helmet, and letting her golden hair tumble to her shoulders, reveals her real identity and attractiveness.[6] During this episode, Ariosto not only presents Bradamante's rhetorical ability to debate and her compassion (32.104) but also shows her heroic and erotic charm as an alternative to Ullania's helpless beauty and to Marfisa's masculine womanhood. While the latter's bearing and sense of self distance her from her gender, Bradamante displays a composite

---

5. About Tasso's religious scruples, but also his complex political agenda in the *Liberata* and *Conquistata*, see Brand 1965: 125–32; Cavallo 2004: 218*ff.*; Hampton 1990: 109–13. For reevaluations and new assessments of the *Conquistata*, see Brazeau 2014: 42–44.

6. "E la scopriro a un tratto / e la feron conoscer per donzella, / non men che fiera in arme, in viso bella" "at once revealing and making her known as a maiden no less fierce in battle than beautiful in her face" (*OF* 32.79.6–8); cf. *Floridoro* 2.28.1–2: "Si tolse l'elmo e discoprì le bionde / chiome dell'or più terse e luminose," "She took off her helmet and uncovered her blond hair more clear and luminous than gold."

woman who combines femininity with physical strength.[7] Risamante, like Bradamante, is equal to yet different from men.

Cloridabello confirms Risamante's charm and similarity to her sister:

> Meraviglia non è s'ella mi vinse
> Poi che prima m'avea preso e legato,
> Ché altri che costei mai non mi strinse
> Tanto, né potea pormi in tale stato.
> Ma presso la bellezza, onde m'avinse
> Non credea che valor tanto pregiato
> Regnasse in lei, né so per qual cagione
> Abbia voluto far meco tenzone.
> (*Fl.* 13.67)

It is no wonder if she defeated me, since already before she had captured me
and tied me up; except for her no one had ever constrained me so much,
nor was able to put me into such a state. Yet besides the beauty by which she
conquered me I did not believe that there was so much precious valor reign-
ing in her, nor do I understand for what reason she wanted to fight with me.[8]

The sequence concludes with a note of irony and comic relief. The rescued
king cannot understand why his beloved is fighting him, but he understands
well why she has the better of him. Cloridabello is a prisoner of love. After the
fight, his metaphorical imprisonment becomes real: he becomes hostage to the
woman he believes to be Biondaura.

The situation reminds us of the fight between Bradamante and Ruggiero,
disguised as Leone, and of Bradamante's reflections after her defeat in Canto
45 of the *Orlando Furioso*. At 45.99.1–4, Bradamante had proposed a fight with
her future husband because she knew she could not have beaten the man she
loved but would be victorious over everybody else. Defeated by the man she
believes to be Leone, she is shocked and desperate.[9] In Ariosto, Bradamante is
aware of Ruggiero's martial strength, but in Fonte the strength of Risamante/
Biondaura takes Cloridabello by surprise. In stanza 68, he finally recognizes
the "virtue" of his woman, identified not as chastity nor beauty but as ability
on the battlefield:

---

7. Benson 1992: 131; Benedetti 1996: 37–38.

8. The word *meraviglia* and the dynamics of the fight remind us of the battle between
Galiziella and Riccieri in the anonymous *Cantari d'Aspromonte* (Riccieri "who had received
such a great blow, wondered" "che avea ricevuto sì gran il colpo si meravigliò" I.xxxi, quoted
by Jacobs 2013: 14). About "marriage by duel" and Galiziella, see Stoppino 2012: 33–55.

9. On the fight between Bradamante and Ruggiero and Bradamante's acceptance of Ruggiero's authority, see Benson 1992: 148–55.

Felice inganno, se ingannar mi volse
Per mostrar forse a me la sua virtute,
Beate piaghe e 'l sangue, che mi tolse
Quando col guardo suo mi dà salute.
M'aggreva sol (né d'altro unqua mi dolse
Tanto) delle percosse ricevute
Da lei per me, dei colpi iniqui e rei
Che per troppa ignoranza io diedi a lei.
(*Fl.* 13.68)

Happy deceit if to deceive me she wanted perhaps to show me her valor; blessed wounds and blessed the blood she took from me, when with her glance she gives me health. I only grieve (not for anything else have I ever grieved so much) for the blows she received by me, for the iniquitous and guilty strokes *that for too much ignorance* I gave her.

Here the tone is light, as epic discourse is bent into the molds of lyric poetry: the soldier conquered by love is also the defeated hero. We will see in chapter 3 how Marinella fruitfully uses the Ovidian reshuffling of epic and elegiac themes to elevate wives forgotten and misjudged by heroes in pursuit of glory. Fonte replays the Ovidian formulation of love as a military service[10] as well as the Petrarchan lyric code, not to construct woman as a silent object of desire but to shape her into an active player. Risamante is described according to the stock symbolism of Petrarchan poetry (pretty face, blond hair, 65.4), and Cloridabello's initial ignorance resonates with that of men who see in women only physical beauty without recognizing other qualities.[11] Yet in the mistaken impression of Cloridabello, Fonte suggests to Biondaura and to all, that women can be an even match on the battlefield.[12] In an ironic context, the author, with grace and originality, manages to create a woman who is victorious at least in the eyes of her lover, who in his deception finally sees the truth: his beloved has other virtues besides beauty. In these lines the importance of love opens up the possibility to read beneath the surface and against the grain. Fonte's appreciation of virtue as non–gender specific stands in stark contrast

---

10. The most famous formulations of the *militia amoris* are in *Amores* 1.1 and 1.9; see Murgatroyd 1975; Cahoon 1988. For Ovid in the Renaissance, Javitch 1991: 71–86; Guthmüller 1981, 1997. For Ariosto's use of Ovid, see Looney 1996: 32–54, 96–123.

11. For a discussion of women's love lyric in the late European Renaissance, see Jones 1990: esp. 1–10, 155–78; Rodini 1996: 69–77.

12. In *Il merito delle donne,* one of the characters suggests that men "never tell the truth except by mistake" (Fonte 1988: 41). The comment aptly applies to the situation.

to the views of her contemporaries. As noticed above, Ludovico Dolce in his
translation of the *Aeneid* underscored womanly virtue as mainly chastity.[13]

In the last lines of her epic (13.68–70), Fonte indirectly affirms the importance of gender equality and love. If the love theme in the Risamante story
(Cantos 2, 3, and 13) was suppressed by Fonte's decision to depict a protagonist
who does not fall in love, it reemerges in the final battle as a positive value
in Cloridabello's illusion of facing his lover. In this description the Venetian
writer uses some of the insights gained in lyric poetry through Neoplatonism
to the advantage of women: love obliges lovers to recognize the equality of
women and men. Neoplatonic love as a sublimation of the object of desire was
mainly the rediscovery of the fifteenth-century philosopher Marsilio Ficino.[14]
In Neoplatonic love, both lovers provide the stimulus for spiritual life, the
step that allows the ascent from nature to divinity; in the epic under consideration, a defeated lover obtains a better understanding of women's spiritual and
physical qualifications. Love is viewed as a force that can help men to admit
the true nature of women.

The acknowledgment of women's worth in the *Floridoro* goes hand in
hand with Fonte's dedication of the poem to Bianca Cappello, a Venetian lady
famous, if not infamous, for her intelligence and skills as well as for the love
that the Grand Duke of Tuscany Francesco de' Medici had for her.[15] Bianca
was a noblewoman who in 1563 escaped to Florence with her lover (and future
husband), the lowborn Pietro Bonaventuri. With great effort, but to no avail,
the Venetian government tried to bring her back to Venice. Eventually her
beauty attracted the attention of Grand Prince Francesco, who, as soon as
his wife Joan of Austria died, married her—by then Pietro was already dead.
Then, the city of Venice, putting aside its resentment for Bianca, celebrated
her marriage and declared her "daughter of the Republic," an honor formerly
bestowed only on Caterina Cornaro, queen of Cyprus, a patrician woman who
had displayed great obedience to the Republic of Venice when ordered to give
up her kingdom and retire to the village of Asolo in 1489.[16] Fonte's appreciation of Bianca's intelligence and resourcefulness was underlined by Emilio
Zanette, an early and unfriendly reader of *Floridoro*. Zanette interpreted the
motto *et animo et corpori,* "to spirit and body," crowning the engraving reproduced at the end of every Canto,[17] as alluding not to Bianca Cappello's physical

---

13. Terpening 1997: 32–59, 116–28; Kallendorf 1999: 201 shares the same understanding.

14. For the importance of Neoplatonism and Ficino in Italian humanism and the debate
about gender, see Allen 2002: 856*ff.*, about love esp. 889–90.

15. Mariotti Masi 1986; Zanette 1953: 455–68; Malpezzi Price 2003: 119–21 connects Cappello with Circe and reminds us of Fonte's admiration for women with "controversial and transgressive real and fictional lives" (119).

16. Van Kessel 2010: 280.

17. Zanette 1953: 467. I owe this observation to Julia Kisacky.

beauty but to her ingenuity. Furthermore, the engraving showed two cupids, each presenting a laurel wreath in a powerful symbol of love, poetry, achievement, and reputation. Similar conclusions can be found in Fonte's masterpiece *Il merito delle donne*. Here Leonora, echoing Petrarch's line (*Rime Sparse* 105, 11) *Ch' amore regge suo imperio senza spada* ("That love reigns over his empire without need for a sword"),[18] underscores love's role in maintaining peaceful alliances. It seems that here Fonte is distancing herself from the advice she had given to women (at *Floridoro* 5.3.1–4) to stay away from love. Love is presented not as something to avoid, but as an aid for the peaceful success of human compacts.

WOMEN'S WORTH IN THE *FLORIDORO* AND *MERITO*

In the final lines of Canto 13 of *Floridoro,* Fonte criticizes violence as the inevitable postulate and result of the epic world: physical strength cannot be the sole characteristic of human nobility. Like Bradamante in the *Furioso,* Risamante rejects "a system that demands life-and-death struggle for their own sake."[19] She also proclaims that chastity and beauty are not the only qualifying characteristics of women: they can be stronger and wiser than men (e.g., Cloridabello), who can more easily see this fact when they are in love. The conclusions reached in the *Floridoro* are taken up more vigorously and directly in her later work.

In *Il merito,* in the conversation of the First Day (*Giornata Prima*), besides beauty and grace, Leonora defends women's physical prowess:

> And besides that (their physical beauty and grace) women have other merits that should give them a claim on men's love. There is our fortitude, for one thing—fortitude of mind and body, for if women do not bear arms, that isn't because of any deficiency on their part; rather, the fault lies with the way they were brought up. Because it's quite clear that those who have been trained in military discipline have turned out to excel in valor and skill, aided by that peculiarly feminine talent of quick thinking, which has often led them to outshine men in the field. (Fonte 1997: 100)[20]

---

18. Fonte 1988: 134 = Fonte 1997: 192: "con l'oblazion . . . che vi facciamo . . . di esservi più che mai per l'avenir amorevoli e soggette, per amore però e non per forza. Ch'Amor regge suo imperio senza spada" "and we pledge in future to be even more loving and submissive to you than ever—submissive that is, as a free choice, out of love for you, not under compulsion. For Love reigns over his realm without need for a sword."

19. Robinson 1985: 175.

20. "Oltra di ciò non manca alle donne per esser meritatamente amate, oltre la corporal bellezza e leggiadria, fortezza di animo e di corpo e in quel che non vagliano per armeggiare,

She corroborates her point with a long list of mythical and historical heroines famous for their martial ability. More importantly, however, Fonte is interested in assessing women's "fortitude of mind" to demonstrate their superiority over men. She does not propose that women's virtues are the same as men's, needing only greater cultivation and recognition. Rather, against the Aristotelian-Galenic tradition, establishing women as defective males and underlining their tendency to be soft, lascivious, despondent, querulous, and deceitful (*Hist. An.* 608a32–b19), Fonte, through Corinna, declares that less bile and blood makes women kinder and more able to overcome their appetites:[21]

> For women's nature is such that ferocity cannot dominate in it, since choler and blood make up a relatively minor part of our constitution. And that makes us kinder and gentler than men and less prone to carry out our desire, while men by contrast, being of a hot and dry complexion, dominated by choler—all flame and fire—are more likely to go astray and can scarcely dominate their tempestuous appetites. (Fonte 1997: 83–84)[22]

Furthermore, while male Renaissance writers conceived female morality in terms of chastity and urged women to enter the convent, transforming them into social nonentities,[23] Fonte undercuts theological demonstrations of women's presumed ethical insufficiency by criticizing the usual interpretation of the Bible's second creation myth. In fact, none of Fonte's characters uplifts the view of man as woman's head, and instead insists that women have the moral capacity, and ought to have the material means, to be their own heads.[24] Besides female moral superiority, in the *Floridoro* as well as *Il merito*, women's restraint and tolerance are central factors for a successful marital life.

---

non è lor mancamento ma di chi dà loro creanza, poiché si è visto chiaro di quelle che sono state già da tempo allevate sotto tal disciplina, quante son riuscite valorose ed esperte, avendo appreso quel particolare e proprio dono del presto conseglio, co'l quale hanno avanzato gli uomini in mille occasioni." Fonte 1988: 62. Cf. Malpezzi Price 1994a: 205. Leonora's quoted lines echo *Floridoro* 4.2.

21. The idea that women are more compassionate than men can also be found in *Hist. An.* 8.608b8. For the Aristotelic-Galenic tradition, see Cox's introduction and the series introduction, in Fonte 1997: viii*ff* as well as Hacke's "Einleitung" (Fonte 2002: 41–47), besides the seminal discussions in Mclean 1980; Mayhew 2004.

22. "Che noi siamo di tale natura, dove non domina alcuna ferocità, per non vi avere molto luogo la colera ed il sangue e però riusciamo più umane e mansuete e meno inclinate ad essequire i nostri desideri che gli uomini, dove all'incontro gli uomini di complession calda e secca, signoreggiati dalla colera, essendo tutti fiamma e fuoco, sono anco più inclinati ad errare e manco si ponno astenere da i loro disordinati appetiti" (Fonte 1988: 47).

23. King 1980: 66–90; Schiesari 1992: 71–73.

24. Jordan 1990: 255.

Fonte's view, in part, may have been suggested by Ariosto's *Orlando Furioso*. In certain segments of his poem, Ariosto not only describes women's chastity and inner strength (e.g., Ginevra's fidelity toward Ariodante, Cantos 4–5) but also questions society's laws built on the belief of women's moral inconstancy and men's superiority.[25] For instance, in Cantos 27–29, the narrator praises Isabella's devotion to her late betrothed and her self-reliance in defending that devotion. At the same time, he openly criticizes Rodomonte and men's fickleness ("O degli uomini inferma e instabil mente! / come siàn presti a variar disegno" "O uncertain and unstable mind of men! How ready they are to change their plans," 26.117).[26] Ariosto suggests something even more alarming than men's fickleness when in Cantos 42–43 Rinaldo's distrust of his wife triggers her ethical downfall and reveals men's greater capacity for wickedness.[27]

Yet, even when dishonest, men are considered by Fonte necessary for women's happiness and social living. In *Il merito* the argument for acceptance of men (vs. rejection) is developed in the conversation of the Second Day.[28] There, a debate most resonant with the ending of the *Floridoro* starts when the ladies imagine going into battle against men.[29] Leonora, Lucrezia, and Helena try to decide on the best emblem and color to wear to manifest their view of men. Emulating Ariosto's Marfisa, Leonora expresses her preference for a helmet with the image of a phoenix.[30] The phoenix, a mythical bird eternally reborn from its own ashes, represents isolation and resistance to natural and institutional constraints. It is a suitable emblem for characters who, like Marfisa and Leonora, militantly resist marriage. Leonora's choice of the color white, symbol of chastity, for her coat of arms and of a broken golden yoke, symbol of freedom, for her shield marks once again her will to distance herself from men. At the opening of the book, emphasis on seclusion, chastity,

---

25. Benson 1992: 94–117; D'Amico 2015.

26. At *OF* 8.1–73, the story of King Astolfo, Jocondo, and their unfaithful wives seems to take for granted that women are fickle, but it must be evaluated in the polyphony of the sequence.

27. The above mentioned episodes are insightfully discussed by Benson 1992: 91–122. Ariosto's "protofeminism" remains a debated issue; cf. Cox 1997: 140–41.

28. The programmatic theme of the *Giornata Seconda* is the following: "Why it should be that, even though men are a thoroughly bad lot, as we proved in so many different ways, many women—decent, sensible women—still love them very deeply" (= Fonte 1988: 74–75 = Fonte 1997: 120).

29. Fonte 1988: 163 = Fonte 1997: 230.

30. Cf. *OF* 36.17–18: "Marfisa emerged from the gate; the crest on her helmet was a phoenix, which she wore either out of pride, to denote that she was unique in the world for martial prowess, or else to celebrate her chaste intention of living forever without a husband" (trans. Waldman, adapted). For *fenice* in the classical and Renaissance tradition, see Chemello in Fonte 1988: LVII.

and freedom appears in the description of the garden where the ladies meet. The importance of the garden as well as verdant and lush natural enclaves (*locus amoenus*) within epic poems, is discussed in Part III. For now, it suffices to observe that even in this dialogue the garden plays an essential role. In the garden, Fonte places an allegorical fountain decorated with statues, each holding in the right hand an emblem (*impresa*) and an olive branch, and in the left hand a scroll containing a motto. Among the *imprese* displayed on the fountain we find the ermine, the phoenix, and the sun, respectively symbolizing chastity, self-sufficiency, and freedom. These virtues, framing femininity as a hostile desire to take charge of one's own body and to affirm superiority before coming to terms with the opposite gender,[31] remind the reader of Risamante's hatred toward Macandro, culminating in his killing (*Floridoro* 1–2). In *Il merito*, during this segment of the conversation, Lucretia's preference for vermilion, a color symbolic of revenge against men, confirms such hostility.[32]

But this aggressive attitude is strongly opposed by Helena, who has the last word communicating to the group her ideas about a more sociable kind of female excellence. Helena rejects vermilion and revenge, selecting red, the color of charity, which in her mind is a more appropriate symbol of what ought to be women's disposition toward men:

> "No, no," said Helena. "Since the desire for revenge has no place in a magnanimous heart, such as we claim ours to be, we would do well to wear dark red, signifying our happiness not at the prospect of our hoped-for victory, but at the thought of winning men over entirely to our side. Because, after overcoming them in combat, I'd want us to overcome them in *courtesy* as well and *to redouble our glory by showing clemency* toward them." (Fonte 1997: 232)[33]

---

31. For the significance of the animals, see Malpezzi Price 1989: 171, 174: "The ermine and the phoenix, conventional representations respectively of chastity, rebirth and solitude, become in Leonora's words the emblems of women's desire to live alone and to defend their bodies against any violence. . . . The recovery of one's body is certainly one of the first steps toward women's emancipation and the strongest and most enlightened of Fonte's characters, Leonora and Corinna, state that they would die rather than become subjugated to a man (13; 16)." Jordan 1990: 254 observes that "the statues of women from whose breasts flows the water of the fountain at the garden's center represent a comprehensive allegory of woman kind. The first three embody aspects of the happy condition of the single woman and are all, paradoxically, generative; 'chastity,' an ermine, destroys what attacks it; 'solitude' a phoenix, dies to be reborn; and 'liberty' a sun, gives light to itself and to the planets." The generative power of these figures seems limited to me.

32. Fonte 1988: 164 = Fonte 1997: 231.

33. "Anzi—seguì—perchè il desiderio della vendetta non regna in magnanimo cuore, come asserimo esser il nostro, faressimo bene a portar il rosso scuro, significando l'allegrezza non pur della sperata vittoria, ma di far gli uomini tutti nostri; perchè vorrei che dopo il vincerli di

These words reflect her concern for women's ethical excellence, already framed in the *Floridoro,* and her awareness of women's engagement in love games as being necessary for their participation in society. After all, the *Giornata Seconda* is an attempt on the women's side to understand why, even if men are so bad to them, they still love them. Harmony, not chaos or division, is the hallmark of this second part of the dialogue.[34]

Helena, newly wed, reminds her friends that victory over the body of men is not all they want—they would rather conquer their minds. *Cortesia* and the extension of *clemenza* are crucial means to achieve this end. Helena's words square perfectly with the *Floridoro*'s benevolent conclusion and remind the reader of the longing for compassion and humanity characterizing the debate over the *Aeneid*'s ending. Risamante's triumph is not a "long Pyrrhic victory of the human spirit"[35] but a sign of hope for a new age. In conclusion, in the *Tredici canti del Floridoro,* as in *Il merito delle donne,* Fonte wants to expose women's unfair condition and the cruelty of war as the product of male moral perversion. The failure of men to act in a fully human fashion justifies elevating women's status but also makes it integral to the reformation of humanity.[36] The argument is significant: against the Aristotelian position that women are more imperfect (and less human) than men, Fonte states the opposite, that they are in fact more fully human. Finally, clemency and love are essential to breaking the cycle of revenge and restoring the foundations of a healthy society.

Reflections analogous to those of Fonte about the worth of women and their ability as warriors appear in the literary production of Marinella, whose positive evaluation of women's nature is found in her book *The Nobility and*

---

valore, gli vincessimo anco di *cortesia* e gli usassimo *clemenza per raddoppiar la nostra gloria*" (Fonte 1988: 164).

34. At Fonte 1988: 182 = Fonte 1997: 258–59, almost the end of the dialogue, Leonora highlights that she has spoken not out of "hatred for men, but rather in a spirit of charity" and compassion toward women. Men, Leonora continues, see the world in a crooked way and feel justified to mistreat women, "but if they could be persuaded of their error, they might just change their ways" ("ma restando con ciò avvertiti del loro errore forse che potriano emendarsi.") All human beings, Fonte underlines, are sociable creatures and should help each other. The various points of view among the women in this dialogue confirm Robin's claim that the discussion may be mimicking those of the salons; Robin 2007: 64.

35. Clausen 1966: 86.

36. Similarly, in the *Floridoro,* Biondaura's lack of *pietas* justifies the glorification of Risamante. An excellent summary of the Early Modern feminist debate on the equality of women is in Jordan 1990: 1–64. Fonte's argument about women is in line with what Jordan calls a "relational feminism," proposing "a gender-based but egalitarian vision of social organization" and "the primacy of the companionate, non-hierarchical, male-female couple as the basic unit of society" (Jordan 1990: 7).

Excellence of Women[37] as well as in her *L'Enrico, overo Bisantio acquistato* (1635), a poem composed in the chivalric tradition celebrating both the role of Venice in the Fourth Crusade (1202–04) and women's intellectual, moral, and physical dignity.[38] This poem, like the *Floridoro*, features independent amazons—Meandra, Emilia, and Claudia—whose value and greatness are not narratologically undermined through death by a man or marriage.[39]

MARINELLA'S AMAZONS

In the *Enrico*, while the amazons Meandra and Emilia fight for Byzantium, Claudia fights for Venice. Despite their different political allegiances, all three women are represented as worthy and noble. Lazzari, Cox, Galli Stampino, Malpezzi Price and Ristaino have made interesting observations about the role of these amazons.[40] I follow their suggestions, but I highlight Marinella's debt to the classics in the characterization of her female knights and expand upon the topic of Part I: women's relationship to violence and *pietas*. In connection to the latter, I also compare the behavior of Marinella's female knights to that of Fonte's Risamante.

Marinella displays her knowledge of the *Aeneid* in describing her amazons by alluding to Virgil's descriptions of Camilla and Harpalyce. In the *Enrico*, Claudia is a crusading virginal warrior who "enters into battle and moves like the boisterous wind through the clouds" ("Entra Claudia in battaglia e tal si move / qual tra le nubi impetuoso il vento," *Enr.* 3.25.1–2). She resembles Camilla, "trained . . . to tolerate harsh battles and to be victorious over the wind on foot" (*adsueta . . . proelia virgo / dura pati cursuque pedum prae-*

37. In Marinella 1999: 18, Panizza points out that Marinella certainly knew the *Floridoro*, which is quoted in her work. It is possible that Marinella also knew *Il merito*; see Fonte 1997: 21–22n32–33.

38. I discuss Marinella, the genre, and the topic of her epic more extensively in chapter 3. During the Seicento, besides the *Enrico*, several romance epics were written by women; e.g., Margherita Sarrocchi's *Scanderbeide* (1623) and Barbara degli Albizzi Tagliamocchi's *Ascanio errante* (1640); see Cox 1997: 141. For a list of women's contributions to the genre, see Finucci in Fonte 1995: XII; Beer 1987. In striking opposition to Marinella's and Fonte's desire to praise women and to define their *valore* not simply in terms of chastity stands *Il meschino*, the only known female-authored sixteenth-century chivalric poem preceding the *Floridoro*. This epic epitomizes a superficial reception of Counter-Reformation preoccupations, not only in its displacement of erotic language and obsessive display of a chaste protagonist but also in the elimination of hybridized types (e.g., female knight) and reproduction of misogynistic clichés about women; see Cox 2000: 58–59.

39. See Galli Stampino's introduction in Marinella 2009: 46–56; Cox 2000: 61; Tomalin 1982: 192–93.

40. Cox 2011: 177–96; Galli Stampino in her introductions to Marinella 2009 and 2011; Lazzari 2012; 2010: 61–112; Malpezzi Price and Ristaino 2008: 93–96.

vertere ventos, Aen. 7.807–8). Claudia also resembles Harpalyce of Thrace, who in the *Aeneid* "wearies horses, and outdoes winged Hebrus in flight" (*qualis equos Threissa fatigat, / Harpalyce, volucremque fuga praevertitur Hebrum, Aen.* 1.316–17). Emilia is a Byzantine virgin unsurpassed with the bow. She will kill important Christian fighters and will also attempt to kill the Venetian supreme commander Enrico. Speed seems the qualifying trait of both women, as it is for Camilla. On the other hand, the most important trait of the third virgin fighter, Meandra, is her ability to spur soldiers into battle. Meandra also rallies them in defeat (12.40–41; 14.116–17) and reminds them of glory (14.26). In the *Aeneid*, with her feisty behavior, Camilla, leader of the Volscians, even arouses the women of Latium to protect their city (*monstrat amor verus patriae, ut videre Camillam*, "true love of country shows them the way, as they see Camilla," *Aen.* 11.892).

Marinella's desire to highlight the importance of training and elevate women is evident when, in describing Claudia's military skills, she says "that practice and not nature put fear in one, and courage in the other gender" ("che l'uso e non natura ha messo / timor nell'un valor nell'altro sesso," *Enr.* 2.29.7–8). Here she repeats what Fonte had already expounded in *Floridoro* 4.1, the idea that women in every age have been endowed by nature with sound judgment and a brave heart, and therefore they do not differ from men in substance. Like courageous male knights, Emilia, Claudia, and Meandra are ready to die for their country and leaders. Marinella dwells on their prowess and ability to handle the sword rather than their beauty. She draws believable and realistic profiles of heroines effective on the battlefield, avoiding their objectification.

Apart from the emphasis on the women's martial skill, in Canto 24 we see Marinella's appropriation of ancient sources to celebrate women. While Venier is fighting against Oronte, who receives a long *aristeia* and is described as a formidable enemy, he is killed by Emilia's arrow. If Venier's foreshadowed death by arrow resembles that of the Homeric Achilles, whose end was prophesized by his mother, Venier's way of dying also resembles Camilla's. Marinella recognizes Virgil's ambiguous approach to Camilla and her relationship to battle and in turn uses it in the *Enrico* to comment on Venier's death and the virtue of women.[41]

Let us begin with Marinella's description of Venier's death:

Ecco stride per l'aria acuto dardo,
Che d'Emilia da l'arco or si diparte,

---

41. For Virgil's Camilla, see Arrigoni 1982: 13–24; Basson 1986; Boyd 1992; DeWitt 1924/25; Fratantuono 2007: 336–65; Grandsen 1991: 20–25; Hardie 1998: 85; West 1985.

Ed il Venier, che contra quel gagliardo
D'Oronte, mostra ardir prodezza ed arte,
A ferir aspramente non è tardo
Sopra del fianco a la sinistra parte,
E mentre quel penetra, un altro giunge,
E più del primo a dentro il passa e punge.
(*Enr.* 24.20)

The sharp arrow strung from Emilia's bow is launched and hisses through the air and was not slow to wound harshly Venier who against the strong Oronte displays prowess and skill, and while it penetrated above the flank on the left side another one joins it and more deeply than the first comes and pierces through.

E lo traffigge sì, che fuori appare
Dal lato opposto al forte il ferro crudo,
Venier di quanto pianto a le tue care
Genti sarai cagion, lungo, io conchiudo.
Nel cader suonar l'armi illustri e chiare,
E sopra il petto suo tonò lo scudo;
A gli occhi intorno l'ombra si diffuse
Di morte, e quelli in sonno eterno chiuse.
(*Enr.* 24.21)

And [the arrow] cut through [his body] so that the raw iron came out from the opposite side of that strong man. Venier, you who will cause so much crying to your dear people, on this note I end. As you fell the illustrious and shining weapons clashed and on your chest the shield thundered; the shadow of death spread around (your) eyes closed in eternal sleep.

Con lagrime e con doglie aspre portaro
Li scudieri a le tende il nobil sire,
A cui di gloria il suon fu assai più caro,
Che in vita assai sicura ognor gioire.
(*Enr.* 24.23.1–4)

With tears and harsh sorrow the squires brought to the tents the noble sire for whom the sound of glory was much more dear than the everlasting joy of a safe life.[42]

---

42. For the English rendition of the *Enrico,* I routinely employ Galli Stampino's translation (Marinella 2009); however, this translation is mine since these stanzas were not included in that

Here Marinella draws from Camilla's death but inverts the roles: if in the *Aeneid* a woman is pierced by the arrow of a man (Arruns), in the *Enrico*, a man (Venier) is penetrated by the arrow of a woman (Emilia)![43] Equality of the genders is pursued through the idea that, in war, women and men have interchangeable roles and can be identically (if unwisely) brave. Marinella may have gained this insight from the duel between Risamante and Macandro and by recollecting the similarities between Camilla and Turnus in the *Aeneid*. Both individuals die for war booty while irrationally blinded by fury and accompanied by the narrator's pity. Camilla pursues a beautiful war insignia, forgetting her hostile environment, while Turnus, after having killed Pallas, tears away the boy's sword belt (*Aen.* 10.496), which, triggering Aeneas's anger, will cause his death (*Aen.* 12.887–952). Although the narrator does not endorse Turnus's behavior, through an apostrophe he manifests his understanding for the fragility of the human mind and men's poor choices (*Aen.* 10.501–5).

Marinella's description of Venier's death is inspired by Virgil's sympathetic description of Camilla's death:

Ergo ut missa manu sonitum dedit hasta per auras
Convertere animos acris oculosque tulere
Cuncti ad reginam Volsci. Nihil ipsa nec aurae
Nec sonitus memor aut venientis ab aethere teli,
Hasta sub exsertam donec perlata papillam
Haesit virgineumque alte bibit acta cruorem.
Concurrunt trepidae comites dominamque ruentem
Suscipiunt . . .
(*Aen.* 11.799–806)[44]

As soon as the arrow was thrown, it whirred through the air,
All the Volscians turned their eager minds and placed
Their eyes upon the queen. She did not realize anything
Neither of air, nor of sound, nor of arrow coming from the sky,
till the thrown lance, arriving under the exposed breast,
Remained stuck and avidly drank her virginal blood.
Her companions rushed there trembling and sustained
The falling queen.

---

edition. The Italian text is from Imberti 1635, reproduced in Marinella 1844.

43. Lazzari 2010: 76n8.

44. In Tasso's *Gerusalemme Liberata*, Clorinda's death (esp. 12.68) is also inspired by Camilla's.

Illa manu moriens telum trahit, ossa sed inter
Ferreus ad costas alto stat volnere mucro;
Labitur exsanguis, labuntur frigida leto
Lumina, purpureus quondam color ora reliquit.
(*Aen.* 11.816–19)

Dying, she tugged at the arrow, but the iron tip
Remained, with a deep wound, between her ribs in the bones;
Bloodless, she fell, cold with death
Her eyes sank, the once purple hue left her face.

. . . tum frigida toto
Paulatim exsolvit se corpore lentaque colla
Et captum leto posuit caput, arma relinquunt
Vitaque cum gemitu fugit indignata sub umbras.
(*Aen.* 11.828–31)

Little by little becoming cold
she freed herself from her body completely and tilted her languid neck
and head seized by death, letting fall her weapons
and with a moan (her) life fled, indignant to the Shades below.

Marinella dwells on several details in Virgil's text and approaches Venier's demise with a sensitivity similar to that found in the Latin lines above. Both authors want to highlight the speed of death but, at the same time, they slow the narration, almost trying to delay the end of these brave characters, making their readers feel it more intensely. Both hover over their warriors, follow the path of the deadly arrows, and observe in detail how death comes to their victims. Through the presence and laments of desperate fellow combatants, their demise is deemed catastrophic. Camilla's deadly hit is observed by all the Volscians, and her female companions catch her as she falls. Venier's squires cry and bring his body back to the camp. His death, we are told, is "reason for long crying" (*di quanto pianto . . . cagion*, 24.21.3–4). The arrow that pierces Camilla's body seems to come alive when it drinks the virgin's blood. Venier is penetrated by two arrows; one of them enters the body and goes out on the other side. A kind of satisfaction is apparent when Marinella dwells on Emilia's victory over Venier—her triumph is a sort of female revenge exacted on men who do not believe in their military strength. But here the predominant note is profound sorrow, which also enfolded the death of Camilla. We see and feel death gradually overcoming the hero's slackened limbs. Darkness surrounds Venier's eyes; Camilla abandons her weapons while her body becomes cold. Finally, in both passages, great attention is given to sound. We can hear the hiss of the arrows swiftly traveling through the air, we hear the loud crashing of Venier's weapons over the ground and his body. Virgil highlights the unfairness of Camilla's fate through the line "and with a moan life fled indignant to the shades below" (*Aen.* 11.830), in which the adjective *indignata* and the noun *gemitu* ("with a moan") betray resistance to a death that has been otherwise sought by the amazon. Although a brave death is the natural *telos* of a warrior's life, that adjective and noun signal that there is something unsettling about Camilla's ending. The line will be famously repeated at the end of the epic to describe Turnus's death.

In the description of Venier's end, Marinella also "resists" the epic impulse to glorify death with some ambiguously memorable lines. The foolishness of Venier and war ethics are highlighted in the emphasis put on the youth caring for "the sound of glory" ("di gloria il suon fu assai più caro," *Enr.* 24.23.3) much more than for "the continuous joy of a safe life" ("in vita assai sicura ognor gioire," *Enr.* 24.23.4). Finally, the attention bestowed by Marinella on Emilia's arrow reveals this writer to be an attentive reader of the Camilla episode.

In the *Aeneid,* Camilla (like Creusa or Dido), despite her courage, must be overcome. Programmatically in Virgil's epic, women are juxtaposed with those characters and forces (Juno, Turnus, anger) to which (at least ideally) they should succumb. Yet the narrator admires and pities Camilla. Besides giving her the place of honor in the catalogue of Italian troops (*Aen.* 7.802–17), a long *aristeia* (*Aen.* 11.648–724), and a memorable death (*Aen.* 11.801–35), he apostrophizes her (*Aen.* 11.664–65) like he normally does to display his sympathy. Marinella realizes that in the *Aeneid* Camilla is a complex character who has Virgil's sympathy and yet must surrender to the logic and the rules of the epic agenda that want women destroyed, especially those who keep the hero from reaching his goals and who are not faithful wives and committed mothers. Camilla's unconventional character can be perceived in the contrasting reactions her persona provokes in male characters. Their speeches about Camilla are marked by "the rhetoric of paradox," the concomitant juxtaposition of praise and blame.[45] While Turnus clearly admires her, calling her "glory of Italy" (*o decus Italiae virgo, Aen.* 11.508), Aulus, Tarchon, and Arruns despise her (*Aen.* 11.705–9, 11.732–35, 11.789, 11.792). Likewise, Marinella's amazons trigger discordant judgments. If the female narrator is impressed by her warriors' ability and courage, their opponents express their lack of respect for their choices by making fun of their preference for the sword. For instance,

---

45. Viparelli 2008: 12.

on the battlefield, Argalto reminds Claudia that she should have stayed home attending to womanly tasks ("meglio era assai tra tele ed aghi e fusi . . . temprar di seta e d'or fregi e colori" "it would have been better among cloths and needles and spindles . . . [for you to] mix ornaments and colors with silk and gold," 3.51.1–4), and he feels ashamed to have been brought down by a woman ("cade il meschin, più che 'l morir, l'aggreva / che da man feminil morte riceva" "the wretched one falls and he is aggrieved not so much for his death but for having received it from a female hand," 3.53.7–8).

Although, as mentioned above, in the *Aeneid,* Camilla is at times depicted as a warrior admired for her martial prowess rather than feared as a woman out of control, not only is she killed by a man, but also it is clear from the narration that she dies for *desiring* something too eagerly.[46] As is well known, during the battle Camilla becomes distracted with Chloreus's finery (*Aen.* 11.774–75). She was following Chloreus either to affix his golden armor to the temple of Diana or to wear it when hunting (*Aen.* 11.778–80), since "she burned with a womanly love for booty and spoils" (*femineo praedae et spoliorum ardebat amore, Aen.* 11.782). The syntagm *femineo praedae . . . amore* provokes discussion from the start. Commentators wonder how the blind pursuit of prey is an activity proper for women and how womanly desire could trigger it. Servius defines the adjective *femineo* as "irrational"[47] because women in antiquity and especially in the *Aeneid* are closely associated with passions and erratic behavior. Several scholars assume that the phrase "evokes the passionate nature, inherent in every female, that Camilla has rejected, first as the ascetic devotee of Diana, later as warrior Amazon."[48] Thus Camilla's womanhood would be reawakened and reveal itself (hastening her demise) when she sees Chloreus's beautiful attire. The lust for glory and booty that makes her *incauta* (*Aen.* 11.781) would reveal her otherwise hidden female nature. Marinella will not allow any of her amazons to fall prey to this kind of prejudice. She remembers Virgil's Camilla penetrated by a man's arrow, and not only does she craft a narrative in which a man is overcome and penetrated by a woman, but she also seems to arrive at the opposite conclusion of Virgil. It is not a "feminine desire" that kills Meandra and Claudia, but rather, as I explain later, a *masculine* impetus to kill without thinking.

I mentioned how Marinella is reluctant to punish or undermine amazons by having them killed by men or obliging them to forsake their vocation for

---

46. The suggestion comes from Trudy Harrington Becker 1997, who notices how all women admire Camilla, and men are willing to collaborate with her.

47. Williams 1983: 117.

48. West 1985: 23.

arms or their religious creed.[49] If Fonte could not draw on Tasso's poem as source—it was published in 1581, the same year the *Floridoro* was published—Marinella was certainly familiar with the *Gerusalemme Liberata*. In epic, the virginity of female warriors—as much as their ability to handle weapons—symbolizes their independence and power: in Marinella's poem they lose neither. While at the end of the war Emilia returns to her life in the woods (*Enr.* 27.87–88), Claudia and Meandra kill each other (*Enr.* 24.47–48). Their duel is particularly interesting because if it establishes Marinella's desire not to tame her "deviant" women, in its brutality and tragic inevitability it also marks a failure, especially when compared to the swordfight between Risamante and Cloridabello (in Fonte's *Floridoro*) and in connection with Marinella's ideas about women's moderation. The shortcomings of these amazons' behavior will become most evident after a detailed analysis of their final confrontation, which recalls Virgil's Camilla and Marinella's ideas about women's nature.

THE DUEL BETWEEN CLAUDIA AND MEANDRA

At *Enrico* 24.35, Claudia recognizes Meandra from her banner and attire, but even more for her valor when she sees the Thracian woman fighting the Venetians. In turn, the Greek woman identifies Claudia. They become eager to find out "who between them is more worthy with weapons" ("qual più di lor ne l'armi vaglia," *Enr.* 24.35.8). Marinella recalls the dueling scenes that in the *Floridoro* had Risamante as the protagonist (see chap. 1) and alludes to them by describing Claudia's attempt to win by hitting Meandra on the head and by drawing attention to the warrior's helmet:

Claudia poi s'avvicina là 've stende
La valorosa i guerrier nostri al piano,
La siede orribil sì, ma la difende
L'elmo composto da famosa mano:
Fin sul collo al destrier s'inchina e scende
Sforzata da quell colpo orrendo e strano,
Vide abbagliata in que' funesti lochi
Cento erranti facelle e accesi fochi.
(*Enr.* 24.36)

---

49. These are patterns of submission normally chosen by Ariosto and Tasso. E.g., in the *Gerusalemme Liberata* the amazon Clorinda who fights against the Christians, is killed by Tancredi and renounces her Muslim religion (Canto 12).

Claudia got closer to the place where that valiant woman was felling our warriors to the ground, and she hit her strongly; but her helmet, put together by a famous craftsman, protected her: she bent all the way to her steed's neck and descended from it as that terrible and unexpected blow forced her to do. Stunned, she saw a hundred lights and burning fires in that fateful place.

When Claudia recovers, she invites her enemy to "leave the common war" (*lasciam la comun guerra, Enr.* 24.37.5) and withdraw somewhere else to "test each other with ease until victory or death" ("dove possiam con agio io te, tu ancor / me riprovar, fin che si vinca o mora," *Enr.* 24.37.7–8). The two warriors "pick a wide meadow quite close to the walls" ("scielgono un largo prato assai vicino / alla muraglia," *Enr.* 24.38.1–2) surrounded by "a long row of marble seats" ("di marmo . . . lungo ordine di seggi," *Enr.* 24.38.2–3). The place is historically important because it preserves Constantine's trophies:

> Quivi si dice il magno Costantino,
> Poichè 'n *Mesenzio atroce estinse l'ira*
> Spiegasse i suoi trofei, tal luogo piace
> A l'una e l'altra, poi che occulto giace.
> (*Enr.* 24.38.5–8)

> They say that Constantine the Great, after *extinguishing Maxentius's horrible anger,* displayed his trophies in that very place. Both women liked it for it was hidden.

Through these details, Marinella reminds us of the pivotal fight between Constantine as emperor of the Eastern Roman Empire and Maxentius as the emperor of the Western Empire in 312 AD. Constantine's defeat of Maxentius was narrated by Eusebius and Lactantius as a victory sanctioned by God, whose "sign" (the cross) and religion Constantine had embraced.[50] Therefore Constantine's success is the victory of God against the pagan Maxentius, who is depicted even by Marinella as a despicable man and a tyrant whose "atrocious anger" (*Enr.* 24.38.6) is finally destroyed by a pious and just ruler.[51] It is not clear why Marinella alludes to Constantine and Maxentius at this moment in her epic. If on the one hand she is glorifying the battle as indirectly compared to that of two famous men, on the other hand we cannot help but notice that *both* Meandra and Claudia are worthy individuals. Furthermore, we see that Marinella will not give victory to Claudia, ally of the Venetians. She could

---

50. Lactantius, *De mortibus persecutorum* 44.5; Eusebius, *Vita Constanti* 1.27–29.
51. Stephenson 2009.

have used this match to sanction the victory of the good Catholic West over the wicked non-Catholic East; instead, she refrains from concluding so simplistically, constructing a more complex scenario depicting a commendable enemy. Sadly, "the end of anger" for these brave combatants will coincide with their death.

Having abandoned the crowded battlefield and ready to fight face to face, the amazons approve of the location not for its historical significance but for its seclusion, and there they can fight and measure their skills without interruption. The remoteness of the meadow highlights how these brave female fighters are eager to demonstrate their strength without seeking external notice, approval, or congratulations. In this episode, Marinella extends the rules of knighthood to women and proves that they believe in the importance of *being* brave rather than *appearing* brave.[52] Ludovico di Canossa and Federigo Fregoso famously debated this issue in Castiglione's *Courtier*.[53] With their behavior, Meandra and Claudia respond and contribute to those men's debate and declare that they do not want a reputation that is not followed by accomplishments.

Apart from the allusion to Castiglione, the women's impetuosity in the fight is regularly emphasized while being compared to natural phenomena and angry animals—both are like torrents and lightning (*Enr.* 24.39), both are compared to angry lions (*Enr.* 24.40), and Meandra resembles a snake (*Enr.* 24.37) and a wolf (*Enr.* 12.40). The connection of heroes to animals is common in ancient epic. For instance, *Aeneid* 11—the book featuring Camilla's exploits and death—is replete with animal imagery. Through these comparisons, Marinella underlines women's ability to fight fiercely, just like men (or animals). Camilla was described by Virgil as *aspera* (*Aen.* 11.664). The adjective is normally used by the Roman author to designate inanimate natural forces, war, or some extraordinary character. Among females, only the Fury Allecto and the vengeful Juno are so qualified, and among men only Turnus and Mezentius.[54] These characters have in common a tendency toward excess, irrationality, violence, and anger. Camilla in fighting against Orsilochus "brings her axe down on Orsilochus' face as he prays to her—she offers no reply to his words other than the gory wound" (*Aen.* 11.697–98). It is one of the grisliest death scenes in the *Aeneid,* including the shocking details of Orsilochus's ignored prayers for mercy.[55] In depicting her amazons, Marinella seems directly inspired by

---

52. Marinella 2009: 341n4.

53. For sources, see Marinella 2009: 340. The relationship between appearing and being is also discussed by Machiavelli in chap. 18 of *The Prince* and by Ariosto in Tristan's castle (*OF* 32–33).

54. Harrington Becker 1997.

55. This observation and the previous quote are both from Fratantuono 2007: 342.

Camilla's fierceness, or by that of Tasso's Clorinda, who in the *Gerusalemme Liberata* is modeled on Camilla and interacts with her enemies with a high degree of brutality (e.g., *GL* 9.69–70).[56]

In their final clash, Marinella's amazons are like "two lions . . . burning with wrath" ("due leon . . . d'ira ardenti," *Enr.* 24.40.2). Their wrath grows when neither can immobilize the enemy or force her to admit defeat:

> Claudia, perchè non vede, onde s'adira,
> Sangue nemico, s'ange, arde di sdegno,
> Si duol Meandra, che restar non mira
> De la sua spada memorabil segno.
> Mentre a ciò pensa, foco e rabbia spira,
> Crescono le forze, ferve il caldo ingegno;
> Onde più, che mai cruda il braccio move
> Con modi e con maniere odiose e nove.
> (*Enr.* 24.42)

> Not seeing any of her enemy's blood, Claudia was upset, stung, burning with scorn. Meandra meanwhile was pained at not seeing her sword leaving a mark anywhere. With those thoughts fire and rage breathed into her, her strength increased, and her quick mind raced on, so she was crueler than ever before, and she moved her arms in novel and hateful ways.

Neither can prevail nor understand that virtue does not amount to sheer physical superiority. Both want to inflict a mortal wound "e questa e quella cupida desía / mandar l'altra de l'Orco a i regni tetri," "this one and that eagerly desire to send the other to the dark kingdoms of Orcus," *Enr.* 24.43.1–2). They are confused about what virtue really is, not because they are women, but because its true nature is slippery and hard to assess, especially in extreme situations. Like Camilla, Meandra and Claudia fail to realize what it means to be honorable in war. Camilla forgot her mission and Turnus's commands while foolishly chasing unsubstantial plunder. In Camilla's pursuit of Chloreus's weapons, Virgil explores the strange and undeniable similarity between women's desire for ornaments and men's desire for booty.[57] Recall the surprising phrase por-

---

56. Gerniero is hit twice by Clorinda's arrows: his death is echoed by Venier's death (*Enr.* 24.12).

57. In Camilla, the masculine power of a warrior seeking glory and that of a huntress passionate about the chase coexist: "Role and gender ambiguity—ambiguity between the world of the female huntress that is marginal to masculine society and the masculine world of war, between the *miles Phoebes* [the soldier of Diana] and the Amazon, between the huntress *virgo* and the *Bellatrix* queen—these identify Camilla's character" (Viparelli 2008: 11).

traying Camilla as brought down by a "feminine love of booty and spoil" (*Aen.*
11.782) and how the "commingling of the ancient heroic code, which dictates
the taking of spoils, with unexpected feminine desire for satin and brocade
carries its own garish disharmony."[58] Camilla's weakness—her craving for
beautiful weapons that also symbolize dazzling glory—betrays the fragility
of traditional epic heroism. Through Camilla, the hero's legitimate and yet
dangerous and vain desire to wear the armor of the slain enemy is indirectly
compared to the empty love of a girl for pretty ornaments.[59] With Camilla
distracted by attractive weapons, Virgil criticizes the heroic ethos, reminding us not to confuse external signs of virtue for virtue itself. Camilla forgets
her safety, mission, and leadership to obtain what does not add anything to
the bravery she already possesses. Turnus displays a similar kind of forgetful-
ness and vanity when he despoils Pallas and decides to wear the youth's sword
belt (*Aen.* 10.500–502). Since Aeneas's sight of the trophy will trigger Turnus's
death, moderation in victory and on the battlefield is not a minor theme, and
Marinella ponders it when narrating the death of her amazons.

Beyond Camilla's extreme desire for prey, Virgil suggests another problem connected to her story and noticed by Marinella. In the *Aeneid,* when
Diana describes her devotee Camilla newly set on the war against the Trojans,
we perceive the goddess's disappointment. She says to her attendant Opis:
"Camilla walks towards a cruel war . . . she carries my weapons to no purpose"
(*graditur bellum ad crudele Camilla / . . . nostris nequiquam cingitur armis,
Aen.*11.536–37) and adds, "I wish such an obsession with war had not seized
her, daring to face the Trojans" (*vellem aut correpta fuisset / militia tali, conata
lacessere Teucros, Aen.* 11. 584–85). Diana is saddened because her favorite
huntress is in danger, but also because she believes that Camilla's desire to
fight in a real war is foolish. Diana's statement implies that the girl would be
better off living in the woods and hunting animals with her female companions. In the *Enrico,* the amazon Emilia, after having fought in the war, will
choose the fate that Diana wished for Camilla. Unable to kill Enrico Dandolo,
aware that her side is defeated beyond hope, Emilia ponders the situation and
wisely decides to return to the happy life of the woods. By remaining chaste
and away from the city, she acquires the reputation of a goddess:

Emilia che quel giorno ultimo scerne
De le achive grandezze, qua, là, move,

---

58. Rosenmayer 1960: 161. Cf. Roche 1988: 115: "Virgil is ambiguous about the cause of
Camilla's lack of prudence and advances two reasons: either she was eager to have this armor
as a triumphal trophy or she was eager to have it because of the innate covetousness of women."
59. West 1985: 24.

Faretrata donzella, e da le interne
Parti sospiri altissimi remove;
Molti ha feriti, e fece a le superne
Stanze del ciel salire in sen di Giove;
Ma, che pro, se già rotto è il campo e gito
Di Misia il duce e 'l Greco re fuggito?
(*Enr.* 27.87)

Emilia, the maiden with a quiver, saw on that day the end of Greek greatness, she moved here and there, lifting great sighs from her heart. She wounded many, she sent many to Jove's lap in the highest parts of heaven, but what good was that, when the camp was routed, the king of Mysia gone, and the Greek king in flight?

Tarda, dolente, e disdegnosa torna,
De' boschi amici, a la bramata pace,
Vinta guerriera, ma di spoglie adorna,
Famose e chiare, in cui pur si compiace,
E l'armi sue volanti ancor ritorna
Nel petto a tinger d'animal fugace,
Per castitade illustre al fin divenne
Diva Silvestre e 'l nome suo ritenne.
(*Enr.* 27.88)

Vanquished as a warrior, she finally went back to the much-desired peace of her friendly woods, feeling pain and scorn. Still, she carried rich and shining spoils, and she was proud of them. She went back to dipping her flying weapons in the chests of quick animals, and at last she became a sylvan goddess by the same name, due to her famous chastity.

Although in part like Camilla and Turnus—the text reveals that she rejoices in "famous and shining spoils" (*Enr.* 27.88.3)—Emilia also displays a new awareness, prompting her to abandon the war at the right moment. She understands and accomplishes what Meandra and Claudia cannot. She has fought bravely and realizes that it would be pointless to keep fighting; therefore, she returns to a "wished-for peace" ("bramata pace," 27.88.2) and unproblematic hunting games. Her blessed fate in a pastoral and serene environment is like that enjoyed by the prophetess Erina, whose character and dwelling place are studied later in this book.

Not so peaceful a destiny is reserved for Marinella's other amazons. As Meandra's blow fatally penetrates Claudia's throat and cuts her beautiful hair, she receives Claudia's sword into her side:

Come lupo da fame afflitto e vinto,
Notturno insidiator la mandra infesta,
Urla, intorno s'aggira, a strage accinto.
E 'l muggito più in lui la brama desta;
Così costei, ch'ha il cor di ferro avvinto,
La nemica crudel batte e molesta,
Qua, là tenta d'aprir, studia a si sforza
Col brando acuto la ferrata scorza.
(*Enr.* 24.46)

A wolf anguished, indeed vanquished by hunger that plagues a herd at night, plotting against it, going around it ready for slaughter, it howls, and its noise awakens its hunger even more. In the same manner this woman [Claudia], *whose heart was bound with iron,* rained blows on her cruel enemy, causing her pain, trying and attempting here and there to find an opening into her armored cover with her sharp sword.

La pertinace Greca non oblia
Il luogo di periglio e 'l ferro caccia
Là, 've 'l candido avorio il varco apria
A fredda morte, e l'elmo il colpo slaccia;
Tal la ferita fu che fuori uscia
Per la bionda cervice e 'l bel crin straccia,
A un tempo il ferro, l'Itala donzella
Move, a Meandra fa piaga novella.
(*Enr.* 24.47)

The tenacious Greek woman had not forgotten the riskiest place. She pushed her sword where white ivory opened up a path to cold death, and the hit took off her [Claudia's] helmet. The wound was such that the sword came out of her blond neck, simultaneously cutting off her beautiful hair. The Italian damsel then moved again and inflicted a new wound on Meandra.

La ricca vesta e l'innestata maglia
Rompe, e nel molle lato a pieno immerse

La fatal spada, tal de la battaglia
La Tracia afflitta il duro fin scoperse.
E quanto l'una e l'altra in armi vaglia,
Stupido il mondo riconobbe e scerse;
Caggiono entrambe e questa, e quella gode
L'onor de la vittoria e de la lode.
(*Enr.* 24.48)

She [Claudia] tore her rich garment and mesh mail, sinking her sword deep
into her soft side: the anguished Thracian woman [Meandra] thus discovered
the harsh ending to their battle, *and the stunned world saw and knew their*
worth in battle. Both fell, and both enjoyed the honors of victory and praise.

In chivalric poetry, pity in a duel is represented as a viable alternative, especially when the duel is anticlimactic. But in the passage above, the damsels
do not consider this option. They instead employ extreme violence until a
brutal ending catches them almost by surprise: as Claudia "deeply buries her
fatal sword" ("a pieno immerse / la fatal spada," *Enr.* 24.48.2–3)[60] into Meandra's side, the Thracian "discovers" her mortality ("il duro fin scoperse," *Enr.*
24.48.4). Like Cloridabello finally aware of Risamante's worth, "the world now
recognizes" (*Enr.* 24.48.6) these amazons' courage, but it is a minor consola-
tion since it coincides with their death, does not serve any larger purpose, and
does not even establish the physical superiority of one over the other. They
could have followed Risamante's example and spared each other; instead, they
stubbornly fight to the end.

A pitying instinct appears in Ariosto's *Orlando Furioso* in connection with
Bradamante, who as amazon prefers to defeat her enemies without killing
them. It is particularly fitting that the woman at the origin of the Este family
behaves this way, because the Este women in Ariosto's poem, besides being
celebrated for their generative qualities, are singled out for their moderation.
In the encomium of Canto 13, they are described as "mothers . . . protective
and sturdy columns of illustrious houses" ("madri . . . reparatrici e solide col-
onne di case illustri," *OF* 13.57.2–3) and considered praiseworthy for their great
"pity," "generosity," "prudence," and "continence" (*OF* 13.57.7–8). In this same
passage the comparison between ladies and knights ("che men degne non son
ne lor gonne, / ch'in arme i cavalier," "in their feminine attire, they are not
less worthy than knights in their armor," 13.57.5–6) anticipates Bradamante
the merciful maiden skilled in arms and mother of illustrious progeny. She

---

60. Here is an allusion to the way in which the "angered" Aeneas "buries his sword" into
Turnus's chest (*ferrum . . . condit / fervidus, Aen.* 12. 950–51) in the final duel.

is the embodiment of fertile restraint that produces stability and harmony. Bradamante gathers many of the qualities that the Stoics attributed to the self-controlled sage, and not accidentally she qualifies herself as a "rock of true faith," unmovable even when hit by waves and wind ("immobile . . . di vera fede scoglio / che d'ogni intorno il vento e il mar percuote," *OF* 44.61.5–6). The rock is an important symbol in Stoic imagery.[61] Seneca famously compares the wise man to a rock lashed by the sea yet preserving its strength (*De constantia sapientis*, 3.5). In the *Aeneid*, Latinus is similarly compared to a rock (*rupes immota, Aen.* 7.586ff.) when he resolutely opposes the war.

Self-restraint is clear in Fonte's lady knight, whose sparing of Cloridabello in a final duel is contrasted with the morally disappointing endings of the *Orlando Furioso* and *Aeneid*. In her refusal to kill her enemy, Fonte's Risamante leans toward compassion. As we saw, Fonte endows her female protagonist with *pietas* not so much for religious reasons, but rather to establish women's ethical superiority over men in assessing war situations and making proper moral choices. In the *Enrico*, however, Claudia and Meandra cannot embrace Risamante's generosity and ethical clarity. Their reciprocal killing is a reminder of the foolishness of war and immoderate men. During the battle the cutting of Claudia's hair is a gruesome detail in an episode seemingly crafted to contrast starkly with those in which amazons reveal their hair, femininity, and superiority. In *Floridoro* 2.28.1–2 and 13.65, after defeating her adversaries, Risamante's shedding of her helmet divulged her gender by exposing her long hair; in *Orlando Furioso* 32.79ff. in Tristan's castle, Bradamante's gender—as well as ethical, rhetorical, and martial superiority over men—was first demonstrated through her behavior and then revealed once she took off her helmet, letting her golden hair tumble down. While in the *Aeneid* Virgil affirmed that Camilla's female nature was finally manifested and allowed to play a role in her death, Marinella asserts the opposite: Claudia and Meandra are suppressing their femininity in their final duel. Claudia's lacerated hair and neck remind us that the violence of the fight is taking something away from the women, obscuring and injuring their true selves. The wrath of Marinella's amazons robs them of their beauty by chipping away their female identity and destroying what makes them special and unique. The author realizes it but cannot help determine a different outcome.

Marinella underlines Claudia and Meandra's harshness while she remembers Risamante's leniency. In *Enrico* 24.46.5, Claudia is described as a knight ("ch'ha il cor di ferro avvinto" "whose heart is bound by iron"). The clause alludes to *Floridoro* 13.63, where Risamante, in the act of sparing her enemy, is "the warrior whose heart is soft and human" ("la guerriera, c'ha 'l cor molle

---

61. For the importance of Stoicism in the *Orlando Furioso,* see Ascoli 1987.

e umano"). If in her poem Marinella identifies a typical shortcoming of the
epic project—the male urge to undermine female knights by forcing them to
accept traditional lives or by eliminating them through death by a man—and
resists it by refusing to give men victory over women in a fight or in marriage,
she fails to find a fully satisfactory conclusion for these two amazons, whose
violent behavior reflects that of their male colleagues. In the duel between
Risamante and Cloridabello, Fonte denounces brute force as thoughtless and
ultimately inconclusive, while Marinella's amazons slip back in and reproduce
the epic pattern of violence that Fonte was careful to avoid. Like Aeneas and
Ruggiero, Claudia and Meandra fall prey to ire. This conclusion is particularly
disappointing, because in her best known work, *La nobiltà et l'eccellenza delle
donne,* Marinella had associated women's superiority with their manifest moderation while she had linked wrath to men.

Marinella dedicates one entire section of her *Nobiltà* to "wrathful, eccen-
tric and brutal men" (Second Part Chap. IV). She begins by defining anger
with the help of Speusippus and Aristotle's words:

> The vice of proud and precipitate wrath is hateful and disgraceful to every-
> one and always worthy of reproof and often of punishment. It obscures the
> light of reason from those who commit incontinent acts to such an extent
> that some people refer to wrath as incontinence. O how many homicides
> it has caused, wrath being, as Speusippus states, "a challenge of the iras-
> cible part of the soul to take revenge." Wrath frequently drives angry men to
> these excesses in order to avenge themselves. Often, for the smallest offense,
> they take the dear life of another. This happens because reason is blinded by
> anger as we read in *Politics,* Book 5, chapter 10, and it is certain that anger
> obscures the intellect—as when occasionally we see a dear friend or obedient
> son transported in an instant by such rage. (Marinella 1999: 149, translation
> slightly modified)[62]

---

62. "Tanto detestabile, e uituperoso il uitio della fiera, et precipitosa iracondia, da ogn'uno,
che sempre senza dubbio merita riprensione, e spesso castigo, nè meno ella oscura il lume della
ragione di quello, che facci l'incontinenza, ancorche alcuni l'ira incontinenza chiamassero. O
di quanti homicidij ella è cagione; percio che essendo l'Ira, come dice Speusippo: *Prouocatio
irascibilis animae partis ad ulciscendum.* Spinge souente gli huomini adirati a commettere simili
eccessi per uendicarsi, e ben spesso per leggierissimo oltraggio uien leuata la cara uita ad altrui,
e questo accadde; perciochè l'ira il più delle uolte accieca affatto la ragione, come si legge nel lib.
5 della *Politica,* al capitolo decimo; et ch'ella offuschi l'ingegno è cosa certa; perciochè si uede
non rare uolte un carissimo amico, un'obbediente figliuolo in un subito lasciarsi trasportar tanto
dalla colera" (Marinella 1601: 166).

In the rest of this chapter, Marinella provides several examples of men (Alexander the Great, Ajax, Tydeus, Achilles) prone to anger. In the first part of her work she states that women are characterized by moderate behavior:

> Io credo, si come affermano tutti gli scritori, che raccontano i costumi delle genti, e come per esperienza si uede per il più che i paesi, oue nascono, e la temperatura de' corpi ne sia origine, e cagione: *percioche un corpo temperato, come è quello delle donne, è molto atto alle operationi moderate dell'anima. cosa che non è nella calda temperatura de maschi,* come dimostreremo al luogo suo. (Marinella 1601: 31)

> I believe, as all writers who describe people's customs confirm and as can be seen by experience, that in general, the origin and cause of these matters [temperature, virtues, and vices] are one's country of birth and one's bodily temperature. *For this reason a temperate body like a woman's is most adapted to moderate workings of the soul, which do not accord with men's hot temperature,* as we will show when the time comes. (Marinella 1999: 77–78)

Marinella argues that Aristotle was right to conclude that women are usually, if not always, cooler than men, temperate rather than cold. She links this cooler physical state with the capacity to execute more proficiently the soul's operations, reasoning that those who are physically temperate are also psychologically and morally temperate. When men behave virtuously and show temperance, they have become more similar to women—more moderate in temperature—which is what they normally experience in maturity.[63] Here we see the cleverness of Marinella, who on the one hand asserts on the authority of Aristotle and scripture that men and women have rational souls and belong to the same species, but on the other insists that this fundamental sameness

---

63. Marinella 1601: 119–20 = Marinella 1621 (Combi): 158–59: "I believe that Aristotle does not consider with maturity of mind the operations of heat and what it means to be more or less hot, and how many good and bad effects derive from it; if he had considered better how many effects are produced by heat which exceeds that of women, he would have not said the least word. . . . There is no doubt, as Plutarch writes, that heat is an instrument of the soul; it can be good, but also not very appropriate to the operations of the soul, necessitating in it a certain measure between too little and too much; since too little heat, as it happens in old people, is quite impotent towards operations. Too much makes them precipitous and excessive. Therefore, not every heat is good and useful to serve the operations of the soul, as Marsilio Ficino says. But it is good [when present] in a certain measure and convenient proportion as that of women. . . . Therefore, we will say that women are less hot than men, but more noble; that if a man operates excellently, it happens because he draws near to the nature and temperature of women, having a calm and not exceeding heat, and in fact [a man] having reached adulthood and cooled the heat proper of young age and being more similar to female nature, he behaves more wisely and more maturely" (my translation). This segment of the *Nobiltà* is not in Marinella 1999.

allows for distinctions in merit. The superiority of women's desires and behavior can be traced to their temperate physiology and is manifested in their physical beauty.[64]

The argument about temperature was not entirely new. It had been used by Fonte in *Merito*[65] and by Castiglione in the *Cortegiano* (Book 3) when Magnifico Juliano defends the excellent nature of women against Gasparo Pallavicino:

> Women are cold in temperament only in comparison with men. In themselves, because of their excessive warmth, men are far from temperate; but in themselves women are temperate, or at least more nearly temperate than men since they possess, in proportion to their natural warmth, a degree of moisture. (Castiglione 1967: 222, trans. G. Bull)

The case is interesting because it does not bestow on heat the positivity that Aristotle did.[66] Marinella, Fonte, and Castiglione do not object to the established fact of men's greater amount of body heat, but argue about its meaning.

Having established temperance as women's best trait, Marinella depicts Meandra and Claudia as being unable to remain temperate during war. Yet Marinella's innovative attitude toward her heroines allows them to die undefeated by men and to measure each other's strength in a serious duel, which previous male authors had not granted to any of their amazons.[67] Despite the amazons' death and inability to fully embrace their female identity, Marinella praises the damsels and reminds the world of their courage and worth:

> Se invida non è sorte al valor vostro,
> E a vostri chiari preghi il ciel nemico,
> Vi trarrà rozza penna e basso inchiostro
> D'alta immortalità nel campo aprico;
> Ma il vostro bel seren del lume nostro
> Uopo non ha, già indarno m'affatico,

---

64. Deslauriers 2012. The importance of the observations about heat has already received critical attention; see Malpezzi Price and Ristaino 2008: 111*ff.*; Jordan 1990: 255–61; Santacroce 1999–2000: 83–96.

65. Fonte 1988: 47. For the exact citation, see note 22 above.

66. Because of insufficient heat, according to Aristotle, women were unable to concoct semen. See Deslauriers 2009: 218 discussing *Gen. An.*: "The female receives, but is incapable both of forming and of ejaculating semen that can transmit form. Nonetheless, the female does produce a kind of 'semen'—the menses or *katamenia*, which Aristotle explicitly says is the same as that in the male, although incompletely processed (765b36–766a2)"; see also Meyhew 2004: 114–18.

67. The duel between Marfisa and Bradamante (*OF* 36.21*ff.*) is comic, not intended to bestow honor but rather to ridicule the warriors; see MacCarthy 2007.

Altissime donzelle, per voi sole
Splendete sì, ch'appo voi tetro è 'l sole.
(*Enr.* 24.49)

If fate does not envy your valor, if heaven is not enemy to your clear merits,
a rough pen and lowly ink will lead you to the open field of immortality.
Yet the clarity of your light doesn't need that, so I work in vain: you, highest
damsels, shine by yourselves, and the sun is dark next to you.

In an apostrophe, a rhetorical trope common in epic, Marinella praises the
women, whose valor is said to exist independently from tributes granted in
works of art. Yet she is keen to record their worth with her pen because merits
are not easily recognized unless immortalized in poems. If in the *Enrico* she
classically attempts, following Horace, to build a *monumentum aere perennius*
to the crusading troops, less classically, her loquacious narrator also builds
a monument to female characters who traditionally do not play as large a
role in epic.[68] Marinella's desire to praise these amazons is probably triggered
by her awareness of the similarities between women who use the sword and
those who use the pen.[69] The juxtaposition of warriors and intellectual women
may appear strange, but both groups were known to Renaissance readers for
pursuing fields not normally open to women. Margaret King highlights the
societal shortcomings experienced by women who dared to write during the
Renaissance and understood that wielding a pen was the equivalent of bearing arms.[70]

By featuring amazons, Fonte and Marinelli highlight women's ability to
accomplish anything if given the proper training and their capacity to choose
what is morally best even in extreme situations. Women's ethical lucidity is
celebrated in the *Floridoro,* when Fonte reconsiders the violence of epic conclusions by fashioning an ending that features in Risamante a wise amazon
who spares her enemy without hesitation. Here Fonte echoes the endings
crafted by her male predecessors (especially Virgil and Ariosto) to ensure that
her readers compare Risamante's upright behavior with that of her male epic
predecessors. If Risamante at first behaves like them, eventually she learns

---

68. Galli Stampino 2014: 81.

69. For the similarities between amazons and humanists, see Benedetti 1996: 52–58. These
two categories of women were paired by Ariosto, who celebrated at *OF* 20.1.1–2 "the ancient
women" ("le donne antique") who "accomplished marvelous deeds" ("hanno mirabil cose /
fatto ne l'arme e ne le sacre muse;") thanks to weapons and the sacred muses. Ariosto mentions
Harpalyce and Camilla, "knowledgeable about war" (*OF* 20.1.6) side by side with Sappho and
Corinna "because they were wise" ("perché furon dotte," *OF* 20.1.7).

70. King 1991a: 244. The essay summarizes King 1991b (esp. chap. 3).

to overcome their mistakes, promoting a more humane and explicitly feminine kind of victory. In this light, Fonte emerges as belonging to a strain of
Renaissance critics debating and criticizing the ending of the *Aeneid*. Even
in Marinella's *Enrico,* at least one of her female warriors (Emilia) learns from
her errors and retreats from war to embrace a pastoral existence. Fonte and
Marinella's treatment of amazons reflects how their epic poems are practical
representations of the philosophical ideas about women's roles and nature that
they expressed elsewhere.

Fonte's emphasis on female mercy is also accompanied by a reevaluation
of love, which, in her view, can help correct prejudice against women. Men in
love can see what society does not want to see; through love, men acknowledge the worth of women. While the theme of compassion is echoed in Fonte's
Il merito through the words of Helena, who hopes that women will become
famous for their mercy, the theme of love is highlighted in the remarks of
Adriana, who realizes love's importance for married couples, promising to
give her daughter in marriage to a man who is wise rather than rich. Although
Adriana's statement is uttered in a dialogue and is in part undercut by the
presence of the varied opinions of her interlocutors, it is remarkable in a book
published in a city in which forced monachization and marriages dictated by
the financial interests of the leading aristocracy were the norm.[71]

---

71. Adriana's words are analyzed in chap. 7.

PART II

Lovers at War

Virgil, Ovid, and Resistance

CHAPTER 3

~

Epic and Elegy

IN 1635, MARINELLA with editor Imberti published what some critics consider her masterpiece, *L'Enrico, overo Bisantio acquistato* (*Henry, or Byzantium Gained*). Rooted in historical events, the poem celebrates the conquest of Byzantium under the lead of Enrico Dandolo during the Fourth Crusade (1202–04). This event catapulted Venice toward political and economic greatness. The expedition was originally organized to capture Jerusalem but stealthily redirected against the Byzantine Empire and Constantinople. Venetians celebrated the Crusade as a holy victory that provided an immense profit to the city, but in reality it was propelled by the desire to release the fighting spirits of European nobles who did not heed the pope but rather used the crusade to legitimize their thirst for conquest.[1] Ultimately, the Venetians systematically subordinated the interest of the crusade to their advantage, leading them to the conquest of Zara and Byzantium.[2] While Pope Innocent III at first exploited the Venetian desire for power by convincing them to build ships for his crusaders, he then found himself exploited by Venetian interests. He

---

1. Nicol 1988; 1995: 155–83. There is no contemporary Venetian account of the Crusade; our closest Venetian source is Martin da Canal (ca. 1275), who blatantly revised the story of what happened, hoping to prove that Venice's participation was blameless, had the blessing of the pope, and brought only glory to the Christian Republic. Later Venetian chroniclers adopted this version of events. The main eyewitness accounts of the Crusade are Geoffery of Villehardouin, Robert of Clari, and Nicetas Choniates (Nicol 1988: 124–25).

2. Meschini 2008: 32–37.

reacted with indignation to the siege of Constantinople. In a letter to Baldwin of Flanders, he accuses him and the Venetians of ignoring their vows to liberate the Holy Land and instead of fighting Christians in the invasion of Constantinople.[3]

How aware was Marinella of this situation? Although she superficially describes the war according to the dictates of Venetian propaganda, she subtly challenges it by endorsing characters whom she qualifies as wise and good but definitely hostile to the war. Marinella was influenced by pro-Venetian sources because she obliterates the disquieting conquest of Zara and shows the crusaders as moved by the noble desire to help Alexius to recover the throne (e.g., *Enr.* 1.28) and then wanting to avenge his murder;[4] in Canto 24, she celebrates the conquest of Constantinople, framing it as a battle between good and evil. But as Zorzi has proven, Marinella was also familiar with the only Byzantine exposition of the Fourth Crusade available at the time, the account of Nicetas Choniates.[5] By the sixteenth century, the Venetian memory of the Fourth Crusade had been complicated and contextualized, becoming "a multilayered strata of competing narratives" probably available to Marinella.[6] Ultimately, in the *Enrico,* she produces a work that extols Venetian history while raising doubts about its validity by giving a voice to female characters who do not endorse the war and try (unsuccessfully) to keep the men they love away from it. In previous chapters I highlighted how Fonte belongs in the tradition of readers who see the shortcomings of epic and war. In a similar vein, in Marinella's work, the reemployment of Virgil's *Aeneid* and texts such as Ovid's *Heroides* and *Metamorphoses* muddles what at first sight seems a laudatory heroic poem written to praise her city.

---

3. Andrea 2000: 173.

4. Zorzi 2004–5: 419; see also Queller and Katele 1982.

5. Zorzi 2004–5: 415–28. Marinella cites Choniates in Marinella 1999: 172, Dunhill explains that the citation comes from Choniates's *Rule of Alexius,* 605. Information coming from Choniates is also in Marinella 1999: 178–79.

6. Madden 2012: 337–44, 340: "The fact that many Venetian chroniclers from the late thirteenth century onward omitted the narrative of papal support for the crusade's diversion suggests that they either questioned or outright rejected it. The willingness of other chroniclers to include this narrative suggests a contested space within Venetian historical memory. . . . The problem was made more acute with the formal presentation to the Council of Ten of a manuscript of Villehardouin that was brought from the court of Charles V in Brussels. The Ten commissioned Paolo Ramusio [the young] to translate Villehardouin into Latin, but the humanist scholar did much more than that. Instead, he produced a new critical history of the Fourth Crusade based not only on Villehardouin but also on a long list of other Byzantine, Venetian, and Continental sources." See also Cicogna 1828: 33/1; Marin 2000. For the sources and fortune of Martin da Canal's history, see Marin 2010: 71–121. For Choniates, see Carile 1967: esp. 104; Marin 2008: 113–23; Simpson 2009: 13–34.

NOT-SO-MINOR THREADS: STORIES OF WOMEN

In style and content, Marinella's epic poem imitates Torquato Tasso's *Gerusalemme Liberata* (*Jerusalem Delivered*, 1581), and it is less obviously influenced by Ludovico Ariosto's *Orlando Furioso* (*Mad Orlando*, 1532). Following Tasso's example and Aristotle's dictates in the *Poetics,* Marinella prioritizes one sequence of events linked to her main hero and, as she states in her introduction, keeps digressions to a minimum:[7]

> Gli episodi ed altre digressioni . . . ho procurato che sieno così unite colla principale azione, che non si potesse facilmente levarne una parte senza confondere il tutto. (Prefazione dell'Autrice, Marinella 1844: 2)[8]

> Episodes and the other digressions . . . I have connected to the main action so that you cannot get rid of them without confusing everything.

Despite what she affirms, some episodes appear so expanded and rich in detail that they are hard to justify within the logic adduced above. Presumably they are secondary segments developed beyond what is natural or necessary, because in them—rather than in the main narrative sequence—she can articulate some of her more progressive positions, such as describing women as morally upright subjects and criticizing Venice's militaristic agenda. It is in one of these minor episodes that we find the ill-fated love between Lucillo and Clelia, while in another is the twin tale of Corradino and Areta. In these episodes Marinella is interested in the love theme as much as Ariosto was; she wishes to remind the readers of those who are left to suffer at home; and she focuses on the love of women for the husbands who leave them to go to war. For instance, love is prioritized over war and political concerns when the narration focuses on Clelia, a loving wife, and in its denouement Lucillo, the male protagonist who puts military glory before love and family matters, is punished and defeated. If in Marinella's work, especially on a structural level, Ariosto is undermined, her allegiance to him is demonstrated in her will to challenge traditional misogyny as well as that more intrinsically linked to

---

7. For the Renaissance controversy between "digression" and "linearity," see Finucci 1999 (introduction). For Tasso's influence on Marinella, see Costa-Zalessow 1981: 141. For Marinella's *convenzionalità,* see Prosperi 2011: 25–37. The controversy is also connected to the rediscovery of Aristotle's *Poetics* and his unities of time, space, and action, which are in turn tied to the debate over whether romance epics constituted a new genre.

8. For the *Enrico,* there is only an edition printed in 1635 in Venice by the editor Ghirardo Imberti. The text I routinely quote in Italian is that from 1844 (from a Harvard microfilm), which does not differ from the original and is also available on Google books.

the epic genre.[9] Although Ariosto is generally committed to rescuing women from their typical epic fate of oblivion and calumny, at times he treats them in a traditional fashion and chastises those who, like Angelica, rebel against Cinquecento norms. Like Ariosto, who removes Angelica from the *Furioso*'s plot for her recalcitrant and antipatriarchal behavior, Marinella eliminates Lucillo from the plot because he cannot serve the poet's pro-women agenda.[10]

Besides adopting Tasso's structure in her poem, Marinella is influenced by Tasso also in another way: by reproducing the tension she detects in his *Gerusalemme*. When we carefully consider Marinella's articulated aims and commitment to Tasso's poetics, we can determine in both authors, for different reasons, a double allegiance. In the *Gerusalemme Liberata,* from the first stanzas (*GL* 1.1–5), while Tasso's protagonist Goffredo di Buglione and his patron Alfonso d'Este are characters who promote unity and health, the poet aligns himself with elements of the story (i.e., women and infidels) that foster physical and ethical chaos and that are ultimately destined to be overcome. In Canto 4, Tasso hopes that Alfonso will "guide him safely into port" and compares himself to a "wondering pilgrim" who is "tossed among the reefs and amid the waves, almost overwhelmed" ("guidi in porto / me peregrino errante, e fra gli scogli / e fra l'onde agitato e quasi absorto," *GL* 1.4.2–4). While at a theoretical level the poet condemns the ideology and structure of romance, in practice he has a hard time repudiating it or excluding "romantic tendencies" and characters from his epic.[11] This attrition—the conscious desire to praise certain characters and ideals while being attracted to opposite characters and ideals—also informs Marinella's *Enrico*.

In his seminal work on Tasso's *Liberata*, Sergio Zatti recognized at the heart of the poem a tension between "Christian unity" and "pagan variety" ("l'uniforme Cristiano" and "il multiforme pagano").[12] He underscores how Tasso cannot help but identify with the enemies of God and the very forces he intends to chastise. Zatti's revisionist approach followed that of Virgil's *Aeneid,* which, after ages of being considered an imperialist poem illustrating the moral progress of his hero and the celebration of Augustus's empire, in the 1960s was studied by the Harvard School for its ambiguous stance toward

---

9. Bloch 1991: 7; Bernard 1999: 295.

10. Not only does Angelica refuse the most distinguished knights who would like to wed her, but she also chooses to marry an insignificant soldier. The abnormality of a woman who selects her own object of desire becomes apparent in the poem when Ariosto obliterates her from the plot; see Shemek 1998: 45–77; Newman 2003: 317. The bibliography on narratology and narrative theory is large. Important contributions include Booth 1961; Chatman 1978; Culler 1975; Hagedorn 2004: esp. introduction; Hawkes 1977; Prince 1982; Rimmon-Kenan 1983.

11. Zatti 1996: 2.

12. The book in question is Zatti 1983.

the political establishment and allegiance to the defeated side. Zatti cleverly highlights how Tasso gives a voice to the enemy (Satan, the pagans, Rinaldo as rebel to the Christian cause) and fosters the reader's sympathy for an ideological content (and characters) that he claims to be eager to thwart.[13] Similarly, Virgil had treated enemies of Aeneas sympathetically and successfully stirred readers' pity for them. Zatti's reading of Tasso's poem follows the Harvard School's approach to the *Aeneid* and what, with Kallendorf or Thomas, we may call "pessimistic" ways to interpret the *Aeneid*. These scholars illustrate the multilayered, even sometimes contradictory nature of Rome's national epic, which was a significant precedent for writers with doubts and anxieties about the exercise of power based on violence and promoting imperialism or state control over individual liberty.[14] Such a dynamic is present in Marinella's attitude toward facets of her poem that do not neatly or easily belong to a pro-Venetian epic; we see her sympathy for women, especially those who do not endorse war and who in the name of the family (Clelia/Areta) oppose agendas that privilege political militarism or absolute prioritization of the state. Therefore, I focus on women who resist their husbands' commitment to martial glory and war. Later in Part II, I expose how Marinella openly grants authority and a strong voice to Erina, who not only does not hide her spite for war but also tries to convince the soldier Venier not to return to it. Beyond the flaunted praise of Venice and its brave heroes, she constructs an elusive yet essential discourse that magnifies women and their resistance to war. Her discussion builds on what men wrote and thought before her, and her reflections arise from a careful and deep evaluation of texts like Ariosto's *Orlando* and Tasso's *Liberata*, which can be considered meditations on classical epics. There is no sharp caesura between Marinella's *Enrico* and the poems of her predecessors, although her gender makes her more sensitive to women's voices and prejudices against them.

ABANDONED WOMEN: OVID VERSUS ARISTOTLE

Although Tasso's and Ariosto's epics were the primary generic sources of inspiration for Marinella, almost programmatically in her introduction she emphasizes Aristotle's *Poetics* and her Greek and Latin sources:[15]

---

13. Zatti 2006: 193.

14. Important explorations of Tasso's internal ambiguities are Caretti 2001: 90, 105; Chiappelli 1981: 14–31. For polyphony in the *Aeneid,* see Parry 1963; Lyne 1994. For the Harvard School and the *Aeneid,* see chap. 1.

15. At the end of the fifteenth century the *Poetics* became known in Western Europe, and by the second half of the Cinquecento it was studied and commented upon, especially in Flor-

Il quale [poema] ho voluto formare secondo li documenti di Aristotile nella sua poetica, . . . e se in alcuna parte parerà ad alcuno che abbia imitato li moderni poeti, vedrà poi onde ne abbia pigliate le invenzioni, se leggerà i primi e veri fonti della poesia greca e latina, e scoprirà che *primis gratiae sunt habendae*; siccome nelli primi libri della Metafisica si legge. (Marinella 1844: 2)

I aimed to fashion my poem according to Aristotle's directions in his *Poetics* . . . and if anyone believes that I have followed modern poets in some respects, he will see where I gleaned my inventions if he reads the first true sources of Greek and Latin poetry; he will then find that *thanks are due to the very first models,* as we read in the first books of *Metaphysics.* (Marinella 2009: 77)

Marinella points the reader to the sources of her poetic inspiration and Aristotle. In practice, she seems eager to advertise her dependence on classical authors and their principles while minimizing her reliance on Renaissance authors.[16] Her claim and debt to the classical tradition are particularly visible in the tales of Clelia and Lucillo and Areta and Corradino. These two episodes echo the cases of Ceyx and Alcyone in Ovid's *Metamorphoses* and those of Protesilaus and Laodamia in the *Heroides.* Clelia and Areta are wives abandoned by husbands eager to acquire glory in war, exactly as Alcyone and Laodamia were abandoned by their consorts.

Ovid's portrait of love and loving women had been widely imitated and admired in the Middle Ages and, besides the portrait of Dido in *Aeneid* 4, had become the paradigmatic representation of abandoned women.[17] In Ovid's *Metamorphoses,* in a rather counter-classical vein, the Roman author replays the most important epic motifs available to him and emphasizes the love

---

ence and Venice; see Tigerstedt 1968: 10; Halliwell 1992.

16. The massive presence of the "ancients" in Marinella's text was highlighted by Enrico Levi Catellani at the end of the 1800s: "Venier welcomed by Erina, reads in the future his own death among the victories of his people, like Achilles foresaw his end among the victories of the Greeks; at Erina's banquet, Altea sings the miracles of nature as Iopas at Dido's feast; Iacete from Biarnia wants to destroy Minerva's icon, which brings bad luck to Greece, in the way in which Laocoon cried 'Equo ne credite Teucri' ["Do not trust the horse, Teucrians"] and a dragon comes out of the earth and kills him like Laocoon had died . . . Idilia, daughter of Artabano is about to be sacrificed like Iphigenia . . . the night raid of Meandro, Dione and Ernesto to the Latin camp to free Asdelio is similar to that of Euryalus and Nisus, of Cloridano and Medoro" (Levi Catellani 1879: 518, my translation).

17. McKinley 2001. During the Middle Ages, a text such as *L'Ovide moralisé* facilitated the reading of Ovid's work; see Copeland 1991: esp. 107–26; Black 2011: 123–43. According to Parker 1997: 250–67, Ovid's *Heroides* and *Metamorphoses* play a large role in some of Angela and Isotta Nogarola's poems.

theme.[18] Besides the importance given to the erotic motif, he is often ironic about or critical of the values and agendas promoted in hexametric poetry. In his *Heroides,* too, we have a denunciation of the epic world paired with a focus on love and female lovers. The deheroization of the mythical material and rejection of the male viewpoint can certainly be interpreted as a denial of the Augustan and Virgilian prioritization of politics.[19] The collected letters, called *Heroides* or *Epistulae heroidum* (*Letters of Heroines*), in terms of subject matter and meter owe much to the founders of Latin love elegy (Catullus, Gallus, Propertius, and Tibullus), but they also break new ground by linking elegy to the epistolary tradition and by featuring women not as objects but subjects of desire.[20] Sara Lindheim summarizes the main features of elegy as a genre antithetical to epic:

> The lover-poet sees himself as a slave to his private passion, a weak creature who refuses traditional values, turning his back on public affairs of state, especially war, on heroism, and on socially sanctioned moral behavior. Instead, he celebrates his personal suffering, complaining about his beloved's faithlessness, accusing her of betrayal, lamenting her lack of love, supplicating her to remain his. Upholding private emotions over public action, the lover-poet redeploys terms from the public sphere—*fides* ("faith"), *pietas* ("pity"), *foedus* ("bond/treaty"), for example—attributing new significance in the realm of individual emotion and personal relationship to these words used traditionally to describe a range of relations within an accepted mode of (male) socio-political interaction.[21]

In elegy, the poet-lover prioritizes his inner feelings and private world. He undermines the world of politics, but also marriage and having children—tra-

---

18. For a definition of "counter-classical," see Johnson 1970: 123–51, esp. 126: "For a long while I have felt . . . that there exists an important body of poetry in Western literature that uses classical forms and classical themes in a way that I should prefer to call counter-classical. I feel, furthermore, that this body of poetry has been too frequently misjudged both as to its nature and to its quality by critics. . . . This kind of poetry is created not to refute the moral experience that classical poetry reveals but to view that moral experience in another way. Counter-classical poetry tends to underline possibilities of disharmony even as classical poetry tends to underline possibility of harmony."

19. Jacobson 1974: 7.

20. I employ the term as Finucci 1992: 147.

21. Lindheim 2008: 16–17. Basic information about the genre can be found in Conte 1994a: 321–24; Miller 2002: 1–37. Seminal reflections about the importance of elegy for women's studies began in the 1970s with Hallett 1973: 103–24. The "difficult integration" of the citizen and the lover in Propertius is discussed by La Penna 1977. For a survey of current critical trends on elegy, see Wyke 1995: 110–28. For elegies written in Latin during the Renaissance, see Parker 2012: 476–90.

ditional social configurations on which Roman society is built.[22] Elegists highlight the importance and nobility of their objects of desire by framing them
and their feelings for them through words normally employed in political contexts (*fides, pietas, amicitia, foedus,* etc.). Love assumes a totalizing dimension
for the elegiac male subject who rejects his usual duties and socially oriented
obligations in favor of love and the celebration of his mistress. For this reason,
elegy can be considered a rather countercultural genre in the Roman literary
landscape, one that redraws the profile of the world by putting love—not politics, war, or public life—at its center. In addition, Ovid's decision to celebrate
(in the *Amores* as well as in the *Ars Amatoria*) the flimsy pursuits of women
and to ignore Augustus's moralizing campaign has been rightly interpreted as
a veiled but palpable criticism of the political status quo.[23] Ovid's criticism of
the political regime can also be heard in the laments of some of his heroines
who reveal the costs of male glory.[24]

   Ovid, perhaps more than his predecessors, is aware of the boundaries/
rules of his chosen poetic genre and strives to redraw them. He is keen to
innovate within the genre. He realizes that elegy's success is built on the poet's
ability to create variations on well established themes and on his revision of
previously discussed amorous trends, on new angles that contradict what his
predecessors or he himself had proposed and previously explored.[25] Clearly, in
the *Heroides* the "remapping" of the genre that puts women (instead of men)
at its center can be considered a further development of elegy. In the *Heroides,* women redeploy the elegiac framework, and the collection reveals how
well suited elegy is for the female voice: elegy becomes a model of the world
that accurately duplicates women's lives of suffering, humiliation, and *servitium.* They create a literary genre rooted in women's sociocultural condition.
In Conte's famous definition, the *Heroides* "are the declension of the elegiac
paradigm in the feminine gender."[26]

   The *Heroides* enjoyed a remarkable circulation during the Renaissance,
with more than forty editions published before 1500.[27] The tale of Protesilaus
and Laodamia was featured in Ovid but also appears, with minor variants, in

---

   22. Miller 1994: 119–38, esp. 128*ff.*

   23. Davis 1999: 431–49, esp. 49. For the ongoing critical debate about the nature of Latin
love elegy, see Fear 2000: 154; Miller and Platter 1999: 403–7; Janan 2001: 3–12; Hallett 1973:
103–24; Gold 2012: 1–7; Thorsen 2013; James 2003: esp. 146–48.

   24. Davis 2006: 49–70. Although I do not fully endorse Davis's argument, his book helped
me to formulate some of my ideas.

   25. Barsby 1979: 8–18.

   26. Conte 1994b: 117; Veyne 1988; Verducci 1985.

   27. Moore 2000: 40–64; Black 2004: esp. 247–62; White 2015. McKinley 2001 deals with the
women of the *Metamorphoses* as well as the *Heroides* in their commentaries. For the influence
of the *Heroides* on Gaspara Stampa and Veronica Franco, see Phillippy 1992.

other important ancient sources, including Homer (*Iliad* 2.695–710), Euripides (fr. 655 Nauck), Catullus 68, Propertius 1.19, and Virgil (*Aen.* 6.447).[28] Marinella was probably conversant with many of them and was certainly familiar with Ovid's version because she explicitly talks about it in her *Nobiltà,* where Laodamia's ill fortunes are described this way:

> But shouldn't we consider Laodamia, daughter of the Thessalian Acastus, who conceived so ardent a love for her husband Protesilaus that, when he went to the Trojan War, she lived in continuous tears and pain, always calling him until his body was brought back to her—he had been killed by Hector—and, consumed by cruel sorrow by his dead body, she let herself die? (Marinella 1601: 93)[29]

After this brief review of the history of elegy in the Roman world and its main transformations, we can see how apt Ovid's letters were for Marinella as the primary subtext for the Clelia and Areta narratives.[30] Essential to Marinella's project and program of allusions in these episodes is her focus on abandoned women. By drawing on stereotypes from subversive manipulations of the epic and elegiac tradition, Marinella explores gender and genre. On the one hand she realizes that women like Virgil's Dido, Ovid's Laodamia, Ariosto's Olimpia, or her Clelia ask themselves what to do and realize that nothing can be done because "their complaints articulate the unofficial story, their stories point to the 'hole' in the middle of history and derail the heroic image, their pleas express the power of words to persuade and move to action and the failure of words to do anything for those lacking an avenue for effective action."[31] On the other hand, she skillfully makes these women larger than reality and removes them from the male narrative economy that wants them to be silenced and defeated by endowing them with their own voice and, as we will see, by allowing them to survive. Even if Marinella's heroines (like their ancient predecessors) in their desperation and powerlessness are represented according to societal stereotypes and therefore Marinella proposes pre-

---

28. Lyne 1998: 200–212.

29. Translation mine; this segment is not in Marinella 1999. Ovid's *Heroides* 13.43–48 with Laodamia's description of Paris and Menelaus is also recalled in Marinella 1601: 117–18 = Marinella 1999: 129–30.

30. Like Marinella, Laura Cereta had echoed Ovid's female speakers in the *Heroides;* see Cereta 1997: 12, 96–97 (letter to Alberto degli Alberti).

31. Ciccone 1997: 13. About Olimpia and the transhistorical significance of the figure of the abandoned woman, see Zanini-Cordi 2007: 37–53; Migiel 1995: 22–44. For the soliloquy of the forsaken woman, see Barchiesi 2001: 29–48. For Olimpia, see Gilardino 1982: 429–44. For Picchio 2007: 63–65, Olimpia, like other male characters, follows a path of redemption and in the end recognizes her limitations and the importance of a divine horizon.

scriptions she is trying to counter, she can—within those fossilized images of passivity—grant them their own voices and thematize their suffering and discontent. Significantly, by identifying with all women traditionally discouraged from engaging in political action, she is eager to represent their powerlessness. She gives them a voice in a work of art that allegedly should celebrate male accomplishments but ultimately also becomes a conduit for the memorialization of female greatness. If Marinella's heroines (like their author) are aware of their static poetic and political lot and inhabit a master narrative that marginalizes their desires and actions, they nevertheless struggle for control over their destinies by disturbing men's plans and epic journeys. In this attempt they are like Gaspara Stampa, Veronica Gambara, Chiara Matraini, and Vittoria Colonna, who had acquired some control of the narrative space linked to love poetry. The experience and voice of these female poets—especially when lamenting the absence of the lover—can be heard in the way abandoned women in love speak in Marinella's epic poem.[32]

As has emerged in critical work produced in the last decades, the victimization and subjection of abandoned women grant them poetic momentum because by their very nature they are subversive figures, "for they call into question not only the integrity of individual heroes, but the necessity for heroic action—and even—action itself."[33] The passivity of the abandoned, however ineffectual, however irrelevant for action, can attain a power of its own.[34] These women resist closure, and their "poetics of abandonment" stand outside the "laws" that Aristotle expounded in his *Poetics*. The poetry and reasons of abandoned women are intrinsically subversive by posing a threat to fictions and their rules. As Aristotle realized, the entelechy of a work of art requires a sequence of events brought to their natural and logical conclusion, "epic and dramatic poems must arrive somewhere, and so must their heroes."[35] And yet abandoned women reject this logic. They know that action is not on their side, that their fates are not in their hands, that they can only exist in their inert suffering and wailing. To the Aristotelian reader who concentrates on the end of the story, on the macronarrative of the war and its

---

32. For women's use of Petrarchan building blocks in their love compositions, see Borsetto 1990: 105–38. In recent decades, good critical work on female-authored love compositions has been published; see Cox 2005: 583–606 (also her expanded Italian version 2006: 117–49); Cox 2008: esp. 45–76; 2011: 51–76; Jones 1990; Robin: 2007: 41–78; Smarr 2001: 1–31. Although in 1559, the appearance of the Index of Prohibited Books negatively affected women's publications, lyric poetry was widely read by women and contributed to their writerly matrix, Cox 2011: 54–55ff. Particularly important for the relationship between women and war is Sears 1996. On the theme of mourning women, see Schiesari 1992: 160–91.

33. Hagedorn 2004: 9.

34. Lipking 1989: 4.

35. Ibid., 3.

hero, Marinella's women, with their own stories, offer an opportunity to look at the "middle," and in the *Enrico* that middle changes how we see the ending.[36] Marinella is aware of the paradoxical strength of abandoned women and lets them be heard. She insists on giving victims a voice that disrupts the heroic economy of her poem and undoes (or problematizes) the claims and progress of male heroes. She offers abandoned heroines who like Ariadne in Catullus 68 or Dido in *Aeneid* 4 remind us about the vanity of warriors and the need for plots to consider feelings and suffering.[37] With her abandoned Clelia and Areta, Marinella, despite her professed allegiance to the *Poetics*, with Ovid's help covertly but effectively minimizes Aristotle's poetic rules. In addition, her ingenious reuse of Latin elegy for the characterization of loving wives proves her willingness to experiment with erotic themes within the boundaries of epic and her success in using Ovid's techniques to accentuate the power of women.[38]

---

36. Fulkerson 2005: 18, describing the stories of Ovid's heroines.

37. Lipking 1989: 4. Similarly, Galli Stampino 2014: 82 notices the narrator's ability to represent Eudocia's "tears, moans, sighs and words" (*Enr.* 25.74.1–2) even "if in the end these cannot stop the progression of the plot and the poem."

38. Here I disagree with Cox 2008: 158, who frames Marinella as uninterested in experimentation with love themes.

CHAPTER 4

~

Love and Lamentation

IN CANTO 4 of the *Enrico,* the Venetian Venier goes to Cyprus to look for allies for his war against Constantinople, and Lucillo, the ambitious prince of the island, decides to accompany him despite the wishes and ominous premonitions of his wife, Clelia. Venier was charged with enlisting allies by Enrico Dandolo, the Doge of Venice, so (in a certain way) he becomes Dandolo's surrogate. While Marinella is not able to criticize Venetian politics directly by making accusations against Enrico—Dandolo was too much of a hero in the Venetians' eyes—by criticizing figures near him or representative of his authority, she manages to resist Dandolo's power through the narration. Venier is offered a chance to remain on Erina's island to cultivate learning and contemplation but he refuses it, returns to war, and dies a mediocre death. Marinella's strategy—the silencing of the heroic temper through the defeat of men close to the Doge and by the same token the magnification of characters who do not value war—is at work when dealing with Lucillo and Clelia. Marinella's complex attitude toward war is also visible when she draws on canonical epics such as the *Iliad* or the *Aeneid* and, choosing problematic passages, highlights conundrums and contradictions present in her ancient sources. Marinella echoes specific episodes of these works as she retells the story of Clelia and Lucillo with the intention of manifesting her profound skepticism toward the easy celebration of political success, especially if linked to the prioritization of war over family bonds. One of these classical episodes is the encounter between Dido and Aeneas with the subsequent abandonment of Dido (*Aeneid* 4).

Aeneid 4 is an important model for Canto 4 of the *Enrico*: while Clelia is cast as Dido, Lucillo, about to abandon his wife, is cast as a second Aeneas. Like Dido in *Aeneid* 4.296–97, Clelia seems to know that something will go terribly wrong. She is frozen ("par ch'occulta paura il cor l'agghiacci," "it seems that a hidden fear freezes her heart" *Enr.* 4.67.6). She "is worried about uncertain evils" ("e teme incerti mali," *Enr.* 4.70.6) before learning of her husband's plan to go to war. Even if she does not have any real reason to suspect anything untoward, she feels uneasy. A similar situation appears in Book 4 of the *Aeneid*. As Aeneas prepares to leave Carthage, Dido is at first portrayed by Virgil as "unaware and unable to think that such a great love can be broken" (*nesciat et tantos rumpi non speret amores, Aen.* 4.292), yet a few lines later, without a tangible reason, she becomes suspicious of some machination. Dido, Virgil explains, "has a presentiment about the deceit" (*praesensit dolos,* 4.297) and "although confident, fears everything" (*omnia tuta timens,* 4.298). On his part, Lucillo, behaving like Aeneas, does not "mention / his departure: he hates to disturb her peace / thus hesitantly he pretends and remains silent" ("Non le fece cenno / del suo partir; aborre la sua pace / sturbare, onde sospeso finge e tace," *Enr.* 66.7–9). When Aeneas talks to Serestus and the other leaders, he bids them to prepare for departure but also to hide the truth (*et quae rebus sit causa novandis / dissimulent,* "let them dissimulate the reason for the changes" *Aen.* 4.290–91). Eventually both women learn about the trip. Clelia begs her husband "to be merciful for the first sign of love and faithfulness" once shown to her ("per quel primo d'amor segno e di fede / ch'a me mostrasti," *Enr.* 4.79.1–2) by renouncing the project or by bringing her with him. In a similar fashion, a profoundly distressed Dido in 4.311–19 implores Aeneas to stay in Carthage "in the name of their union and initiated relationship" (*per conubia nostra, per inceptos hymenaeos,* 4.316).

In *Nobiltà*, Marinella declares that Virgil had not recounted the truth when narrating the reasons for Dido's suicide, attributed to the queen's shame for having been abandoned by her lover Aeneas.[1] The statement proves that

---

1. Marinella is reluctant to establish connections between Clelia and Dido because she does not endorse the Virgilian treatment of Dido. In the *Nobiltà* (Marinella 1601: 46–47), she includes Dido among the ranks of virtuous women and rectifies Virgil's story: following Justin and the pre-Virgilian tradition endorsed by Petrarch, she records that, after having founded Carthage, the queen received warning of King Iarbas's threats to destroy the city unless Dido married him. To remain chaste and to preserve peace and the well-being of her newly created state, she committed suicide. See also Marinella 1999: 97: "For as long as Carthage endured Dido was worshiped like a goddess, as Tarcagnota relates . . . even if Virgil pretends (and Passi follows him) that Dido killed herself for love of Aeneas, which is false." For Dido in the Renaissance, see Kallendorf 1985: 403–4; the two most important sources for the Dido myth before

she was familiar with *Aeneid* 4, which in the *Enrico* is reemployed for the magnification of Clelia and denigration of Lucillo. Marinella's direct use of *Aeneid*
4—one of the most famous and problematic books of the *Aeneid*—is an interesting narrative strategy that shows her as a keen reader of Virgil's nuanced
masterpiece. She understands that the *Aeneid*'s imperial project is at risk not
only when Aeneas delays his departure to Italy to indulge himself with the
Carthaginian queen. The priorities of the empire and of *pius* ("duty and god
bound") Aeneas are also undermined when the reader takes pity on Dido,
doubting the orthodoxy of a hero who meddles with truth and abandons the
woman who saved his life and offered him a kingdom. Through Dido's story,
Virgil highlights the conflicting allegiances of *pietas* to fatherland, gods, and
family. In Carthage, Aeneas must forget what he owes Dido as his partner and
rescuer in order to fulfill his political mission. The Trojan hero must forsake
the ties of *hospitium* (hospitality). The queen who so generously welcomed
him becomes the victim of the future greatness of Rome, the plaything of
the gods.[2] Book 4 is a powerful example of the complexity of Roman *pietas*
and the competing allegiances that, in its name, an individual experiences.[3]
Although we see that the gods summon Aeneas and what is at stake is a future
greater than the man himself (the foundation of Rome and its empire), Virgil
fails to prove (at least in this book) the *pietas* of Aeneas and his moral superiority. Even if only for a short while, Book 4 enlists the audience's sympathy
for Dido and engages the audience against the cause of empire.[4] Augustine's
writings demonstrate how successfully Virgil employed this strategy, pushing
the reader to favor Dido. By his own admission, Augustine as a reader of the
Aeneid became engrossed with the passion of Dido. In *Confessions* 1.13.20–21
he remembers how much he cried for the queen.[5]

   All of Aeneas's ethical shortcomings (in *Aeneid* 4) appear even more pro-
nounced in the *Enrico* when applied to Lucillo, Clelia's husband, and who
has children, a father, and a kingdom in need of leadership. Clelia implores
Lucillo to show compassion in the name of their son and of his father ("del
padre tuo, di me, del caro erede / pietà ti mova," "have mercy for your father,
for me, for your darling heir" *Enr.* 4.79.5–6). Besides alluding to Dido's request
for sympathy in 4.315–19, these words are reminiscent of the Ulysses episode

---

and around Virgil's time are Timaeus's *Histories* and Justin's Epitome of the *Philippic History* of
Pompeius Trogus. Cf. Burden 1998; Desmond 1994: 23–73; Franklin 2000: 117–18; Quint 1993:
21–50.

   2. Farron 1980; Johnson 1965: 360; Gibson 1999.

   3. King 2003.

   4. Spence 1999: 95.

   5. For Augustine and Virgil, see MacCormack 1998; Hagedorn 2004: 2.

in Dante's *Comedy*, which underlined how, for his excessive desire to acquire knowledge, the hero from Ithaca no longer valued "his son's sweetness, nor the reverence for his old father nor the love he owed" to his wife Penelope ("né dolcezza di figlio, né la pietà / del vecchio padre, né 'l debito amore / lo qual dovea Penelopè far lieta, / vincer potero dentro a me l'ardore," *Inf.* 26.94–96). The allusion to Dante's *Comedy* anticipates Lucillo's demise—like Ulysses, he will be crushed by the waves—and it criticizes his desire to leave his fatherland for reasons felt by the narrator as being illegitimate.[6]

Marinella's sustained references to *Aeneid* 4 remind us of the unbridgeable ethical gaps at the heart of the epic universe and reveal crucial similarities and differences between the two male heroes. In forgetting his wife and fatherland in the pursuit of problematic goals, Lucillo is just as culpable as Dante's Ulysses and more culpable than Aeneas. When he left Carthage, the Trojan hero was simply betraying Dido; Lucillo, by leaving Cyprus, is forgetting his role as husband, father, and leader of his people. If Aeneas could maintain credibility with his audience by claiming that he had never agreed to marry Dido and was abandoning a city that was not his own (*Aen.* 4.339, 349), Lucillo cannot claim the same motivations. His desire to gain glory appears much more selfish and foolish. If the Trojan hero had to desert a worthy woman for the foundation of a new city and a glorious future that he could demand not simply for himself—but, above all, for his descendants, and ultimately for the civilization of the West—the king of Cyprus abandons a worthy wife, city, and children in the name of someone else's city. Marinella skillfully inserts the Virgilian background to highlight the shortcomings of *pietas* and Lucillo's unreasonable behavior. She also borrows details from the Virgilian description of Dido to show the concern and deep love Clelia has for her husband. How Clelia resembles (and is different from) Dido will become clearer in the following sections: if Lucillo is worse than Aeneas, Clelia is better than Dido.

---

6. Lazzari 2010: 139. There is another allusion here to Altamoro's wife in Tasso's *Gerusalemme Liberata*: "Nor could you, Altamor, be kept at rest / in her chaste bed by your beloved bride. / She wept and tore her blond hair and her breast / to avert your fated absence from her side. / 'ah! do you, cruel man,' she said, 'desert / my face, to woo war's visage, bleary-eyed? / Shall weight of weapons hold a dearer charm / than does your infant toying on your arm?'" (*GL* 17.26, trans. Wickert). According to Stephens, Goffredo's salvation of Altamoro (*GL* 20.142–3) is important because it saves his wife from the fate of Andromache; Tasso's allusion to Homer's Andromache would be emblematic of his repudiation of a masculine ethos in favor of a feminine ethos (Stephens 1995: 302). *Pietas* must take women into consideration. If *pius* Aeneas was constantly forgetting about his women, for Stephens, Tasso wants to construct a hero who is not blind to their suffering.

STORMS, APOSTROPHE, AND LAMENTATION

Lucillo and his crew, as suggested by Clelia in her anxious premonition, become the victims of a terrible storm. To no avail, the woman warns her husband about the threats of the sea. Like Alcyone in Ovid's *Metamorphoses*, she does not trust any human skill against the waves, which in both texts are personified as malignant creatures deaf to prayers and eager to flaunt their relentless anger.[7] "The sea," Clelia says, "doesn't fear the swaying or glitter of your sword; it doesn't fear derision, prayer or cries. With stormy screeching it calls on the winds to fight with itself, as it is thundering and proud; its angry, dark, and powerful waves jump all the way to the sky; land and shore are affected. In the end the fury of the waves leaves ships destroyed and sailors drowned and dead" (*Enr.* 4.74.1–8). When Lucillo reveals her his plan to leave, she stiffens with despair:

> Ma come a te sua luce, il chiuso petto
> Scoprì pien di desio, d'eterno onore,
> Tosto un rigido ghiaccio, un mesto affetto
> Occupò i lassi membri, e strinse il core;
> Fuggir le rose, e forse ne l'aspetto
> Più che di bosso, un orrido pallore;
> Si sforzò dir tre volte e tre le note
> Restaro, e sol di pianto ornò le gote.
> (*Enr.* 4.72.1–8)

But as soon as he revealed to you, his light, that his chest enclosed a desire for eternal honor, a stiff ice and sad affection filled your tired limbs and enveloped your heart. Your rose color fled, and a horrible paleness spread over your face, darker than boxwood. She tried to speak three times, and three times her voice broke; only tears covered her cheeks.

We have here two precise allusions to Alcyone in *Met.* 11:

> Consilii tamen ante sui, fidissima, certam
> Te facit, Alcyone; cui protinus intima frigus
> Ossa receperunt, buxoque simillimus ora
> Pallor obit, lacrimisque genae maduere profusis.
> Ter conata loqui ter fletibus ora rigavit

---

7. For the myth of Alcyone and Ceyx, see Fantham 1979; Griffin 1981; Hardie 2002: 273–82; Rudd 2008; Stadler 1985.

Singultuque pias interrumpente querellas.
(*Met.* 11.415–420)

Nevertheless, before he set out, he discussed it with you, most faithful Alcyone; deep in her marrow she was invaded by a chill, immediately, her face grew boxwood-pale, and her cheeks were drenched in flowing tears. Three times she tried to speak, three times her face was wet with weeping, and sobs interrupting her loving reproaches. (trans. Kline)

Like Alcyone, Clelia wants to keep her beloved by her side or at least to go with him: "Turn your mind away from the sea," she implores "remove this pain from my heart . . . but if you have resolved to go, take me along" ("Volgi dal mar la mente, e questa pena / toglimi al cor . . . ma se fisso hai d'andar, me teco mena," *Enr.* 4.77.3–5; cf. "But if . . . you are resolved to go, then take me with you" *Si . . . nimiumque es certus eundi, / me quoque tolle simul, Met.* 11.439-41). Both Clelia and Alcyone turn cold, and in tears three times they try to speak without success. Lucillo (like Ceyx) does not yield: he leaves his island and finds himself in the storm that destroys his boat and kills him.

Storms are important tools in the hands of epic writers. Although the tempest in Book 5 of the *Odyssey* (262*ff.*) is a starting point for Marinella's storm by providing the motif of the epic hero separated from his homeland and wife, thus establishing the combination of epic and erotic elements, Virgil's and Ovid's treatment of the storm in the *Aeneid* and *Metamorphoses,* respectively, are the essential points of reference for this specific episode. In the *Aeneid* (like in Genesis), the storm assumes the level of a cosmic phenomenon appropriate to highlight the themes of divine justice and order.[8] The pattern visible in *Aeneid* 1—a storm caused by an angry Juno helped by Aeolus, the king of the winds, immediately followed by Neptune's pacification of the water—embodies, in a powerfully constructed sequence, the altercation of chaos and order that is central to the Virgilian epic universe. In *Aeneid* 1.148-54, Virgil compares Neptune's actions in calming the storm to those of a human statesman who employs his authority to quell a riot. In its correlation of divine power in the cosmos and human power in history, the comparison establishes one of the *Aeneid*'s most ambitious goals: to assess as attainable an ideal synthesis of the natural order and of Rome's historical order.[9] Juno's storm in Book 1, and her anger later in the narration, are allegedly destined to subside under the benevolent and rational leadership of Jupiter and Aeneas.

---

8. Bate 2004; Huxley 1952; Kardulias 2001.
9. Feeney 1991: 137.

The storm of *Aeneid* 1 is echoed by Ovid in *Metamorphoses* 1 and, above all, *Metamorphoses* 11 with a different agenda. Brook Otis observes how Virgil emphasizes the divine causation and termination of the storm.[10] In reverse, Ovid reworks the Homeric simile of *Iliad* 2.144ff., where a riot is compared to a storm. Homer is recalled via Virgil who, as I mentioned, juxtaposes Neptune to a man of authority able to quell an insurrection not with weapons, but through his charismatic personality. Following Virgil's lead but also Ovid's response to Virgil, Marinella depicts a storm with angry and uncaring winds. The sea and winds wage an almost titanic war against the elements: "the sky gathers its weapons" ("l'olimpo s'arma") while the wind "sinks ships, uproots trees, rips off roofs" ("navi affonda, arbor svelle, e tetti atterra," *Enr.* 5.9.4). In *Metamorphoses* 11, the storm's assault on the fleet resembles the siege of a city: "Again and again the force of the flood strikes the sides with a huge crash, sounding no lighter a blow than when, sometime, an iron ram, or a ballista, strikes a damaged fortress" (*Saepe dat ingentem fluctu latus icta fragorem / nec levius pulsata sonat, quam ferreus olim / cum laceras aries balistave concutit arces*, *Met.* 11.507–9). In a similar fashion, when the sea is beating the ship and prevailing against the helmsman, Marinella observes that "perhaps with less strength a fortified battering ram pushes and hits a tall wall" ("forse con minor forza urta e percuote / ben ferrato ariete alta muraglia," *Enr.* 5.12.1–2). Here the elements are personified and the gods are unwilling to help Lucillo. In contrast to the *Aeneid* and more in line with the *Metamorphoses*, Marinella does not depict the moment when this storm ends, nor thanks to whom. She employs the same vocabulary adopted by Virgil in Book 1 but, as I will point out, the effects of her narration are starkly different from those produced by the Augustan epic.

In the *Aeneid*, "clouds suddenly tear from the Trojans' sight sky and day, a dark night weighs on the sea" (*eripiunt subito nubes caelumque diemque / Teucrorum ex oculis; ponto nox incubat atra*, *Aen.* 1.88–89); in Marinella's poem, "thick rain and dark horror deprive people from sight" ("le pioggie folte / toglion la vista e l'orror denso e nero," *Enr.* 5.10.3–4). Marinella describes "the frequent thunder, the bright lightning" ("spessi suoni, i luminosi lampi," *Enr.* 5.14.4) and how "what is seen and heard brought darkness, fear, and death" ("ciò che si vede e ode avvien che porte / tenebre a gli occhi lor, spavento e morte." *Enr.* 5.14.7–8). Similarly, in Virgil, "it thunders from the pole, and the ether flashes thick fire, and all things threaten immediate death to men" (*intonuere poli, et crebris micat ignibus / praesentemque viris intentant omnia mortem*, *Aen.* 1.90–91). Virgil also describes the storm's consequences: "swimmers appear here and there in the vast waste, men's weapons, planks, and the

---

10. Otis 1966: 231–78.

Trojan treasure in the waves" (*adparent rari nantes in gurgite vasto, / arma virum, tabulaeque, et Troia gaza per undas, Aen.* 1.118–19). Marinella does the same: "you saw men, tools, planks and oars wander in the water" ("uomini vedi, arnesi e travi e remi / errar per l'acque in que' perigli estremi," *Enr.* 5.15.7–8). The stars are no longer visible to Lucillo ("a le stelle il guardo gira / (benchè stella non sia")), "he glanced towards the stars, though no star is visible," *Enr.* 5.16.5–6), and Venier, like Odysseus, overwhelmed by the storm in *Odyssey* 5.308–12, begins to fear an inglorious death at sea ("che senza gloria, oimè, sarà ch'io cada / dal campo lungi senza oprar la spada?" "Alas, will it be that I will fall without glory, far from the battlefield, and without using my sword?" *Enr.* 5.17.7–8). He regrets not having been able to die during a fight at the hands of powerful enemies:

> "Deh perchè, oh Cielo! Oh Fato! Io non cadei
> Per le man greche nel contrasto atroce
> Di Scutari ne' campi, e non potei
> Da te aver morte, o Licaon feroce;
> Or ora senza onor fra i flutti rei,
> Che morte tal, più assai, che morte noce."
> (*Enr.* 5.18.1–6)

> "Heavens and Fate, why, o why, was I not felled in a ferocious battle by a Greek hand on the battlefield at Scutari? Why couldn't I have received my death from you, cruel Licaone? Now I shall die without honor among the waves, and this death hurts more than death itself."

These lines reveal Venier's character and his desire for fame in war and his nostalgia for a glorious death in Scutari,[11] recalling Odysseus's words in a similar situation:

> "Thrice blessed, four times blessed those Danaans who died long ago on Troy's wide plain working the will of the sons of Atreus. I wish I had met my fate like them, and died on that day when the Trojan host hurled their bronze-tipped spears at me while we fought for the corpse of Achilles, son of Peleus. Then I would have had proper burial, and the Achaeans would have trumpeted my fame, but now I am destined to die a miserable death." (*Od.* 5.300–310, trans. Kline)[12]

---

11. In front of Constantinople, at Scutari (modern Üsküdar) in 1203, the Venetians fought the Byzantines.

12. The speech of Aeneas facing the storm (*Aen.* 1.94–101) is also modeled on Odysseus's speech.

Immediately after Odysseus's invocation, the hero is rescued by Ino-Leu-
cothea. But Marinella does not tell us what will happen to Venier, and readers
cannot help but imagine that he has reached the hour of his death. Following
the Homeric pattern, Virgil in the storm narrative describes the help from
the gods in rich detail; he tells us about Neptune's intervention, how the sea
and the waves were returned to a state of calmness and order. In Marinella's
poem, however, we do not see the conclusion of the storm. No god ends the
crisis, and for many lines, without knowing Venier's fate, we assume that he is
dead like his companion Lucillo. While the wild forces of nature confuse sea,
sky, and men without providing any conclusion, Marinella relates how Clelia
is impatiently waiting at home for the return of her husband. We have Ovid's
chaos but not Virgil's peace, at least not at this point in her narration. We can
see how Virgil's model has been modified by what has been left out.

Virgil highlights the responsiveness of the gods, while Ovid focuses on
Ceyx and Alcyone's piousness toward the gods and loyalty toward each other
to emphasize the gods' lack of interest in human affairs when they do not rescue Ceyx, Alcyone's faithful husband, from the storm. Ovid counters the universe constructed by Virgil and populated by benevolent gods with a world in
which decent human beings are abandoned. In Ovid's narration, the gods do
not care enough about Ceyx or any human being to intervene. Even Lucifer,
Ceyx's father, when invoked by his son for help, is not allowed to get involved,
"since it was not allowed to him [Lucifer] to come down from the sky, he covered his face" (*quoniam excedere caelo / non licuit, densis texit sua nubibus ora*,
Met. 11.571–72). Lucifer's covering of his head, suggesting indignation for not
being allowed to help his son, reflects the gods' refusal to intervene: Lucifer
would like to act, but he seems constrained by a higher will intensely present and active in that *non licuit* ("it was not allowed").[13] Marinella's narration
remains suspended between the Virgilian and the Ovidian model; it does not
want to establish God's apathy. This would be inconceivable for a poem written after the Counter-Reformation, and for a writer who is normally careful to
reveal God's benevolence toward humankind. Therefore, we must assume that
she had a different reason for keeping God from rescuing Lucillo. I believe
that Marinella insinuates, with the help of Virgil and Ovid, that Lucillo's death
at sea is a form of divine punishment. Lucillo dies not because of God's lack
of concern, but because he has let himself be captured by the allure of an
unworthy war, by selfishly wanting glory and foolishly desiring an unneces-

---

13. The passage alludes to Hercules's suffering for being unable to save the young Pallas
(*Aen.* 10.464–65) and to Juturna's inability to keep her brother alive; in pain she covers her head
and hides herself in the stream (*Aen.* 12.884–85).

sary entanglement with chaos. The storm is depicted as a proud warrior, a giant who wants to climb up to the sky, symbolizing war and its risks. Lucillo chooses to side with this problematic character: he has forgotten his wife and family, letting pride and self-centeredness prevail.

Only at the end of the episode, when facing death at sea, in the same situation as Odysseus, is Lucillo able to gain a new sort of understanding through the memory of Clelia's desire to keep him home. He is no longer sad because of his lost glory but because suddenly he realizes the foolishness of his actions and wishes. Lucillo is a hero who at the end of his life denies the importance of martial glory, conforms his will to that of his wife, and repents:

> Sospira gravemente, e non asconde
> Il dolor del suo petto acerbo e fero.
> *Si pentisce; ma tardi, assai si duole,*
> *Che non restò di Clelia a le parole.*
> (*Enr.* 5.19.5–8)

> He sighed gravely and did not hide the harsh, ferocious pain in his heart.
> *He repented, too late alas; he felt sorry that he had not stayed as Clelia's words asked him to do.*

While the lamentation for a watery death, as we saw before, is completely traditional for a hero, this repentance—in a man with heroic aspirations—is absolutely new. Marinella highlights it not only by communicating in the third person how Lucillo is feeling but also by making him openly confess: "Why can't I hear you, dear, my sweet one, consoling me in my extreme moments? I deserve this, my dear soul, since I could leave you in your pains, to risk my life in those vicious waves" ("Deh perchè a consolarmi dolce e pia / in quest' ultimo fin non posso udirti? / Ciò merto, anima cara, che potei / lasciarti in pene, espormi a' flutti rei," *Enr.* 5.20.5–8). He then adds:

> *Di me non già, ma ben di te mi doglio,*
> *Che rimanesti segno a un fier dolor;*
> *Al mar del tuo gran pianto un duro scoglio*
> *Fu sì, non nego, il mio ferino core;*
> Or mi traffigge il sen grave cordoglio,
> *Che pel lume acquistar di un breve onore*
> *Lontan dal regno e da la patria a morte*
> Corro, senza con l'armi usar mia sorte.
> (*Enr.* 5.21.1–8)

I am not sad for myself, but for you since you are left as a target for deep pain.
I do not deny that my beastly heart was a hard rock against the sea of your
many tears. Now a cruel pain pierces my heart, since I ran away from my king-
dom and my land, towards death, and since I will use up my destiny without
fighting, though *I wanted to gain the light of a quick honor.*

With these words, the reaction of the hero to the archetypical motif of the
death at sea present in *Odyssey* 5 and *Metamorphoses* 11 is drastically altered.
Lucillo sees, better than any other epic hero, how, blinded by glory, he deserted
his fatherland. "What good is it to me that I have a happy kingdom? What
good is it to me that I have a gentle father and an honest and grateful wife?
I will lose forever my beloved life, alas, because of these waves and this horrible ordeal ("L'aver regno felice a me che giova? / padre cortese, sposa onesta
e grata; / se di tal flutto, tra l'orribil prova / perdo per sempre, oimè, la vita
amata," *Enr.* 5.22.1–4). The value of life and private actions here finally receive
the importance and recognition they deserve. Furthermore, such repentance
and recognition of the importance of conjugal matters are brought about by
the words and memory of a woman. That a female character can influence
an epic hero is a remarkable accomplishment. Lucillo does not just miss his
wife; through her, he learns something essential about himself and his priorities. Present here are fruitful echoes brought by the words and behavior of an
abandoned woman.

Only in death does Lucillo understand his foolishness. He drowns invoking Clelia's name:

Lucillo ai tronchi de l'infausto legno
Con contrasto de l'onda al fin s'apprende,
E de la sposa il nome amato e degno
Chiama, ch'ai propri affanni afflitta attende.
La voce sua dell'acque tra 'l disdegno
Gorgogliando indistinto il suono rende,
Brama che portin l'onde anco nemiche
Il corpo suo sul le riviere amiche.
(*Enr.* 5.27.1–8)

Lucillo at last grabbed onto the logs of the unlucky ship to fight the waves.
He called out the beloved dignified name of his wife, who busied herself with
her own grief. The gurgling sound of the scornful water made his voice faint.
He wished that the enemy waves would push his body onto friendly shores.

The passage closely reproduces the actions of Ceyx, who "with one hand grabs a fragment of the boat" (*tenet ipse manu . . . / fragmina navigii Ceyx, Met.* 11.560–61), while thinking about Alcyone ("On the mouth of the swimmer is Alcyone his wife" *nantis in ore est / Alcyone coniunx, Met.* 11.562–63), as he "wishes that the waves may bring his body . . . towards her friendly hands" (*ut agant sua corpora fluctus, / optat, . . . manibus . . . amicis, Met.* 11.564–65).[14] Clelia dreams of the dead Lucillo, whose body is sent home by "an unknown power and kind heaven" ("potenza ignota e il ciel cortese," *Enr.* 5.41.7–8), just like Alcyone dreamt about her shipwrecked husband (*Met.* 11.650–709) and found his body on the shore (*Met.* 11.716–25).

As Lucillo is drowning, the narrator poignantly apostrophizes him, calling him an "unfortunate lover in whose noble breast the thirst for glory was stronger than love" ("misero amante nel cui nobil petto / più che d'amore potè di gloria affetto," *Enr.* 5.29.7–8). Earlier in the Canto, she had qualified Lucillo as "misero amante" ("poor lover," *Enr.* 5.3.3) in a precise reversal of Virgil's apostrophe *fortunati ambo* ("you both are fortunate," *Aen.* 9.446) directed to the lovers Euryalus and Nisus, destined to die together:

Fortunati ambo! Si quid mea carmina possunt,
Nulla dies umquam memori vos eximet aevo,
Dum domus Aeneae Capitoli immobile saxum
Accolet, imperiumque pater Romanus habebit.
(*Aen.* 9.446–49)

You both are lucky! If my poetry has some power,
No day ever will remove you from the memory of time,
As long as the house of Aeneas dwells on the unshaken rock of the Capitoline
and Roman father maintains his empire.

In the *Aeneid,* Euryalus and Nisus are Trojan warriors who volunteer for a dangerous mission to gain glory and to help Aeneas during a war crisis. Ultimately, both die during the mission. This apostrophe highlights a solemn and tragic moment in the story—the youths' death—marked by a narrator who makes his presence felt. In this passage, the rhetorical figure glorifies friendship and love. Virgil's narrator is certain that the memory of the two friends will last forever; it will be imperishable like the Roman *imperium.* The adjective "fortunate" corrects Nisus's previous judgment about his friend's and

---

14. Cf. *OF* 29.26.1–2, when Isabella dies invoking Zerbino ("e funne udita chiara / voce, ch' uscendo nominò Zerbino") and Ariosto magnifies her exemplary behavior in the apostrophe of 29.27.

his own lot in *Aeneid* 9.427–30, where he had begged the enemy to spare his beloved Euryalus, described as a "luckless friend" (*infelicem . . . amicum,* 430).

This story is interesting because it is not simply one of heroism, of two brave soldiers who want to help their general. It is a rare episode, in the world of Virgil's *arma,* when love and private feelings are prioritized and celebrated. In the narrator's words, Euryalus and Nisus *are lucky* despite their terrible death. Although the passage lends itself to multiple interpretations,[15] here we must consider that of Gordon Williams. Williams is convinced that the two combatants are called lucky because "loving one another, they died together . . . Euryalus was lucky because he did not die alone and abandoned; Nisus was lucky because he did not outlive his lover, and his death on his lover's behalf was noble."[16] If at the beginning of the tale the two young men have in mind personal glory (*Aen.* 9.184–87) and in the name of this glory Euryalus forgets his duty and love toward his mother, at the end of the episode we see his companion Nisus forgetting his epic mission and undermining its initial goal (i.e., finding Aeneas to inform him about the crisis at the camp) to try to save his beloved companion. Williams argues that in the adjective "fortunate" we would have Virgil's recognition that what redeems and ennobles the warriors' final action is love as a private feeling, directed not toward the fatherland but each other. I am convinced that Marinella favored lovers over soldiers and that she would endorse Williams's interpretation. She calls Lucillo "misero amante" because—in marked opposition to Nisus and Euryalus—in the end he cannot die near his wife, who loves him the most. Marinella does not excuse him but feels close to this "unlucky lover." She pities him, especially when he realizes his mistake and endorses Clelia's point of view, or, to anticipate myself, when Lucillo has transformed himself into an elegiac character.

Virgil's narration of Euryalus and Nisus's tragic death is made particularly poignant by the employment of apostrophe, which is a rhetorical device common in epic from Homer to Tasso. The strength of apostrophe resides in the emotional intensity it grants to the narrative sequence. Apostrophe is a figure of pathos employed to stir emotions and guide the reader's response. Marinella uses this technique to attract readers to the characters she likes best and identifies as most vulnerable. She uses it above all to address female characters or, as in the case of the dying Lucillo, characters she endorses. According to some critics, apostrophe in the *Aeneid* is a manifestation of the narrator's sympathy for characters who die young or are defeated, and it expresses his

---

15. Hardie 1997b; Conte 1986: esp. 169–72.
16. Williams 1983: 206.

emotional participation in their suffering.[17] This rhetorical figure is intrinsically tied to the representation of grief as well as that of closure and narrative
coherence, for it reveals how the narrator is willing to comment on the suffering caused by Aeneas's war in Latium. Through apostrophe, the narrator
manifests his sorrow for the victims of Rome and also his discontent about
the imperial project imposed on him by the gods. Something similar happens
in the *Enrico*. While Marinella often describes events and characters from the
point of view of the Venetians, and therefore justifies the war waged by Dandolo and his city, when she apostrophizes women, she assumes their point
of view and seems to admit the uselessness of the same war. We perceive an
unresolved clash between what this poem asserts at the level of its general plot
and what we feel when we read about the fates of some of its minor characters. Apostrophized and lamenting women play a crucial role in Marinella's
ideological agenda.

In an important article, Sheila Murnaghan highlights the importance of
lamentation in the Greek epic tradition. Initially, lamentation's chief practi-
tioners were women, and it barely survived being incorporated into larger—
male-made—epic structures, which probably bear traces of authentic women's
voices and perspectives on actions sung and performed primarily by men,
promoting male interests.[18] Murnaghan highlights how the content of lamentation bears an equivocal relationship to epic:

> As a grieving response to the loss of an individual, lamentation is an urgent
> expression of that person's value, and so is a form of praise. Lament is thus
> prototypical of epic as a genre that confers praise—*kleos* in Homeric epic—
> on the actions of heroes, and more particularly on the actions of dead
> heroes, who have earned their right to be praised through the manner of
> their deaths. Thus laments, along with panegyrics delivered to living leaders,
> lie at the source of many traditions of heroic poetry. But, unlike panegyric,
> lament is praise inspired by the speaker's sorrow and regret at the subject's
> loss. As C. M. Bowra puts it, "Lament is born from grief for the dead, and
> though praise is naturally combined with it, grief has the chief place."[19]

---

17. Block 1982: 7–22; Heinze 1993: 234. The importance of apostrophe in Marinella's *Enrico*
has been noticed by Galli Stampino in several of the notes to her English and Italian editions
of the *Enrico* (Marinella 2009, 2011).

18. The connection between contemporary laments and those preserved in ancient Greek
literary sources was established by Alexiou 1974 and further analyzed by Holst-Warhaft 1992.
For the female lament in the Middle Ages, see Jones 1997: 15–41. About Juturna's lament in the
Aeneid, Perkell 1997.

19. Murnaghan 1999: 204, quoting Bowra 1952: 10.

Lamentation undermines the *kleos*-conferring function of epic because it reminds us of the suffering caused by heroic death rather than the glory obtained by it. This powerfully articulated expression of grief calls into question such glorification advertised by martial societies and their epics.[20] In the general economy of an epic work, the female-dominated subgenre of lament can play a role analogous to that played by female characters in the heroes' realization of their goals: laments hinder the hero's ability to obtain glory and political success. Lamentation is one of the most important rhetorical tools Clelia uses to thwart Lucillo's epic march toward *kleos*.

But Virgil's attitude toward Euryalus and Nisus is nuanced; in the apostrophe to the "fortunate" youths he tries to preserve the memory of their love while also seeming to glorify Rome. Marinella in her epic reuses ambiguities in Virgil's account of Euryalus. Lucillo's conduct is misconceived in the light of Marinella's allusions to Euryalus's similar behavior at *Aeneid* 9.176–449. As we saw above, Euryalus is a young warrior who risks his life in a dangerous mission to gain glory and to help his general in a difficult war situation instead of remaining in the camp at the side of his old mother. He ultimately dies and, as predicted by Virgil's apostrophe, owes his memory not so much to his failed war mission but to his special bond with Nisus. But Euryalus is famous not only for having in Nisus an exceptional friend but also for having an excellent mother. Tired of roaming around the Mediterranean, most women in the *Aeneid* remain in southern Italy. Only a few follow Aeneas and the rest of the warriors to Latium; Euryalus's mother is one of them. Despite her old age, she chooses a path of hardship to stay close to her son, and she eventually suffers his loss during the night raid.

Euryalus and Nisus's night incursion develops as an intricate episode in which the reader must evaluate conflicting emotions and allegiances. To some extent, Euryalus's catastrophic action results from the opposing claims of *pietas* to his mother and to the state. But at one point his civic *pietas,* spurred by a great desire for personal glory, overcomes his domestic *pietas.*[21] Euryalus's desire to aid Aeneas and his thirst for glory make him forget his duty to his mother. In a similar fashion, Lucillo's eagerness to join Venier and help Venice makes him forget his old father, wife, and kingdom. His behavior cannot be considered ethically irreproachable. Marinella will echo the lamentation of Euryalus's mother before her dead son when Clelia is obliged to stare at the dead body of her beloved consort brought back to her by the waves. "Alas!" she will weep, "in such a state I see you again" ("Oimè! Qual ti riveggio, oimè,"

---

20. Fantham 1999 offers similar observations within the Roman environment.

21. Pavlock 1985: 221. For the night raid of "lover-friends" in heroic literature, see Cabani 1995.

Enr. 5.50.1). Here it impossible not to recall Euryalus's mother's matching cry: "In such a state I see you, Euryalus? (*Hunc ego te, Euryale, aspicio, Aen.* 9.481). Such verbal allusion alerts us to the similarities of the two episodes. Moreover, identically, both women wish to die rather than be separated from the object of their affection (*En.* 5.52; cf. *Aen.* 9.493–97). They consider their lives worthless without the men they love.

REUNIONS AND MIRACLES

Marinella alludes to *Aeneid* 4 as well as to Ovid's Ceyx and Alcyone in her description of the storm and beyond. Clelia resembles Alcyone at many different levels: both women fear the violence of nature and are described in similar terms when receiving the news of their beloved's departure. Equally significant in Clelia's story are Marinella's echoes of Ovid's *Heroides* 13, a text that recounts Protesilaus's departure for the Trojan War and abandonment of his wife Laodamia. By featuring a husband and wife separated by war and reunited thanks to their great love, the myth must have been attractive and appears in the Lucillo-Clelia episode. The myth features a man who is summoned back to life to be reunited with his wife and a woman who dies consumed by grief, suggesting that love is more powerful than death.[22]

Lucillo dies at sea, but his ghost visits Clelia to let her know about his sad destiny. The appearance of the dead Lucillo recalls that of Sychaeus to Dido in *Aeneid* 1.335–70, where he reveals to his wife the truth about his cruel end at the hands of his brother-in-law, Pygmalion. Conspicuous in the representation of *Aeneid* 1 is the great love shared by the Tyrian couple (Sychaeus is described as *magno miserae dilectus amore*, "loved with a great love by the wretched girl," 1.344); the hatred between Sychaeus and Pygmalion (*quos inter . . . venit furor*, "madness came between them," 1.348); Dido's complete unawareness of her husband's sudden end, kept hidden by the assassin (*factumque diu celavit*, "and he hid the fact for a long time," 1.351); and the pallor of the ghost displaying his wounds to the wretched woman (*ora modis attollens pallida miris / . . . traiectaque pectora ferro / nudavit*, "lifting his pale head in a wondrous manner / he showed his heart pierced by a knife." 1.354–56) to show her what had happened. Finally, Lucillo's specter is reminiscent of that of Hector in *Aeneid* 2.270ff., when the ghost of Hector manifesting itself

---

22. Marinella may also have been influenced by Propertius's version of the myth since at 1.19.7ff. he tells of Protesilaus's desire to be reunited with his wife after his death: "There in the regions of darkness, the hero Protesilaus could not be unmindful of his sweet wife (*iucundae coniugis . . . / . . . immemor,* 7–8), but, desirous (*cupidus,* 9) to reach his joys with false hands, the Thessalian came to his ancient home a shade (*venerat umbra domum,* 10)."

"saddest of all and pouring out great tears" (*maestissimus Hector visus / . . . largosque effundere fletus*, 2.270–71) "with a ragged beard and hair incrusted with blood" (*squalentem barbam et concretos sanguine crinis / vulneraque ille gerens*, 2.277–78) also shows his wounds and delivers important instructions for Aeneas. Sychaeus, Hector, and Lucillo all appear to their beloved in a miserable state and bring terrible news. In the *Aeneid*, the sequences of mutilated figures are combined to offer a striking, compound image of the ironies and devastation produced by the traditional heroic code and the need to transcend it.[23] The three men have undoubtedly been defeated and, in the case of Lucillo, deluded by a promise of fame.

Significantly, in the Italian poem, it is Clelia who is cast in the role of the surviving hero, while Lucillo functions as the ghost of Hector or Protesilaus, men who have lost everything and, at the moment of their appearance, have already been overcome by death. We do not see a powerful Lucillo at the height of success, but rather during a tragedy, when the prophetic words of his wife have come true. Earlier I drew a connection between Dido and Clelia, apprehensive before their men's departures and eventually completely overwhelmed by sorrow and tears. Yet upon her death, Clelia's behavior departs from that of the dying Carthaginian queen. This narrative switch enhances her heroic profile and grants her a kind of victory. She has been already magnified by her dying husband, who has realized the validity of her prayers and the foolishness of his epic dreams. Her honor and heroic stature will further develop when she stoically faces her end in what can be described as a suicide *manqué*.

After recalling her sad fate, her inability to prevent the evil death of her husband, whose "soft heart was transformed into jasper," after lamenting Lucillo's doom and pronouncing her last words, Clelia promises that she will soon reach him. At this point, she fully regains her composure:

> Nè più rivolse al cielo i lasssi lumi;
> Nè sospirò, nè sí percosse il seno;
> Nè si vider da gli occhi amari fiumi:
> Scender pel volto a far molle il terreno;
> Nè tremò, nè si scosse; ma costumi
> Casti e colmi d'amor scoperse a pieno
> Mentre abbracciato il tiene, *cangia stile*,
> *S'aggela e affredda, a lui diviene simile.*
> (*Enr.* 5.54.1–8)

---

23. Fuqua 1982: 239.

She no longer turned her tired eyes heavenward, she didn't sigh, she didn't hit her chest. Neither could one see bitter rivers flowing out of her eyes across her face to soak the ground. She didn't tremble, she didn't move. She made manifest her modest customs full of love: as she held him in her arms, *she changed, she became cold and icy and similar to him.*

This series of negative statements is striking. Marinella stresses all the actions that we would expect from a frantic, suffering woman, highlighting them through their very absence. It is also as if Clelia is purposefully avoiding doing what Dido had done in her last moments. The Carthaginian queen was portrayed by Virgil as completely beset by her fury and desperation: "restless, wild with desperate purpose, rolling her bloodshot eyes, her trembling cheeks stained with red flushes, yet pallid at approaching death . . . furiously climb[ing] the funeral pyre" (*Aen.* 4.642–46).[24] Dido also "lingered a while, in tears and thought" (*paulum lacrimis et mente morata, Aen.* 4.649) while pronouncing her last words and finally "tried to lift her heavy eyelids again, but failed . . . three times she fell back onto the bed, searching for light in the depths of heaven, with wandering eyes, and, finding it, sighed" (*illa gravis oculos conata attollere rursus / deficit . . . ter revoluta toro est oculisque errantibus alto / quaesivit caelo lucemque ingemuitque reperta, Aen.* 4.688–89, 691–92). While Dido is crying, frantically driven to death by her passion and guilt (she was unfaithful to her husband Sychaeus out of love for a foreigner who abandoned her), Clelia is controlled, silent, and blameless. Wanting to die seems to her the next logical step after Lucillo's death, a rational consequence of her love and desire to be with him. She embraces him and becomes ice-cold. In *Nobiltà*, Marinella deemed Dido's representation false, and, following Petrarch and Tarcagnota, she was eager to clear the queen's reputation, explaining that she did not die of a furious passion for Aeneas, but because she wanted to preserve her vow of chastity for Sychaeus and reject her African suitor Iarbas.[25] Here Marinella once again distances herself from Virgil. Her dying Clelia is instead inspired by strong and innocent girls like Polyxena, whose glorious death is described by Ovid in *Metamorphoses* 13.451–80 and quoted in Latin in *Nobiltà* (chap. 3, "Donne forti e intrepide," Marinella 1601: 61). Polyxena's braveness is fully manifested in her dry face and courageous demeanor in front of the crowd (*dixerat et populo lacrimas, quas illas tenebat / non tenet,*

---

24. At *trepida et coeptis immanibus effera Dido / sanguineam volvens aciem, maculisque trementis / interfusa genas et pallida morte futura . . . conscendit furibunda rogos* (*Aen.* 4.642–44, 646).

25. Marinella 1601: 47.

"She spoke, and the crowd could not restrain the tears, that she restrained," *Met.* 13.474–75).[26]

Clelia's death resembles Ovid's transformations in the *Metamorphoses* also in terms of style, content, and narrative technique. Like Ovid, Marinella focuses her attention on specific physical details, reminding the reader that a change of form is taking place. Echoing *Metamorphoses* 11, Canto 5 of the *Enrico* adopts a somber tone while unforgettable elements soften the tragic events. As Clelia slowly grows cold, she becomes one with Lucillo; almost imperceptibly, the boundaries between their bodies disappear as those between life and death begin to merge. When Lucillo departed for the war, Clelia wanted to go with him, affirming that it would have been enough just to die with him ("Sarò beata se vivremo, e ancora / felice a pien, se sia che teco io mora," "I will be blissful if we were to survive, and still fully happy if it were to pass that I die with you," *Enr.* 4.77.7–8). Now that her desire is fulfilled, their bodies in death are reunited. As soon as Clelia utters "yet soon I am coming with you" ("ma teco tosto vengo," *Enr.* 5.52.5), we see her cooling off; no longer willing or able to cry, she "gives cold kisses to the icy face" ("dà freddi baci alla gelata faccia," *Enr.* 5.52.8). Having "placed her face right next to his desired visage" ("giunta ha la faccia alla bramata faccia," *Enr.* 5.55.3), she twists her arms around his neck, and she becomes inextricably tied to his body ("nè già le belle e delicate braccia / da que' nodi amorosi alcun può sciorre," "nobody could untie her beautiful and delicate arms from that loving knot," *Enr.* 5.55.1–2). Clelia's dying kisses are also inspired by Ariosto's description of Isabella's embrace of Zerbino—"pale . . . and cold like ice" ("pallido . . . e freddo come ghiaccio," *OF* 24.85.5).[27] Yet the clearest prototype for the scene is Ovid's Alcyone, who as a bird enfolds in her wings the bloodless body of Ceyx and kisses his frigid face with her beak:

Ut vero tetigit mutum et sine sanguine corpus,
Dilectos artus amplexa recentibus alis
Frigida nequiquam duro dedit oscula rostro.
(*Met.* 11.736–38)

---

26. The absence of tears and irrationality at the moment of death is prominent in Boccaccio's characterization of Ghismonda, one of the most eloquent and determined women in the *Decameron* (4.1). At the end of the novella, Ghismonda and her lover Guiscardo are buried in the same tomb.

27. "Who can fully express how the maiden grieved when she saw her dearest Zerbin lying in her arms pale and limp and cold as ice? She abandoned herself to grief over the bleeding corpse and bathed it in copious tears. She shrieked so loud that the woods and countryside for miles around echoed with it" *OF* 24.85.5–8, 24.86.1–4 (trans. Waldman).

When she reached the mute and bloodless corpse,
She clasped the dear limbs with her new wings
And kissed the cold lips in vain with her hard beak.

Alcyone's icy embrace is directly recalled in *Enrico* 5.54.1–8 ("s'aggela e
affredda, a lui diviene simile," "she turns icy, becomes cold, similar to him"),
where there is also another pointed allusion to the Ovidian text. As death
encloses both lovers, Clelia, instead of releasing Lucillo's body, embraces it
more "avidly" ("avidamente," *Enr.* 5.53.1). The intensity of Clelia's desire continues to be felt in the way she "clings to" ("circonda e stringe") the "beloved
trunk" ("il caro tronco") of her husband:

Non così avidamente edera cinge
A l'amato marito il collo adorno;
Nè cupida così circonda e stringe
Vite amorosa il caro tronco intorno;
Come costei, che già al morir s'accinge
Ne l'amplesso di morte.
(*Enr.* 5.53.1–6)

Ivy does not encircle anything with as much zeal as she adorned her beloved
husband's neck. Loving vines do not surround and squeeze with such desire
a dear tree trunk as she did, about to die in a deadly embrace.

When the woman hugs Lucillo's dead body, she is compared to an ivy, a love-
filled vine.[28]

The adverb "avidly" and the fusion of the two bodies remind us of the
Ovidian story of Salmacis and Hermaphroditus (*Met.* 4.285–388). In *Metamorphoses* 4, after narrating the love story of Salmacis and the beautiful son
of Hermes, Ovid recounts how the gods answered her prayer to be forever
united with the lovely youth:

Vota suos habuere deos: nam mixta duorum
Corpora iunguntur, faciesque inducitur illis
Una, velut, siquis conducat cortice ramos,
Crescendo iungi pariterque adolescere cernit.

---

28. The image and the wording recall Ruggiero and Alcina's embrace on the enchantress's
magic island: "Ivy does not cling so closely to the trunk round which it is entwined as the two
lovers clasp each other" ("Non così strettamente edera preme / pianta ove intorno abbarbicata
s'abbia, / come si stringon li dui amanti insieme," *OF* 7.29.1–3).

Sic ubi conplexu coierunt membra tenaci,
Nec duo sunt et forma duplex, nec femina dici
Nec puer ut posit: neutrumque et utrumque videntur.
(*Met.* 4.373–79)

Her prayers were heard: now the entwined bodies of the two were joined together, and one form covered both. Just as when someone grafts a twig into the bark, they see both grow joined together, and develop as one, *so when they were mated together in a close embrace, they were not two, but a two-fold form,* so that they could not be called male or female, and seemed neither or either. (trans. Kline)

The tale of Salmacis and Hermaphroditus surprisingly mirrors the story of Menander in Plato's *Symposium* 189c–191d. The union of the male and female forms, in both narratives, becomes the symbol of an otherwise unobtainable perfection. Marinella knew well Plato's *Symposium,* whose fame had been increased by Ficino's commentary. Apart from Plato's account and Ficino's work, it is also possible that she was familiar with the commentaries that flourished in the Judeo-Christian tradition around the ambiguous switch from singular to plural in Genesis 1:27: "So God created man in his own image, in the image of God created he him; male and female created he them." Philo and Origen believed the passage to mean that (like in *Symposium* 189c–193e) the original man was androgynous and that, only later, the unified body split and degenerated into two genders.[29] Elliot Simon underscores how this quest for wholeness appears in Renaissance humanist syncretism based on the unity of all beings in God and, more specifically, is predicated on "the biblical assertion that the human being—both the Hermaphrodite Adam (Genesis 1.26–28) and the divinely undifferentiated Adam and Eve before the Fall (Genesis 2.21–25)—was originally created in the 'image and likeness' of God."[30] In the Renaissance, this interpretation had been enthusiastically embraced by Giovanni Pico della Mirandola, Agrippa of Nettesheim, and Leone Ebreo, writers extensively known and quoted by Marinella in her *Nobiltà.*[31] Through the allusion to Salmacis's fusion, we would have in Marinella's description of the dying Clelia the suggestion that in death, as two

29. Almond 1999: 7.
30. Simon 2010: 14.
31. For instance, Leone Ebreo is mentioned in Marinella 1621: 21. For connections between Marinella and Pico, see Shapiro 2005: 227. Nagel 2011: 97–99 underlines how the resurrected Christ of Rosso Fiorentino is depicted as androgynous. See also Sivelli 2011; Bottoni 2002.

souls are reunited, even their bodies are newly joint and become one, as it was in the beginning of time.

The special tie and spiritual symbiosis between Clelia and Lucillo appear in other portions of the text. For instance, recall how Clelia was brought down: physically pushed to the ground when Lucillo departed the shore. Marinella describes the fall in detail: "She didn't bend; she fell, attracted downward by the weight of the anguish that filled her heart" ("Non si piegò, caddè, tratta dal pondo / di quella angoscia, che nel cor ritiene," *Enr.* 5.49.1–2). This scene is reminiscent of Ovid's Laodamia in the *Heroides*, where, on the pier unable to see her husband, she fell to her knees (*at postquam nec te nec vela fugacis vidi . . . succiduo dicor procubuisse genu*, "after I could no longer see you nor your sails . . . it is said that I fell on my knee," *Her.* 13.20–24). Protesilaus's sailing away is focalized through Laodamia's eyes and suffering. Likewise, as Lucillo sails away, "Clelia could barely stand because of her pain, she barely responded to his goodbye. She stood as if stunned and unmoving" ("Clelia a fatica sta per doglia in piedi, / a pena al salutar, salute rende, / sta qual stupida e immota," *Enr.* 5.3.5–7)—the woman's frozen countenance ominously anticipates Lucillo's disappearance at sea and her own demise. Marinella uses the Ovidian motif to highlight the mental anguish and physical pain felt by the woman. The separation of husband and wife is perceived as a rape that unnaturally disrupts the symbiotic union of the couple. From this premise it is not difficult to anticipate their demise.

Even the glory-driven Lucillo acknowledges the inextricable union with Clelia when he begs her not to cry at his departure: "it is my very blood which wets and soaks your beautiful cheeks with tears" ("è sangue mio quel che tue belle gote / irriga e bagna volto in pianti tali," *Enr.* 4.83.3–4), or when his ghost tells Clelia that his love for her is alive even while he is dead: "I love and adore you, and the flame of my love will not be extinguished, as it burns on among the dead" ("Io t'amo e t'adoro, nè sia d'arder priva / fiamma d'amor, ch'ancor ne' morti è viva," *Enr.* 5.42.7–8). Clelia's reply confirms her belief that their fates are indissolubly linked, that separation is not actually possible:

"Ben de l'anima mia teco infelice
Me infelice condurre ormai ti piaccia:
Che a me senza di te viver non lice,
Ch'io viva e 'l mio Lucillo estinto giaccia,
Ah! Ver giammai non sia; s'era tua vita
Mal grado mio da me sarai partita?"
(*Enr.* 5.43.3–8)

"My soul will let you take sad me with sad you wherever you want: it is not possible that I live without you, it is not possible that I live when my Lucillo lies dead. This will not happen! Since I was your life, how could you leave despite me?"

As Clelia laments her tragic destiny, becoming a symbol of women who cannot determine their own futures, she underlines the special union of husbands and wives and indirectly affirms that this compact should not come undone under any circumstance. Finally, Marinella's description of the couple's union in death is physically and mystically charged, pitting love against fury:[32]

> Ne già le belle e delicate braccia
> Da que' nodi amorosi alcun può sciorre,
> Giunta ha la faccia a la bramata faccia,
> Nè concess'è di moverla o disciorre.
> Oh miracol d'amor! Chi sia che 'l taccia?
> E non tra le altre sue queste ancor porre
> Supreme meraviglie, *Amore congiunse*
> *Quei che del Fato ira e furor disgiunse.*
> (*Enr.* 5.55.1–8)

> Nobody could untie her beautiful and delicate arms from that loving knot. Her face was joined to his most beloved one, and it wasn't possible to move it or separate it from it. What a miracle of Love! Who could not talk about it? One must put this among love's highest wonders: *Love joined those that the wrath and furor of fate had separated.*

Although the tale of Clelia and Lucillo ends tragically, as readers we are consoled by the knowledge of their union after death. Virgil employs the same technique at the end of the Euryalus and Nisus passage celebrating their union in death. Marinella refuses to be silent; she extols this miracle of love and informs us that in the end fury and anger have been defeated. Later, the narrator invokes heaven directly and again expresses her approval that Clelia has joined her husband: "Most pitiful heaven, you brought an end to her harsh anguish with her death, and you joined her with her . . . beloved" ("Pietosissimo Ciel, quando al dolore / acerbo, il fin con la sua morte desti, / e col suo caro e tanto amato amore / dopo tanto martir lei congiungesti," *Enr.* 5.56.1–4). In a scene reminiscent of the death of Pyramus and Thysbe in *Metamorphoses* 4 (*vota tamen tetigere deos . . . / quodque rogis superest, una requiescit urna,*

---

32. Marinella 1999: 35.

"however, the gods listened to her prayers . . . whatever was left from the pyre, rests in a single urn," Met. 4.164–66), Clelia's demise is framed as a remarkable miracle, making it more acceptable to a Christian audience.[33] Heaven's intervention seems to confirm that Clelia's desire to remain with her husband was good (and endorsed by God), while her husband's decision to leave her was bad and went against the plans of providence. God could have rescued Lucillo to allow him to pursue his war mission, but instead God showed sympathy to a woman unwilling to live alone by allowing her, through a miracle, to follow her husband in death. Fury and anger in the end are trumped by wifely devotion. Through love—and a female writer—Clelia acquires a reputation.

Marinella's memory of Ovid's Ceyx and Alcyone appears to be an essential matrix for the death of Clelia for another reason. Pierpaolo Fornaro in his book *Metamorfosi con Ovidio* notices that what happens in the Ceyx and Alcyone story is a sort of resurrection:

> The love of Alcyone now transformed into a bird surrounds him [Ceyx] and this vital force (Ovid would consent with the biblical *Song of Songs* that love is as strong as death) reawakens the senses of the dead body *"at ille senserat"* "he had felt" Met. 11.740. Here the metamorphosis does not keep death away nor prepares for it; it arises in death and compensates it [*la risarcisce*] with a regeneration which is more effective than in assumptions to heaven or in the apotheosis of Hercules or emperors which can be subject to irony.[34]

If at times Ovid can be a supremely ironic poet and can manipulate a situation or a metamorphosis to incite skepticism and laughter, we notice that no irony imbues Alcyon's death, where instead we perceive Ovid's will "to compensate" the lovers for their doom. Through this finale, Ovid wants to glorify love and, in the name of love, he reintroduces the pity of the gods (*et tandem, superis miserantibus, ambo / alite mutantur*, "and at last through the gods' pity, both were changed into birds," Met. 11.741–42). In Ovid's story the couple always behaved piously, and the transformation can be interpreted as triggered by

---

33. Cf. Cereta 1997: 96–97, where she calls fortunate those women of antiquity who died or changed shape after the loss of a beloved one: "No less fortunate is Halcyon, who on account of her weeping for Ceyx after he drowned, changed into a bird. . . . Ah me, battered by disconsolate lamentation, for whom death, though hoped for, still waits in the wings: life, cruel and inexorable, does not withdraw. O that I might at least die a pagan, since it is not possible according to Christian dogma to elect not to live. Would that those changers of forms, the gods, now summoned so sorrowfully and humbly, might help me in my misfortune." Cereta lost her husband, Pietro Serina, eighteen months after their marriage in 1484. Here she is perfectly aware of how problematic invoking death is for a Christian writer. Marinella was familiar with Cereta and mentions her in her work; see Ross 2009: 288.

34. Fornaro 1994: 69–70, my translation.

divine pity and as a kind of recompense for their misfortune.[35] The gods who had been absent during Ceyx's death and completely deaf to his prayers seem to care about Alcyone, and are almost forced to act because of her love:

> Tandem, superis miserantibus, ambo
> Alite mutantur. Fatis obnoxius isdem
> Tunc quoque mansit amor, nec coniugiale solutum est
> Foedus in alitibus: coeunt fiuntque parentes,
> Perque dies placidos hiberno tempore septem
> Incubat Alcyone pendentibus aequore nidis.
> Tunc iacet unda maris: ventos custodit et arcet
> Aeolus egressu praestatque nepotibus aequor.
> (*Met.* 11.741–48)

> At last through the gods' pity, both were changed to birds, the halcyons. As they suffered the same fate, their love remained as well: and their conjugal bond was not nullified by their feathered form: they mate and rear offspring, and for seven calm days in the wintertime, Alcyone broods on their nest, floating on the water's surface. Then the waves are stilled: Aeolus imprisons the winds and forbids their roaming, and controls his grandsons' waves. (my translation)

Not only do the gods transform the couple into birds that fly together above the sea, but they also grant peace to the sea and men while those birds are nesting. This episode, which began with the fury of the winds, is magnificently concluded with those winds finally at peace, reminding us that the protagonist of Ovid's tale is not the gods but Alcyone's attachment to her husband. In this story the impossible becomes possible—the lovers are birds flying together with a love preserved *ad finem* (750) "until the very end," and not yet extinguished.[36]

Marinella remembers how Ovid concluded the story. She cannot resurrect a man or reproduce the impossible metamorphosis into birds, but she captures the story's spirit by introducing a miracle, not to save a hero, not to exalt a city or the piousness of character, but to celebrate the love of a wife. This miracle commemorates the love of a woman for a man. We do not know whether Clelia is prepared to kill herself: Marinella does not want to cast the slightest shadow of blame on this wife, so she creates a pitiful God who fulfills her wishes and takes her life, preempting her suicide. It is a memorable conclu-

---

35. Fantham 1979: 333.
36. Fornaro 1994: 136.

sion, a rare instance in which erotic love and marriage are considered by our author in a positive way. If in her characterization of amazons Marinella had created women who preserve their identity by remaining free from male ties, here she seems to suggest that the essential role of a woman is in preserving the marital bond. In the end, Clelia's fidelity drives the plot and is sanctioned by God in a miracle: the love of Clelia for Lucillo is recognized and rewarded by a compassionate God, who allows their reunion in death.

OVID'S *HEROIDES* AND ELEGIAC IDENTITIES

In the world of elegy, Ovid's *Heroides* are unusual for the importance that the Latin poet grants to the abandoned female lovers. In fact, the collection draws us into the illusion that we are hearing various women lamenting their abandonment. Since these women speak in the first person, Ovid's narrator is fictionally trying to obliterate himself: he wants the reader to experience the woman's voice, not his own. It is easy to forget the revolutionary place that a collection like Ovid's *Heroides* occupies in the Roman world and, above all, to overlook the significance of Marinella's awareness of Ovid's peculiarity and her use of some of his techniques in granting a voice to the women of the *Enrico*.[37]

I have mentioned above how the most significant "remapping" of the genre in the *Heroides* involves putting women at its center. Besides the prioritization of the female point of view, what is peculiar to *Heroides* 13 is Ovid's elegiac revision of the *militia amoris*—that lovers and soldiers have much in common.[38] The most important result of the *militia* or *servitium amoris* of the poet/narrator of Roman elegy is to remain by the girl's side, continuously exposed to her beloved presence. For Ovid, a lover is like a soldier, able to endure all kinds of hardships to conquer and remain with his love. In *Amores* 1.9, Ovid codified these similarities; however, in *Heroides* 13, he proposes a shift, namely, that a lover *is not* and *should never be* a good soldier. Marinella uses this suggestion to pursue a double objective: criticizing the obtainment of traditional honor if undertaken at the expenses of family and wives, and praising women's subjectivity and heroism in patiently accepting values that are imposed on them against their will. In the *Enrico,* women have their own agendas and ideas, even if altruistically, in the end, they conform their desires to those of their beloved. In Marinella's narration, Clelia never accuses Lucillo

---

37. For the importance of putting a woman at the center of the narration, see Lindheim 2008; Baca 1969: esp. 2–5.

38. Thomas 1964: 11–65; Baker 1968; McKeown 1995. For the similarities between elegy and the *Heroides,* see Mack 1988:17–20, 69–83.

directly, but at the end of the story, through Lucillo's own indictment of his misplaced ideals and echoes of several ancient sources, she firmly criticizes Lucillo's choice of war.

In Canto 4, Clelia speaks of Lucillo as a devoted lover, yet his departure for war clarifies that he has placed greater value on his militarist duties than on his love and family. In this way, Lucillo's stance differs from typical elegiac stances such as those of Septimius in Catullus 45 or of Propertius in 1.6 or 2.15, which feature characters ready to disown their political identities for the sake of their private lives. Furthermore, by evoking Ovid's Laodamia, Marinella urges us to remember how the heroine encouraged Protesilaus to avoid battle and risking his life in the Trojan War.[39] Clelia (like Laodamia) obviously endorses the elegiac neglect of war-related matters. For a long time, until his death is imminent, by pursuing his war mission and fulfilling his desire for glory, Lucillo continues to follow the ideals and behavior set forth by traditional epic heroes such as Hector, Aeneas, or Protesilaus, who most clearly embody the notion of the dutiful soldier. Only in the end does he learn better.

Clelia would like to keep Lucillo home, but, like Protesilaus, he rushes to war. According to *Iliad* 2.695–710, Protesilaus was the first Greek who, disregarding an oracle predicting his death, set foot on the battlefield of Troy. In Marinella's treatment of Clelia, Ovid's *Heroides* seem to be a particularly important archetype because through them she exploits the theme of abandoned women.[40] Also in these letters, Ovid lets women speak about themselves and gives them traits that previously characterized the male protagonist of elegy.[41] In elegiac texts the male lover is the speaking, although weak, element of the couple: he is the one who complains about the *duritia* (harshness) of his female companion, feels abandoned by her, and fears that he is going to die for pain. He often delights in imagining his own death and the tears of his mistress, finally seeing how much he loved her only as she stares at his dead body (e.g., *Amores* 1.3.17–18). In *Heroides,* there is a switch: now the heroines follow this script; *they* become the *speaking* protagonists. They voice their devotion to their beloved, how they live to satisfy their companions, how empty and useless they feel without them. In many epistles, being a wife or somebody's companion is the only condition substantiating a worthy existence and providing an identity (e.g., 1.83*ff.*, 5.157*ff.*, 6.15–18, etc.). The woman's *servitium* toward the lover or husband has become in the *Heroides* a fulfilling vocation, so much that even if or when the beloved is inconstant and dishon-

---

39. Laodamia is also featured in Catullus 68, esp. 73–86.

40. Zanini-Cordi 2007: 37–53; Ciccone 1997: 3–16; Hagedorn 2004; Lipking 1989; Pavlock 1990: 113–46 (about Ovid's Ariadne and the Catullan epyllion), 147–70 (about Ariosto's Olympia).

41. Fulkerson 2005; Spoth 1992: 29–30; Spentzou 2003.

est, the woman persists in her commitment to the values of unconditional love and commitment (*fides*).[42]

Like Ovid's heroines and the male protagonists of elegy, Clelia voices her elegiac conception of life even if the claim of mutual love and devotion between her and her husband is problematized by the very development of the story, with Lucillo's abandonment of his homeland and inability to return home safely. Clelia's marked idealization of her husband when probed deeper appears questionable, and the reader realizes that Lucillo's credibility as a lover is developed *in extremis*. It can only be found in death and in the admission of his fault, a revelation that, as emphasized above, can be qualified as Marinella's most innovative addition to traditional (male-related) stories of abandonment. Readers finally sympathize with Lucillo only when he realizes the foolishness of his aspirations, when he admits to being unworthy of his wife's love and care. Only at this point—after repentance and ultimately useless suffering, Lucillo gains a new understanding of love and personal bonds—the waves grant him (or at least his dead body) a return home and a reunion (of sorts) with his wife. Having been unable to endorse the values of elegy during his life, Lucillo dies rediscovering them. Ovid had fantastically allowed some of his characters to save themselves or obtain what they wanted through metamorphosis. Marinella subtly employs this technique when Lucillo turns into a lover, creating closure. Only once he has realized his mistakes is Lucillo allowed to return home and join the person he has discovered as most important in his life. Finally, at this point, nature, which had been portrayed as hostile to the hero's plan to help Venier in war, becomes agreeable again.

THE TWIN STORY OF ARETA AND CORRADINO

The juxtaposition and attrition of the epic and elegiac codes are also considered in the episode featuring Corradino and Areta (*Enrico*, Cantos 17–18). Although their story takes place in the enemy camp, the man and woman are described as exemplary individuals who deeply love each other but must separate because of the war. Their parting replays that of Hector and Andromache in *Iliad* 6.369–463, which, in conjunction with *Heroides* 13, appears to be the most important ancient source Marinella uses in her characterization

---

42. Rosati 1989: 45–46 and 1992: 92. Recently, Lindheim 2008: esp. chap. 8, in which she notices how the women of the *Heroides* focus on their men as their point of reference for self-definition: even if they could cast themselves as protagonists, they continue to grant preeminence to their companions.

of the episode.[43] Areta plays Andromache and Laodamia at the same time. This overlapping gives the narration a tortuously entwined texture in need of being properly assessed. Even if Areta accords tremendous power to Corradino and yields to his desires, a careful examination of the language and sources she uses to describe herself and her husband suggests that the woman's self-marginalization is also self-empowering. Furthermore, the focus on female lamentation sensitizes the reader to the presence of a community of women whose suffering and abandonment counter and condemn the masculine heroic ethos.[44]

Alessio III, the illegitimate ruler of Byzantium and the king against whom the crusaders are fighting, orders Corradino into battle. When saying goodbye to Areta, he tries to justify his decision to follow Alessio. Corradino is fully armored and already wearing his helmet:

> Come il guerrier del suo signor intese
> Il bisogno, i pensieri, e quanto brama,
> Lieto più de l'usato l'armi prese
> Ardendo nel desio di nuova fama:
> Se ne adorna, si cinge e poi discese,
> A ritrovar colei che cotant' ama,
> Cinto di ferro il giovin più rassembra
> Nobil di faccia, e assai maggior di membra.
> (*Enr.* 17.69.1–8)

As soon as this warrior heard of his lord's needs, thoughts, and wishes, he took up his weapons and more happy than usual, burning with desire for new fame: he put them on and arranged them, then he went to see the woman he loved so. Clothed in iron this young man's face looked even nobler, and his limbs seemed more powerful.

At this point, the situation sounds familiar, as it repeats the parting encounter between Clelia and Lucillo. Corradino, eager for new fame, embraces his weapons with alacrity and puts on his war suit. Marinella's description

---

43. In the last decades, the *Odyssey* has been analyzed for the narrator's treatment of women. E.g., Stephens 1995: 302: "Recent Homeric scholarship, especially concerning Penelope, has shown dramatically that the Homeric narrator's empathy with women surpasses the attitudes of even his most humane heroes."

44. Phillippy 1995: 105–6 views the *Heroides* as crucial for Gaspara Stampa's *Rime*: "Stampa's vision of Petrarchism as an authoritative discourse that the female speaker must challenge exploits the *Heroides*' similar view of the limitations of the epic. Thus on both literal and figurative levels, the antimartial informs Stampa's *Rime*" (120).

emphasizes the armor ("cinto di ferro"), just as in the Homeric precedent of Hector meeting Andromache by the Scaean Gates. During this encounter, the husband is qualified by the epithet "of the shining helmet" (κορυθαίολος). Hector's helmet is also the focus of attention and fear of his young son, Astyanax, for the sake of whom, at least for a short while, the hero puts it aside (*Iliad* 6.466–70). James Redfield insightfully comments on how Hector remains imprisoned by his mask-like helmet: "Hector in his armor is a terrifying, alien figure to his own son; for a moment he can set aside the costume of his role and play with the child, but he must then again put on his helmet and his task."[45]

At *Heroides* 13.135–46, Ovid alludes to that Iliadic scene and to the helmet when Laodamia imagines how a newlywed Trojan woman helps her husband put on his helmet and weapons before battle (*nova nupta marito / imponet galeam Dardanaque arma dabit*, "the new bride will put on the husband the helmet and will give Dardanian weapons," *Her.* 13.139–40). But Ovid's bride counteracts the gesture with her advice "to be careful to bring back the weapons of Jove" (*referas ista fac arma Iovi*, 13.144). She is sure that her man will remember her words: "By keeping in his heart the orders recently given by his woman, he will fight cautiously" (*Ille ferens dominae mandata recentia secum, / pugnabit caute*, 13.145–46). Paralleling this image and emphasizing the warrior's attire, Marinella's Areta helps Corradino put on his helmet and more:

> Li allaccia l'elmo, or con dolce riso
> Lo mira e lo vagheggia, or d'acque amare
> Bagna il vago splendor del nobil viso,
> E più ch'altra dolente e mesta appare.
> (*Enr.* 17.92.1–4)

She tied his helmet, then she admired and gazed upon him with a sweet smile. Then she soaked her beautiful, splendid, and noble face with bitter tears, and she appeared more sorrowful than all the other women.

The juxtaposition of Areta's gesture with her tears is intriguing. On the one hand, Areta endorses Corradino's martial urges by fastening his helmet. On the other, she disapproves through her tears. Later she redraws the contours of the parting scene, imagining that her husband promised her to be careful, while in truth for ten stanzas (17.77–87) he explained why he felt compelled to fight bravely.

---

45. Redfield 1975: 123.

During the Iliadic encounter, Andromache begged Hector not to go to battle in the name of his love for her:

> "My dear husband, your warlike spirit
> Will be your death. You've no compassion
> For your infant child, for me, your sad wife,
> Who before long will be your widow . . .
> . . . .
> . . . As for me,
> It would be better, if I'm to lose you,
> To be buried in the ground. For then I'll have
> No other comfort, once you meet your death . . .
> . . . .
> . . . So Hector, you are now
> My father, noble mother, brother,
> My protecting husband. So pity me.
> Stay here in this tower."
> (*Iliad* 17.498–501, 503–6, 526–29, trans. I. Johnston)

Echoes from this segment of the *Iliad* can be heard in Areta's plea to her husband. She implores Corradino to have pity on her and on himself ("pietà di te, di me che sia," "have pity on yourself and on myself," *Enr.* 17.71.5),[46] and after stressing how she has already lost her father, brother, and mother (*Enr.* 17.72–73), she adds:

> Di tanti solo tu sostien la vice,
> Per te mi sono i dì lieti ed adorni;
> Per te seren m'è l'aere e 'l ciel gioioso,
> Padre, madre, fratel, compagno e sposo.
> (*Enr.* 17.73.5–8)

You are the only one to support me, instead of those many, you make my days happy and full, you make my air serene and the sky joyful: you are my father, my mother, my brother, my companion, and my husband.

Here Areta speaks in the first person. Her happiness is completely dependent upon her husband's fate; everything in her life acquires color and meaning only through him. Corradino is her sun and the only family member left, hav-

---

46. Notice also an echo of Laodamia's bid to Protesilaus: "Let the care you have for yourself, be a care you have of me" *Si tibi cura tui, sit tibi cura mei* (*Her.* 13.163).

ing lost everybody else in this war. Achilles-like Enrico is the cause of her tragedy and losses. In these lines, Areta repeats what she had already confessed
in *Enrico* 17.72, in turn duplicating Andromache's words from *Iliad* 17.429–30:

Tu padre caro e veneranda madre
Mi sei, tu fratel dolce e sposo amato.
Poscia che tra guerrieri il mio buon padre
Spirò lo spirto al Ciel devoto e grato;
Il fratel mio tra coraggiose squadre
Cadè su l'età prima al crudo fato,
Ohimè nel dì, ch' Enrico Pera vinse,
E del sangue de' nostri il suol dipinse.
(*Enr.* 17.72.1–8)

You are to me a dear father and venerable mother, a sweet brother and a
beloved husband, now that my good father has exhaled his soul to heaven in
devotion and service to his warriors. My brother fell to a cruel destiny in his
prime among courageous warriors on the day Enrico took Pera and painted
the ground with our soldiers' blood.

Besides placing her husband at the center of a world made empty by the
war, like Clelia (and Laodamia), Areta wishes she could follow Corradino
onto the battlefield (*Enr.* 17.75.1–2); in the end, however, she accepts his decision to leave without her (*Enr.* 17.88).[47] Corradino's response to his wife's pleas
reflects his desire to be obedient to his king and evidences his longing for
glory already highlighted in *Enrico* 17.69.1–8. Laura Lazzari emphasizes how
Corradino's undermining of love in favor of duty, his renunciation of personal
advantage for the good of the community, distances him from chivalric values
and draws him closer to the ideal of the new hero, in whom order and allegiance to the state prevail.[48] Marinella, following Tasso's example in *Gerusalemme Liberata,* wants to present heroes who, completely bound to the state
and never postponing their civic obligations for private or amorous duties,
dissociate themselves from the love-enslaved paladins found in Ariosto's
Orlando Furioso and Arthurian legend. Corradino's answer to Areta, modeled
on Hector's reply to his wife, corroborates this point and enforces the image
of an *epic* man committed to his city and military duty:

47. Cf. Arethusa in Propertius 4.3; see Janan 2001: 53–70.
48. Lazzari 2012: 142.

Ma che giova, o mio cor, de la vergogna
L'avvertenza mi tragge a pigliar l'armi,
E dal sen mi ti svelle e la rampogna
Temo del re, che'n me di sdegno s'armi;
Un desio forte e coraggioso agogna
Gloria, ch'ognor pur seguo e giusto parmi.
(*Enr.* 17.85.1–6)

Awareness of shame pushes me to take up my weapons, and it tears me away
from you. I fear the king's reprimand, I fear that he will conceive scorn for
me. A strong and valiant desire pines for that glory that I follow all the time,
and it seems right to me to do so.

The emphasis on shame and the desire to acquire fame echoes *Iliad* 6.441–
43, where the hero confesses to Andromache how a terrible sense of shame
pushes him to face death in battle ("'Lady,' said Hector of the gleaming helm,
'I too am concerned, but if I hid from the fighting like a coward, I would be
shamed before all the Trojans and their wives in their trailing robes'"). Corradino's expression "de la vergogna l'avvertenza . . . dal sen mi ti svelle" (*Enr.*
17.85.3) alludes to Hector's shame and signals the violence through which the
hero must suppress his desire to be by Areta's side. Corradino seems to know
("so ch'avverrà questo," "I know that it will happen," *Enr.* 17.84.7) that the city
is doomed and wishes that heaven "would strike [him] . . . with lightning" and
the "earth open up and offer a tomb" before he can see his wife "teary and sad
prey and servant to faithless people" or "burdened with lowly, harsh, trouble-
some servitude" ("pria mi fulmini il cielo, e s'apra questa / terra e sepolcro al
miser corpo dia, / ch'io ti rimiri lagrimosa e mesta / preda e serva di gente
infida e ria; / che bassa servitù, grave e molesta / t'opprimi," *Enr.* 17.84.1–6). Yet
he leaves, as Hector had, fearing the opinion of the Trojans and dreading the
day when his wife would be dragged away in servitude:

My heart and mind know well the day is coming / when sacred Ilion will be
destroyed. . . . My pain concerns you, / when one of the bronze-clad Achaeans / leads you off in tears, ends your days of freedom . . . May I lie dead,
hidden deep under a burial mound, / before I hear about your screaming
as you are dragged away. (*Iliad* 6.447–48, 454–55, 464–65; trans. Johnston)

Juxtaposing *Iliad* 6 with *Enrico* 17, we see that Corradino's reply to his wife
confirms that he embodies the traditional epic warrior so much that he can

repeat almost verbatim the words of a prototypical epic hero like Hector.[49] But we also realize that by composing the tale of Areta and Corradino's separation, Marinella wants to create a twin story to that of Clelia and Lucillo, focusing on women. The *mise en abîme* confirms her willingness to explore situations in which personal allegiances are pitted against each other and women's suffering is prioritized.

Corradino goes into battle, and Areta, having climbed up a tower not far from the Golden Horn, watches the raging conflict. While keeping her eyes fixed on the object of her devotion, she speaks to the enemy ranks ("spesso anco volta a l'italiane schiere / dicea cose," "often turning towards the Italian squads, she would tell them things," *Enr.* 18.4.5–6):

"Tenete lungi da le membra amate
Le mani, i ferri, l'ire e i vostri sdegni,
Perdonate a lui solo in tra cotanti.
Ch'usciro in pugna giovani prestanti.

Chè a voi lasciare a un sol l'alma e la vita?
Temer non v'è d'un sol, benchè feroce;
Torni a dar gioia a l'anima smarrita
Del mio sposo fedel l'amata voce."
(*Enr.* 18.5.5–8, 18.6.1–4)

"Keep your hands, swords, anger and scorn away from the limbs of my beloved and forgive him alone among the many strong youths who came to battle . . . what is it to you if you grant life and soul to one only? You mustn't fear one, even if he's fierce. Let my faithful husband's beloved voice come back to give joy to my lost soul."

---

49. Even in Corradino—a character impersonating a stereotypical epic hero—there are resurfacing "chivalric" elements. His emphasis on courtesy is one of them. According to Corradino, what binds him to Alessio is not so much an obligation to a superior, but the allegiance to a worthy friend. He says to Areta that "the wise emperor added his plea to his command" ("ma 'l saggio imperator perch'io non neghi / sua voglia a far, giunse a comandi i prieghi," *Enr.* 17.77.7–8); the plea makes it impossible for him not to fulfill his wish. Alessio is old and can no longer defend his city. He is distressed not about his defeat but the devastation and suffering of his subjects (*Enr.* 17.78–80). He talks to Corradino "sweetly" ("in dolci modi," *Enr.* 17.78.1) and calls him "only friend" ("unico amico," *Enr.* 17.78.2). Corradino's devotion recalls of that of Medoro toward Dardinello, a leader who was always "humane" toward him (*OF* 18.168.5–8). It is Dardinello's kindness that Medoro holds dear and compels him to go bury his body.

These lines bring us back to Laodamia's address to the Trojans, when she urged them "to spare him [Protesilaus] alone among so many enemies" (*parcite, Dardanidae, de tot, precor, hostibus uni, Her.* 13.79). Also, Areta is concerned not with the fate of the battle or the victory of Byzantium but her groom—she wants to be happy again and hear his voice. Her behavior resembles Laodamia's, whose involvement with Protesilaus produces "the peculiar vision of the whole great external world through the narrow lens of the heroine. International affairs and military strategies are reduced to egocentric concerns . . . The focus of the war—or Laodamia's view of it—is limited to one man."[50]

These episodes help Marinella break up the dichotomy of personal versus political by uncovering the links between them, and illustrating how men's choices influence not only their public lives but also those of their families and wives; moreover, she reminds us how a woman can behave heroically by staying home and facing the suffering that being abandoned entails. Most importantly, Marinella shows us how a female writer can embrace a quintessentially political genre (epic) and turn it into something different: a meditation on the costs of war, the physical and psychological suffering of those who stay behind, allegedly safe. The exceptionality of Marinella's poem resides in her ability to make the epic more elegiac. As a woman, she inhabits the minds of other women, more authentically than any other male poet before her. The political world of men dissolves and is silenced for a while, and we enter a kind of feminine echo chamber in which the private and the public mingle, elegy and history appear to be made of the same substance, and both originate from autopsy.[51] Clelia and Areta participate in the autopsy together with the author in a struggle to extract from the unconscious what has been silenced.

Unfortunately, fate proves adverse to Areta's prayers, and Plautio kills Corradino (*Enr.* 18.17.1–3). When she receives the sad news, she reacts like Clelia upon learning of Lucillo's death. As if injured by a real wound, she turns pale and is unable to speak, move, or cry:

> Rimase tal, qual resta quello, al quale
> Ferro crudele da man nemica è sceso,
> A rapirli lo spirto, e di mortale
> Piaga nel cor da quel si senta offeso;
> Tace, sta immota, a lamentar non vale,
> Chè del travaglio è troppo grave il peso,
> Nè 'l suo penoso affetto è in pianto sciolto,

50. Jacobson 1974: 202–3.
51. I owe these observations to Anne Carson's *Nox*.

Né in sospir gravi è 'l suo dolor disciolto.
(*Enr.* 18.24.1–8)

*She was left like one hit by an enemy hand with a cruel sword that takes his
spirit away, and who now feels the pain of a mortal wound.* She was silent
and motionless, as it was no use moaning, for the weight of her pain was too
great. Her feelings of grief were not expressed in tears, nor was her pain let
loose in deep sight.[52]

Remarkably, Areta's pain is like that of a soldier suffering from a wound in
the battlefield. Ovid's *militia amoris* is replayed by framing Areta as a soldier
of love. For a while she is frozen, unable to cry or speak. There is the sense
that, like Corradino, she is already dead. Areta stresses that she cannot have
a life apart from her husband. It is not meaningful to live without Corradino;
her best part—formerly sheltered in his heart—died with him (*Enr.* 18.33.1,
7–8). In this admission, we find the idea—promoted already by the Clelia and
Lucillo episode—of a special union between lovers. Areta's awareness of her
deep ties to Corradino ("come possibil è che io vivi e spiri / se chi fu l'alma
mia qui giace estinto?" "how is it possible that I live and breathe / if the one
who was my soul lies dead?" *Enr.* 19.33.1–2) resembles that of Clelia and Laodamia with their respective partners. In *Heroides* 13, Laodamia claims a special physical and spiritual union with her husband, a bond that makes her
vulnerable when they are apart. Laodamia suffers Protesilaus's hardships and
imitates him in attire and behavior (13.41*ff.*). She faints as soon as he leaves her
(13.19*ff.*). The two are one, fused so much so that we are told that Laodamia's
blood runs through Protesilaus's body (*ne meus ex illo corpore sanguis eat!* "do
not allow my blood to be spilled in your body," *Her.* 13.80). For this reason, in
Laodamia's final advice to Protesilaus, she urges him to concern himself with
his body to show concern for *her* body (*si tibi cura tui, sit tibi cura mei,* "let
the care you have for yourself, be a care you have of me," *Her.* 13.163). This line
contains the suggestion of a "mystic union" of these lovers and foreshadows
Christian mysticism.[53]

The motif of the lovers' union beyond death is old; it was variously
employed by many authors from Boccaccio to Shakespeare and, relevantly
for my argument, it is featured at the ending of *Heroides* 13 in Laodamia's
statement, "I will come as your companion, wherever you call me" (*Me tibi
venturam comitem, quocumque vocaris, Her.* 13.161). Laodamia depicts herself
as Protesilaus's perfect companion, and the *comes* motif in this text is realized

---

52. The description also echoes that of the abandoned Sappho at *Her.* 15.110–13.
53. Fränkel 1969: 21, 183n37; Merklin 1968: 461–94.

in two different ways: in Laodamia wanting to share in spirit her husband's labors at Troy and also in her willingness to die with him.[54] The motif was already present in Marinella's treatment of Clelia's death.

BURIALS

The exemplarity of Areta emerges after Corradino's death when, distressed and only half alive, she cannot stand the thought that her husband lies dead and exposed ("dai cani sia sbranato, ed insepolto / rimarrà l'amor mio nel sangue involto?" "will he be torn by dogs? Will my love remain unburied, covered by blood?" *Enr.* 19.36.7–8). With the help of her maidens, she finds the body and carries it home:[55]

> E dal soave pondo oppresse . . .
> . . . .
> Urlo, latrato, o dirupati sassi,
> Non pon tardar la via che incominciaro;
> E dove il marital suo letto stassi,
> Gementi e sospirose lo posaro,
> Quivi di nuovo al lamentar si volse,
> E quasi in acqua il vago corpo sciolse.
> (*Enr.* 18.38.1, 3–8)

They were laden with the sweet weight . . . no yell or bark or steep rocks could delay the trip they had started. Finally, they placed him on the couple's wedding bed, sighing and moaning. There she again turned to wailing, almost melting her beautiful body in water.

The ottava is replete with allusions. Besides a reference to Ovid's Cyane, "wasted away with weeping" (*Met.* 5.127), and to her dissolution into water, in these lines the marriage bed and a woman crying profusely allude to Boccaccio's Ghismonda (*Decameron* 4.1) and Lisabetta (*Decameron* 4.5).[56] Areta's desire to bury the dead Corradino also makes her similar to Medoro, who in the *Orlando Furioso* carried his dead captain Dardinello on his shoulders with the help of Cloridano ("fu il morto re sugli omeri sospeso / di tramendui,

---

54. Öhrman 2008: 9; Landolfi 2001.

55. Another example of burial performed by women is that of Argia and Antigone (Marinella 1601: 97).

56. For women's dissolving into water in the *Metamorphosis,* see Robinson 2013: 105–7.

tra lor partendo il peso," "the dead king suspended on the arms of both who shared his weight." *OF* 18.187.7–8). The same allegiance of Medoro to a good captain that characterizes Corradino at the beginning of the episode is this time felt by a devoted wife toward her husband. She is ready to risk many dangers to bury him. Once again, Areta's behavior is like a good soldier's. Medoro with his pitiful lamentation for Dardinello "could stop the winds to hear" ("potea ad ascoltar fermare i venti," *OF* 18.186.8); when Areta cries on her husband's dead body, "air itself felt pity" ("facea pietoso l'aere," *Enr.* 18.30.7). Areta is also a new Antigone who demonstrates the importance of burials and the care of the dead by women. Antigone-like, she dedicates her existence to burying her family members, and eventually we learn that, after having retired to a cell, she is welcomed into paradise (*Enr.* 18.47).

Only after Corradino's body has been recovered, while staring at his beauty now deprived of his vital breath, is she finally able to give voice to her sadness:

> O del mio core anima eletta e cara;
> O de la vita mia più degna parte,
> *Ov'è la fé promessa?* Ah sorte avara,
> A la tua sposa, ahi, fur parole sparte!
> *Giurasti di guardarti in quella amara*
> *Guerra e contrasto de l'orribil Marte,*
> *Per non offender me,* che nel tuo petto
> Avea di casto amor ricetto.
> (*Enr.* 18.32.1–8)

My heart's chosen and dear soul, better part of my life, *where is the faith you promised?* Stingy fate! You scattered your words to your wife, *you swore to take care of yourself in horrible Mars's bitter war and fight, so that you wouldn't hurt me*—the noble shelter of the chaste love in your heart.

Here we detect a note of reproach, and we can also fully grasp the distortion of Corradino's epic identity: he did not repudiate his loyalty to the king while leaving Areta for the battlefield. He did not promise to be careful while protecting his wife's well-being. Looking back to Canto 17, we see that, in an opposite fashion, Corradino explained that he had to do whatever he could to help his king, begging his wife to be happy to please him (*Enr.* 17.86.7–8). Yet Areta seems to remember what she wants to, constructing an ad hoc image of her husband as a lover who swears that he will be careful on the battlefield so as not to "offend" her. In practice, Areta fashions a husband who promises to follow Laodamia's advice to Protesilaus of "fighting cautiously," remembering "his homecoming and the loyal embraces of his consort" (*tu tantum vivere pugna, / inque pios dominae posse redire sinus . . . pugnabit caute respicietque domum, Her.* 13.77–78 and 146).

Marinella goes beyond what Ovid had done by redrawing, with the aid of Clelia and Areta, the identities of two heroes who are also husbands. In Areta's description, Corradino preserves his heroic traits, but the lover prevails. In Corradino's fictional promise, Areta is the object of his desire, and he is eager to please her; at the same time, in Clelia's episode, Lucillo ends up as a man who values love more than war. In Areta's story, Corradino's metamorphosis happens through the manipulation of her memory. In apostrophizing his dead body, she seizes control of the narrative, and she memorializes him as the perfect lover he never was.[57] Even the statue that in the end is erected by the king to honor him is granted not so much to the brave warrior, but as a favor to the lamenting wife:

> La clemenza real vinta e conquisa
> Da le lagrime sue, dal suo lamento,
> Fa che in marmi pregiati resti incisa
> La virtude e 'l valor del guerrier spento;
> Credendo in parte ancora in questa guisa
> Alleggerir di lei l'aspro tormento.
> (*Enr.* 18.40.1–6)

The king's clemency was conquered by her tears and moans, so the king ordered that the merit and valor of that dead warrior be carved in valuable marble, as he believed that her deep anguish would be partially dulled in this manner.

THE WORTH OF WIVES

This stigmatization of the female point of view and undermining of women's desire, phenomena that define epics written by men, do not really occur in the episodes explored above, in which war-loving men die and love-loving women

---

57. According to Jones 1997: 27, 32–34, a similar rhetorical maneuver is discernible in Heloise's letters to Abelard. Here not only does she adopt a powerful emotional stance and arguments modeled on Latin authors such as Seneca, Lucan, Cicero, and Ovid, but by insisting on the insuppressible nature of her sorrow, she seems to challenge Abelard's authority and maintain narrative control.

live and control the narrative.[58] Clelia displays intellectual and practical assertiveness in trying to stop Lucillo from going to war and by making it clear
that to her nothing is more important than marital fidelity. If at first, from
a narratological point of view, Marinella condemns her to become an abandoned woman, eventually she is restored to the plot without having changed
her mind. Marinella displays her endorsement of Clelia by allowing her to be
reunited with a husband who realizes his shortcomings and misplaced priorities. Areta's narrative adventure is also significant. Although left behind,
she gets revenge by memorializing Corradino the lover rather than Corradino
the fighter, and by convincing the king, through her lamentation, to erect a
statue for him.[59] In describing these abandoned wives, Marinella redeploys
Ovid's *Heroides* to undermine her own declared allegiance to Aristotle's *Poetics* and to give his women the voice and rational capacity to discern what is
right; moreover, the deaths of Clelia's and Areta's husbands are portrayed as
senseless and unheroic, in contrast with their wives' thoughtful reasoning and
soldierly heroism. In the end, we see in Marinella's treatment of Clelia and
Areta the same attitude shown toward her amazons. Even when they die, she
compensates for their demise by praising their virtues and punishing the men
who do not heed their wishes. She avenges them through narrative dynamics
borrowed from classical texts. Although minor characters, these women capture the attention of the reader, which can hardly be considered a coincidence.

Clelia and Areta are dramatizations of what Marinella had expounded in
Nobiltà, namely, the heroism of true love and the importance of the family. In
chapter 10, "Dell'amore delle donne vs i padri, mariti, etc." ("About Women's
Love Towards Their Fathers, Husbands, etc.") this author defines true love as
an emotion that "does not have as its object pleasure or utility" instead, "for
the beloved the lover is content and rejoices to suffer a cruel and harsh death,
without expecting delight or any kind of advantage."[60] Marinella invokes Aristotle's authority in the *Nicomachean Ethics* and that of Propertius to qualify
true love. She writes:

---

58. Pezzini 2005: 201–2 underlines how during the Counter-Reformation amorous paren-
theses included in heroic poems are contained by stereotypical devices such as the death of one
or both lovers, suicide, the retirement of the woman into a monastery, etc. I argue that although
Marinella uses these strategies and creates narrative impasses, she finds alternative ways to give
relevance to women in love and maximize their subversive strength.

59. The statue may have been inserted as a faint memory of the wax image of Protesilaus
mentioned in *Heroides* 13.152–56.

60. My translation for "Quello è sincero, e uero amore, che non ha per oggetto il piacere, o
l'utile: anzi per la cosa amata si contenta l'amante, e gode di patire una cruda, e acerba morte,
non aspettandone diletto, od utilità alcuna" (Marinella 1601: 92).

Onde dice Aristotile nell'ottauo dell'*Etica: Argumento sunt matres, quae amando gaudent reamari non curant, sed satis ipsis uidetur, si liberos suos bene agentes inspiciant, amantque ipsos.* Et questo è un uero amare, un perfetto e sincero amore e perciò disse Propertio: *Verus amor nullum nouit habere modum.* (Marinella 1601: 92)

Because of this in the eighth book of the *Ethics* Aristotle says: "As evidence I cite mothers who rejoice in loving and do not care to be loved back but it seems enough to them if they see their children prosper and they love them." And this is true loving, a perfect and sincere love and for this reason Propertius said: "True love knows no measure."

In the *Nicomachean Ethics*, Aristotle discussed friendship and love "not as entailing obligations or as based on kingship, but as an altruistic desire."[61] He uses as an example of true friendship the affection of mothers for their children, who might not love them back.[62] Marinella also quotes Propertius (2.15.30) as an authority that "true love knows no measure." The immediate context of Propertius's citation is appropriate because the Roman elegist, using hyperbole, affirms that rivers may call their waters back to their springs and sea creatures live on dry land before he transfers his love pangs to another: in life or in death he belongs to his woman (2.15.33–36). Therefore, Propertius's essential point is that the true lover does not care whether he is dead or alive so long as he can love. Marinella remembers the Roman elegist as well as Aristotle's ideas on friendship. In fact, in describing the special friendship between a wife and a husband, she uses the example of mothers. She deems only sacrificial love as true love, exemplified by the unconditional love mothers have for their children, husbands, and brothers. The gift of love from wives to unworthy husbands echoes and exceeds Aristotle's definition. It also recalls Christian love, because the love of somebody who "gode di patire una cruda, e acerba morte" ("rejoices in a cruel and harsh death," Marinella 1601: 92) resembles that of Christ. In this part of her work, Marinella mentions women

---

61. Konstan 2006: 212.

62. Aristotle in *NE* 8.4: "But in its essence friendship seems to consist more in giving than in receiving affection: witness the pleasure that mothers take in loving their children. Some mothers put their infants out to nurse, and though knowing and loving them, do not ask to be loved by them in return, if it be impossible to have this as well, but are content if they see them prospering; they retain their own love for them even though the children, not knowing them, cannot render them any part of what is due to a mother" (ed. J. Bywater and trans. H. Rackam 1894). The bibliography on friendship in the Greek and Roman world and how it relates to our modern notion is massive. Konstan 2008 provides an insightful overview. See also Smith Pangle 2008; Nussbaum 2001. For Jordan 1996: 56*ff.*, *amicitia* among women, in Fonte's *Il merito*, is the foundation of a new kind of society.

like Laodamia and Artemisia, the wife of Mausolus. The selfless love that Clelia and Areta nourish for their husbands is of this type.[63]

Marinella's description of marital love is also conditioned by the portrait of conjugal love in Fonte's *Il merito*. Here in Leonora's garden, Corinna points out that women's altruistic love for men can be compared to divine mercy "which lavishes love and concern on all creatures, however much they may offend it and however little they return love" (Fonte 1997: 121). She adds that women's patience and kindness have been employed by men "to set themselves up as tyrants" ("ci vogliono tiranneggiare," Fonte 1997: 59) over women. Fonte also observes, through Corinna, that sadly the benefits of women's friendship cannot be experienced outside the garden in a society founded on "the malignity of men" who "rarely find these very rare and close friendships among themselves" or with their wives. Corinna's description of men's relationships resembles Aristotle's description of the inferior friendship of utility. She explains that men are so obsessed with their reputation and commanding respect from others that they behave stiffly and formally; they pretend to follow rules dictated by courtesy, but in fact their behavior is dictated by artifice. Instead of honoring their friends, by behaving in this absurd way, they dishonor friendship and its sacred laws (Fonte 1997: 124). Ultimately, women's true friendships foster a better, if ideal, society, since "true friendship is the cause of all good. For it is friendship that keeps the world alive; friendships seals marriages which preserve the individual of the species, while the friendship and bonding of the elements maintains health in our bodies" (Fonte 1997: 128).

When dealing with the nature of women and endorsing Ficino and Plato's conception of beauty, Marinella praised women's beauty, through which they elevate men to the knowledge and contemplation of the divine essence (Marinella 1601: 17). Marinella had shown that while "men are obliged and forced to love women . . . women are not obliged to love them back, except for courtesy."[64] Interestingly, the chivalric term *cortesia* is used to qualify the behavior of women.[65] Recall that *cortesia* in conjunction with *clemenza* had

---

63. The relationship between Beatrice and the character Dante in his *Commedia* may have played a role in Marinella's and Fonte's conceptualization of friendship. On Dante's understanding of *amicitia*, see, most recently, Modesto 2015. The topic of friendship in Marinella and Fonte (in relation to the classics and to modern understanding) awaits a more systematic account.

64. "Ma uoglio che passiamo più innanzi, e che mostriamo, che gli huomini sono obligati, e sforzati di amar le donne, e che le donne non sono tenute à riamarli, se non per semplice cortesia" (Marinella 1601: 17–18).

65. *Cortesia* plays an essential part in the history and literature of the West: "Courtesy, courtliness, and chivalry, understood broadly, were ethical and social values widespread over the continent from the Carolingian period onwards, with discernible origins in Roman thought. They were concepts that guided lives at court and within the warrior class, as well as of those

been almost programmatically used by Helena, one of the characters of Fonte's *Il merito,* to describe the spheres of action in which she wished women
would assert themselves over men ("I'd want to overcome them in courtesy
as well and to redouble our glory by showing clemency toward them," Fonte
1997: 232). Besides revealing Marinella's pessimism toward men deemed
unworthy of love, the assertions reveal her trust in women's steadfastness
in their love of underserving men. Despite unfavorable circumstances and
men's indifference or undermining of their wives, women are serious about
pursuing their conjugal duty of love. Lucillo and Corradino are examples
of undeserving men whom, despite their unfitness their spouses, Clelia and
Areta love to the very end.

---

who dwelled in both worlds, forming a crucial and inherent part of articulations of civilization
throughout the medieval and early modern period. To study courtesy, courtliness, and chivalry
in their various permutations in courtly literature, troubadour poetry, Arthurian romance, and
conduct literature from the time after the Carolingian era up to the sixteenth century (*Il libro
del Cortegiano* by Baldassar Castiglione) is nothing less than to survey the history of thought
on civilization, not just a literary trope" (Olson 2014: 4–5); see also Scaglione 1991.

PART III

Women in the Garden

Enchantresses Erina and Circetta

CHAPTER 5

❦

Ancient and Modern Prototypes

IN HER BOOK analyzing the role of epic in the contemporary world, Susan Wofford reflects on the nature of epic. She explains that when we look at the most important epic tales about origins, we should consider "to what extent they are narratives about the naturalization of force or violence—to what extent they are stories in which a sudden, revolutionary, and instantaneous act of force is made to seem a natural event."[1] According to Wofford, epic is structured as a genre that mystifies rather than reveals origins not only by giving the impression that the catastrophic endings generated by those chosen acts of force are unavoidable—that is, by creating false causalities—but also because it evades the straightforward representation of aetiology.[2] In the opening of the *Aeneid*, for instance, the poet's question about what caused the anger of Juno towards Aeneas receives a rather indirect answer through three mythological tales that displace it onto a different narrative level.[3] Though the *Aeneid* includes Lucretian allusions and the narrator asks the muse to remind him of "causes" (*mihi causas memora, Aen.* 1.8), the poem more often resists knowledge of causes, resembling, in this obfuscation, a work of imperial ideol-

---

1. Wofford 1999: 244.

2. Ibid., 257.

3. Ibid., 241, for Lucretius (*DRN* 1.55) to know "the beginning of things" means to overcome the fear of death and false illusions that make men miserable.

ogy.[4] This ambiguity towards causality would explain why, for instance, Virgil distinguishes the writer of epic from the happy man of *Georgics* 2 who knows causes.

But although epic poets seem ultimately unable to relate in a straightforward fashion reasons which can explain the present and provide ethical or factual clarity, even in this genre there are moments when origins are narrated, when muddling of events, if not openly revealed is at least made palpable, and a submerged counter-narrative surfaces.[5] The episodes of Fonte's and Marinella's poems that I analyze are such tales, and reveal an agenda that differs from that normally visible and "naturalized" in the genre of their choice. Beyond being stories written to amplify the role of women, the tales centered around Risamante, Clelia, and Areta allow a different perspective about "the arms" of men and their society. Another episode in which "the naturalization of violence" is revealed and opposed in the *Enrico* is that featuring the encounter between Erina and the Venetian soldier Venier. Religious, philosophical, and political matters are explored in the meeting, which, totaling five cantos, cannot be relegated as a useless incident. As a matter of fact, it is the only digression of the poem that threatens its unity of action.[6] In the encounter, Venier, like a new Achilles, receives Erina's prophecy about the future glory of his city as well as the gloomy news of his premature death (*Enr.* 24.21–24); like his Homeric archetype, Venier will be killed by an arrow.[7]

At *Iliad* 9.410–16, Achilles recounts that his mother Thetis told him about his choice: either return home and live a long life, or remain at Troy, dying young and winning endless renown.[8] In a similar fashion, thanks to the prophecy of Erina, Venier receives a chance and a choice: he could remain alive on her island, peacefully busy in the cultivation of learning and self-knowledge, or return to his war games and death. Both heroes pick death. In Book 9, Achilles, offended by Agamemnon's abduction of his war prize, Briseis, is begged to return to the war but rejects the proposal and the prizes presented to him in compensation for the loss of the girl. For a while he is unable to choose the currency of his heroic world. Although in the *Iliad* Achilles's glory and fame are strictly dependent on his death on the battlefield ("I have

4. For Lucretius and Virgil, see Farrell 1991: 169–206; Gale 2000; Giesecke 1999; Hardie 1986: 157–240 and 2009: esp. chaps. 3 and 5.

5. Wofford 1999: 257, 241.

6. Lazzari 2010: 100 states that the episode "threatens the unity of action of the poem" (my translation).

7. In chapter 1, I discussed Venier's death as modeled on that of the Virgilian Camilla. Marinella's familiarity with the *Iliad* is proven by her citation of *Iliad* 1 in the *Nobiltà*, where she considers Achilles's anger towards Agamemnon, providing a loose translation in verse of *Iliad* 1.188–89, 223–28, probably borrowed by Luigi Grotto; see Marinella 1999: 153.

8. Nagy 1999; Wofford 1992: 3–4. Recently, Burgess 2009: 17, 43–56.

lost a safe return home, but I will have unfailing *kleos* (glory)," *Il.* 9.413), in this episode, through Achilles's hesitation, the *Iliad*'s commitment to war and renown is undermined, for in Achilles's refusal of the rewards and offerings of the Achaean leaders lies the suggestion (although in actuality it is ultimately denied) that one may decide to live a long life *without* battlefield glory.

Achilles once again reviews the option of a long and quiet life, quite significantly in the *Odyssey* when, in the Underworld, his shade meets Odysseus. In his reply to Odysseus, Achilles "implicitly repudiates the choice he perforce made in the *Iliad* of a short and glorious life over a long and obscure one":[9]

> O shining Odysseus, never try to console me for dying.
> I would rather follow the plow as thrall to another
> Man, one with no land allotted him and not much to live on
> Than be a king over all the perished dead.
> (*Od.* 11.488–91; trans. Lattimore)

Pointedly, M. Suzuki notes that this passage is found not in the *Iliad* but in the *Odyssey*, a text that, in her mind, explicitly challenges the Iliadic heroic code and the idea that martial glory should be the highest pursuit in a man's course of life. In Achilles's reply to Odysseus, the sheer act of existence—no matter which kind—appears to be the most important value.[10]

The possibility of living honorably without fighting does not really exist in the *Iliad*, but Marinella's poem explores this theme in the encounter between Venier and Erina. While in the *Iliad* Achilles's greatness is built on his choice of war—which, according to Gregory Nagy, is paradigmatic to the Homeric poems[11]—Erina disapproves of Venier's choice. Also, in the *Enrico*, criticism of the war between Venice and Constantinople cannot be made openly against the main protagonist, Enrico Dandolo. But a kind of denunciation develops in the digression featuring Erina's island and in Erina's attempt to stop Venier, Enrico's narrative surrogate, from resuming his military activities. If on the one hand Venier must be considered Enrico's alias because he is devoted to his cause, sent to enlist forces to help the Venetians, because of his youth he is cast as a sacrificial lamb thanks to Marinella's multiple allusions to the *Aeneid*.

In the end, Venier does not accept Erina's offer to remain on the island. He refuses a life of contemplation and returns to fighting, but even so he is not able to die a glorious death. Above all, he is unable to grow ethically, to

---

9. Suzuki 1989: 58.

10. Cf. Ahl and Roisman 1996: 144. For the differences between Iliadic and Odyssean heroes, see Rinon 2006: 201–23.

11. Nagy 1999: chap. 10 (§14).

gain the insight that all great heroes like Achilles, Aeneas, Goffredo, and even Enrico eventually gain in some moments of their epic journeys. He never understands that war should not be an end in and of itself and that human fulfillment can also be obtained in a life of tranquility and peace. Venier fails to grasp the lesson he learns on Erina's island, a place presented to him and all readers as a reminder that glory, especially military glory, is not the only path toward personal and public fulfillment. In Marinella's judgment, higher values such as inner happiness and knowledge of God can be more easily obtained away from violence and bloodshed through a life devoted to contemplation and study. In Marinella's text, Erina takes the role of the philosopher-scholar and suggests an alternate course of action: a life dedicated to learning and in harmony with God and the universe. By openly condemning Venier's choice and by giving him a mediocre death in battle, Marinella disrupts the male epic agenda. Moreover, by dwelling upon Venier's death, forcing us (and Enrico) to regard his dead body, she obliges her external and internal audience to feel the costs of the war more intensely.

Marinella's depiction of the island and of Erina—enchantress, prophetess, philosopher, hunter, and scholar[12]—employs a variety of classical and modern authors. She has read a multitude of epic texts and imitates them. Chapter 5 is dedicated to Erina and her links to other enchantresses, magicians, and prophetic figures from important classical and Renaissance texts (Homer's Circe, Calypso, and Nausicaa in the *Odyssey*; Virgil's Dido in the *Aeneid*; Ariosto's Alcina in the *Orlando Furioso*; Tasso's Armida in the *Gerusalemme Liberata*; Fonte's Circe and Circetta in the *Floridoro*). My claim is that Marinella successfully constructs in Erina a new kind of positive enchantress. I use the term "enchantress" to characterize Erina even if Marinella has emptied the character of every negative connotation and refashioned it to resemble a philosopher and a scientist. Erina can really be seen as a counterpart of Marinella since this author pursued scientific knowledge and natural philosophy by employing them in literary discourse not only to shed light about the physical world but also to disclose women's intellectual potential and criticize bigotry built on ignorance. Marinella (but also Fonte) use their understanding of scientific discourse and philosophical training as weapons in the *querelle des femmes* to reveal prejudices and to improve men and women's lives.[13]

Since the narrative nucleus and ideological center of Marinella's indictment of excessive thirst for power and dominion is launched on Erina's luscious island which is described according to the dictates of the *locus amoenus*,

---

12. *Lamia* is the premodern term for this complex character. See Capodivacca 2007, especially her introduction.

13. Ray 2015: 13.

the pastoral arcadia that she inhabits and in which she finds fulfillment and peace is the topic of chapter 6.[14] I clarify that this Venetian author has been influenced by pastoral and philosophical reflections about human flourishing, and that her concerns and views go beyond the selfish interests and martial ambitions depicted in classical epic or those advocated by specific political interests. On Erina's island, politics begins with "care of the self," and Erina's seemingly private project has a much wider significance.[15] She advocates an aesthetics of existence, a cultivation of the self that culminates in autonomy but is also connected to the rest of the cosmos. As Arnold Davidson has written about the movement of the philosophically inclined soul from the inside to the outside as described by M. Foucault, it is correct to emphasize the ancient care of the self, because conversion to self is a precondition of the spiritual transformation that constitutes philosophy. Such a conversion "does not shrink the world to the size of the self," but rather, "dilating the self beyond itself, brings about that cosmic consciousness in which one sees the human world 'from above.'"[16] Apart from Marinella's focus on a peace- and wisdom-loving Erina, who lives on an Edenic island in isolation from the city, her criticism of the war and earthbound dreams is constructed through allusions to segments from Homer's *Odyssey*, Cicero's *Somnium Scipionis* (*Dream of Scipio*), and Virgil's *Aeneid* 6. While the *Odyssey* is chosen for its positive depiction of women in general and the enchantress in particular (Circe, Calypso, and Nausicaa), the other two texts are deployed for their nuanced and pessimistic attitude toward politics and human accomplishments. The dependence of Marinella on Cicero's *Somnium* and *Aeneid* 6 is another theme of this chapter.

In chapter 7, I return to Fonte and recognize that her treatment of the topic in the *Floridoro* constitutes an essential prelude to Marinella's development of the virtuous enchantress. In the *Floridoro*, Fonte had already created a good enchantress in Circetta and reflected on the story of Circe in Homer's *Odyssey* by showing sympathy for the woman. A high degree of optimism can be observed in Fonte's development of Circetta, whose character is scrutinized and compared to that of Erina. Chapter 7 also lays out some conclusions about women's lives in Venice and during the Renaissance.

---

14. *Locus amoenus* literally means "pleasant place." It refers to an idealized place of safety and comfort, usually a beautiful, shady lawn or open woodland, sometimes with connotations of Eden. See Russell 1998: 21.

15. Yates 2010.

16. Davidson 2006: 37.

CALYPSO, CIRCE, NAUSICAA, DIDO, AND ERINA

In the *Enrico,* the enchantress-prophetess Erina is important because she provides a commentary on similar figures previously elaborated on in works written by men. I am categorizing her as an enchantress although she embodies features that distinguish her from traditional female sorceresses. Far from being a seductress, Erina is a chaste maiden, a good daughter, and committed scholar. She lives on a peaceful and verdant island, and by studying the hidden causes of the universe pursues perfection and union with the divine. Often when a Circe-like figure appears in narratives by men, she is a powerful individual who can reduce men to brutish copies of themselves or (more rarely) lead them to joy and salvation. Male writers tend to highlight the negative aspects of these female figures, their power to hinder the hero's mission and transform him into a self-pleased individual oblivious to his duties to society. The fact that the enchantress also appears in artifacts and stories created by Renaissance women suggests that she is employed as a reply to those created by men. Marinella's elaboration of the enchantress follows that of Fonte's Circetta in the *Florido* and reveals something important about women's experiences and perspectives.[17] Significantly, in their epic poems, Marinella and Fonte recount the story of the magnificent and powerful enchantress with some distinctively female twists.

The Erina episode in the *Enrico* is inspired by Homeric women such as Circe, Calypso, and Nausicaa. We cannot say for sure whether Marinella could read Greek, but surely she consulted Latin translations of the *Odyssey* since already in 1362 Leontius Pilatus had completed a line-by-line Latin translation of both Homeric poems.[18] In the *Odyssey,* these handsome ladies live in solitude, immersed in nature far from the inhabited world. Their relationship with Odysseus is often sexual, and frequently they try to control him by making him stay with them. Although in the beginning they appear selfish, threatening, and domineering, they turn out to be benevolent and help the hero return home. Like her Homeric predecessors, Erina is a beautiful young woman who lives in a magnificent palace on a lush island away from city life and structured societies. Female companions assist in daily activities while she is devoted to hunting and contemplating the mysteries of the universe. She has special powers, like the control of a magic chariot and foreknowledge of the future. After Venier has been shipwrecked, she welcomes him to her island and invites him to remain with her, but upon the realization that it is not the

---

17. Fonte in the *Floridoro* employs the Homeric Circe (Book 5) to characterize the encounter between a hero and a woman of prophetic powers (see below).

18. See the introduction to this volume.

hero's desire to leave his people and the turmoil of the war, she lets him go. Only thanks to her aid can he return to the war in Byzantium. Erotic suggestions are present in the encounter between Venier and Erina, who does not want to seduce the hero with her physical allure and carnal pleasures but with the wonders of the universe and the appeal of peace and knowledge. Erina's earthly paradise is not fashioned as bait pulling Venier away from essential concerns but rather as a place of reflection that brings him closer to God, toward a world better than his own. Erina offers him a chance to stay not because she is in love with him or for her own satisfaction, but because she wants the hero to be happy and flourish.

Erina resembles the ageless Calypso, who lives far away from gods and men "in a distant island . . . out of the violet sea" (*Od.* 5.55), "across a huge expanse of sea" where "there is no city of mortal men who offer sacrifices or choice gifts to the gods" (*Od.* 5.101–3). The nymph sings and weaves in her lovely house built in a splendid forest, which is described as a *locus amoenus:*[19]

> But when he [Hermes] reached the distant island, he rose up,
> Out of the violet sea, and moved on shore,
> Until he reached the massive cave, where Calypso,
> The fair-haired nymph, had her home. He found her there,
> A huge fire blazing in her hearth—from far away
> The smell of split cedar and burning sandal wood
> Spread across the island. With her lovely voice
> Calypso sang inside the cave, as she moved
> Back and forth her loom—she was weaving
> With a golden shuttle. All around her cave
> Trees were in bloom, alder and sweet-smelling cypress,
> And poplar, too, with long-winged birds nesting there—
> Owls, hawks, and chattering sea crows, who spend their time
> Out on the water. A garden vine, fully ripe
> And rich with grapes, trailed through the hollow cave.
> From four fountains, close to each other in a row,
> Clear water flowed in various directions,
> And all around soft meadows spread out in full bloom
> With violets and parsley. Even a god,
> Who lives forever, coming there, would be amazed
> To see it, and his heart would fill with pleasure.
> (*Od.* 5.55–76, trans. Johnston)

---

19. For the *locus amoenus* in early Greek literature, see Thesleff 1981: 31–45.

The "ashes, beeches, and myrtles" (*Enr.* 7.72.4), the fertility of the soil, the precious metals, and the abundance of water on Calypso's island become recurrent elements in Renaissance chivalric narratives that describe the dwelling places of magicians. These features are also highlighted in Marinella's description of Erina's home and island:

> Giunser poscia al palagio, il qual nel monte
> Ha loggie, ampi verron, camere e sale,
> Di saputo scarpello opre alte e conte,
> A cui non vede il sol nè vedrà eguale;
> Scioglie per mille fori un chiaro fonte
> Sopra lui l'acque in copia tanta e tale,
> E con tanto furor dal monte scende,
> Che quasi un nuovo Nil l'udito offende.
> (*Enr.* 5.83)

Finally, they reached her palace. Inside the mountains it had loggias, wide balconies, rooms, and halls, all noble and skillful work of a well-trained chisel: the sun had not seen anything like it, and it never will again. A clear spring let its water out by thousands of holes above it—so much water that it came down from the mountain with such fury that it bothered the ears almost like a new Nile.

> Cantan per le campagne ampie le bionde
> Spiche il valor de le lor grevi chiome;
> Verdeggiano appo i sposi le feconde
> Viti, già onuste di gradite some;
> Vedi in schiera scherzar tra le lucid' onde
> Gli agili pesci, par che mostrin come,
> E la terra abbondante e ricca e lieta,
> Ov'ogn'agio, ogni ben s'accolga e mieta.
> (*Enr.* 6.41)

Blond ears proclaimed the value of their heavy hair through the fields. Nearby fecund grapevines were green and loaded with their happy weight. One could see swift fish frolic among clear waves in schools. All this seemed to show how fruitful, rich, and happy that land was, where everything good was present and ready for the plucking.

Similar to Calypso's home, Circe's is erected "through dense brush and trees" (*Od.* 10.197), and she lives in a "splendid palace built of polished stones"

(*Od.* 10.211, 253). Homer's description emphasizes Circe's enchanting voice and hospitality toward Odysseus by bathing and feeding him and his men (*Od.* 10.350–71, 449–53) and, in the end, her unwillingness to keep him against his will. If at first Circe manifests her power over nature and hostility to men by changing Odysseus's companions into pigs, later in the story, once Odysseus begs her, she becomes a benevolent helper:

> . . . I went to Circe,
> In her splendid bed, and clasped her knees.
> The goddess listened to me as I begged,
> Speaking these winged words to her:
> "Circe, grant me the promise which you made
> To send me home. My spirit's keen to leave, as are
> The hearts in my companions, too, who, as they
> Grieve around me, drain my heart, whenever you are
> Not among us." I spoke. The lovely goddess
> Answered me at once: "Resourceful Odysseus,
> Laertes' son and Zeus' child, if it's against your
> Will, you should not now remain here in my house."
> (*Od.* 10.480–89, trans. Johnstone)

Correspondingly, Erina's home is found "among wild animals and trees" (*Enr.* 5.80.8), and she does not try to keep Venier on her island after receiving his entreaty to depart:

> S'orna, d'illustre spoglie il corpo cinge,
> Che dono fur de la mirabil figlia;
> A gli amici tornar desio lo spinge,
> Onde di pregar lei baldanza piglia:
> La trova, la saluta e a dir s'accinge
> De la veduta somma meraviglia;
> De le grandezze d'Adria, e quando tace
> Il silenzio nel volto e più loquace.
> (*Enr.* 21.2)

He [Venier] put on the noble clothes that were a gift from that admirable daughter. His desire to go back to his friends urged him, so he found the courage to plead with her: he sought her out, greeted her, and started to talk about the great wonder they had shared, about the greatness of Adria. When he stopped, the silent expression on his face was more telling.

Poi con atto modesto gli occhi inchina,
Dal cor premendo il desiderio ad arte:
Di' se naviglio alcun, donna divina,
Mi trarrà salvo a la natìa mia parte:
Ond'io la tua bontà, la mia ruina
Nota faccia nel mondo a parte a parte.
(*Enr.* 21.3.1–6)

Then he modestly cast his eyes down, craftily repressing his heart's wish: "Divine lady, tell me if a ship will bring me back safely to my land, so that I can share your goodness and my ruin with the entire world," he said.

Ma colei che regina era del grande
Ricco palagio, n'avea intense doglie,
Conoscendo ei voler che lo rimande,
Contra il suo intento a le guerriere soglie.
Vede che pesca, caccie, ozii e ghirlande
Non piegano di lui l'accese voglie:
Vorria quel far contento.
(*Enr.* 21.16.1–7)

The woman who was queen in that great and rich palace felt great pain knowing that he wanted to go back to battle against her wish. She saw that fishing, hunting, resting, and flowery garlands didn't break his intense desire. She wanted to make him happy.

"Non t'astringo restar, vattene." (*Enr.* 21.18.5)

"I cannot hold you here; go away then."

Both texts emphasize how women have power, that they could do with the heroes as they wished. Erina is particularly distressed because she knows that Venier's return to Byzantium will cause his death. Yet both Erina and Circe are unwilling to keep the men against their will. Without Circe's advice, Odysseus would almost certainly have died before reaching Ithaca; it is Circe with her counsel who makes possible Odysseus's homecoming and his reunion with Penelope. Similarly, Venier's homecoming depends on Erina. She will help the Venetian hero to leave her island, conforming her will to that of her father and renouncing Venier's company.[20]

---

20. An identical psychological state of mind characterizes Calypso, who ultimately conforms her will to that of Zeus and lets Odysseus go (esp. *Od.* 5.204–5).

For a long time, Circes's positive features were not recognized. It was the task of a female critic in the 1990s to put aside the negative connotations of the evil "witch" Circe and reevaluate her as a positive character. According to this critic, Judith Yarnall, what is actually defeated in the Homeric encounter between Odysseus and Circe is the notion that "one of them must have clear dominance over the other . . . from the moment when Circe swears her oath and Odysseus enters her bed, the powers of both are shared and accepted."[21] An interaction between equals is also what Marinella is keen to highlight in her description of Venier and Erina's encounter. Although Erina is obviously in control, she never uses her power unwisely or against Venier's desires.

Besides the resemblances with Calypso and Circe, in Cantos 5–6 the meeting between Erina and the Venetian has as its most important prototype the encounter between Odysseus and Nausicaa on Phaeacia in *Odyssey* 6. Richly adorned palaces, fertile lands, and singing bards characterize both episodes. The abodes of Alcinous and Nausicaa are at the edge of the world. Fountains and fruit trees surround the premises (*Od.* 7.86–131). Near Alcinous's palace there is a spectacular fruit garden that resembles the Garden of Eden and generates produce year-round. Men work in the fields only at the time of the harvest; there is no tilling, sowing, or planting.[22] It is an extraordinary land, and its inhabitants seem to live closer to the gods. In fact, Ahl and Roisman title their subchapter on Phaeacia "Gods or Men?" and suggest that the world of the Phaeacians represents a kind of Hesiodic, yet civilized, Greek Bronze Age (*Works and Days,* 144–68) in which men were better than they are now. Even Erina's island is depicted as a world in which nobody worries about subsistence and handmaids take care of chores while Erina spends her time cultivating her spirit. Erina's palace is a place without equal, where people acquire special knowledge and proximity to the divine. It is no coincidence that the woman tells Venier: "It is possible to live happily, joyful and blessed here among wild animals and trees" ("Chè qui tra fiere e tronchi ancor lice / viver beato e 'n sè lieto e felice," *Enr.* 5.80.7–8) and urges him to visit her house ("vieni al mio tetto, in cui gran saper pose / somma bellezza," "come to my home: great knowledge has created the highest beauty there" *Enr.* 5.81.5–6).

Marinella portrays Erina's palace as incomparable also when Armano shows it to her ancestor Pietro Candiano,[23] who is amazed and wonders whether Armano may be leading him to heaven ("io non so dove / mi guidi

21. Yarnall 1994: 21.

22. Ahl and Roisman 1996: 119.

23. Armano is a servant of Pietro and also has special powers. He rescues Pietro and his young son from death (6.33.1), carrying both to the island where Erina will be born.

forse in ciel," *Enr.* 6.40.7). Eventually Pietro lives in perfect happiness in this fantastic palace immersed in natural beauty:

> I vaghi siti, l'alta mole e queste
> Piacevoli acque, i verdi prati e l'ore
> Godeva Pietro, in boschi ed in foreste
> Con fauni e Dei e traeva in pace l'ore;
> Or contemplava del giardin celeste
> De' lumi erranti il moto e lo splendore;
> Così premea gli affanni, e di natura
> Desia sublime e al ben l'alma assicura.
> (*Enr.* 6.42)

Pietro enjoyed everything: the happy places, the tall palace, the pleasant waters, the green meadows, and he spent his time there in woods and forests with fauns and gods. At night, he observed the motion and splendor of the wandering stars in their heavenly garden. In that manner he suppressed his disquiet, enjoyed sublime nature, and connected his soul with goodness.

The Nausicaa episode shares several other features with the Erina interlude: besides the remoteness of the island on which these encounters happen and the mystical, almost divine beauty, we find an emphasis on Nausicaa's chastity and wisdom, the suggestion of a possible erotic union between Odysseus and the girl, and finally a harmony that characterizes life on the island and the supremacy of Queen Arete.[24] Similarly, Erina is depicted as a chaste and most wise young girl who rules over the island, living harmoniously with her maidens. The Phaeacians are described as a people dwelling apart from other groups, far away at the end of the sea (*Od.* 6.204–5).

Nausicaa is a *parthenos* (virgin), inexperienced with men, yet she demonstrates character and strength. When facing the shipwrecked, potentially dangerous Odysseus, she shows courage ("the daughter of Alcinous remained still . . . and stood in front of him," *Od.* 6.139–41).[25] In the Homeric text, Nausicaa goes to wash her brothers' garments because she is thinking about her imminent marriage. She plays ball with her handmaids, and upon seeing Odysseus, while the other girls cry and run away, she remains still (*Od.* 6.116*ff.*)

---

24. For an old-fashioned reading of the island of the Phaeacians as a matriarchal society, Boas and Campbell 1967: 86.

25. Marinella recalls this moment in the *Nobiltà* when discussing Speroni's *The Dignity or Nobility of Women*. She rejects the idea that a woman is her husband's servant and quotes Odysseus's words to Nausicaa: "Lady, you fill me with reverence and fear" (Marinella 1999: 137). Marinella also cites *Odyssey* 8.168 in Latin: "te mulier valde equidem admiror, et metuo" (1999: 127).

and meets the stranger. At 6.102-4, Homer conveys the virginal beauty of the young Nausicaa through Odysseus's comparison of the girl to Diana (*Od.* 6.102-8).

Erina behaves like Nausicaa when facing Venier for the first time. As soon as she sees him, she blushes, her heart trembling, but she is able to face him and speak wisely ("come la donna [Erina] in lui fissa le ciglia, / tremò nel cuore e impallidì nel viso; / poi com'è rosa nel mattin vermiglia, / venne, il passo fermò con saggio avviso," *Enr.* 5.64.1-4). Erina lives on an island of women, has experienced the pain of losing her father, and has never confronted the possibility of meeting another man, so she is shocked and fascinated upon meeting Venier. Like Nausicaa, she is compared to Diana:

Vede venir di venerando aspetto
Donna d'età perfetta, inculta e bella
. . . .
Li dardi ha in man, son sue bellezze altere
De' boschi onor, terror dell'empie fere.

Tal ne va forse all'abito, al sembiante
Nelle selve a cacciar ninfa o Diana,
Con gli occhi casti e con maniere sante;
. . . .
Segue le vaghe fere, amor non cura,
Prende le belve e doma ancor sicura.
(*Enr.* 5.62.1-2, 7-8; 5.63.1-3, 7-8)

He [Venier] saw a woman approaching whose appearance was worthy of reverence. She [Erina] was of perfect age, beautiful, and without makeup ... both her stars resembled a bright sun, and she held arrows in her hands.

A nymph or Diana herself might share her clothes and her appearance when they go hunting in the woods. Her eyes were chaste, her manners saintly; ... she followed handsome prey, disdained love, and caught and tamed wild animals.

At first sight, Erina appears to be a huntress. Like the amazon Emilia, she is an excellent archer and hunts wild animals (*Enr.* 8.89-95).[26] Erina's similarity to Diana anticipates her imperviousness to erotic love. Like a new Artemis, the young woman does not think at all about love but is attracted to Venier who

26. For Emilia, see chapter 1.

represents "the other," the real world (made up of men with dissenting opinions), and the opportunity for an exchange of ideas between equals. A reciprocal seduction between the two is implied but erotic entanglement is quickly dispelled, not so much because our protagonists are related (as we learn in *Enr.* 6.16–17) but because Marinella does not want to confuse the reader about what Erina and her island stand for: Erina has no desire to entrap Venier through the enticement of the senses nor through marriage.[27] Marinella highlights her attachment to virginity through the parallelism with Diana (the Greek Artemis) as well as her innocence and good intentions by alluding to Nausicaa's meeting with Odysseus, a stranger in a condition of absolute need, whom the princess will promptly aid. Like Odysseus, Venier has been shipwrecked and needs Erina's care.

Nausicaa's awakening sexual maturity and thoughts about marriage are triggered by the stranger, who is perceived as a desirable suitor once he has washed, oiled, and dressed himself in the fine clothes offered by the princess. At that point she realizes his attractiveness, admires him (*Od.* 6.237), and, speaking to her handmaids, compares him to the gods, wishing that her future husband may be like him: "Before he seemed to me uncouth, but now he is like the gods, who hold broad heaven. Would that a man such as he might be called my husband" (*Od.* 6.242–44, trans. Murray). In the beginning of the episode, the simile was reversed: Nausicaa was compared to a goddess by Odysseus in his address to her. As he recounted his recent misfortune at sea, put his life into her hands, and begged for pity, he wondered whether she was mortal:

> I am at your knees, o queen: are you a goddess or a mortal?
> If you are a goddess—one of those who hold the vast sky—
> You are quite similar to Artemis
> . . . .
> Yet, o queen, have mercy, after much suffering, I as a suppliant come to you
>   first
> (*Od.* 6.149–51, 175–76, my trans.)

In a parallel fashion and situation, the shipwrecked Venier calls Erina *dea*, wishing she would pity him, and asks for help:

27. Ultimately, the affection that ties Erina to Venier is chaste: "sorse e scintillò per gli occhi fuore / gli onesti rai di consanguineo amore" (*Enr.* 6.15.7–8). See Cox 1997: 143; Finucci in Fonte 2006: 26; Galli Stampino in Marinella 2009: 57–59; highlighting erotic nuances, Ristaino and Malpezzi 2008: 89.

Ed egli: "O dea, che dagli empirei chiostri
Scendi or pietosa a consolar mie doglie,
Diva all'aspetto, ai panni, al dir ti mostri,
E dea t'inchino, e diva il cuor t'accoglie;
Come tal dammi aita."
(*Enr.* 5.66.1–5)

He replied, "Goddess, you have come down from your heavenly abode
to console my pains with your pity. You look like a goddess from your
demeanor, your clothing and your words, so I bow to you as a goddess, and
as a goddess my heart accepts you. And if you are a goddess help me."

The symmetry of the genders, which according to Nicole Loraux typifies the
Homeric poems, is evident in the reciprocal comparisons of the man and
woman to gods.[28] Marinella adopts this strategy by allowing her characters to
give each other identical compliments. Having compared Erina to a goddess,
once Venier has been bathed, oiled, and clothed, *he* becomes the object of her
admiration and seems to be "more than a man":[29]

Più ch'uom sembrava in regal manto involto,
Nel parlar saggio e nel leggiadro volto.

Più, che mai bello avea fatto ritorno
L'ostro già in pallor volto al morto viso;
Nel suo sembiante di grandezza adorno
De l'altezza del cuor dà certo avviso.
Par ch'abbelli d'Erina il gran soggiorno
Con modi onesti *e mansueto riso*;
Stupisce la donzella e tace e mira,
E spesso gli occhi e 'l cor ver lui raggira.
(*Enr.* 5.87.7–8; 5.88)[30]

He looked more than human, wrapped in a royal mantle, wise in his speech,
and handsome in his appearance.

---

28. For more on gender symmetry in the Homeric poems, see Loraux 1995.

29. In this octave and the one following, the man's "superhuman" beauty and his "laughter"
could allude to Sappho's famous ode (fr. 31 = Campbell 1982: 78).

30. Sexual awakening is also suggested by the presence in Venier's room of a marble Pan
"wounded by love" (*Enr.* 5.97.8). More prominently, the allusion to a love story like that of Dido
and Aeneas appears when Erina retires to her apartments and, like Dido after the banquet with
Aeneas, keeps thinking about him (*Enr.* 5.98.6–8).

The color that had turned to pallor in his almost dead face was back, more beautiful than ever; it was a sure sign of the nobility of his heart, displayed in his face adorned with greatness. It seems that he made Erina's great home more beautiful with his good manners and *temperate smile.* The maiden was astonished, she observed quietly and often she turned to him her eyes and her heart.

Nausicaa's yearning for Odysseus presupposed a widening of horizons for the girl, who begins to appreciate a stranger, a non-Phaeacian man, something that no other young woman on the island had ever done. Odysseus's presence challenges Phaeacian beliefs about the outside world, and triggers her admiration for him. Nausicaa becomes well disposed toward him even if, as we learn, Phaeacians normally have deep-seated xenophobia (*Od.* 7.31–33).[31] With Odysseus's arrival, the islanders have a chance to experience his cleverness and strength, and the princess appreciates him as eloquent and attractive. If Nausicaa, for a while, imagines a life with Odysseus, his departure puts an end to that fantasy. His departure leaves her desire unfulfilled: the chance of a new kind of life and the alternatives made possible for Odysseus by an endogamous society remain unexplored options in the *Odyssey.*[32] Likewise in the *Enrico,* Venier returns to his usual existence, and the episode is there solely to signal the road not taken, a universe that remains unexplored.

The encounter between Erina and Venier also alludes to that between Dido and Aeneas. We saw in chapter 2 that Virgil's *Aeneid* is a text frequently remembered and evoked by Marinella. Even if Dido is not an enchantress, in *Aeneid* 4 the Carthaginian interlude between Aeneas and the queen corresponds, from a narratological point of view and in content, to the stories of Odysseus being shipwrecked and receiving the attention of beautiful and capable women. Given the erotic premises of *Aeneid* 4, Dido's extreme reluctance to let Aeneas go, her curse on the Trojan leader, and her suicide, Marinella is not keen to allude too closely to the episode and tie Erina to Dido. Yet we do see some allusions to her. In *Aeneid* 1.498–502, when Dido is surveying her newly founded city, Virgil compares her to Diana:

Qualis in Eurotae ripis aut per iuga Cynthi
Exercet Diana choros, quam mille secutae
Hinc atque hinc glomerantur oreades; illa pharetram

---

31. Rose 1969. We see this preconception against strangers during the banquet of Book 8, where the Phaeacian Euryalus considers himself superior to any voyager who travels by sea.

32. See Buchan 2004: 200–202.

Fert umero gradiensque deas supereminet omnis.

. . . .

Talis erat Dido. (*Aen.* 1.498–501, 503)

Just as on the banks of the Eurotas or along the ridges of Mount Cynthus
Diana leads her throngs, a thousand Oreads who, here and there, cluster
around her. She bears a quiver on her shoulder and as she walks towers
above all the goddesses . . . such was Dido.

In Virgil's *Aeneid* the connection of Dido to Artemis/Diana is prominent
in the description of the queen at the height of her power, when in Book
1 she perfectly controls her fate and people. At this moment the assimilation of Dido to Diana does not imply virginal beauty—Dido is not a virgin,
although she has sworn to remain faithful to the memory of her dead husband
Sychaeus—but suggests that the queen's success as a leader is linked to her
chastity and remoteness from men.[33] Typically within epic, a woman can cross
the boundaries between the masculine and feminine only if she gives up her
sexuality—if she, by behaving like Diana, renounces all contact with men.[34] I
elucidated in chapter 4 how the prototype of the amazon is particularly attractive for women authors who wish to explore women's independence. Dido, in
Virgil's version of the story, is not an amazon, but she maintains control over
her people so long as she remains single and does not fall in love. This seems
to be the case also with Erina, whose flourishing is guaranteed by her solitary
existence in the woods, far from men, love, and sex.

Her perfect happiness is partly undercut when she meets Venier and begins
to feel the "uneasiness" of being alone. After an evening with the stranger, as
she rests in bed, Erina is disturbed and unable to sleep:

Erina parte, ma col cor doglioso
Su le solite piume il corpo stende;
Pensa, come l'eroe tra pochi giorni
A gli onori, a le guerre, al campo torni.

Ma non sa come i suoi pensier molesti
Le aprono il petto, alquanto di duol pieno.
(*Enr.* 5.98.5–8; 99.1–2)

---

33. By Catholic doctrinal definitions, Dido is *casta* until she meets Aeneas. Her wifely
devotion to Sychaeus is like that of Clelia and Areta. This may be one of the reasons why Marinella felt attracted to the character.

34. Suzuki 1992: 108. In the *Enrico* this is also the case with the amazon Emilia, who, thanks
to her status as virgin and warrior, is never victimized.

Erina departed and stretched her body on her usual bed *with anguish in her heart.* She thought about that hero going back to his honors, his fight, and his camp in a few days.

She did not know why, but these worrisome thoughts got into her heart, already filled with anguish.

In the description of Erina's confused state, Marinella echoes Dido's love pangs and insomnia (*at regina gravi iamdudum saucia cura / volnus alit . . . nec placidam membris dat cura quietem*, "But already the queen tormented by a profound anxiety / nourishes the wound . . . her concern does not grant placid rest to her limbs" *Aen.* 4.1–2. . .5) after meeting Aeneas, whose look and deeds had triggered her amazement (*obstipuit primo adspectu*, "she marveled at first meeting him," *Aen.* 1.613) and an invitation to her splendid home for an opulent banquet:

> . . . Simul Aeneam in regia ducit
> . . . .
> At domus interior regali splendida luxu
> Instruitur, mediisque parant convivia tectis;
> Arte laboratae vestes ostroque superbo,
> Ingens argentum mensis, caelataque in auro
> Fortia facta partum, series longissima rerum
> Per tot ducta viros antiqua ab origine.
> (*Aen.* 1.631, 637–42)

> So she speaks, and leads Aeneas into the royal house
> . . . .
> The interior of the palace
> Is laid out with royal luxury, and they prepare
> A feast in the center of the palace: covers worked
> Skillfully in princely purple, massive silverware
> On the tables, and her forefathers' heroic deeds
> Engraved in gold, a long series of exploits traced
> Through many heroes, since the ancient origins of her people.

Venier, like Aeneas, receives warm hospitality in Erina's sumptuous house. Besides the beauty and richness of the room, the objects at the banquet, and the protagonists' attraction, the element that makes the two dinner parties particularly similar is the presence of a bard who, during the feast, does not sing the typical theme of "the arms of men" but about the wonders of the universe.[35]

Poignantly, in the *Aeneid* at Dido's court we have the wise Iopas, who sings about different natural phenomena and their causes:

> . . . Cithara crinitus Iopas
> Personat aurata, docuit quem maximus Atlas.
> Hic canit errantem lunam solisque labores,
> Unde hominum genus et pecudes, unde imber et ignes
> Arcturum pluviasque Hyadas geminosque Triones:
> Quid tantum Oceano properent se tinguere soles
> Hiberni, vel quae tardis mora noctibus obstet.
> Ingeminant plausu Tyrii, Troesque sequuntur. (*Aen.* 1.740–47)

> . . . Iopas, the long-haired
> Who learned from great Atlas, plucked his golden lyre
> And sang of the wandering moon and the sun's labors,
> Where men and beasts came from, the origins of rain and fire,
> Of Arcturus, the rainy Hyades, the two Bears:
> Why the winter suns rush to dip themselves into the sea,
> And what delay makes the slow nights linger.
> The Tyrians redoubled their applause, the Trojans did the same.

On Erina's island we have the female bard Altea, who sings at the banquet for Venier. The presence of a bard in the royal houses of epic poems signals civilized life. Odysseus encounters the bard Demodocos in the palace of Nausicaa, and then there is the bard Phemios in Ithaca. Yet only Iopas entertains the court with "causes," which she knows like the happy man of *Georgics* 2:

> Felix qui potuit rerum cognoscere causas
> Atque metus omnis et inexorabile fatum
> Subiecit pedibus strepitumque Acherontis avari.
> (*Geor.* 2.490–92)

---

35. Adler 2003: 9–17; Brown 1990; Farrell 2014: 8off. Kinsey 1979; Segal 1971. For the importance of Iopas in the Italian cultural world of Boccaccio and Dante, see Carranza 2002. The best description of "Dido's Phaeacian heritage" is in Gordon 2012: 61ff., esp. 63. For Lucretius as an intertext for *Aen.* 4, see Hardie 1986: 90ff., 180ff.; Dyson 1996; Kinsey 1979; Poschl 1962: 161–64. For *Aeneid*'s adaptations in the Italian Cinquecento, see Savoretti 2001.

Happy is he who has been able to learn the causes of things and has set all
fear, and unrelenting fate, and the noise of greedy Acheron, under his feet.

According to Servius, "a song about philosophy fits well a banquet organized
by a chaste woman" (*bene philosophica introducitur cantilena in convivio regi-
nae adhuc castae*).[36] Virgil's Iopas undoubtedly signals the importance of philosophy and Epicurean science. P. Gordon underscores how in the Epicurean
tradition "learning and pleasure take place at the same time (*Sent. Vat.* 27)."
She also stresses the connection between happiness and physics in Epicurus by
citing the *Letter to Herodotus,* where the philosopher writes: "we must believe
that obtaining accurate knowledge of the causes of the most important matters is the point of natural science, and that happiness depends on the knowledge of celestial phenomena."[37] The mention of causes and Virgil's attention
to philosophical discourse are of great interest to Marinella, who in Erina's
palace inserts a female bard singing about similar themes and entertaining
the guests with the aid of science rather than with a war song. Altea and her
regard for natural phenomena confirm not only Marinella's desire to fashion
an enchantress interested in philosophy but also her wish to insert women
into the nascent scientific discourse. In addition to functioning as an important factor in Marinella's defense of women's moral and intellectual prowess,
scientific discourse "serves more generally in these narratives to position them
within an evolving cultural transition from Neoplatonic approaches to natural
philosophy and 'natural magic,' to the rationalism that characterized Galileo's
'new' science."[38]

   With her "sweet cithara" and "the song of the Sirens" ("dolce cetra, e
canto di Sirena," *Enr.* 5.87.2), Altea sings about the universe. Her knowledge
of nature represents for our narrator the most attractive allure. The content
of the song is described for several stanzas (*Enr.* 5.89–93). Like Iopas, Altea
sings about air condensed by cold (89), comets and hail (90), why seawater
rises (91), and more:

   Come poi chiuso de la terra in seno
   Vento crudel gli alti edificii scuote;
   Perchè si mostri il ciel chiaro e sereno,
   Mentre trepido il pian crolla e percote:
   Perchè dal sol la luce venga meno,
   Mentre più splende ne l'eterne rote,

---

36. Servius, ad. *Aen.* 1.742.
37. This quote and the previous one are from Gordon 2012: 64.
38. Ray 2015: 99–100.

Ed eclissi la luna, a che si mostri
Or ritonda ed or scema a gli occhi nostri.
(*Enr.* 5.92)

[She sang about] how a cruel wind in the bowels of the earth shakes high
buildings; why the sky is clear and bright when the anxious plain is shaken
and hit; why the light of sun dims when it shines the most in the sky,
eclipsing the moon, and why the moon appears round or missing a part to
our eyes.[39]

The lines inspired by Iopas's song (*Aeneid* 1.740–77) in turn evoke *Georgics*
2.475–82:

As for me, may the sweet Muses, supreme above all,
Whose rites, I celebrate, stirred by a great love,
Receive me, and show me heaven's roads, and the stars,
The sun's many eclipses, the moon's labors,
Where earthquakes come from, forces that swell the deep seas,
Bursting their barriers, then sinking back again into themselves:
Why winter suns rush so to dip themselves in the ocean,
And what it is that holds back the slow nights.
(*Geor.* 2.475–82, trans. Kline)

If ultimately in *Georgics* 2.484 the narrator renounces the celebration of
nature, he is convinced that he will receive blessedness in the enjoyment of
the countryside and anonymity away from political turmoil:

But if the chill blood around my heart prevents me
From reaching those regions of nature, let the country
And the flowing streams in the valleys please [*placeant*] me,
Let me love [*amem*] the rivers and the woods, unknown [*ingloriosus*].
(*Geor.* 2.483–86, trans. Kline)

He who's been able to learn the causes of things is happy,
And has set all fear, and unrelenting fate, and the noise
Of greedy Acheron, under his feet. And he's happy too,
Who knows the woodland gods, Pan,
And old Sylvanus, and the Nymphs, his sisters.

---

39. Marinella 2009 (adapted). Cf. Ray 2015: 106: "Echoing Corinna's words about the per-
petual transformation of natural elements in the second day of Fonte's *Worth of Women*, Altea
explains the cycle of production and disintegration that is essential alchemical in nature."

The honors of the crowd, royal purple, won't move him,
Nor the discord stirring treacherous brothers,
The Dacians swooping down from perjured Danube,
The wealth of Rome, or doomed kingdoms.
(*Geor.* 2.490–98, trans. Kline)

The text here may be separating the physicists who by following Lucretius and rejecting the gods have lost their fear of the afterworld (2.490–92) from "the ruralists" who promote religion and interaction with minor divinities (2.492–94).[40] Ultimately, however, both categories seem to fare well, being described as "happy" and "lucky." Contemplation—whether of the heavens or the countryside—is presented as an activity absorbing and satisfying in and of itself.[41] Furthermore, philosophers and lovers of the countryside are associated with a neglect of public life. They do not care and are not moved by people's reputation or by a will of distinguishing themselves in war. They are immune to the pleasures of wealth and greed. Erina is this kind of individual: appreciative of the solitude necessary for studying, eager to immerse herself in the knowledge of nature, and spiteful of political activity that she deems treacherous. Her bard Altea celebrates the topics she appreciates the most.

Apollonius of Rhodes's Song of Orpheus in *Argonautica* 1.496–511—with its emphasis on oblivion—appears as another possible reference for Altea's song. Apollonius explains how Orpheus, singing about the earth, heaven, and sea and different natural phenomena (lines 512–18), enchants and pacifies the hearts of the warriors. The song is sung to pacify the unruly and belligerent Argonauts.[42] Similarly, Altea's song should charm and calm the Venetian. Like Odysseus on the islands of Circe, Calypso, or Nausicaa, Venier is eager to leave Erina's island, but he forgets about his sorrow and eagerness to fight when he listens to Altea ("l'eroe pose in non cale, a i dolci carmi / le tempeste del mare, l'amor de l'armi," "thanks to these sweet songs, our hero forgot the tempest at sea and his love for fighting," *Enr.* 5.94.7–8). It is the only time that oblivion occurs in the mind of the soldier, who otherwise is troubled about the island's remoteness and yearns to return to the war.

Marinella uses many ancient sources in the depiction of Erina's island, framed as an idealized place in which women, happy and isolated, can rule themselves and pursue knowledge as their ultimate goal. Symbolically, it corresponds to the beautiful garden described by Moderata Fonte at the beginning of *Il merito,* where the seven women protagonists of the dialogue gather

---

40. Adler 2003: 11–12.
41. Miles 1980: 153.
42. Perkell 1999: 29–49.

to talk at ease. Unfortunately, but realistically, women's thriving and ability to speak freely can occur only in a community of women; their state of blessedness appears built on the absence of men.

WOMEN AND THE *LOCUS AMOENUS*

Although Nausicaa is the most important ancient prototype for Erina, the reception of Circe in Renaissance Italy must be considered when approaching any representation of the enchantress in this period. Circe, as the most famous sorceress of classical mythology and the transformer of the companions of the wandering Odysseus into beasts, was an immensely popular subject in the art and literature of the late Renaissance. The lesson of the deep complementarity and essential equality of the genders embedded in Homer's version of the Circe-Odysseus myth was forgotten in the work of later writers, many of whom considered beautiful and powerful women dangerous and inferior to men. This is the notion assigned to Circe by Boccaccio's text *On Famous Women*: "If we consider human behavior," Boccaccio writes, "we can well understand . . . that there are many Circes everywhere and many other men are changed into beasts by their lustfulness and their vices. And Ulysses, instructed by Mercury's advice, obviously signifies the wise man who cannot be bound by the trickery of deceitful people and who by his example often loosens the bonds of those who are held" (*Famous Women*, 75–76).[43] The typical source for Circe's visual and literary depiction during the Renaissance was not Homer's *Odyssey*, but the writings of Boccaccio, Virgil (*Aeneid* 7), Ovid (*Metamorphoses* 14), Augustine (*City of God*, 17.17–18), and Boethius (*De consolatione philosophiae*, 38.1), in whose works the woman was an emblem of spiritual enslavement.

The most important transformation in the depiction of Circe in post-Homeric writers is her reduction from understanding goddess and benevolent lover to wicked enchantress and whore. Virgil presents Circe as a "cruel Goddess" (*dea saeva, Aen.* 7.19) who lives "in a lofty palace" (*tectisque superbis, Aen.* 7.12) on a "dreadful shore" (*litora dira, Aen.* 7.22) and who "with her powerful herbs" (*potentibus herbis, Aen.* 7.19) can transform men "into the form and pelts of brutes" (*in voltus ac terga ferarum, Aen.* 7.20). Ovid also makes Circe the embodiment of lust. In his *Metamorphoses*, she is aggressive and vengeful, perfectly able to control nature (*Met.* 14.406–15) and ready to transform men into animals if they do not submit to her sexual advances (e.g.,

---

43. Translation from Boccaccio 2003. Background information about Boccaccio's text can be found in Kolsky 2003.

Picus, *Met.* 14.320–96). Above all, the Homeric allegorists and several Christian writers crafted the image "of a voluptuous Circe, beckoning the rational, temperate Odysseus to drink from her poisoned cup" and possessing "obvious similarities to the figure of Eve holding out the fruit of the Tree of Knowledge to a still-innocent Adam in Genesis 3."[44]

Writers like St. Paul, St. Augustine, and Boethius were particularly harsh on women and enchantresses throughout the Middle Ages, and in the Renaissance women's status worsened. Almost inexorably, the identification of women with nature, sensuality, and ultimately with sin was set in opposition to the spiritual superiority of men, so that the encounter of Odysseus and Circe for the next several centuries was considered a conflict between good and evil, soul and body. A practical exemplification of Circe's degeneration appears in European books of emblems. Here the view of Circe as sexual seductress—drawn from a long medieval allegorizing tradition that also included the *Moralized Ovid* and John of Frankfurt[45]—became widespread. This new genre, beginning with Andrea Alciato's *Emblemata*, published in Augsburg by Heinrich Steiner in 1531, used pictures, poems, and mottoes to impart moralizing messages to their readers. One of the earliest images of Circe appeared in the 1546 edition of the *Emblemata* published in Venice by the sons of Aldus Manutius.[46] In this collection we can see how in the sixteenth century the metamorphosis of Odysseus's men is interpreted as a loss of human reason, and Circe embodies the vice that enslaves reason.[47]

In Renaissance chivalric poems, the negativity of Circe-like figures continues to be visible in characters like the lovely Dragontina (*Orlando Innamorato*); the gorgeous Alcina, who in the *Furioso* entraps Ruggiero; and the enchanting

---

44. Yarnall 1994: 91; Franco 2012: 7–23.

45. *Ovide moralisé* (*Moralized Ovid*) was composed in the early fourteenth century in France and offered readers a verse adaptation of Ovid's *Metamorphoses* in Old French as well as more than 60,000 lines of philosophical and theological commentary. The text of Ovid was therefore informed by the Christian Bible and other Latin and vernacular authorities, through which the anonymous Franciscan friar who composed the text guides his Christian readers on a redemptive quest. For John of Frankfurt, see Kieckhefer 2000: 29. A negative view of Circe informed Neoplatonic thinkers such as Cristoforo Landino and Giovanni Pico. The history of the reception of Circe is of paramount importance when we evaluate Marinella's different approach to a Circe-like character such as Erina.

46. Zika 2002: 24; 2007.

47. In the 1546 Venetian Aldine edition, the image includes Circe with a rod in front of a group of swine. The title "Beware of Whores" is accompanied by the following words: "So great, we are told, was the power of Circe, daughter of the Sun, that she turned many persons into new monstrous shapes. A witness to this is Picus, tamer of horses, and Scylla with her double form, and the Ithacans who became pigs after drinking the wine. Circe with her famous name indicates a whore and shows that any man who loves such one loses his reason." For this edition I have consulted Alciato at Glasgow: http://www.emblems.arts.gla.ac.uk/alciato/index.php

Armida, who in the *Liberata* entices knights (above all Rinaldo) away from their military duties to pursue pleasure and idleness.[48] In *Orlando Innamorato,* Dragontina's lures are dramatized in her Garden and Loggia (6.47–48), whose walls portray the tale of Ulysses and Circe as *luxuria* (6.49–50). It is not difficult to realize that "Alcina's island is Ariosto's 'Island of the Blest' (Pindar II.72), his milk-and-honey land of eternal youth and beauty where Ruggiero will follow in the footsteps of Ulysses, Aeneas, and Hercules."[49] In chivalric poems the brief account of the earthly paradise of Genesis, from which Christian authors draw, becomes interwoven with the splendid gardens of classical myth and the Golden Age. The luscious garden in which these women live can be read as representative of their erotic allure, of their attempt to confuse upright men with their luxuriantly seductive beauty. Yet both Ariosto and Tasso, elaborating on the theme, go beyond simplistically warning against a temptation of the senses embodied by beautiful ladies. I argue that Marinella's description of Erina's island, besides being inspired by Homer and the classical texts analyzed above, capitalizes on Ariosto, Tasso, and Neoplatonic explorations of the topic.[50] Ultimately, Erina's earthly paradise is a symbol of men's desire for a perfect union with God, once enjoyed in Eden.[51] Her island is fraught with spiritual implications; it suggests inner happiness and balance, "the Paradise within"[52] of the good man (and woman). In addition, the role of Marinella's enchantress turns out to be important because she embodies a model for the scientist-philosopher who strives to be closer to God by using her mind. Finally, in her ability to enlighten Venier with the sheer force of her eloquence despite being removed from the world, Erina is a double for the poet who is eager to influence her society through books rather than through public action. Erina is the narrative embodiment of Marinella.[53]

Nature offers itself to Venier in all its allure when, after being shipwrecked, he discovers the delightful Erina and her island. It is an Edenic world of natural plenty. At first, their encounter resembles traditional encounters between beautiful women and warriors who, against their will, find themselves in a distant and verdant corner of the earth. The context and setting activate the

---

48. In the *Orlando Innamorato,* Angelica, Dragontina, Falerina, Origille, and the nymphs of the Laughing Stream function as sensual distractions; see Cavallo 1993: 42–48 and 146. For an overview of the dynamics between men and women in Tasso's poem, see Benedetti 1993.

49. MacCarthy 2004: 325.

50. Lazzari 2012: 16, for whom Marinella is eager to provide "alternative endings to corresponding episodes in Tasso's *Gerusalemme Liberata.*" For a Neoplatonic framing of Ariosto's poem, see Marinelli 1987: esp. 11–17; Ascoli 1987: 109; Picchio 2007.

51. Cf. Harrison 2008: x: "one way or another, in their very concept and their humanly created environments, gardens stand for a kind of haven, if not a kind of heaven."

52. The expression is from *Paradise Lost* 12.587.

53. The same idea can be found in Galli Stampino 2014: 82–83.

expectations of a *locus amoenus*: in a beautiful, wooded, and remote corner of the earth similar to an earthly paradise we find a woman who threatens the hero's progress toward his goal.[54] As Peter Brand observes:

> The most prominent gardens in Cinquecento narrative poetry are of course the enchanted creations of wicked women, which provide not reverence or spiritual uplift but temptation and moral confusion. An almost obligatory stage in the epic hero's adventure is his exposure to a beautiful garden inhabited by a seductive female who distracts him from his Christian purpose until he discovers the falsity of this seeming paradise, turns his back on its creator and resumes his duty: Boiardo, Francesco Bello, Poliziano, Ariosto, Trissino, Tasso all compose some of their most memorable verse on this theme. Central to most of their versions is the recollection of a Golden Age when men and women enjoyed nature's blessings unadulterated and unhindered.[55]

The gardens of Renaissance romance epics are not rewards for virtue, but function as temptations and illusions. They must be discovered as counterfeit before man can access true paradise. Yet in Marinella's story the garden and the woman work in a different way.

Brand's description is a starting point. His views record a well established polarity in the Renaissance imagination that, shaped by ancient and medieval gender prejudices, routinely identifies women as the negative pole. But this interpretation of earthly paradises does not do justice to the complex exploration that authors like Tasso and Ariosto enact by introducing the enchantress and the *locus amoenus* motif in their poems. Often the *locus amoenus* and the beautiful woman occupy the same space, not simply embodying a threat but advanced even as a tool to survey an intricate set of related and tussled issues. Not only does the garden becomes the sight of a struggle in a man's soul wrenched between earthly pursuits and more spiritual objectives, but it is also a locus of deep reflection, where Christian values and classical heritage confront each other, spirit and matter collide, romance and epic tendencies wrestle. In Ariosto's *Orlando Furioso,* Alcina tries to lure Ruggiero away from

---

54. Curtius 1953: 182–202 documents the tradition of the *locus amoenus* beginning with Homer's epic and continuing into the Middle Ages. Cf. Ceccantini 1996; Duncan 1972; Giamatti 1966; Patanè 1996. Boccaccio famously spells out the connection between the *locus amoenus* and paradise in *Decameron* (day 3, intr.): "The sight of this garden, so beautifully laid out, with its plants and the fountain and the watercourse fed by it, so that, were it possible to build a heaven on earth, they would be at a loss to know how else to embody it but as this garden" (trans. Waldman). For the *locus amoenus* in the *Decameron*, see Raja 2003.

55. As quoted in Saccone 1997: 11.

the fighting, but in the end the hero pries himself from her magic tricks. Alcina's story can be interpreted allegorically, with the woman cast as temptation, the archetypical Circe turning her lovers into beasts and making them forget about their duties toward their companions, but this interpretation has shortcomings. In the Alcina segment, Ariosto seems influenced by philosophical tendencies, and it can be understood as a "self-contained Neoplatonist philosophical fiction" in which the triad of women-sorceresses Alcina, Melissa, and Logistilla represent sensual love, human love, and intellectual love, respectively.[56] Ruggiero is exposed to all three, but their different revelations and lessons do not help him to change. Even after he has experienced Logistilla's wonderful castle immersed in a perennially lush wood (*OF* 10.61–62) and learned to drive her hippogriff (*OF* 10.67–68), he does not become detached from the senses nor does he attain intellectual enlightenment, because in *OF* 10.114–15 we see him trying to rape Angelica.

In the light of this episode, Ita MacCarthy, undermining philosophical interpretations, concludes that there is no ascending route at work in the *Furioso,* but rather "the oscillatory pull of the seemingly bipolar and mutually exclusive impulses of sensuality and reason."[57] Ariosto does not blame Ruggiero for his sensual attraction nor chastise Alcina, which is why her island is depicted so delightfully and memorably.[58] Besides the aesthetic import of the description, Alcina's significance is also highlighted through her sorrow and because she is allowed to survive in the story. When she is defeated, she remains alive even if she wishes to die after losing her beloved Ruggiero. In her suffering, as she captures our compassion, her status of villain is compromised. The complexity of the character of Alcina, born from a tangle of emotions that stir the heart and mind, helps us to grasp the sophistication of Ariosto's treatment of the topic. In the *Orlando Furioso,* the archetypal seductress becomes a victim who challenges the reader's capacity to assign well defined roles and to distinguish between good and bad. Finally, confusion and displacement of tidy borders can be seen in the similarity between the fake garden of Alcina (*OF* 6.20–22) and the real garden of Logistilla: even if one is the product of misleading magic and the other is the genuine fruit of attentive cultivation (*OF* 10.63), they look alike.[59] By juxtaposing real paradises

---

56. In the *Orlando Furioso,* Melissa is a good sorceress helping to bring together Ruggiero and Bradamante. Logistilla is also a good fairy, as well as Alcina's sister (Canto 10).

57. MacCarthy 2004: 340.

58. Brand 1974: 67.

59. Even the terrestrial paradise to which Astolfo ascends with the hippogriff at *OF* 34 is shaped as a *locus amoenus.* This garden is not the product of magic, and it provides a sort of perfect paradigm against which the regular world should be measured. When Astolfo looks at it, he undermines his world: "Astolfo on his steed ambled slowly . . . admiring the beautiful

to replicas and underlining their similarity, Ariosto suggests that all kinds of beautifully wooded enclaves must be evaluated carefully in order to discover what exactly it is that they reveal, if indeed in them a man will thrive or be destroyed.

The *locus amoenus* appears again, and with an altogether different meaning in Canto 1 of the *Orlando Furioso*. Here Angelica, the beautiful princess of Cathay, after stirring the desire of countless knights in Charlemagne's court, flees and finds herself in a grove filled with trees and two limpid brooks (*OF* 1.35.3–8). The wood is conceptualized not as Dante's dangerous dark wood from which one wants to escape but rather as a place where anything can happen, as "the locus, *par excellence,* of communication and adventure, where *errare,* to wander is both positive and negative."[60] The grove signals a fork in the road, a place where a significant shift can occur. Marinella develops this aspect of the *locus amoenus,* conceiving of Venier's arrival on the island as a momentous time for his development.

Other gardens lingering in Marinella's mind while composing her poem are those of Tasso. In the *Gerusalemme Liberata,* the cipher of the garden has an even greater resonance and looms large. Armida's garden(s) appear to have all the characteristics of the *locus amoenus* (trees, water, ornate palaces), and Tasso indulges in their description. In *GL* 14.57*ff.,* we see Armida's garden by the river Orontes, and in octave 68, Armida, mounting a magic chariot, transports Rinaldo to the Island of Fortune, in the most secluded corner of the earth "in the immense ocean, where boats rarely or never touch the shore" ("nell'Oceano Immenso, ove alcun legno / rado o non mai va dalle nostre

---

scene on every side. As he compared what he saw with this rank world we live in, he dismissed our world as ugly and evil and loathed by Heaven and nature in comparison with the sweetness, light and happiness up there" (*OF* 34.5, trans. Waldman). Astolfo's voyage echoes a variety of different works, such as Lucian's *Icaromenippus,* Cicero's *Somnium,* and Dante's Paradise in the *Divine Comedy.* Its ultimate meaning is elusive and, to me, intentionally so. In his lunar travel, Astolfo discovers how "pride and idolatry are thus two sides of the same coin, both forms of worshiping the human, of trying to assign intrinsic value and substance in a world of shifting appearances and uncertain identity" (Ascoli 1987: 280). Yet Astolfo's episode can be viewed as an exploration "of religious faith, with the suggestion that an ethics of words cannot survive at all without a transcendent guarantor" (Ascoli 1987: 285). I find Ascoli's perspective on this topic sound. Although scholars usually dismiss the metaphysical side of Ariosto's text, it remains an important aspect of the *Furioso,* especially when we consider a character like John the Evangelist, who ponders how "the medicine" for Orlando cannot be found on earth and necessitates another kind of travel ("altro viaggio," *OF* 34.67.1). Whether Astolfo's education follows Neoplatonism, secular humanism, or a Christian faith that combines and transcends the two—the fetching of his and Orlando's wits would playfully yet effectively depict this educational ascent—he clearly obtains it, not for the purpose of going farther up but because he wants to bring it down on earth. See Ascoli 1987: 271; Quint 1977; Parrett 2004: 33–34. Interesting observations on Astolfo's voyage can be found in Bassi 2004; Gulizia 2008: 160; Segre 1966: 85–95.

60. Saccone 1997: 4.

sponde," *GL* 14.69.5–6). Again this place features wild animals, luxuriant and fruitful nature, and a richly decorated palace. In his analysis of "the spectacle of the world," which includes the above-mentioned gardens and their women, Giovanni Getto stresses the importance of the "figurative state" of the *Gerusalemme*. Getto notices that at times, with great enthusiasm, Tasso abandons the theme of arms to give substance to other worlds (characters, emotions, values) that are far away from war and help the narrator and other characters escape it.[61] The longest among these detours is that featuring the love between Rinaldo and Armida, so that "the beautiful enchantress not only tears the Christian knight away from the camp, but embodies a temptation for the poet, determining a kind of break of equilibrium in the compositional structure of the *Gerusalemme*. Cantos 14, 15, and 16 represent the most lavish holiday for Tasso's imagination along the itinerary of the Crusade."[62] Getto (and Tasso) expose their readers to exotic landscapes interpretable as temptations into worlds and ideals that an orthodox Catholic writer should, at least a priori, reject. All of Armida's residences are segregated and gladdened by "grottoes and waters and flowers and grasses and plants" ("antri ed acque e fiori ed erbe e piante," *GL* 14.59.3), and by lingering in the reader's memory mysteriously, hypnotically, and powerfully dispel the allure of *fama*, worldly renown.

At *GL* 14.62–64 the warning about the futility of fame, although coming from Armida qualified as an "illusory siren" ("magica larva," 61.4), rings true and has the flavor of a philosophical reflection:

Folli, perché gettate il caro dono,
Che breve è sì, di vostra età novella?
Nome senza soggetto, idoli sono
Ciò che pregio e valore il mondo appella.
La fama che invaghisce a un dolce suono
Voi superbi mortali, e par sí bella,
È un ecco, un sogno, anzi del sogno un'ombra[63]
Ch'ad ogni vento si dilegua e sgombra.
(*GL* 14.63)

Fools, why do you throw away the gift
Of your youth which is so short?
Virtue and honor themselves

---

61. Getto 1977: 179–209. The first citation alludes to the title of the chapter (*Lo spettacolo del mondo*), and the other, which I translate as "figurative state," appears in the original Italian as *condizione figurativa* (179).

62. Ibid., 179–80.

63. Cf. Pindar, *Pythian* 8.95 ("man is a dream of shadow").

Are but idle names, idols, prized by the world.
Fame which bewitches with tickling pleasure
You proud mortals and seems so beautiful
Is an echo, a dream, the shadow of a dream
Which disappears and goes away with every wind. (my trans.)

Even if one realizes that what Armida offers his guest—peace satisfying the fragile senses ("l'alma tranquilla appaghi i sensi frali," *GL* 14.64.2)—is not more substantial than the object she deems fleeting and illusory (fame granted by the world), with a philosophical undertone her gift is presented as a more natural goal: "This is knowledge," she explains, "this is the happy life: this nature teaches and commands" ("questo è saver, questa è felice vita: / sí l'insegna natura e sí l'addita," *GL* 14.64.7–8). Human commitment to the goals of the active life (virtue and honor) is redrawn as foolish in its tendency to make one forget about mortality. The futility of success and earthly renown are again perceived when Carlo and Ubaldo, en route to free Rinaldo, traverse Hercules's pillars on the magic Vessel of Fortune, depicted as a woman who shows them the entire world, including the site where Carthage once rose:

Giace l'alta Cartago: a pena i segni
De l'alte ruine il lido serba.
Muoiono le città, muoiono i regni,
Copre i fasti e le pompe arena ed erba,
E l'uom d'esser mortal par che si sdegni:
Oh nostra mente cupida e superba!
(*GL* 15.20.1–6)

Great Carthage lies, barely the coast
Preserves the signs of its great ruins.
So cities fall, kingdoms perish
Sand and grass cover their immensity and pomp
While human beings seem to fret at the idea of mortality:
O our mind eager and proud! (my trans.)

In this exclamation, political success and urban greatness are dismissed, and Fortune is the prophetess of men's foolish beliefs and their constant desire to neglect and forget their impermanence. From the magic skiff, the entire universe is observed, and Carlo and Ubaldo must confront their "smallness" in the vastness of the world and in the movement of time. Marinella uses a similar strategy in the episode of Erina showing Venier the world from her magic chariot.

Jo Ann Cavallo does not discuss Armida's environment; instead, she sur-veys how Tasso's poem innovatively develops the typology of the enchantress. She claims that in the *Gerusalemme Liberata,* through Armida's union with Rinaldo, Tasso's epic breaks with the stereotypical image of the wicked *maga* and creates a different model. In this interpretation, the centripetal geom-etry of Tasso's epic is compromised by Armida, who pushes the order of the poem centrifugally toward romance. Cavallo's reading is captivating because it illustrates a wider and deeper way to view this subject, and her interpreta-tion resonates with Getto's.[64] In the representation of Armida, she sees a rap-prochement of forces that are normally felt as opposed and inimical (men vs. women; Christian vs. pagan; reason vs. appetites, etc.). When in Canto 20 Armida and Rinaldo finally come together, each of them professes to be the other's servant; Armida becomes a Christian, and Rinaldo confirms himself a courteous knight desirous, above all, to satisfy his beloved. This reunion must be used to reevaluate the plot: if in Canto 16 Armida could be constructed as a traditional obstacle—the beautiful woman hindering the hero in the fulfill-ment of his mission[65]—at the end of the poem, it is rather the holy war that is a parenthesis for Rinaldo, who is reminded by a defeated Armida about his vow ("e gli sovien che si promise in fede / suo cavalier quando da lei partia," "and he remembers to have promised in faith to be her knight when he left her," *GL* 20.122.3–4). Therefore, their story happily concludes when he manifests his will to the woman. He does not intend to preserve her in order to enslave her, but wants to rule with her; he will remain her servant and champion ("Armida, il cor turbato omai tranquilla: / non a gli scherni, al regno io ti riservo; / nemico no, ma tuo campione e servo." "Armida, bid your stormy heart be still: / I keep you for a kingdom, not for spite—/no enemy, but your faithful champion knight," *GL* 20.134.6–8, trans. Wickert). It is an important moment of closure featuring a Christian and his enemy coming together productively. Their union will create a long and famous lin-eage.[66] Diversity is reconciled, and the generation of offspring underlines the fruitfulness of the encounter. Love proves long-lasting and offers a resolution against wrath ("sorse amor contro l'ira," "love rose against anger," *GL* 20.63.1). Many of Cavallo's observations are insightful, although she does not stress enough that Armida can have a place in the *Liberata* only after she accepts Rinaldo's religious creed: Armida must renounce her pagan prerogatives and

64. Cavallo 2004: 213 (Tasso is "the only epic poet to merge woman as deviation and woman as endpoint . . . into the very same person"); Getto 1977: 149–78, esp. 175.

65. When Armida goes to Goffredo's camp to persuade him to fight for her, her eloquence is called stronger than Circe or Medea (*GL* 4.86). See Migiel 1987: 149–66; Gough 2001.

66. The vow was contracted at *GL* 16.54. For an overview of Armida and Rinaldo's relation-ship and the renewed emphasis on reciprocity and reproduction, see Schachter 2010: 234–39.

be absorbed by the world of Rinaldo, masculinity, and Christianity before she can be integrated into the text.[67]

Ultimately, when Marinella decides to include an enchantress and a *locus amoenus* in her poem, she draws from the classical tradition (especially Homer and Virgil) but also from her most immediate predecessors (Ariosto, Tasso, and Fonte). Erina can and must be allegorically interpreted, but not as an Eve. Marinella plays with the clichés of the pagan woman and the sorceress, ultimately creating a unique figure who, despite being unbaptized, wants to bring the epic hero closer to inner happiness. Erina is a redemptive figure committed to leading men to salvation.

---

67. Benedetti 1993: 34.

CHAPTER 6

Away from the City

ERINA'S ISLAND REMINDS us of the peaceful environment of pastoral poems, which is not accidental. E. R. Curtius defined the *locus amoenus* as a beautiful, shaded, natural site where lovers can meet and embrace. But at the heart of pastoral poetry is the desire to take refuge in a bygone era (the Golden Age) by seeking a perfect place or environment, or by devising a differently arranged society (the world of the sophisticated albeit melancholy shepherd).[1] In other words, what appears as a constant element in pastoral literature is the recognition of a contrast (implicit or explicit) between pastoral life and a contemporary, more complex, type of society.[2] Certainly Marinella does not insert Erina into a lovely landscape to let her and Venier delight each other in it, but uses the woman and her island to highlight the contrast between an almost ideal society of peace and contemplation (where women are prominent) and another more realistic one, of turmoil and anxiety, led by men.

---

1. Curtius 1953: 195; Fernandez-Cañadas De Greenwood 1983: 131.

2. Bernard 1989 (about the interconnections between pastoralism, politics, and philosophy) remains seminal; Greg 1906: 4; Fernandez-Cañadas De Greenwood 1983; Giamatti 1966; Leach 1974; Lerner 1972: 11–41; Poggioli 1975; Putnam 1970; Williams 1973. In 1600, Marinella composed a pastoral romance called *Arcadia Felice* (*Happy Arcadia*). The modern text is edited by Lavocat (Marinella 1998). Even in this poem the sojourn in Arcadia is considered an initiation into moral progress, and the protagonist Ersilia is not in love. Cf. Marinella 1998: 43; Malpezzi and Ristaino 2008: 25–37. For women and the pastoral genre, see Bossier 2010; Campiglia 2004 (introduction); Cox 2011: 92–119; Torelli 2006.

The dynamics at work in pastoral literature are those archetypically employed by Virgil in *Eclogue* 1, where we meet Tityrus, who lives a blessed life in the country while Meliboeus toils in the urban environment.[3] The setting is the *locus amoenus* where Tityrus can rejoice in a peace that recalls philosophical ataraxy, the productive stillness of the sage and the gods. Epicurean philosophy characterizes Virgil's *Eclogues,* in which the philosophical *otium* (leisure) practiced by Tityrus is morally justifiable and conducive to the cultivation of the divine.[4] In the *Enrico,* Erina, like Tityrus, lives in peace and strives to get closer to nature; Venier, on the other hand, comes from a world of violence and is attracted to earthly glory. Their dialogue unfolds outside the city within an ideal landscape like that in Plato's *Phaedrus* (230b–c), where Socrates and Phaedrus discuss the immortality of the soul. This space, away from the disorder of cities, is prototypical of enchantment and rapture and is meant to lead the characters to the essence of things.[5] In *Phaedrus,* Socrates, at first maintaining that he has nothing to learn from trees and the countryside, eventually praises his interlocutor for having pointed out how to link nature to his desire to know (230d). Erina will similarly try to use nature as a philosophical tool to guide Venier toward a better understanding of human life.

At this point, it should be clear that "pastoral" does not designate a genre but "a state of mind."[6] It is possible to find pastoral moments even in the heart of an epic poem. The juxtaposition of epic and pastoral invites reflection because they mirror contrasting ways to perceive the world. From the pastoral viewpoint, the subject matter of epic celebration (e.g., quests and conquests) reveals the degeneration and decadence that characterize the world. Epic literature "celebrates what the pastoral regrets."[7] Erina and Venier respectively embody these two different approaches to history, so that Venier celebrates and seeks what Erina spurns and rejects. The peace of Erina's island helps to bring into focus the cruelty and chaotic violence of Venice's history and Venier's world. Her voice and opinions are at odds with those of the famous writers of this age who praise communal life in the city and believe that solitude and isolation vilify human nature.[8]

3. Wright 1999: 119–23; Jenkins 1989: 26: "The *Eclogues* form probably the most influential group of short poems ever written: though they themselves take Theocritus as a model, they were to become the fountainhead from which the vast and diverse tradition of pastoral in many European literatures was to spring."

4. Rundin 2003: 165.

5. Milani 2009: 35.

6. Heninger 1961: 257.

7. Macedo 1990: 32. She is talking about Camoes's *Lusiads.*

8. E.g., Stefano Guazzo in his *La Civil Conversazione* (*Civil Conversation,* Brescia 1574), reprinted thirty-four times between 1574 and 1631, states that he who departs from civil life and lives in solitude returns to being a wild animal and takes back the name of beast or tyrant

In the *Enrico*, Erina's "pastoral vocation"—the aspiration for a better life away from the city, allowing for the development of moral perfection—is summarized in the octaves where the young woman informs Venier about the benefits of living in isolation removed from positions of power, keeping within the boundaries of reason and praising the joy of a simple existence in a natural surrounding:

> Quant'assai meglio sia frenar le voglie
> Dentro il confin d'una ragion capace;
> E saper che col regno inferno, e doglie
> Pigliansi e d'astio al cor pena vorace;
> Ecco congiure e insidie, ecco le spoglie
> Di venen tinte, e laccio e ferro e face;
> E 'l nome accorre con dispregio e danno,
> Divorator di genti e di tiranno.
> (*Enr.* 21.39)

It would be much better to keep one's wishes within the boundaries of good reason. If only one knew that with the rule one takes on hell and pain and a devouring grief and resentment! There are conspiracies, deceptions, clothing marred by poison, nooses, swords, and torches. The name of devourer of people and of tyrant circulate with contempt and damage.

> Quanto più giova a le bell'ombre o appresso
> Di un vivo fiume a le piacevol onde,
> Con dolce avena a la sua greggia spesso
> Porger diletto e far l'alme gioconde.
> D'augelli il canto udir vago e dimesso;
> E l'aura sussurar tra le foglie e fronde;
> E i tondi pomi in cibo e care l'acque
> Fur più che Bacco, al saggio e l'erba piacque.
> (*Enr.* 21.40)[9]

It is much more beneficial to enjoy one's herd and make souls happy with sweet oats under a cool shade or by the pleasant waves of a lively river! Or to listen to birds sing prettily and humbly, and to breezes whisper among

---

because he does not realize that cities and human congregations are the foundations of justice (Guazzo 1589: 13; citation in Benzoni 1991: 26). Similarly, Paolo Paruta's *Della perfezione della vita politica* (*Perfection of Political Life*, Venice 1579) is a eulogy to human virtue as civic virtue. See Benzoni 1991: 32; Garin 2008: 523.

9. Cf. Lucretius, *DRN* 2.29–33.

leaves and fronds! A wise man likes round apples and grass for food and water better than wine.

Recall that in *Eclogue* 1 Tityrus similarly describes his good fortune as *otium,* in which one can live in harmony with nature, surrounded by natural bounty and withdrawn from society.[10] Earlier in the story, to a Venier preoccupied with returning to civilization, the young maiden presented her island as a kind of escape. She reminded him that hers was a special location where he could find happiness and a chance to become divine:

> Non ti doler se 'l tuo malvagio tanto
> Destin ti ha spinto in parti erme e remote,
> Chè qui tra fiere e tronchi ancora lice
> Viver beato e 'n sé lieto e felice.
> (*Enr.* 5.80.5–8)

Do not be in pain if your very evil destiny pushed you to the wild and far-off places, because it is possible to live happy, joyful, and blessed in oneself here among wild animals and trees.[11]

> Col contemplar delle cagioni ascose
> Gli alti principi e le mirabil opre,
> Vien l'uomo divin, sue voglie gloriose,
> Per cui l'ascoso e occulto apre e discopre.
> Vieni al mio tetto, in cui gran sapere pose
> Somma bellezza, e l'oro il vela e copre.
> Io mortal donna in bel, ma frale albergo
> Vivo e l'alma e i miei strai polisco e tergo.
> (*Enr.* 5.81)

Man becomes divine by pondering the main principles of hidden causes and wonderful deeds. This is how his desires become glorious:[12] by opening to view what is hidden and unknown and by discovering it. Come to my home: great knowledge has created the highest beauty there, veiled it and covered it with gold. I am merely a mortal woman, I live in a beautiful but flimsy home, where I polish my soul and clean my arrows.

---

10. For Lucretius as an inspiration and source for Virgil's *Eclogues,* see Giesecke 1999.

11. "In oneself" ('*n sé*) is my addition to Galli Stampino's translation. It highlights the importance of inner life and is key to the notion of personal contentment.

12. Marinella 2009 (slightly adapted).

E lodo lui, che tra le stelle e 'l sole
Di sua diva bellezza eterno regna,
Che lungi dal sentier di scherzi e fole
Sè tra nebbia mirar mi fece degna:
Ed a mente mortal, che Dio ben cole
Far parte del cielo seco non isdegna.
(*Enr.* 5.82.1–6)

There I praise him who rules eternally among the stars and the sun in his eternal beauty. He made me worthy that I would stay away from tricks and illusions when I look around in the fog. And he does not scorn even a mortal mind who cultivates God to be a part of heaven with him.[13]

It is an extraordinary moment in the history of the depiction of women who live on verdant islands. Erina pronounces words that have never been uttered before by a woman, sounding more like Plato or Pico della Mirandola than Eve. She invites Venier to inquire into the causes of the universe and in that process become godlike. She praises the beauty and mercy of God, who considered her worthy of initiation to this eternal truth. She is aware that God allows "a mortal mind" who "cultivates" him ("che Dio ben cole," *Enr.* 5.82.5) to become part of his majestic order. Erina is proposing that Venier explore the benefits of the *vita contemplativa,* a path that will lead him away from his world but take him closer to the sublime structure of the universe through the study of nature. To her, this endeavor is the most important goal a man can pursue. Erina's project is a religious one, but it is also quintessentially philosophical and humanistic.[14]

Erina's character can be considered a double of the Mago d'Ascalona of Tasso's *Gerusalemme Liberata.* From his first entrance (*GL* 14.30*ff.*), the man of Ascalona appears "courteous" and "wise" (*GL* 14.31.3–4). He can walk on water (*GL* 14.33.7–8) and has knowledge of the future, which he uses to help people (*GL* 14.36.3–4). He takes Carlo and Ubaldo (*GL* 14.37)—who were looking for Rinaldo—to his home, gives the knights hospitality, and shows them what is hidden inside the earth, the source of all waters and precious metals (*GL* 14.36–40). The Mago's dwelling place, at the center of the earth, abundant with

---

13. I have modified the last two lines of the English translation by Galli Stampino.

14. Erina also resembles Erato in Marinella's *Arcadia Felice.* About her, Ray 2015: 104 has written, "Certainly, Erato embodies Marinella's model for the learned woman. Chaste and virginal, her feminine reputation is irreproachable (indeed she goes largely 'unseen' in the text); her mind is exceptional. A Diana-like figure, she is described as both hunter and 'virgin sovereign' or 'virgin oracle.' She is also a new Hypatia who contemplates and interprets the secrets of the heavens from her garden, located above the clouds."

gold and jewelry, resembles Erina's dwelling place. The wonders displayed by
Erina and the Mago evoke the marvels and mysteries of the universe pursued
by Renaissance scientists like Leonardo da Vinci and Copernicus, as well as
the natural wonders celebrated by Erina's bard Altea (cf. *supra*). In *GL* 14.43–
44, the Mago contemplates the heavens and the stars. In the *Liberata*, he represents wisdom, allowing him to place earthly goods in the right perspective. He
also stands for the failure of the intellectual tied to the court and engaged in
civil society because only in a liminal space away from the tumults of history,
beyond fallibility and action, is it plausible to assess human accomplishments
and perceive the truth that makes history meaningful.[15] Before his conversion,
he could see and reveal the secrets of nature ("spiando . . . da lor vestigi," "spy-
ing . . . give them a form," *GL* 14.42.5). After his baptism (*GL* 14.45.5–6), his
knowledge is enhanced and given a new focus (*GL* 14.46–47). He continues in
his "usual arts" (14.46.6) as God wishes, but now he finds peace only in God
("in lui m'acqueto," 14.47.1) and laughs at his previous blindness:

> Conobbi allor ch'augel notturno al sole
> È nostra mente a i rai del primo Vero;
> *E di me stesso risi* e de le fole
> Che già cotanto insuperbir mi fero.
> (*GL* 14.46.1–4)

> I saw then how like a night bird in the sun
> Is our mind in the rays of the first truth:
> *And I smiled at myself* and at my folly
> That had made me grow so proud.

The Mago and Erina live separated from history and understand what is valuable, and indirectly criticize the compromises typical of the active life.[16] They
do not withdraw from helping those in need, but are aware of the vanity of
what the world considers important. They both become symbols of the superiority of the *vita contemplativa* and represent scientific knowledge linked to
the knowledge of God.

The meditation on the *vita contemplativa* occupies the works and minds
of many Renaissance and Christian poets.[17] Even Jacob Burckhardt, a scholar
who celebrated the Renaissance as an era promoting a new kind of individual-

---

15. Ardissino 1999: 20.

16. See Alpers 1996; Bernard 1989; McGushin 2006: 136–39; Patterson 1997. The Mago and
Erina also remind us of the Muslim prophet Apollino, who in *Orlando Innamorato* is described
as "wise enchanter, astronomer and prophet" (*OI* 2.1.57).

17. Bernard 1989: 39–48.

ism, was able to recognize the motif of deification as central for many Renaissance thinkers, aware of how, "by recognizing God, the soul of the individual can draw *Him* into its narrow boundaries, but also by love of Him it can expand *itself* into the Infinite."[18] Burckhardt considers this particular way of conceiving and approaching reality (and the divine) "the blessedness on earth."[19] Recently, Jens Zimmermann again summarized the Christian character of Renaissance humanism and highlighted how Renaissance humanists reacted to failures of medieval Christian cultures out of religious concerns. The increasing rift between the church and public life triggered their renewed attempt to "forge a synthesis between faith and reason."[20] The Renaissance desire to combine faith and reason can be clearly seen in a scholar like Nicholas Cusanus (1401–64), whose ideas resemble Neoplatonic thinking but are also aligned with those of the Christian fathers. Cusanus presumes a natural religious sense and human openness to the divine, the rational pursuit of which will lead all rational creatures to the recognition of God.[21] In the creation of a character such as the unbaptized but pious Erina, Marinella promotes a similar agenda and asserts herself as a writer participating in the Renaissance milieu *and* the Catholic Reformation.

Marinella's Erina remains unbaptized, but she is framed as an enlightened pagan.[22] Venier does not offer baptism to her and she does not request it—her knowledge of nature brings her closer to God. She knows about Christ, praises his vicar on earth (*Enr.* 6.67–69), and is a firm believer of the immortality of the good souls (*Enr.* 6.63–64). Remarkably, after recounting the story of her ancestor Candiano and father Fileno, who became like God in his pursuit of science, she cries because she is aware of not being baptized. Yet she is confident that God will have mercy on her, reserving a special place for those who live a pious life (*Enr.* 6.64.7–8):[23]

Benchè di noi la salutifer' onda
La colpa original non purghi e lave,

---

18. Burckhardt 1960: 385 (emphasis original).

19. Ibid.

20. Zimmermann 2012: 107.

21. Ibid., 112. On the topic of *theosis* (deification) in Cusanus, see Hudson 2007.

22. E.g., against the Augustinian tradition, Thomas Aquinas was convinced that pagans could acquire real wisdom. His philosophical system was built on the teachings of Aristotle, and the nature of his construction was meant to demonstrate a seamless transition from the truths of human philosophy to the ones supplied by divine revelation (Marenbon 2015). Even Dante makes the pagan Cato an example of true virtue.

23. In this revelation, Erina is flirting with the idea of salvation by faith alone. Vittoria Colonna, the most famous female poet of the Early Modern Period, at times also seems to endorse the idea. See Mazzetti 1973; Bardazzi 2001.

Tant'è la fede onde il cor nostro abbonda,
Che del drago infernal timor non àve;
E l'alma qui vive si pura e monda,
Che non è che delitto uman l'aggrave;
Nè stima error il Ciel, quel che ci nega
Necessità, se l'alma a lui si piega.
(*Enr.* 6.67)

Salvation-giving waters do not cleanse and wash away our original sin, still through the great faith that is abundant in our hearts we have no fear of the infernal dragon. Our souls live so pure and innocent here that no human crime can soil it. If a soul is devout, heaven does not hold it a sin when something is denied by necessity.

Ma forse quella eterna, alta bellezza,
Non avrem noi, che serba a i più felici,
Ma gli agi, il ciel sereno e la docezza,
Che sua bontà concesse a i primi amici,
Allor che nel gran dì la somma altezza
A l'alme, o buone o ree, liete, o infelici
Darà la gran sentenza, i più perfetti
Vedranno Dio, n'avran gioie e diletti.
(*Enr.* 6. 68)

Perhaps we won't have that eternal, high beauty that the happiest will enjoy, but the comfort, the clear sky, the sweetness that his goodness bestows on his first friends. On that great day when his highness will render his mighty judgment on souls (good or bad, happy or unhappy), the most perfect will see God and will draw happiness and delight from that.

In questo ella stillò, da i chiari lumi
Lagrime di dolor per tanto danno.
(*Enr.* 6.69.1–2)

As she spoke her clear eyes shed tears of pain for such harm.

Erina's affirmations and lack of baptism are astonishing in a book written after the Counter-Reformation, since they reveal an author siding with the more liberal interpreters of Church doctrine who believed in the moral goodness and salvation of pagans (e.g., Abelard, Thomas Aquinas, Marsilio Ficino, Pico della Mirandola).[24] Despite its chronological collocation, Marinella's epic does not seem overly saturated by the ideological backlash produced by Luther's *protest.*[25] Instead, it appears consonant with Christian humanist ideas that had blossomed earlier in the works of authors such as Erasmus and Pico della Mirandola, who eventually were condemned by the Church and whose works were listed in the Index of Prohibited Books in the Cinquecento.

A MAGIC CHARIOT RIDE

Venier remains deaf to Erina's perspective. After having enjoyed the beauty of her palace and the whole world on her winged chariot, he asks to use her power to allow him to see his general Enrico (*Enr.* 22.58.3–4). This fact reveals the circularity of Venier's thinking: he does not care about the beauties and mysteries of the island; from the chariot he wants to see things and people he is already familiar with, and he wishes to return to where he had started. While Ariosto's Ruggiero, having gained control of the hippogriff, was eager to see the world and put aside his desire to return to his beloved Bradamante (*OF* 10.70–71), Venier remains indifferent to this exploration. He asks to see Enrico and learn about the war left behind against his will. Erina obliges, but not without replying in such a way that leaves no doubt about her low opinion of Venier's priorities. She agrees to show him the battlefield and the gathering ranks put together by Giovanissa to assist Byzantium (*Enr.* 22.40). In 22.59, Venier sees the war and is reassured that his people will win, but he also learns that he will not survive the final battle:

> "Nè tu l'invitto fianco sottrerrai
> Da quella pugna nel gran dì prescritto,
> Chè cadrai tra quell'armi in tempo corto
> Glorioso e immortal, mortale, e morto."
> (*Enr.* 22.59.5–8)

---

24. Marembon 2016, esp. chap. 12.

25. About the influence of the Counter-Reformation on women's writing, see the sound and nuanced approach in Cox 2008, chaps. 5 and 6. E.g., while we cannot ignore ecclesiastical censorship as a factor negatively influencing women's literary production, Cox (2008: 153–93) sees women writers' willingness to prove themselves in more influential genres (i.e., epic) as a sign of their literary integration. Such willingness was facilitated by their newly established employment of "Counter-Reformation" themes and concerns.

"You will not be able to protect your unvanquished body during the fight on that great day either: you will quickly die among those weapons, glorious and immortal, yet mortal and dead."

The war will make Venier "glorious and immortal," but he will have to pay a high price for that glory. Marinella asserts indirectly that no glory acquired on the battlefield can compensate for death, especially if other ways to conquer fame and immortality exist. The revelation of his own death leaves Venier untouched and set on departure, while Erina keeps manifesting his desires as misdirected and narrow:

> Essa che vede *l'animo feroce*,
> Tutto avvampare al marziale aspetto:
> *Sorrise alquanto*, e con benigna voce
> Apre la bella bocca a simil detto:
> "*Quell'incendio d'onor, che t'arde e coce*,
> *Ti lacera così, ti rode il petto*,
> *Che 'l caro e 'l bel non curi*, onde si mostra
> Ricca e abbondante la mia regia chiostra."
> (*Enr.* 22.63)

She saw *his fierce soul* ablaze in his martial countenance, and *she smiled broadly*, then with a kind voice she uttered the following words with her beautiful mouth: "*That fire of honor burns you and tears you apart and eats at you to such a degree that you don't care for what's dear and beautiful* (and there's plenty of that in my royal home)."[26]

> Dunque n'andrai là dove il fero Marte
> Tra lancie e spade, e ben ferrati scudi:
> *D'uccider e ferire insegna l'arte*
> *A i cor d'amore e di pietade ignudi*;
> Tu coloro imitando in quella parte
> Li tuoi teneri affetti acerbi e crudi
> Farai *d'umanità spogliato*, e 'l core
> Potrai far lieto ne l'altrui dolore?"
> (*Enr.* 22.64)

Therefore, you will go among spears, swords, and well reinforced shields where *fierce Mars teaches the art of killing to hearts deprived of love and*

---

26. Marinella 2009 (adapted).

pity. Will you change your tender feelings into harsh and cruel ones? *Will you deprive yourself of your humanity* and make your heart happy in other people's pain?

In the name of honor, considered by Erina a negative force that burns and bites one's breast, Venier will abandon the island and reject what is beautiful and precious. Away from her, "fierce Mars" will become his teacher, and Venier will shed his humanity and imitate those whose hearts are empty of love and pity.

The chariot ride Erina grants to Venier is her last attempt to enlighten the hero. Looking at the world from afar, she voices the wisdom of philosophically inclined minds. Here Erina is a philosopher, and the chariot ride is a *mise en abîme* of her island; it is a place where, through distance, the world can be assessed more justly. Erina bears a strong resemblance to Plato's philosopher-king (*Republic* 5.473d) or the Stoic sage. In his *Republic,* Plato reminded readers that through erotic sublimation, philosophers can rise to the Forms and perfect knowledge, because their souls' association with the Forms makes them akin to them (500c). In this way, philosophers resemble the objects of their rational love, and do not wish to engage in human business: "'there's nowhere else their minds would ever rather be than in the upper region' (517c–d). Such beings can be trusted to use their power wisely and well."[27] After being exposed to continuous contemplation of what is most noble, Erina has become detached from the material world. In defining perfection, she looks beyond the obligations of political community or ordinary life; in her commitment to ethical growth, she understands that perfection cannot be structured in terms of political good alone, but must consider a person's *askesis,* an internal itinerary of elevation that often occurs more easily in a quiet place traditionally associated with a moral project of individual ethical improvement. In this way, Marinella develops in Erina a figure that is critical of the epic and urban agenda. Women's de facto centuries-long exclusion from political and public life facilitates their realization that the attainment of wisdom is sufficient for happiness.

Besides alluding to Plato's philosopher-king, Marinella elevates Erina to the status of a philosopher through specific allusions to classical texts. In fact, Erina speaks like virtuous Roman heroes who fulfilled their service to the state but, thanks to correct evaluations of the hierarchy of the universe, also retained their ethical stature and detachment from reality. The enchantress resembles the judicious leaders of Cicero's *Somnium Scipionis* (*Scipio's Dream*) and Virgil's *Aeneid.* Marinella is inspired by these texts, but she is also attuned

---

27. Klosko 2006: 144.

to the discordant notes that problematize their message. Like Cicero and Virgil, she feels caught between divergent impulses, the desire to praise her excellent city and its accomplishments, and the limits of politics and human affairs. Finally, in the octaves connected to the chariot ride, as a religious perspective becomes palpable, we realize that even religion seems to be criticizing the status quo.

Already in Canto 7, with past and future glories frescoed on her walls for the sake of Venier, Erina had evidenced the shockingly violent actions of men living in society and the foolishness of their dreams. On the chariot, patiently, again, she tries to lift Venier's soul toward more durable and worthy goals. At 21.36–37, she presents to the Venetian soldier the sight of a miserable earth. As they are flying, the planet appears as a tiny, insignificant point in the universe. Erina invites Venier to reflect about it and the vanity of human pursuits:

> Or volgi, amico, gli occhi e guata dove
> Hanno gli *egri mortali* or gioie, or pianti;
> Cui la destra del Ciel benigno piove,
> Or grazie e doni, or folgori tonanti;
> Come, ch'al petto de l'eterno Giove
> Sembran degni *i miseri* abitanti;
> *Ove tra lunga guerra e pace breve*
> *Nasce, e si strugge il mondo infermo e leve.*
> (*Enr.* 21.36)

Now, my friend, turn your eyes to observe where *weak mortals* find their joys and tears, where benign heaven's right hand showers courteous good and gifts or thunder and lightning. See to what extent its *miserable dwellers* seem worthy to eternal Jove's heart. *See where our sick and unsubstantial world is born and troubled between long wars and short periods of peace.*

> Benchè per l'aere puro il carro mova,
> Non siamo in cielo, o ne la sfera ardente;
> Nulladimen rimira, *qual si trova*
> *Picciola in grembo al mar la terra algente;*
> *Picciola sì, ma grande desta e cova*
> *Guerra e tumulti in lei l'umana mente,*
> Chè del regnar l'ambiziosa lode
> Tesse al frate e a l'amico e morte e frode.
> (*Enr.* 21.37)

Though our chariot travels in pure air, we're not in heaven or in the burning sphere. Nevertheless, admire *how small is the cold earth*[28] *surrounded by the sea! Though it is small, human minds elicit and harbor in it great wars and troubles*: the ambition for and praise of ruling prepare tricks and death for friends and brothers.

Nè solo a lo inimico lo inimico
Tesse inganni, il crudel, morte ed esiglio,
Ma l'amico tradisce il vero amico,
Il fratello, il fratello, il padre il figlio:
S'uomo non c'è ch'abbia odio novo o antico,
Nel proprio petto il ferro fa vermiglio.
O secolo infelice, ch'offre chiaro,
Ch'esser più de la vita è il regger caro!
(*Enr.* 21.38)

Not only does an enemy prepare tricks (or death or exile) against his cruel enemy, but friends betray their true friends, brothers betray each other, and fathers betray their sons. If a man doesn't harbor a new or an old hatred, then he marks his sword with his own blood. O unhappy age! You show clearly that ruling is far dearer than living.

Seeing earth from a distance has a long and prestigious literary history that, beginning with Cicero's *Somnium* and Virgil's *Aeneid,* also includes Dante's *Divine Comedy* and Petrarch's *Africa.* Erina's comments follow a long line of observations on the *vanitas mundi* theme found in some of the most prominent texts of the Western tradition and customarily put in the mouth of wise statesmen or heroes. In Marinella's work, the "enlightened individual" knowledgeable about past and future and aware of what makes life worth living is a woman who dismisses war, violence, and political power in the name of more fruitful endeavors. In the eyes of Erina, who—godlike—can glance at the earth from above, human beings appear "sick" and "wretched" ("egri . . . miseri," *Enr.* 21.36.2, 6) and the world a cold and tiny island in the sea, an insignificant place that nourishes perverted ambitions, death, and treachery. Erina highlights how small the earth is—"picciola" appears twice (21.37.4–5)—and how vast ("grande," *Enr.* 21.37.5) the war produced by men on it. Not accidentally, the landscape of devastation and treachery is populated, above all, by men.

---

28. I have slightly modified Galli Stampino's translation (Marinella 2011).

These observations echo those of Dante in *Paradise* 22.141, where earth is a "tiny place which makes us so ferocious" ("aiuola che ci fa tanto feroci").[29] In the heavens, Dante looks down from the constellation Gemini, and at that moment the terrestrial surface is described as an *aiuola*, a small, insignificant spot that nevertheless makes man cruel. It is linked with lines 133–38 of the same canto, in which the pilgrim glances at the globe, smiling with detachment:

> Col viso ritornai per tutte quante
> Le sette spere, *e vidi questo globo*
> *Tal, ch'io sorrisi del suo vil sembiante;*
> E quel consiglio per migliore approbo
> Che l'ha per meno; *e chi ad altro pensa*
> *Chiamar si puote veramente probo.*
> (*Paradise* 22.133–38)

> My eyes returned through all the seven spheres
> *And saw this globe in such a way that I*
> *Smiled at its scrawny image*: I approve
> That judgment as the best, which holds this earth
> To be the least; *and he whose thoughts are set*
> *Elsewhere, can truly be called virtuous.* (trans. Mandelbaum)

Similarly, having acquired a more detached view of human affairs, Erina cannot help but smile ("sorrise," *Enr.* 22.63.3) when she notices the incendiary passion that devastates Venier's heart. Her behavior reminds us of Goffredo, whose smile in the *Gerusalemme Liberata* revealed his detachment from the world:

> . . . E l'altro in giuso i lumi
> Volse, quasi sdegnando, *e ne sorrise,*
> Ché vide un punto sol, mar, terre e fiumi,
> Che qui paion distinti in tante guise,
> Ed ammirò che pur a l'ombre, a i fiumi,
> La nostra folle umanità s'affise,
> Servo imperio cercando e muta fama.
> (*GL* 14.11.1–7)

---

29. Traina 1980: 305–35. For Goffredo's dream and the *Somnium,* see De Sanctis 1958: 2:670; Getto 1977: 183; Vivaldi 1983: 80. Cf. also *OF* 34.67.1–4: "Here Astolfo had a double surprise: what a big place the moon was from close up, when to us, who look at it from down here, it seems but a little sphere" (trans. Waldman).

... The other, as in disdain
Gazed down and smiled, for everything that
So, varied in our world he now saw wane
And shrink to one small point—seas, lands, and streams,
He marveled that on smoke and shades our vain,
Humanity pins all its aims and dreams
Of slavish empire, glories mute and dumb.
(trans. Wickert)

Goffredo's dismissive attitude towards earthly accomplishments magnifies how, despite Erina's superficial similarities to classical enchantresses, she functions in an opposite way: she is more like the pious Goffredo than the stunning Armida. *Contemptus mundi*—"the contempt of the world" and earthly matters, a recurrent theme in the intellectual reflections of both classical and Christian authors—is a hallmark of Dante, Goffredo, and Erina, their mindset highlighted by their ability to smile when facing human foolishness. Their wording and approach also draw from that of Africanus in Cicero's *Somnium Scipionis*.

THE WORLD FROM AFAR

In a famous passage of the *Somnium*, Scipio the younger (Aemilianus) stares at the small size of the earth while Africanus reflects upon it:

> While I marveled at these things, however I soon cast my eyes again upon the earth. Then Africanus said: "*I perceive that you are now fixing your eyes on the abode and home of men, and if it seems to you small, as it really is, then look always at these heavenly things, and despise those earthly.* For what reputation, or fame worth seeking, can you obtain from the speech of men?" (*Somn.* 6.19, trans. A. Peabody)[30]

Thanks to Macrobius's commentary upon the *Somnium*, the work was well known, widely imitated, and often cited in the medieval and Renaissance periods.[31] In Cicero's *Somnium*, the younger Scipio, from a lofty perch in the

---

30. "Haec ego admirans referebam tamen oculos ad terram identidem; tum Africanus: 'Sentio' inquit 'te sedem etiamnunc hominum ac domum contemplari; quae si tibi parva, ut est, ita videtur, haec caelestia semper spectato, illa humana contemnito. Tu enim quam celebritatem sermonis hominum aut quam expetendam consequi gloriam potes?'" I am using Powell's edition (Cicero 2006: 142).

31. Warner 2005: 81.

heavens, has a vision of his adoptive grandfather, who reveals that protectors of justice proceed from and return to heaven after death (*Somn.* 6.13). He makes the younger Scipio aware that the truly alive are only those who have fled the chains of the body, and what is known as life in reality is death (*Somn.* 6.14). Yet, he explains, good men must abandon earth only when God decrees—their devotion to the commonwealth and respect for justice will ultimately grant them access to the sky (*Somn.* 6.15). As Scipio the younger concentrates his attention on the small size of the earth and brilliance of the sky, at 6.18 he is lectured about the constitution and operations of the heavens. He can listen to the music of the spheres and learn that gifted men, imitating this harmony on stringed instruments and in song, have earned a return to this region (*docti homines nervis imitati atque cantibus, aperuerunt sibi reditum in hunc locum*), as have those who during their life have devoted their exceptional abilities (*qui praestantibus ingeniis in vita humana*) to a search for divine truth (*divina studia coluerunt*). Erina had reminded Venier that men can acquire eternity by the sword or by searching for truth ("Although an unconquerable heart falls in a fight or searches the world pursuing knowledge, he does not die," *Enr.* 21.14.5–6). Scipio must look up to his eternal salvation rather than for fleeting fame; he should "not place his hopes on human rewards" (*nec in praemiis humanis, spem posueris, Somn.* 6.23) but rather focus "on virtue itself that leads to true honor" (*ipsa virtus trahat ad verum decus, Somn.* 6.23).

To encourage Scipio Aemilianus to serve his city, Africanus describes the recompense of the statesman in the afterlife and introduces the two most important themes of the *Somnium*: the immortality of the soul and the relationship between human society and the divine order of the universe:

> He answered: "Go on indeed, and be convinced that you are not mortal, but only your body is mortal. This external form is not yourself; the spirit is the true self, not that physical figure which can be pointed out by the finger. *Know, then, that you are a god (deum te igitur scito esse)*, because he is a god who lives, feels, remembers, and foresees, and who rules, governs, and moves the body over which it is set, just as the supreme God above us rules this world. And just as the eternal God moves the universe, which is partly mortal, so an immortal spirit moves the fragile body." (*Somn.* 6.26, my trans.)

Here Africanus separates the body from the spirit, the fragile world from God. While on the one hand Scipio is told to concentrate on the future and scorn earthly accomplishments, Roman government and rule are justified in the name of natural law; all those who have preserved and helped the state to flourish are destined for heaven (*Somn.* 6.13), and nothing is dearer to God than human associations (cities) based on law (*Somn.* 6.13). Therefore, in the *Somnium,* as Macrobius points out, there is not only praise for the contemplative life and the cultivation of philosophy but also an understanding that blessedness can come from a life of political engagement. Scipio is considered outstanding for both.[32] Cicero considers happiness and *virtus* as independent from the outside world and yet is aware that this autonomy does not prohibit the individual from caring for the world.[33] Erina, Socrates, Dante, Goffredo, and the Mago d'Ascalona agree with Scipio about the pursuit of heaven; they value the outside world, but they emphasize cultivation of the spirit much more. This double attitude—detachment and concern, scorn for the body and concern for the soul—is also present in Anchises's answer to Aeneas in Book 6 of the *Aeneid,* for which the *Somnium* has been credited as a major intertext.

In the underworld (*Aeneid* 6.703–51), Aeneas's father Anchises lectures him about the universe's structure. He explains that a divine soul animates the whole universe and that all living things are born of it; while human souls are made of divine fire, their bodies are marred by emotions, and even after death they must be purified. For Thomas Habinek, in Anchises's answer to his son we find a philosophical explanation of human nature which undermines the body and earthly deeds; at the same time, Anchises's words include a hortatory speech in which history and political accomplishments are magnified (*Aen.* 6.752–885).[34] Anchises emphasizes the glory of Rome by showing his son a parade of future Roman heroes. Habinek finds the two segments—the philosophical "lecture" and the parade—coherent and corroborative.[35] Other scholars, however, deem the two segments to stand in opposition. They remain skeptical about Virgil's optimistic view of Roman history and focus on the negative undertones of *Aeneid* 6. They notice that while in the first part of Book 6 Aeneas's body makes him real, in Anchises's speech the body becomes the principal cause of deception and delusion.[36] We detect Virgil's pessimism about earthly life when a horrified and puzzled Aeneas asks his father why the

---

32. Bernardo 1962: 120–21, quoting Macrobius; Gregory 2009: 57.

33. Hill 2004: 57.

34. Habinek 1989.

35. Similarly, Zetzel (1989: 276) explicates that in the Virgilian catabasis of *Aeneid* 6, "the combination of myth, religion, philosophy, and history bears a close resemblance to one of the texts to which Virgil, in the composition of Book 6, was most greatly indebted, Cicero's *Somnium Scipionis,* in which the Platonic myth of Er is extended and altered to allow a place for Rome in the cosmic order, in which the Roman state acquires a religious and moral importance in the universe at large"; see also Leach 1999; Dufallo 2007: 116.

36. The inherent tensions present in Virgil are highlighted in Tarrant 1982: 54. See also Hardie 2014: 25; Bacon 1986.

misguided shades of Elysium desire to return to earth, where once again they will receive a flawed body:[37]

> *Aeneas shuddered at the sudden sight* (*horrescit visu subito*), and, in ignorance,
> Asked the cause: what river he was glancing at in the distance,
> Who were the men crowding the banks in ranks so numerous.
> Then his father Anchises answered: "They are spirits,
> Owed a second body by fate, and they drink
> The happy waters, and long oblivion at Lethe's stream.
> For a long time I've wished to tell you about them,
> And show you them, to enumerate my children's
> Descendants, so that you might rejoice with me more at finding Italy."
> "O father, is it to be thought that some spirits go from here
> To the sky above, returning again *to dull bodies* (*ad tarda reverti / corpora*)?
> What *frightful eagerness* (*dira cupido*) for the light possesses *the pitiable ones* (*miseris*)?"
> (*Aen.* 6.710–21, my trans.)

Notice here the disturbing presence of *dira cupido,* which at 721 animates the souls of the blessed, who must be reborn to the sufferings of earth.[38] Aeneas cannot help but wonder why the souls of Elysium are eager to leave such a peaceful place to return to the dark reality of earth. He qualifies the souls destined to be reincarnated as "pitiable" (*miseris,* 6.721); Erina uses the same term for the inhabitants of the world busy killing each other in *Enrico* 21.36.6. Anchises disputes whether those souls are "miserable" (*miseri,* 6.721) but does not object to their being driven by a *dira cupido.* This specific cluster ("frightful eagerness") is also used at 9.185, when Nisus's desire to face a dangerous mission with his friend Euryalus is called a *dira cupido* because, like that of the soul's longing for the light at 6.721, it is for something dazzling but illusory.[39] Similarly for Erina, Venier's desire to return to the war in Byzantium is dazzling but fearfully deceptive. She cannot understand why anyone having arrived at her Elysium could wish to go back. The negative nuances of *Aeneid* 6 are redeployed by Marinella in Erina's speech (*Enr.* 21.36–37) during the chariot ride, in which the emphasis is not so much on a divinely structured providential order or human political accomplishments, as on the fallibility and short-sightedness of men.

---

37. Among those scholars who detect a deep pessimism in this passage is Boyle 1986: 169.
38. Warden 2000.
39. Boyle 1986: 169. I have already discussed Euryalus and Nisus's night raid.

Even if in octaves 22–30 of Canto 22 Anchises's parade of heroes is transformed into Erina's display of Venetian conquests, through which the prophetess celebrates the greatness of Venice, and although in *Enrico* 21.37 she mentions "gifts and graces" bestowed upon men by God, the stress is on the struggle produced by human passions, on human fragility and wickedness. Following Cicero's lead, Marinella could have highlighted God's endorsement of human political compacts as essentially directed by divine will, and she could have rehashed the idea of a providentially ordered history so persuasively crafted in the myth of Venice, but, Aeneas-like, her Erina calls mortals "sick" (*egri*, 21.36), regretting men's misplaced hopes and their trust in fleeting political success. Furthermore, her description of the greatness of Venice is darkened by Venier's awareness of imminent demise. The chariot ride (overlooking Venice) is her final reward to the hero, who can see his beloved city for one last time before he dies ("ma 'l veder la tua patria, anzi che morte / di te," "but [I want you] to see your fatherland before death triumphs over you," *Enr.* 21.41.7–8).

PEACEFUL ISLANDS AND TREACHEROUS CITIES

Erina lives in a place of pastoral serenity, and in Canto 7—like Circe and Calypso had done for Odysseus—she highlights for Venier the hardships of his future indirectly juxtaposed with the tranquility at hand. In *Odyssey* 5.206–8, Calypso tells Odysseus that if he knew all the sufferings he was destined to experience before arriving home, he would remain with her. Nevertheless, she also gives him instructions for successfully confronting those future perils (*Od.* 10.483–540, 12.25–141). In her awareness of Venier's suffering and desire to save him, Erina is cast as Calypso and Circe (preoccupied with the hero's physical safety), but even more as Ariosto's Melissa, who can advise Ruggiero and Bradamante thanks to her prophetic abilities. For instance, in *Orlando Furioso* 3.8, Melissa portends the marriage of Bradamante and Ruggiero and later interprets the embroidery on the wedding pavilion (*OF* 46.76–102). In Canto 7, Erina displays her prophetic skills, depicting on her walls Venice's past and future glories.

In epic, prophecy is normally a tool to extol the present of the author and to persuade internal and external audiences to accept hardships in the name of future greatness; Marinella uses prophecy in a different fashion.[40] In *Enrico*

---

40. Prophecy in epic is a complex topic upon which I can only barely touch. See Albis 1996: 11–16; Ascoli 1987: 390*ff.*; Edmunds 2005: 42–43; Hunter 1993: 90–96; Kugel l990; McPhail 2001; Moore 1921: 100*ff.*; O'Hara 1990; Stoppino 2012.

6–7, Erina interprets for Venier the future carved on a wall of her palace. In Erina's prophecy the emerging image of Venice, despite the superficial praise of the city, is far from idyllic. In a move paradigmatic of the Venetian masculine ideology of conquest, the artist Albino has depicted on Erina's walls major events of Venetian history. We see men violating different spaces and, in a parallel but opposite fashion, Erina peacefully inhabiting her island and proposing this lifestyle to Venier. While Maria Galli Stampino emphasizes the "civic religion" of the Serenissima, the "cohesion" and republicanism of the Venetians as dominant elements of the portrayal of Venice in the poem (and in its prophetic moments), Virginia Cox notices how in these prophetic paintings cruelty, violence, and disturbing feelings dominate.[41] We read:

> Non Apelle, nè Zeusi a l'uomo o al cielo
> Scoprì del lor saper sì chiaro segno,
> Quanto il pennel d'Albin nel sottil velo
> Mostra del cuor gli affetti, ira e disdegno;
> Vede splender il ferro, arder il telo,
> Sossopra gir del gran Nettuno il regno;
> Par tutto vero, e uscir fumante il sangue
> Da piaga di guerrier, che geme e langue.
> (*Enr.* 7.52)

Apelles or Zeuxis did not show men or heaven such a sure sign of their ability as Albino's brush shows the anger and disdain of their hearts on that thin canvas. One can see iron shine, weapons burn, and great Neptune's kingdom roiled. Everything seems real, including the steaming blood flowing from the wound of a warrior lamenting and growing weak.[42]

Here the focus is on anger, violence, and suffering. I agree with Stampino, that Marinella is fully aware that "suffering and sacrifice cannot be separated from joy and victory" and that Venice would not be what it is without those who gave their lives, whether in the Fourth Crusade, at Lepanto, or in Cyprus,[43] but I am not convinced that Marinella endorses these wars, and to me her goal is a subtle but pointed criticism.

In the paintings, she portrays the city as filled with factional strife and political disorder, with ferocious citizens ready to attack and betray their leaders. After showing Venier the origins of Venice, where good leaders alter-

---

41. Galli Stampino 2014: esp. 82–94; Cox 2011: 175–76; Conti Odorisio 1979: 48; Marinella 2011: 28. Salvatore and Allen 1992: 32 also interpret the scene as uplifting Venice's greatness.

42. Marinella 2009: 179 (slightly modified).

43. Galli Stampino 2014: 94.

nate with bad ones who often have to deal with upset and envious citizens, she emphasizes the human losses at the battle of Lepanto. The depictions are extremely realistic, including "the steaming blood flowing from the wound of a warrior lying and growing weak" ("par tutto vero, e uscir fumante il sangue / da piaga di guerrier, che geme e langue," *Enr.* 7.52.6–8), and "it seems as though one can hear the sighs and the noises of those who fight, of their crossbows and bows. Arrows shriek when bows are bent and released by quick hands" ("par che sospiri s'odano, e il suono / de' combattenti, e di baliste e d'archi. / Mentre stridono i dardi, e spinti sono / da sollecite man curvati e scharchi," *Enr.* 7.53.1–4). This battle, celebrated as one of Venice's greatest successes, is here featured for its bloodshed. The waves are red with blood, the sea is scattered with cut-off limbs, many ships are set on fire, and "you can observe air and sea and heaven troubled by the terror of this horrible battle" ("vedi l'aria ed il mar, e il ciel turbarsi / pel terror de l'orribile battaglia," *Enr.* 7.56.5–6). Sebastiano Venier is mentioned summoning his men, but more lines are given to Marcantonio Bragadin, the Venetian governor of Cyprus, tortured and skinned alive by the Turks (*Enr.* 7.58–59).[44] Not only is the glory of Lepanto immediately deflated by Bragadin's horrific death, but also we get the impression that what makes this man worthy in Erina's eyes is his devotion to God rather than his dedication to the state. She calls him "glory of the world," yet she rushes him to withdraw from the world to ascend to heaven, where, having escaped earthly deceptions, he can be a star ("Vattene sù nel Ciel novella stella, / de gli inganni del mondo ormai satollo," "Go up to Heaven as a new star, fed up with the tricks of the world," *Enr.* 7.59.3–4). Erina's future Venice closely resembles that which Circetta had illustrated for his guests Silano and Clarido (*Floridoro* 12), but while Fonte had optimism for her city, conceived as a stronghold of liberty and virtuous men, Marinella emphasizes chaos, violence, and deception.

Another element Marinella adopts to denounce civic life and conversely amplify the worth of solitude and contemplation is her treatment of Erina's forerunners. Erina recounts their story to Venier in *Enrico* 6.20ff.: entangled in city politics, only their distance from Venice makes them better people. Pietro IV Candiano, twenty-second doge of the Venetian Republic, is presented in the *Enrico* as an ancestor of Erina. With tyrannical aspirations (*Enr.* 6.22, 25, 27), he ended up being killed by the Venetians, who desecrated his

---

44. According to the testimony of Alessandro Podacataro, when Bragadin was asked to surrender, he replied that once food supplies were depleted, "holding his crucifix in his hand, he would go out in the country, making sure he was followed by valorous and honorable soldiers, in order to gloriously end their miseries and life, acquiring the kingdom of heaven" (Podacataro 1876: 22).

and his young son's bodies, leaving them to be devoured by dogs.[45] Fictionally in Marinella's *Enrico*, however, Pietro is rescued and brought to Erina's island. He escapes civil riots in Venice and becomes a far better man than he was in his urban environment. The personal history of Erina's family illustrates how distancing one's self from city politics can trigger moral progress and spiritual growth.[46] It is correct to emphasize "Pietro's awareness of and repentance for his hubristic political ambitions,"[47] but also to recall that Pietro in reality was not given a chance of survival in the mayhem of Venetian life. Marinella in this section is correcting history and reinventing it under the guise of harmony and peace. Enjoying the beauty of the remote island, Pietro spends his days in peace among fauns and gods (*Enr.* 6.42.1–4), and, thanks to the wisdom bestowed on him by Armano—the good magician who in Marinella's story helps him escape (*Enr.* 6–50; 6.33–36)—at the end of his life he is a new man.

These are the words through which Pietro, upon his death, says goodbye to his son:

Abbracciò il figlio, e disse: "Ora m'invio
Per via tanto temuta a la natura
Orribil tanto al sciocco mondo oscura."
(*Enr.* 6.47.6–8)

He [Pietro] hugged him and said: "Now I am going on a much feared road, one that nature believes horrible and that the stupid world finds obscure."

Io poi, che nel gran sol, de la mia mente
Tolta ogni nebbia, affissai pronto i lumi,
E conobbi il mio error, già in tutto *spente*
Calde voglie di fama, ed ombre e fumi;

---

45. Pietro Candiano ruled as doge in Venice from c. 959 to 976 and is remembered in Marinella's *Nobiltà* for his tyrannical behavior and brutal death at the hand of the Venetians: "Where should we place Pietro Candiano proud and with a tyrannical mind? As Pietro Marcello writes, word for word: "Petrus Candianus turned the duchy into a tyrannical government filled with arrogance and threats, he did everything legitimately or illegitimately as he felt like so that the people feared him and in the end he was killed," Marinella 1621: 239 = Marinella 1601: 308–9). In 1574, Pietro Marcello wrote *De vita, moribus et rebus gestis omnium ducum Venetorum* (*About the Life, Customs and Accomplishments of the Venetian Princes*), which was translated into Italian by Ludovico Domenichi as *Vite de' prencipi di Vinegia di Pietro Marcello tradotte in volgare,* Venezia 1557, ed. Plinio Pietrasanta. In Domenichi's translation, Candiano's death can be found on p. 20. See Crouzet-Pavan 2002: 11–12.

46. Pietro also brought to the island his son, who grows up and has a son with Eonide, the daughter of a sylvan god and a goddess (*Enr.* 6.43–45).

47. Galli Stampino 2014: 89.

Lieto rendo al terren la spoglia algente,
E varco d'Acheronte i negri fiumi.
(*Enr.* 6.48.1–6)

"But I stared directly at the great sun after I removed all fog from my mind,
I recognized my mistake, and I feel that all my passionate desire for fame
(which is but shadows and smoke) is utterly extinguished. I happily give my
chilly body back to the earth and cross the black river of Acheron."

This utterance displays his drastically changed attitude. Pietro is no longer
thirsty for fame (6.48.3–4); as a new Socrates, he does not fear death and "happily" (6.48.5) prepares to die. Erina's father Fileno, descendent of Pietro, continues in this path of redemption and is described as an even wiser man: "He
spent his most serene days in obtaining virtue, handsome and gentle" (*Enr.*
6.51.2–3), and his virtue progressed "to such an extent that he was the only
one on earth to be equal to the gods in the heavens." ("oso dir, che in virtù
sì s'avanzasse, / che 'n terra i Dei del ciel solo agguagliasse." *Enr.* 6.52.7–8).
Thanks to him, Erina learns about natural philosophy and the importance of
peace. She is convinced that one day the two of them "will go where glorious spirits find their happy and noble rest" (*Enr.* 6.64.7–8).[48] In his love for
knowledge and solitude, Fileno represents an ideal that Venice has forgotten
or tends to undermine. Through him, Marinella criticizes the complications
of the political environment and the difficulties of handling power. Aston-
ishingly, Marinella chooses an infamous character to be the ancestor of her
alter-ego Erina, demonstrating that she is not simplistically celebrating the
Venetian past or its political order but revealing the brutality that at times
stained its history. History and remembering are crucial activities for Marinella writing a romance epic, a genre only obliquely linked to the memorialization of the past, but more precisely an instrument for ethical, social and
political reflection in the present by means of the past.[49] As Marinella tells
Pietro's story, she suggests paths of improvement for wicked men like him.
She reveals that in the right setting and with the correct education, any man
can become a worthy human being. In her praise of Candiano and the *vita
contemplativa,* Marinella insinuates that the urban environment may not be
the best training ground for ethical growth and inner fulfillment; in Venice,
however, a political and ethical evolution was hardly conceivable outside the

---

48. Fileno can be linked to the character of Erimeno in Marinella's *Arcadia Felice.* See Ray
2015: 102.

49. Raaflaub 2005: 69–70.

city and its demands.[50] By fashioning characters like Candiano and Fileno, Marinella reminds us of men like Ermolao Barbaro, who chose a course of life not recommended by his society. Throughout his existence, Barbaro fought against the republic and his family for the right to live in isolation. Having been released from public obligations, he remained confident that through his solitude, celibacy, and devotion to God he could attain happiness and freedom. Barbaro was considered a traitor for wanting to cultivate his spiritual growth away from the city.[51]

Criticism of the Venetian political agenda is also visible in Erina's magnification of peace openly voiced in *Enrico* 22.30 in her apostrophe to Venice. In her address, she wishes that the city will nurture pacific harmony and follow the example of Christ, the Prince of Peace who gave away his life to save others:

> Rimanti in pace, o terra amica, il Cielo
> Del dolce dì sue grazie il crin t'asperga;
> Turbo nemico, o procelloso gelo
> D'avversa voglia dal tuo sen disperga;
> La giustizia, l'amor, la fede e 'l zelo
> Oltre le vie del ciel t'innalzi ed erga;
> *Vivi felice, sempre a quegli unita,*
> *Che per salvar altrui porse la vita.*
> (*Enr.* 22.30)[52]

Be at peace, friendly land! May Heaven scatter its graces on your hair during sweet days, and may it repel enemy invasions and stormy coldness from your bosom. May justice, love, faith, and zeal raise you beyond Heaven. *Live happy, always together with him who offered his life to save others.*

The apostrophe is important because, like several segments reviewed in this study of the *Enrico,* it highlights the tension at the heart of Marinella's poem. In making Erina deplore enterprises and actions typically considered praiseworthy in epic poems, Marinella lets us perceive a polarization of the moral

---

50. Venetian men were socially enticed to choose a politically active city life. E.g., Gasparo Contarini (1483–1542), a significant figure in the politics of the Serenissima, after having seriously pondered retiring to the Hermitage of Camaldoli, remained active in Venice. Two of his dearest friends, T. Giustiniani and V. Querini, embraced religious retirement. Gleason 1983: 10–11; Hubert 1953: 30–32; Martin 2004. About Contarini, King 2005: 44; Fragnito 1983.

51. King 1986: 192–205. Some ideas in Barbaro's *De coelibatu* (*On Celibacy*) strike me as resonant with those Erina employs to convince Venier to abandon his civic duties.

52. I have modified Galli Stampino's translation (Marinella 2011).

values associated with two literary traditions and respective points of view (epic and pastoral) present in her work. The poem proceeds on two parallel tracks. On the one hand, it praises war and features men committed to it; it encompasses a narrator who wishes that her "humble cetra" may become a "superb trumpet" to celebrate the anger and fury of Mars (*Enr.* 1.1). On the other hand, through apostrophe (such as that cited above or addressed to women) and characters like Erina and Clelia, the poem incorporates its "dialectic counterpoint," that is, condemnation of greed and honor and the exaltation of peace, attitudes associated with pastoral poetry.[53] The integration of pastoral values into epic discourse is not resolved, but brings about an internal strain that can be interpreted as criticism by the author, who, not without difficulty, voices the incongruities she recognizes in her urban environment.

In *Della perfettione della vita politica* (1579), Paolo Paruta praises peace as the highest accomplishment for the state. He explains that the prince or republic that directs all its attention to wars to enlarge its empire does not foster his city's well-being (*felicità*), which consists not in empire but in ruling with justice in peace and tranquility.[54] But between 1580 and 1630, the *giovani* (the young) took control of Venetian politics and sought a more assertive role for Venice, viewing a policy of balance and neutrality as a form of submission to Spanish dominance over Italy.[55] The *giovani* did not tolerate the pope's intrusion into state affairs and defended Venetian rights during the crisis of the Interdetto; they were ready for maritime aggression in the Mediterranean. Under the leadership of the *giovani* and Nicolò Contarini, Venice also fought Habsburg interference in the eastern frontier and the Duke of Ossuna, the Spanish Viceroy of the Kingdom of Naples. War contributed to the decline of the Venetian economy, and eventually around 1628 the coalition of the *giovani* splintered. The bubonic plague of 1630 precipitated the situation. Since the *Enrico* was published in 1635, through Erina, Marinella could be voicing her opposition to the aggressive political orientation inaugurated by the *giovani*. Her preference for moderation is visible also in her decision to dedicate the poem to the doge Francesco Erizzo. Erizzo had held important political offices and distinguished himself for his diplomatic maneuvering and ability to remain neutral. He was doge from 1631 until 1646, and during the end of his mandate he waged a war against the Ottoman Empire for the control of Crete (1645)—like Dandolo, as an old man, Erizzo fought against the Turks,

---

53. The formulation of "dialectic counterpoint" is in Asenso and de Pina Martins 1982: 31–33.

54. Lane 1973: 392–93.

55. Ibid., 394.

which brought on his death in 1646—but, overall, he was opposed to war.[56] In the *Enrico,* Marinella describes him as the man who "removed Italy from peril and opened the path to peace" (*Enr.* 1.5). Giuseppe Gullino presents this doge as a balanced and restrained individual.[57] When the tension between the *giovani* and the pro-Spain and pro-clerical factions was most intense in Venice, Erizzo maintained a position of equanimity. Marinella may have liked this doge for his commitment to peace, diplomacy, and moderation.

Finally, Marinella's commitment to peace can be seen in Canto 21, where Erina again suggests that Venier's thirst for martial success is misplaced. She makes clear for the young captain that no ship will rescue him, and that he should be glad to remain on the island:

"Non aspettar che audace legno,
Giungendo a noi, ti guidi al campo amico:
Ch'invan l'attendi: accheta il vago ingegno
Di gir tra l'armi e 'l marziale intrico:
Lieto starai nel mio piacevol regno,
Da perigli lontano e dal nemico:
Se 'l cor piacer ne prende ancor vedrai
Di mirabil natura opr'alte e assai."
(*Enr.* 21.5)

"Don't expect that a bold ship might arrive here and take you back to your camp; you'd wait in vain! So, appease your eager fancy to walk among weapons and tangles of war: you'll stay happily in my appealing kingdom, far away from dangers and enemies; and if your heart finds it pleasant you'll see many great works made by admirable nature."

Come quel che tra piume infermo giace,
Ma che di speme abbondi, e poscia ch'oda
Dir al medico: Oimé, la vital face
S'estingue e 'legno di tua vita è a proda;
Confuso trema, inorridisce e tace,
Timor li gela il cor, la lingua annoda:

56. Galli Stampino 2014: 77n5 has a different opinion, believing that Marinella's dedication displays a desire to praise her city and her agreement with Venetian political leadership. She also notices that the doge is a striking choice because it stands in contrast with that of other female writers of epic, including Sarrocchi and Albizzi Tagliamochi, who selected female addressees. Marinella's choice also stands in opposition to her own previous practice.

57. Gullino 1993.

Così costui di quella Ninfa al detto
S'attristò in volto e fe' di ghiaccio il petto.
(*Enr.* 21.6)

Like one who's sick in bed but hopes to recover fully, who then hears the doctor say: "Alas, the flame of your life is becoming extinguished, the ship of your life is reaching its destination," trembling in confusion, horrified and quiet, with his heart chilled by fear and his tongue in knots, so Venier's face became sad and his heart froze at the nymph's words.

Ma com'uom delirante fugge e sprezza
Ciò ch'a salute sua buon si discopre:
Il vago, il lieto e 'l bel non cura o prezza,
Ch'ivi de l'arte e di natura scopre;
che la sua stabil mente a l'armi avvezza,
Non piegan fasto, o dilettevol opre;
Nè di sua vita sicurezza e pace
A star constringe l'animo vivace.
(*Enr.* 21.12)

As a raving man he fled, despising what showed itself good to his life, he didn't care for or appreciate what was pretty, happy, and beautiful that art or nature unveiled in front of him. His mind was focused on and accustomed to weapons, so pomp and pleasing things didn't hold any sway over him, and the safety and peace of his life didn't compel his lively soul to stay put.

Venier's behavior is not described positively. Erina's message makes him confused and horrified, unable to utter a word (*Enr.* 21.6.1–2). Disturbed by the idea of having to remain on the island, Venier does not accept Erina's salvific advice. He does not care or value what is "beautiful and pleasant" (*Enr.* 21.12.3); he is like a sick man who will die if he continues his ill habits, but who nevertheless cannot accept the words of his doctor proposing a cure. In his scorn for peace and beauty, Venier is qualified as a "delirious" man. The phrasing and situation underscore a problem that Aristotle had envisaged. The good man establishes his worth and that of his community by sacrificing his life, the most important asset he owns. Fighting and embracing death are, obviously, done not for their own sake, but for the results they bring about. If the same results could be brought about by some other means, the wise man would choose them. In other words, "the upshot is that . . . political and military virtuous actions, however intrinsically valuable they may be given the

circumstances, necessarily look to an independent end beyond themselves."[58]
Sadly, Venier has not understood that fighting is not valuable per se.

   While in *Enrico* 21.5–6 Erina voices her opinion, in the lines below we
learn Venier's perspective. He complains about his bad fortune and does not
understand why God wishes him to stay on an island where his valor is destined to remain hidden and fame cannot be obtained:

> "Crudel fortuna, in sì *solinghe selve*
> *Da la gloria de l'armi, oimè, lontano*
> Tratto m'hai rea, tra sassi, tronchi e belve,
> Di senso prive e d'intelletto umano.
> Dunque il Ciel vuol che *'l mio valor s'inselve,*
> Pur creduto dal mondo alto e sovrano?
> E in giovinetta età che brama onore
> Sopra un diserto scoglio accheti il core?"
> (*Enr.* 21.14)

Evil and cruel fortune, you drove me to these *lonely woods, far away from the
glory of battle,* among rocks, trunks, and wild animals that have no senses
and no human brain. Is it heaven's will, then, that *my valor may become lost
in the wild?*[59] The world believes it to be noble and superior! Is it heaven's
will that I content my heart on a deserted rock in my youthful age that pines
for honor?

> Così dicea, perchè non cura o aggrada
> Vita, la qual per sè fama non merchi;[60]
> *E sdegna l'uom, qual con vindice spada*
> *Per ferma eternità viver non cerchi;*
> Benchè un invitto cuor pugnando cada,
> O 'l mondo *per saper cerchi e ricerchi,*
> Non muor morendo, quando di sua morte
> Miete stato mortale immortal sorte.
> (*Enr.* 21.15)

This is what he said because he didn't care for or appreciate any life that
didn't acquire fame for itself, and because *he scorned any man who didn't
try to live for eternity through his vengeful sword.* Though an unvanquished

---

58. Richardson Lear 2004: 187.

59. "Lost in the wild" is my modification of Galli Stampino's "becomes wild."

60. Rather than meaning "purchase, trade," the verb *mercare* here means something like
procacciarsi or *procurarsi* ("acquire for oneself").

heart may die fighting *or looking for knowledge* all over the world, still it doesn't die when it dies gathering immortal strength through the death of its mortal being.

These two octaves are fundamental to Venier's psychology. In them we see a youth who "spites" ("sdegna," 21.15.3) those who do not try to acquire eternity through their "vengeful sword" ("vindice spada," 21.15.3). Although immortality could be obtained by "looking for knowledge" (21.15.6), Venier believes that the valor of a man "is lost in the wild" ("s'inselva," 21.14.5) when he lives in seclusion among trees and animals. The choice of words in Italian is revealing, as "virtue" (*valor*) is juxtaposed with the present indicative *s'inselva*. The verb is etymologically connected to *selva*, a noun with obvious pastoral and negative implications in Venier's mind. The verb is also important because it reminds us of Dante's *selva*. In the *Comedy, selva* (e.g., *Inferno* 1.1–2) is often a negative term that becomes a metaphor for sin, errancy, and alienation from God.[61] In this story, for the misguided Venier, anonymity is the sin, and immortality can be obtained *only* by fighting ("pugnando," 21.15.5). Venier conceives of the *locus amoenus* as a punishment. Although he realizes that heaven may want something different from him—that ultimately God may want him to renounce something worthy only in the eyes of the world—he is not ready to relinquish his epic dream.

VENIER'S LIFE AND DEATH

If immortality can be reached via two different paths—fighting in battle or searching for knowledge (*Enr.* 21.15.4–5)—Venier is blind to this second possibility. He appreciates only the active life; his creed is that of Achilles, and we cannot be sure that he wants to fight for God's sake. This shortcoming, in part, can be attributed to his youth. In the poem, Venier does not have a chance to mature. Like Pallas in Virgil's *Aeneid,* he is in love with war and reputation and dies without ever understanding the costs of war.

Following some reflections from David Green in his book on English epic, Christopher Bond detects two kinds of hero in most epic poems: a primary hero, who is godlike and almost perfect in virtue but not particularly likable, and a secondary hero, who despite his physical superiority is often ethically weaker and prone to choosing the wrong path. Readers frequently sympathize with this faulty but passionate human being who eventually learns how

---

61. Warner 1995: 449; Freccero 1966. In Dante as well, *selva* in certain passages is Eden (e.g., *Purgatorio* 28.23).

to behave following the example of the primary hero.[62] This pattern is applicable to Dandolo and Venier in Marinella's *Enrico*. If the mature and judicious (although not particularly likeable) Enrico represents the primary hero who frames human glory as subordinate to the glory of God, Venier is the secondary hero who in his desire to gain reputation stirs our sympathy but does not subject his glory to that of God. Although historically speaking Dandolo always prioritized Venice's needs over those of the pope, in Marinella's poem he is depicted as an exemplary religious and ethically irreproachable hero. In the last Canto, we see God's endorsement of Enrico in assigning to the general a guardian angel who protects him from Emilia's arrows and preserves him from death. If on the one hand Venier, differently from secondary heroes such as Rinaldo or Achilles, never abandons Enrico or rebels against his will, he also does not seem to learn anything from him. Like Lucillo, Venier succumbs to his love for martial reputation. Marinella emphasizes the futility of his death and prowess by having him killed by an arrow, and she lingers on the desperation that his death produces in Enrico (Canto 24).

After the siege of Byzantium and the routing of Mirtillo, Enrico returns to camp and cries over the body of "his" Venier. His tears disrupt the epic's celebratory intents and reveal his misery:

> Pria che svesta l'armi, o posa prenda,
> . . . .
> Ritrova il suo Venier, che 'n chiusa tenda
> Giacea per morte impallidito e bianco;
> Come fu giunto, raddoppiar le genti
> Pianti, sospiri, gemiti e lamenti.
> (*Enr.* 24.87.1, 5–8)

> Before he takes off his armor, and rests
> . . . .
> he finds his Venier, who inside the tent
> white and pale laid dead;
> As he arrived, people doubled
> Their tears, sighs, moans and laments.

> Qual di viola il pallidetto fiore;
> O di giacinto tra sue belle foglie,
> Di giglio unito al lucido candore,
> Ch'accresce il bello a le sue belle spoglie;

---

62. Bond 2011: 1–3; Green 1979: 18–22.

Tal giacea cinto d'immortale onore
Il delicato busto, d'aspre doglie
Nobil cagion, sospeso il grand' Enrico,
Mira dolente il suo diletto amico.
(*Enr.* 24.88)

Like the pale flower of a violet
Or hyacinth among its beautiful leaves
Or a lily amid its lucid splendor
Which gives further beauty to his beautiful body;
Such the delicate body
Encircled by immortal honor was lying,
Noble cause of harsh sorrow, kept in suspense great Enrico,
And regretful he stares at his beloved friend.

Il mira, e tace, e pensa, poscia il freno
Scioglie in suon grave ai flebili sospiri,
Indi tai note de l'afflitto seno
Svelle . . .
"Alma beata, che nel bel sereno
Ti diporti e del ciel ne' lieti giri;
Porgi orecchio a colui ch'amasti tanto,
A cui cagione or sei di lungo pianto.
(*Enr.* 24.89.1–4, 5–8)

He looks at him, and remains silent, then
He doesn't curb the grievous sound of dim sighs,
Therefore these words from his afflicted chest
He wrenches away . . .
"Blessed soul, you who wander in serene air
And move in the happy spheres of the sky;
Turn your ear towards whom you loved so much
And for whom now you are the reason of long crying.

Oimè! Che giova, o giovinetto invitto
Se fortuna seconda a noi si scopre?
Di che godo, se tu, come anco è dritto,
Meco non godi il guiderdon de l'opre?
Che farò senza te lasso ed afflitto,
Tra cotanta vittoria? Ora discopre

La fama, che tu pur recasti a noi
Trionfal pregio co' perigli tuoi.
(*Enr.* 24.91)

Oimè! What does it profit, undefeated youth,
If fortune shows herself benign to us?
What enjoyment is there for me if you, as it is right
With me do not enjoy the reward of our work?
What will I do, tired and afflicted,
In such great victory? Now fame discloses
The triumphal reputation which you brought to us
With your dangers.

Veggio la patria tua, la mia sì cara
Città per te meschiar tra l'oro e i pregi
De le nostre alte glorie, ahi parca avara!
Bende lugubri e sanguinosi fregi.
Tra 'l riso, il pianto e tra le gioie amara
Memoria de' tuoi fatti eccelsi e regi.
(*Enr.* 24.92.1–6)

I see your fatherland, my so dear city
For you mixing the gold and the worth
Of our high glory, ahi ravenous Fate (*parca*)
With funereal bands and bloody adornments.
Among laughs and cries and joy, there is the bitter
Memory of your regal and excellent deeds."

Tacque, e con un sospir grave e profondo,
Diede l'estremo vale al caro amico.
(*Enr.* 24.93.1–2)

He fell silent and with a grievous and deep sigh
Gave the last "vale" to his dear friend.

Dandolo's words tarnish his mask of pity. Looking at the youth's dead body, he cannot contain his sorrow. He vents his disappointment as he realizes that there is nothing to be gained in conquering Byzantium, however necessary it might have seemed to conquer it. Even this most loyal general, so devoted to his city, now recognizes the bitterness of a triumph in which his young friend cannot participate. There is distress and irony in Enrico's words when he compares his "dear city" to the "ravenous Moira" ("parca avara"), who cuts the life-thread of a young and most promising man. Although those lines are ambiguous—we cannot be sure that he speaks of Venice as Moira—the way each unfolds suggests that interpretation. Not only is it impossible to celebrate without crying, Dandolo also feels that there is no profit for him in this triumph, nothing that he or his city can bestow on the youth, no reward worthy of his sacrifice. In this loss, even his faith wavers, since the thought that Venier is in heaven does not arrest his tears. Conversely, in the *Gerusalemme Liberata* (3.67–70), Goffredo in front of Dudone's coffin highlighted that "tears were not due" to a man who "although dead to the world had his rebirth in heaven" (*GL* 3.71.1–2), and that if now Dudone could no longer provide "mortal help" (*GL* 3.72.6), he could hear his people's prayers and render "celestial aid" (*GL* 3.72.7). While Goffredo's speech is illuminated by hope and trust in God, Dandolo displays his intense despair. Through Dandolo's lament, Marinella undercuts the Venetian success and shows that she can effectively reuse some of Virgil's most touching lamentations to that effect. In fact, Dandolo's speech is reminiscent of Aeneas's plaint over Lausus's and Pallas's dead bodies (*Aen.* 10.821–26, 11.29–71).[63]

Marinella recalls four moments of Aeneas's visit to Pallas's dead body during Enrico's lamentation over Venier: the mourning and crying of the people around the youth as Aeneas sees his body (*Aen.* 11.34–37); Aeneas's rejection of any sense of accomplishment at the sight (*hi nostri reditus expectatique triumphi?* "Is this our return and the waited for triumph?" *Aen.* 11.54); Pallas's beauty being "like a flower cut from the hand of a virgin, a soft violet or languid hyacinth from which not yet its splendor nor beauty receded" (*qualem virgineo demessum pollice florem / seu mollis violae languentis hyacinthi, / cui neque fulgor adhuc nec dum sua forma recessit, Aen.*11.68–70); and Aeneas's final salutation to his friend (*maxime Palla, / aeternum vale,* "greatest Pallas, an eternal farewell" *Aen.* 11.96–97). Pallas was entrusted by his father to Aeneas, who welcomed the young man as a son into the Trojan camp. Instead of protecting him, the hero is witness to his slaughter by the enemy. By prompting Pallas to fight, Aeneas feels that he condemned the youth to death.

Aeneas's pity and resentment of war are also visible after his murder of Lausus, when he realizes he has killed a worthy youth who was trying to save

---

63. The situation also recalls Orlando's lamentation over Brandimarte's body (*OF* 43). But Orlando seems more resigned than Enrico, and he does not regret his friend's death but rather his inability to share in Brandimarte's peace and glory (*OF* 43.170–73).

his father. As he speaks to the dead boy, Aeneas knows that there is nothing he can do to atone for his death:

> But when the son of Anchises saw the glance and face of the dying youth, a face wondrously pale (*simulacra modis pallentia miris*), he groaned heavily in pity (*ingemuit miserans graviter*) and held out his right hand, and the thought of his own loyalty to his father touched his mind. "What, poor boy, can pious Aeneas give you in return for these glorious deeds, what can he give you worthy of so great a nature?" (*Aen.* 10.820–25, my trans.)

Aeneas's sense of impotence here is like that of Anchises surveying the future heroes of Rome and directing an apostrophe to the prematurely dead Marcellus. While the parade of unborn heroes emphasizes the future greatness of Rome, in Anchises's speech for the dead Marcellus (*epicedion Marcelli*), a deep gloom is communicated through the youth's "sad brow and downcast eyes" (*Aen.* 6.861), Anchises's "swelling tears" (6.867), the fragile beauty of emptily offered flowers (*manibus date lilia plena,* 6.883), and the repetition of *luctus* (sorrow/mourning, 6.868).[64] Marcellus exemplifies all young Romans cut down in the flower of youth to build the Roman Empire, and Anchises stands for all their bereaved Roman fathers.[65] Dandolo's tears over Venier and Erina's display of the world from the chariot manifest a similar grief. Erina is skeptical about men's ability to obtain happiness, especially when they are exposed to war and battles or to political squabbles. She detects in the human mind a preposterous desire to look for unsubstantial things, recognizing how war in the "civilized" world appears or is made to appear as a natural state that young men can foolishly embrace, crave, and idolize. Erina feels toward Venier the pity Aeneas felt toward Lausus, or Anchises toward Marcellus, since they all are destined to die young. Wanting the best for the Venetian hero, she tries to shelter him from danger—like the magician Atlante attempted to shelter Ruggiero in his castle "to save a brave knight from death" (*OF* 4.29.5–6)—by convincing him to remain on her island. She describes the world as a frightful place filled with "conspiracies and ambushes" and "bodies tainted with poison, and the noose and weapons and fire" ("congiure e insidie . . . spoglie / di venen tinte, e laccio e ferro e face," *Enr.* 21.39.5–6); in vain she highlights Venier's ineffective courage and tragic fate.

In the *Aeneid*, the pastoral places that Trojan Aeneas visits have critical significance for his development and for the poem: in them, Aeneas experi-

---

64. Von Albrecht 1999: 115; Markos 2013: 45 "And so, in what is perhaps the most ambiguous moment of the *Aeneid,* Virgil transforms the great march of Roman history and glory into a funeral procession for Marcellus."

65. Segal 1966: 55.

ences psychological crises that help him to mature in his heroic quest. These pastoral enclaves give the hero a deeper understanding of both the divine purpose and his own religious, familial, and patriotic duties.[66] Aeneas as the servant of fate can never free himself from the forces that dominate history, and pastoral *otium* amid the *locus amoenus* is necessarily ill-suited to the needs of the statesman or the warrior. Yet, at least in two significant episodes, Aeneas finds himself in pastoral enclaves and has time to meditate about them: first in the Elysian fields (*Aen.* 6), which are described as a garden of serenity, and then in Book 8 in Evander's land, a kind of moral Arcadia where values such as piety toward the gods and hospitality for guests are paramount. These pastoral moments are not digressions but rather integral to Virgil's goal and to the development of the hero into a morally competent individual. In the *Aeneid*, "Aeneas' sense of lost pastoral virtues is important to the whole epic, and Vergil sees to it that we are reminded of this fact."[67] For Fulgentius, *Aeneid* 6 was the most important part of the poem, since here the hero can contemplate what will help him in his active life.[68] Even if we believe that in his final action—the killing of Turnus—the Trojan hero fails to put into practice what he has realized and to integrate pastoral virtue within a war context, we realize that he has understood their importance. In the *Aeneid*, true heroic action is based on contemplation and reflection, through which the hero acquires self-knowledge. This pattern of learning cannot be applied to Venier. His pastoral experience on Erina's island does not provide new insight into life, nor does it develop his faith. Like the impatient Turnus, his failure to insert the heroic quest within a larger vision suggests that his thirst for personal glory is directly tied to a mistaken sense of self-sufficiency, and his blindness leads him to what can be considered a defeat: a mediocre death at the hands of a woman. Yet we sympathize with Venier because he is young, and Dandolo's tears over his body remind us that he is a sacrificial lamb, an innocent and misguided youth who dies too soon for the aggrandizement of his city.

From distant Scheria, Odysseus returned to Ithaca only because of a magic rudderless boat granted to him by the Phaeacians (*Od.* 8.557–63, 13.70–92); similarly, Venier can go back to his battles in the West thanks to Erina's chariot. While Odysseus's return to Ithaca entailed his transformation and a new understanding of fatherhood, marriage, and friendship, Venier's return does not trigger any such development, and, as anticipated by Erina's prophecy, he dies soon after. He has been given a chance to meditate, to experience

---

66. Rosenberg 1981: 46.

67. Anderson 1968: 7. Even Bernard 1989: 42 points out how from the beginning the *Aeneid* "was held to entail an 'epic duplex' blending outstanding exemplars of the active and the contemplative lives." General observations on the theme can be found in Grilli 1953.

68. Bernard 1989: 43.

and enjoy Erina's world of seclusion, to reflect on the meaning of the active and heroic life more lucidly and at a distance. Yet Venier does not seize the opportunity in any productive way. He does not appreciate that values such as prudence and practical wisdom must be rooted in a larger perspective, and he is drawn (back) to battle. If Erina understands that the successful search for oneself entails the discovery and appreciation of a wider prospective and the risks associated with civic living, neither attitude is congenial to the Venetian young man, who may represent Venice itself. Venier and Erina meet but are unable to establish a dialogue; Venier/Venice is indifferent to Erina's insights.

Even their spiritual beliefs are never dialectically juxtaposed. Although from a religious point of view the two characters may have a lot in common, they do not seriously discuss it: Erina is not offered baptism or a return to city life, and Venier rejects a priori philosophical training. Despite fleeting allusions to a romance between these two handsome and young characters, no such complication occurs, and neither conceives children: Venier will die in battle shortly after his departure, and Erina will disappear with her beautiful island, burying her knowledge with it (*Enr.* 6.63–64).[69] Sterility and incommunicability accompany their destinies. Each remains fossilized in his or her role and fails to be persuaded by the other's point of view. Impervious to the allure of contemplation, Venier goes back to war, Erina cannot stop him (Marinella could not undermine Venice's civic religion and Catholicism so openly), and her inability to comprehend Venier's sense of duty and her isolation reveal a fictional impasse that, in my opinion, must be tied to the reality of Marinella's world: her and women's incapacity to access history in their own name, as individuals rather than as wives or mothers. This failure is not simply Marinella's but that of a society incapable of balancing civic and spiritual aspirations, of fostering the flourishing of men, and of women who cannot thrive in the urban environment without conforming to cultural expectations.

---

69. When Erina shows Venier her father's tomb, she reveals that "his spirit lies hidden" there and will do so until her death. At that time, as the souls of father and daughter "go where glorious spirits find their happy and noble rest," the mountain, the beautiful palace, and the riches contained in it will disappear like smoke or fog, and nature's forests, wild animals, and monsters will take over the island (*Enr.* 6.63–64).

~

CHAPTER 7

Fonte's Enchantress
and Beyond

A POSITIVE CHARACTERIZATION of the enchantress occurs in Marinella's *Enrico*. Moderata Fonte explored the theme in Canto 5 of the *Floridoro* with the episode of Circetta. Here she rewrites the Homeric story of Circe and Ulysses (*Odyssey* 10) and attempts to rescue Circe from her poor reputation while developing the thesis that hostility between the sexes is neither useful nor natural. Fonte confronts the stereotype of the seducer, showing herself to be familiar with ancient and Renaissance stories of Circe, and edits them for the sake of women's worth.[1] The importance of a harmonious relationship between men and women is also featured in Fonte's masterpiece *Il merito delle donne*. Fonte's conclusions in her enchantress episode differ from Marinella's, but both authors are eager to celebrate women and their accomplishments.

In her *Floridoro,* Fonte imagines that Circetta—a daughter she fictionally attributes to Circe and Ulysses—finds the knights Silano and Clarido stranded on her island and tells them about her mother's sad story and the origins of the island (Cantos 7 and 8). She recounts how Circe and Ulysses, having fallen in love, conceived her, and how not only those who accuse Circe of changing Ulysses's companions into animals should be silent ("let those who unjustly say that she turned her men into beast be silent," *Fl.* 8.13.1–2) but also that Circe, "a virtuous and beautiful fairy" ("bella e virtuosa fata," 8.12.7), taught

---

1. Finucci in Fonte 1995: xxxiv.

Ulysses all her wisdom and arts. Circe is described as completely taken by the Trojan's "graceful manners" (8.16.5). No incantation or potion helped her to resist his charm. Ultimately, to help him, she hurt herself ("per gradir altrui nocque a se stessa," 8.16.7–8). Despite her benevolence, love, and teachings, the ungrateful lover abandons her (8.14). Even by superficially reviewing this story we can see how much Circe's behavior differs from Erina's. Although both women have a special connection to knowledge and supernatural powers, while Circe is in love with the foreigner and begrudges Ulysses's departure, Erina cares for Venier like a sister, and is at peace with his choice to leave. Erina's benevolent attitude toward the Venetian is facilitated by the platonic nature of their affection. Circe instead, erotically involved with Ulysses, seems unable to detach herself from the hero. Even after she has lost him, her actions are dictated by resentment mixed with desire to preserve the memory of her unappreciative lover. She waits for Ulysses's death before taking vengeance on his homeland Ithaca. She "covers every city on Ithaca with a dark fog" (8.10.1), then magically fashions lions, tigers, and snakes as sentinels of the island. Soon these animals' fierceness and poisonous nature make the place uninhabitable. Finally, the daughter of the sun creates a mountain and on top of it erects a temple where Ulysses's ashes are preserved for eternity (8.21–24).

While avenging herself and constructing a memorial to her lover, Circe cares for her daughter, giving her eternal beauty and teaching her only good things ("insegna il ben," *Fl.* 8.25.7). She devises a plan to keep the girl on the island away from mankind. As Circetta reveals to her guests, with the sole company of three maids, a sad fate ("sciagura") keeps her shut in these unknown valleys (5.31.3–4), and she "floods her cheeks with tears" ("spargo di lacrime le gote," 5.31.6), hoping for the arrival of a knight who by means of "rare and profound virtue" (5.32.1) will "defeat the wrath of the monsters" ("de mostri avrà vinta la rabbia," 5.32.4) that inhabit the place, free her, and become king of Ithaca. Only a man as courageous as Ulysses can rescue Circetta from the prison craftily devised by her mother; unworthy suitors, unable to defeat those who guard Ulysses's ashes, are quickly turned into trees, and in Canto 5, Clarido and Silano, having arrived on the island, witness with great fear and astonishment how another knight meets this fate (5.27.4–8).[2] Having experienced Ulysses's cruelty toward women's benevolence, Circe wants to protect her daughter from the malice of men like him, yet in the attempt she condemns Circetta to a fate of isolation, deemed preferable to the company of unworthy and selfish males.

But Circetta is not happy in solitude and does not share her mother's rancor toward men. For the sake of Silano and Clarido, who are about to enter

---

2. In *Fl.* 8.30, Circetta explains to her guests what happened.

her fortress, she swears not to harm them nor to use magic to their detriment
("poi che la giovinetta afferma e giura / che d'ogni tradimento gli assicura,"
"since the young woman affirms and swears / that she guarantees them against
any treachery" *Fl.* 5.34.7–8; "io vi prestai salvo condotto / quanto al valor
dell'incantato carme," "I gave you safe conduct / from the power of the magic
spell," 5.38.1–2). A similar oath is prominent in Ludovico Dolce's rendition of
the *Odyssey*.[3] As noted previously, we cannot absolutely assess Fonte's ability
to read Greek or Latin, but, without doubt, we can assume that she read Virgil
and Homer in translation.[4] The vow reminds us of lines 10.345–46 of Dolce's
Odyssey, when Circe, after being confronted by Ulysses, swears that she will
not scheme against him. This is the moment that marks Circe's change, when
she abandons her hostility and becomes friendly. The *Odyssey* is recalled in
Fonte's poem also when Circetta, having used magic to protect her guests
from the hoard of wild animals, takes the two men by the hand, just like Mercury had taken Odysseus by the hand before giving him the magic herb moly
(*Od.* 10.280).[5] Fonte is ingeniously playing with the translated ancient source.
If Homer had created *a* Circe who turned men into beasts, Fonte creates a
daughter of Circe who protects men against beasts and plays the role of Mercury, allowing them to proceed in safety. The assimilation of Circetta, first to a
benign Circe and then to Mercury, clarifies that this character is envisioned as
an entirely positive figure: she has none of her mother's anger and is genuinely
concerned with her guests' safety and well-being.

The elaboration of Circetta seems to be original to Fonte's epic poem.
While the existence of a son of Circe and Ulysses is mentioned in several
sources (e.g., Hesiod, *Theog.* 1011–14), only Lycophron, an obscure Hellenis-
tic source, ascribes a daughter to the two famous lovers.[6] Circetta's presence
would then underscore the relevance of a female perspective—that is, Fonte's
desire to retell the story of Ulysses and Circe from the point of view of a
woman—to underscore the importance of the relationship between a mother
and a daughter as well as to comment on that between women and men. Furthermore, the appearance of a seductress who is unable to hurt her guilty lover
and herself becomes his victim is quite original. Fonte has rewritten the role
of the seductress in the romance epic to highlight the limitations of that role

---

3. In Dolce's translation *L'Ulisse di M. Lodovico Dolce* (Venezia, Giolito de Ferrari 1573)
we read "Fece subito Circe il giuramento . . ." (90).

4. About Fonte's knowledge of Latin and Greek as well as of Vergil, see chapter 1. For
related issues about Marinella, see the introduction, chapter 3, and chapter 5.

5. In Dolce's translation: "Ecco venirmi incontro un giovinetto auanti . . . mi prese per la
man" "a young man [Mercury] came towards me . . . he took me by the hand" (89).

6. About Circe and Ulysses's alleged daughter, see the entry "Cassiphone" in Visser 2017.

for women.[7] Her sympathetic approach to Circe and to her daughter suggests a degree of identification between the writer and the mythological figure.

The Circetta-Silano narrative also gives weight to the idea of the meeting between a man and a woman. We recognize in Fonte's story the epic pattern of a man who arrives at a remote land and finds a woman who grows attached to him. We do not know for sure how the episode was going to be concluded because the *Floridoro* is unfortunately unfinished (see chap. 1), but we do have enough details to suspect that Silano will rescue Circetta, only later to let her down. We also learn that Silano will prevail over the beasts, not through his valor but thanks to Circetta's help.[8] We assume that things will not go well for Circetta because in an apostrophe at 5.30 the narrator pities Circetta for her friendly welcome of the heroes:

Ah, misera, tu cerchi i tuoi riposi
Abbreviar, e 'l cor ferir c'hai sano.
Quanto meglio saria se con ritrosi
Accenti e con parlar fiero e villano
Da te scacciasti i cavallieri arditi,
Che con sì care parolette inviti.
(*Fl.* 5.30.3–8)

Ah, wretched maiden, you try to cut short
Your peace and wound your healthy heart!
How much better it would be if with contrary
Accents and with haughty and discourteous speech
You drove away the bold knights
Whom you invite with such dear little words. (trans. Kisacky)

In addition, we fear the worst for Circetta because the narrator tells us that Silano is not really in love with the young woman but only pretends to be in order to obtain her help. He cannot appreciate her because he pines for another (Celsidea) ("the knight Silano esteemed her little / for by another fire

---

7. Kolsky 1999: 171.
8. After displaying knowledge of Homer's Circe, Fonte seems to fashion the Circetta-Silano relationship according to another famous ancient model, the Medea-Jason liaison in Apollonius of Rhodes's *Argonautica*. Both Medea and Circetta are portrayed sympathetically and as reacting to tyrannical parental wills; both are eager to display their autonomy and "coming of age" by foiling their parents' expectations and falling in love with the wrong man. Eventually both women will be disappointed. We know that according to the version of the myth made famous by Euripides's tragedy, Jason, having been helped by Medea to defeat several monsters and acquire the Golden Fleece, abandoned her for a more profitable royal marriage. It is possible that Fonte in her portrayal of Circetta was influenced by these Greek texts, but more research will be required to assess that.

his desires were kindled," 11.93.3–4), yet he flirts as if animated by love: "he looks at her, he praises her and with ingenuity, every minute he shows her some sign of love" ("la mira, la vagheggia, e con ingegno / le mostra ognor qualch'amoroso segno," *Fl.* 11.93.7–8).

Overall the episode is carefully structured to instruct the readers about the dangers and deceptiveness of men's love. Circetta's meeting with the two knights contains erotic overtones, as the three characters exchange passionate glances that do not substantiate love but appear as "proof of love's blindness among the three so that while Circetta is attracted to Silano, whose heart is already engaged elsewhere, Clarido is hopelessly enamoured of Circetta."[9] Circe's motherly affection and precautions do not ultimately keep Circetta safe from cruel lovers. Fonte's pessimism is confirmed by a narrative remark at the beginning of Canto 8, when she exclaims—perhaps as a reply to Boccaccio's view in *On Famous Women* as well as to Homer—that it is not difficult to change men into animals, for many individuals are more like animals than human beings (*Fl.* 8.3). Everybody, according to Fonte, is a sort of magician who can easily change himself without magic or potions ("alla nostra età gli uomini errando, di lor medesmi son trasformatori; / e con tal facilità girsi mutando / gli veggio, senza oprar versi o liquori," 8.3.3–6). Everybody "is eager to escape from himself" ("d'uscir di sé stesso è così vago," 8.4.5), and most men "like to seem what they are not" (8.4.8). Embedded in this pessimism is a reference to Silano, who acts duplicitously (8.33.3, 8.28), while Circetta, after saving his life, recounts her past with sincerity and without hiding her nature, feelings, and hopes.

The male protagonists of this episode—Ulysses first and Silano later— cannot be improved by women's benevolence and love; instead they are selfish creatures and unrepentant liars. Fonte's judgment here of the interaction between women and men resembles Marinella's in her *Enrico*. In both texts, women want to help men even when they do not deserve their aid. We cannot help but think about Clelia and her unworthy husband and obviously about Erina and the narrow-minded Venier. But women in all situations show themselves as kind, independent, and ready for action. Clelia tries to convince her husband to stay home, afraid for his life; Erina fulfills Venier's wishes even if she realizes that his desires will hasten his death. Through Circetta, too, we see women remarkably unwilling to give up on men: despite what her mother taught her about men's nature, she falls in love with Silano and helps him. It may be innocence or naiveté, or a deeper understanding that it is not possible for a woman to escape from love and relationships if she wants to live in a community and be part of history. Significantly, the episode communi-

---

9. Malpezzi Price 2003: 117.

cates Fonte's understanding that love may be dangerous and may bring sorrow, but solitude as well, especially if it is not freely chosen, can have serious repercussions.

Circetta is also a victim of her parents' ill-fated relationship. She suffers because her father was unwilling to remain in a relationship with her mother, who then starts to hate men and turns her powers against herself and her offspring. Circetta nevertheless sees the shortcomings and value of both parents; she does not approve of her father's behavior but also rejects complete identification with her mother and her beautiful island, perceived not as an idyllic site for a protected existence but as a prison. For a while the girl plays out her destiny according to her mother's will—she remains on Ithaca and witnesses male guests being changed into trees—but eventually, when Silano arrives, she stops conforming to this passive role. The text does not tell us if Circetta had previously and unsuccessfully tried to escape alone from Ithaca, nor if Circe's plan to have her rescued by a man is only a ruse. But it clearly establishes that Circetta is not happy living in the company of her handmaids and has realized that only by collaborating with a knight can she free herself from a sterile present, thus gaining access to the world of sexuality, adulthood, and history. The Circe-created Edenic garden in which Circetta lives is rejected by the girl, who, like Odysseus on Calypso's island, refuses a protected yet fruitless existence.

Circetta becomes the spokesperson for relationships between men and women, and hope for a better future when she decides to help Silano and especially in Canto 12, when she interprets for her guests the meaning of the figures carved by her mother, Circe, on the wall of her magic fortress. We learn that the knights marvel at the beauty of the carvings representing "people of the future" (*Fl.* 12.4.3) but that "they cannot understand the meaning of those figures" by themselves ("né . . . possono interpretar quelle figure," *Fl.* 12.4.7–8). Only Circetta can understand the pictures and the intentions behind them. She elucidates that when her mother sculpted that work of art, her main goal was to celebrate the glory of a city in which "a woman would flourish destined to become the honor of her time and of her sex" (*Fl.* 12.7.7–8). Eventually, Circetta reveals that her mother was "aware of the high and subtle mind of this proud and glorious woman, and of how she will be adorned by sound customs and kind acts, and of how, as a column of sturdy virtue, she will have no equal."[10] The carvings illustrate the political and military history of Venice and climax in the history of Bianca Cappello, a Venetian aristocrat destined to marry a descendant of Ulysses and to become a patroness of Fonte. Bianca

---

10. "Di questa altera e gloriosa donna / prevedendo l'ingegno alto e sottile, / e come vestirà sì chiara gonna / di bei costume e d'ogn' atto gentile / e che fia di virtù salda colonna / sì che null'altra a lei sarà simile" (*Fl.* 12.8.1–6).

had eloped from Venice with a lover of low birth and for that reason was repudiated by her family and city. Later, her marriage to Francesco de' Medici the Tuscan grand duke prompted her rehabilitation; once married, she was celebrated by Venice as a favorite daughter of the republic.[11] Circetta clarifies that Bianca and Francesco's marriage is the part of the story that Circe depicted "more gladly" ("più volentier," *Fl.* 12.9.1) because Francesco was a descendent of Ulysses, "stronger and wiser than the hero himself . . . worthy husband of such a dear consort" ("di lui più saggio e forte . . . di sì degno signor cara consorte," *Fl.* 12.9.4–6).

Circetta's elucidation of the carvings relates to Bradamante's interpretation of Cassandra's pavilion in the *Orlando Furioso.* At the end of Ariosto's poem, the marriage between Ruggiero and Bradamante is celebrated in a pavillion decorated by the mythic prophetess Cassandra with the history of the most illustrious descendant of Trojan Hector (*OF* 46.78–97). This offspring is Cardinal Ippolito d'Este, Ariosto's own patron and the man to whom the book was dedicated. Cassandra, the weaver of the embroidery, is the famous prophetess loved by Apollo and destined to never be believed. Not only do we find in the *Furioso* elements like those emphasized by Fonte—a prophetess who foresees the future of a patron and celebrates a wedding—but also during the ceremony those who see the pavilion, Ariosto explains, just like those who see the carvings in the *Floridoro,* do not understand what they are about:

> The ladies and the knights scrutinized [Cassandra's] embroideries without understanding them . . . Alone Bradamante rejoiced in secret: instructed by Melissa, she knew their full history.[12]

When Fonte introduces Circe's carvings to illustrate a future that only her daughter Circetta can see, she is paying homage to Ariosto and emphasizing women and their role. Thanks to the prophetesses Cassandra and Melissa, Bradamante can see her future. She learns that she can fulfill her destiny and have a powerful family only by embracing sexuality and marriage; in a similar fashion, Circetta, staring at the sculptures of Circe, realizes that, so long as she remains alone on the island, she cannot have true happiness or a major role in political history.

Ariosto frames the union between the amazon Bradamante and Ruggiero as an optimistic conclusion that guarantees the origin of the Este family and stands as a symbol of the perfect family, one in which both male and female share honor and agency. Although the final scene of the *Orlando Furioso* pres-

---

11. Mariotti-Masi 1986; Steegmann 1913: 188–93. *Supra,* chap. 2.
12. Ariosto (*OF* 46.98), quoted by Jordan 1999: 307.

ents a tame Bradamante who must stand by as her future husband Ruggiero fights Rodomonte, she undoubtedly chooses her destiny as a wife, and it may not be a permanent renunciation of fighting as a knight.[13] Similarly, Circetta's exegesis of the carvings with the mention of the marriage of Bianca and Francesco is important because within the *Floridoro* it provides an optimistic ending to a story begun under the sign of hostility with the encounter between Circe and Ulysses. Worthy men who have meaningful relationships with women are exhibited and praised on the wall. Although Ulysses and Silano failed as lovers, Francesco will be successful. Even Circe is rescued in the process because by fashioning the carvings she offered her daughter hope in the future. Finally, in this episode we see how the political history of Venice is inscribed within the personal history of a woman. The many military victories of the powerful city are postponed for Bianca's successful union with Francesco, and the couple's relationship seems to be what Fonte is eager to celebrate. Private history and individual fulfillment seem more important than public success and political welfare. Fonte has made a determined effort to rewrite the myth of Circe and its telos to valorize female achievement, and ultimately to insert women in the context of a universal history.

The episode featuring Circe and Circetta is significant for another reason: in it Fonte depicts a mother preoccupied with her daughter's future. In late Renaissance Venice, aristocratic families tried to secure their daughters' marriage to a suitable party, which normally meant a man of the same economic means and social standing. If Fonte was brought up among learned relatives and friends who encouraged her literary interests and fostered her marriage with an equally educated and liberal man, her masterpiece, *Il merito*, exposes women's worry about being married to or marrying unworthy partners. Although mothers may have desired to do whatever they could to satisfy their daughters' wishes in the choice of a partner, their space for maneuvering was strongly circumscribed by social status.[14] As discussed in chapter 1, the dialogue depicts a group of noble Venetian women in a secluded garden speaking about their lives and lamenting the yoke of marriage. Some of them reveal wealthy widowhood as the most blessed of all situations. At the opening of the book, the emphasis on women's desire for seclusion and freedom is underlined in the description of the garden. There Fonte places an allegorical

---

13. Bradamante's domestication from warrior to wife is suggested by Finucci 1992: 230–53. See also Gunsberg 1987; Schiesari 1991. Against domestication, see Shemeck 1998: 47 and 91*ff*.; MacCarthy 2007: 135–67.

14. Chojnacky 2000: 115–69. The issue is obviously linked to that of forced entry into convents: families preferred to see their daughters as nuns than married to men who were not their equal. Sperling 1999: 18 estimates that 54% of Venice's patrician women lived in convents in 1581, with that number growing in the seventeenth century. For arranged marriages in Siena, see McClure 2013: 36; in Florence, see Klapisch-Zuber 1985.

fountain decorated with statues, each holding in its right hand an emblem (*impresa*) and an olive branch, and in the left a scroll containing a motto. Among the emblems displayed on the fountain we find the ermine, the phoenix, and the sun, respectively symbolizing chastity, self-sufficiency, and freedom. At the end of the dialogue, Verginia, a girl of marriageable age, declares that she now agrees with Leonora, who believes it better not to submit to any man "when one could live in peace and liberty alone."[15] These elements, framing femininity as an antagonistic desire to take charge of one's own body and affirm superiority before coming to terms with the opposite gender, remind us of Circe's hostility toward men, her devastation of Ithaca, and her attempt to isolate her daughter Circetta from male selfishness. They also remind us of Fonte's observation in *Floridoro* 5.3.1–2, when she invited women to "flee the business of love more than sin and death."

Yet at the end of *Il merito* we find in Adriana a different tendency and mind-set. Adriana is a mother who reacts to her daughter's longing to live without a husband. She promises that she will do whatever she can to find not simply a *suitable* husband but a loving one:

> "Non dir così figliola mia—disse la Regina—che *gli è forza* che io ti mariti. Ben ti prometto che quando sia il tempo, cercarò tanto che vedrò di trovarti compagnia, con la quale tu viverai consolata; *perché studierò di trovar uno nobile, savio e virtuoso più tosto che ricco, delicato e vagabondo.*" (Fonte 1988: 170)[16]

> "*I have no choice* but to find a husband for you. But I do promise that when the time comes, I'll keep searching until I find a companion with whom you'll be able to live happily, *for I shall strive to find someone noble, sensible, and virtuous, rather than someone rich, spoilt, and unreliable.*" (Fonte 1987: 238)

Clearly, while Adriana believes that being single is still not a possibility for an aristocratic Venetian woman—"gli è forza," literally "it is necessary" or "I have no choice," said by Adriana, is a strong expression—she also understands that wealth cannot be the only factor when choosing a husband, so she pledges to

---

15. Fonte 1997: 238: "Well, that's it," said Virginia. "I heard so many fine things about men yesterday, and I've heard so many more today, that I'm beginning to feel almost converted to the position of Leonora and her companions. They've made me inclined to think I'd prefer not to submit myself to any man, when I could be living in peace and liberty alone" = Fonte 1988: 170: "Io in somma—disse Verginia—ne ho udite tante ieri e ne odo tante oggi, di questi uomini, che son quasi convertita alle tante ragioni di Leonora e di quest'altre che mi hanno posto il cervello a partito, sì che penso di non voler altrimenti farmi soggetta ad uomo veruno, potendo star liberamente in pace."

16. I have used Chemello's edition (Fonte 1988).

be actively engaged in finding an enlightened husband for Verginia. In a series of important contributions, historian Stanley Chojnacki has documented how and to what degree the wealth of Venetian mothers could make a difference in determining the future of their daughters; through his study we learn that although mothers did not have the authority to dramatically alter the marriage expectations and customs typical of the Venetian patriciate, they had more flexible views on social relationships and were ultimately more inclined toward social change.[17]

If at first Adriana seems to choose the position of marriage almost *by default*—because nothing else seems to be realistically available or appropriate for women in that specific cultural milieu—she expresses a much more positive opinion about marriage when she explains that the worst part of being single is to "be deprived of that companionship that could be the joy of your life" (Fonte 1987: 239), to which Lucrezia adds:

> Ma se per caso, che pur l'aviene, che 'l marito sia buono o in sua qualità avendo ricevuto buona disposizione nel suo nascere, somigliando molto la madre, overo diventi per l'avuta creanza tale che sia essempio a gli altri di virtù e bontà, non si può poi imaginare quanta sia la felicità della donna in questo mondo, unita a tal compagnia che inseparabile dura fin alla morte." (Fonte 1988: 172)

> "But if, by some chance, as sometimes happens, one's husband is a good man (whether because he is innately good-natured, having taken after his mother, or whether his upbringing has been such as to make him a paragon of virtue and kindness, and an example to others), *then it's impossible to imagine how happy a woman's life can be, living with such a man in an inseparable companionship that lasts until death.*" (Fonte 1987: 240)

Adriana and Lucrezia's position is that chosen by Circetta when she goes against Circe's will and, by helping Silano, decides that association despite its risks is better than isolation. Although in the beginning of the episode Fonte had expressed profound doubts about the worthiness of men and the ability of women to thrive at their side, at the end of the *Floridoro* as well as in the *Merito,* she admits that, in a few cases, good men can be found, and their wives can have a fulfilling existence.[18]

---

17. Chojnacki 2000. More recently, Ferraro 2001.

18. Even during the second day, women understand that despite men's unworthiness, they continue to love them. Therefore "Fonte recognizes that women and men coexist—and manage to love one another—despite enduring and institutionalized gender inequity" (Ray 2015: 85).

EPILOGUE

~

MARINELLA AND FONTE'S writings are proof of the effervescent Venetian cultural climate of the end of the Cinquecento, and their intellectual fecundity is a consequence of that environment. While in the early phases of the Renaissance the culture of Venice had been ruled by homogeneous elites, from about 1500 the city resounded with diverse voices and interests, becoming "the most vibrant and tolerant of the capitals of Catholic Europe."[1] Marinella and Fonte's works emerge from this milieu defined by the rediscovered classical heritage, a thriving print industry, the rise of social institutions such as the academies, and an animated religio-political debate.[2] In this monograph I have privileged their knowledge of classical writers, focusing on the arguments and techniques employed by these authors to counter the belief in women's inferiority, primarily drawn from the ancient world and from contemporary authors.

In the Renaissance, higher education was built on the study of classical authors, fostering virtue and persuasive public speech conceived of as denoting the proper qualities of a man (*vir-tus*). Classical learning was defended on the basis that it strengthened children's moral and physical fiber. Boys studied tales eulogizing physical prowess and heroic glory, texts that reinforced reli-

---

1. King 2013: 592, quoting from Nicola Bonazzi's *Il Carnevale delle idee: l'antipedanteria nell'età della stampa, Venice 1538–1553* (Bologna, 2007).
2. Campbell and Larsen 2009: 1–24.

gious, classical, and manly virtues as well as rhetorical skills. In the territories around Venice, texts like Virgil's *Aeneid* were considered appropriate to accomplish these tasks. But during this time, reading the *Aeneid* (and other important classics such as those by Aristotle and Ovid) also fostered and facilitated women's intellectual emancipation. Fonte and Marinella's poems can be framed as examples of negotiations with male-authored texts that provided fertile ground in the pursuit of sensitive topics such as women's character and place in society. Humanistic education with its emphasis on practical decision-making and attention to specific circumstances proved a fundamental tool for women's critical thinking skills and reassessment of social assumptions about their nature and political environment. Humanistic training gave Fonte and Marinella the intellectual basis for a systematic reanalysis of the distinct and biased patterns of their society and the genre of romance epic. Having seriously considered the humanist representation of virtue and having familiarized themselves with the classical tradition, these Venetian authors can be considered humanists who contributed to a debate from which women long had been excluded. Women's heightened ability to contextualize and relativize their situations ties in well with an image of humanism that, despite its conservative social assumptions, tended to destabilize traditional morality. Reception theory offers an excellent conceptual framework for the assessment of female-authored Early Modern texts alongside contemporary and ancient authors. Whether direct or nuanced, these authors' engagement with their predecessors has been taken seriously, developed in close readings of their texts, which reveal women's empowerment but also their limitations. I have tried to carefully gauge their work, pondering the complex nature of their message. By negotiating with their literary past, they have reshaped it and articulated new conclusions that should be considered meaningful products of the *querelle des femmes*.

Fonte and Marinella realize that women's moral worth, goodness, and accomplishments are systematically undermined by their society and in men's books. In epics written by men, women—especially those who are opposed to the hero's epic mission or who behave in ways not codified by societal expectations—are minimized or inexorably expelled from the narrative. In the *Iliad*, Andromache is abandoned, as is Penelope in the *Odyssey*. In the *Aeneid*, Dido—wanting to keep Aeneas from founding Rome—dies; in *Orlando Furioso*, Alcina—threatening Ruggiero's dynastic fulfillment—is rejected. In the same poem, Angelica, having fallen in love with a common soldier not suitable to her rank, marries him but narratively pays for the transgression by quickly being forgotten. In their societies and literary productions, female characters are victimized when their behavior does not conform to patriarchal rules.[3] Marinella and Fonte break with this pattern and do not undermine rebellious women, their behavior, or their point of view. Fonte places at the center of her romance epic an amazon who can control her temper and succeeds where her epic male predecessors had failed; Marinella devotes large segments of her epic to women who are depicted as heroes even when they hinder the martial telos of men.

In the *Floridoro,* Fonte "corrects" the violence of epic conclusions, fashioning a new kind of ending in which she praises women and their ability to make proper moral choices in difficult situations. She creates in Risamante a gentle amazon who spares her enemy Cloridabello without hesitation. In that episode, we saw how carefully Fonte echoes the endings crafted by her male predecessors (especially Virgil and Ariosto), and how important it is for her to remind readers of those male heroes and compare them to the upright behavior of her female protagonist, who avoids violence and irrationality. Fonte's emphasis on female mercy is also accompanied by her reevaluation of love, which should unite men and women, fostering a better society. Love, in her estimation, can be a corrective for a community's prejudices and an antidote to separation and discontent. The knight Cloridabello, in love with Biondaura, more quickly and easily than other men, can appreciate the virtues of his beloved (Risamante mistaken for Biondaura). Since he is in love with her, her military prowess does not surprise him.

The importance of love and mutual esteem in conjugal matters also features in the *Giornata Seconda* of *Il merito delle donne.* Here the words of Helena, who wants to treat men with courtesy and clemency even when they are not worthy of it, highlight Fonte's belief in women's ethical excellence. Moreover, Adriana's and Lucrezia's speeches confirm the worth of a conjugal relationship marked by the love of both husband and wife. Having heard from Corinna and Leonora about the vices and tyrannical behavior of husbands, at first Adriana's daughter Verginia agrees with them and confesses that she does not want to marry or become subject to any man. Eventually Adriana's intervention in the exchange signals a development in the conversation and communicates Fonte's newly endorsed position on love. As Adriana promises to undermine the role of wealth and status while prioritizing a man's virtue and wisdom when choosing a husband for her daughter, she expresses a new way to view men and societal institutions. Ethical goodness (not wealth or blood nobility) should be used to determine a suitable partner and is considered the key for a better world. As a matter of fact, a good man will necessarily love a woman who in turn loves him. Adriana's argument is endorsed by Lucrezia,

---

3. Migiel 1995: 1–14.

who helps Verginia realize that if a woman can marry a man who is "nobile . . . di animo e di creanza" ("noble . . . in his soul and behavior," Fonte 1988: 170), she will have the most blessed of all conditions. A marriage with a good man guarantees happiness and has intrinsic merit.

A positive assessment of the relationships between men and women also appears in the episode connected to Circetta. The story is important for two main reasons: in Circetta, Fonte reshapes the stereotype of the female enchantress/seducer, fashioning a positive character, and she creates a space for the reevaluation of love and marriage. In the *Floridoro*, Circetta refuses isolation from men and understands that her nonparticipation in love games (the fate her mother had chosen for her) not only provokes her frustration but also hinders her entrance into the world of history, preventing her from having a real place in human affairs. If Circetta's mother, Circe, having been disappointed by Ulysses, deemed solitude the best fate for a woman, Circetta judges otherwise. Fonte's celebration of the union between Bianca Cappello and Francesco de' Medici (a descendant of Ulysses) is proof of this author's belief in the power of love and social progress along with women's willingness to accept the shortcomings of men and their deep commitment to family life. Fonte's encouraging conclusions about love square nicely with those established in *Merito* through Adriana and Lucrezia.

The worth of wives is also an important theme in Marinella's romance epic. In the *Enrico*, Clelia and Areta's loving words and actions have an essential role. In their wifely devotion we see their bravery and heroic qualities: they are not afraid of dying to remain near their men. In their tales, Marinella's debt to the classical tradition is particularly visible since the two episodes echo those of Dido in Virgil's *Aeneid*, Ceyx and Alcyone in Ovid's *Metamorphoses*, and Protesilaus and Laodamia in the *Heroides*. Like their ancient prototypes, Clelia and Areta are wives left behind by husbands eager for glory in war. Although in the end they cannot escape abandonment or save their husbands from death on the battlefield, they are an example of resistance to the epic plot, exerting control over the narrative. Intrinsically tied to Marinella's pro-woman and antiwar agenda, Clelia and Areta have independent minds, appreciate peace, and can enlighten men about their misconceived priorities. They are able to turn men into better lovers by means of their wise and loving behavior. They try to persuade their husbands to privilege their families over their reputation as warriors. Even if these women are not successful (their husbands leave), they persuasively voice their point of view, stirring the reader's sympathies. They triumphantly demonstrate (*pace* Aristotle) the power of minor characters over the plot.

In Marinella's poem, the importance of peace is also developed in the encounter between the Venetian soldier Venier and the peace-loving Erina. In her book-length exploration of the *Enrico,* Lazzari questions Venier's precise role in this saga. It is a valid concern, as he does not have a dynastic role in the plot and is not even granted a proper *aristeia.* Venier seems to be invented mostly to give prominence to Emilia, the amazon who kills him, but I would add that above all he gives relevance to the prophetess Erina and her message about the importance of the *vita contemplativa.*[4] Recall that Erina lives in isolation and perfect harmony with her female companions, studies nature, and develops an appreciation for the physical and metaphysical world. Erina's wicked forefathers had to abandon Venice to escape from certain death. Removed from city life, they become better people able to cultivate their spirituality and relationship with God. In this plotline, Erina (and her ancestors) must live on an island far away from the city because urban depravity does not permit them to get in touch with their spiritual needs or embrace values that Marinella's society often dismisses as nonessential. If on the one hand the author pays lip service to the ideals celebrated by the Serenissima by writing an epic poem that praises men, war, and the siege of Constantinople, on the other hand she draws on the philosophical undercurrents of the pastoral topos to argue that the superior man (and woman) shuns the temptations of corrupted or unpredictable politics, instead focusing the mind on seeking the way home to true happiness.

Venier's exposure to Erina and her garden of plenty points him toward spiritual flourishing. It is not a deceptive maneuver, but rather one designed to help him discover the falsity of the ideals he has worshipped. Erina does not propose escapism or enticement of the senses but philosophical contemplation and study. Marinella creates in Erina the equivalent of what Dante created in his Limbo with "la bella scola" (Homer, Horace, Ovid, Lucan, and Vergil, *Inf.* 4.94), an unbaptized individual who can still connect with God and true goodness because of a thirst for knowledge. The Counter-Reformation with its emphasis on spiritual health is an important factor in shaping this episode, but ancient discourses on the importance of *askesis* also play a role. In fact, Erina is more like Socrates than Circe or Alcina. She represents a new kind of lover, a philosopher who cares, above all, for the soul of her beloved. The purpose of Erina's interaction with Venier is to make him aware of the limits of his desires, of the inadequacy of a life dominated by the thirst for battle, and consequently to stimulate a will to *cure* his condition. Erina strongly resem-

---

4. Lazzari 2010: 155–60.

bles Plato's philosopher-kings. After continuously contemplating what is most noble, she becomes detached from the material world. In defining perfection, she looks beyond the obligations of a political community; in her commitment to ethical growth, she understands that perfection cannot be structured in terms of the common good alone, but must consider a person's *askesis,* an internal itinerary of elevation that often can happen only in the "pastoral space" traditionally associated with a philosophical and moral project of individual growth. Marinella's failure to free Erina from her island is the failure of a society that, theoretically, has begun to acknowledge *women as intellect* but is unable to accommodate that important realization in its communal life and institutions. Detached from any practical (societal, economic, or legal) advancement, women's cultural ascendancy makes them aware of their worth but not much else.

UNDER THE SIGN OF FICTION: *PIETAS* AND THE ENDING OF THE *ENRICO*

Beyond Erina, Clelia, and Areta, Marinella reveals her commitment to moderation and peaceful modes at the ending of the *Enrico.* While in the final duel between the amazons Meandra and Claudia she could not draw attention to the importance of restraint and mercy, she rediscovers these values and their crucial role when she describes Baldovino's and Enrico's behavior during the siege of Constantinople.

In the concluding lines, Marinella manages to undercut the traditional male epic agenda committed to military glory by reasserting a pacifist and religious perspective already highlighted by Fonte in her duel between Risamante and Cloridabello. Written under the sign of fiction—we cannot determine from historical sources how Dandolo and the leaders of the expedition behaved in the last hours of the Fourth Crusade—this last segment of the poem idealizes the behavior of the Venetian captains portrayed as superior in *pietas.* In praising this Venetian victory, Marinella creates an ending made memorable not by duels or acts of heroism for the fatherland, but by tears and human compassion. The doge and Bonifazio behave as truly merciful leaders.

While it is impossible to establish precisely how Dandolo behaved during and after the siege, we do know that plundering, rape, and violence spread throughout the city.[5] P. G. Ramusio—one of our most reliable sources—mentions the crusaders' avaricious behavior, which was their last resort in restor-

---

5. Madden 1995; Queller 1997: 193–205; Queller and Katele 1982.

ing financial losses after Alexius's denial of payment.[6] Ultimately, "the sack
of Constantinople was the most profitable and shameful in medieval European history. Oaths sworn on relics to leave the city's churches, monaster-
ies, and women unmolested were routinely ignored. The loss of life and the
destruction of the physical city were great."[7] Marinella fills in the silence of
the sources and in her epic crafts an ending that stresses the personal piety of
the men in charge.

Bonifazio "gives some help ("procura agio") to the inhabitants of Constantinople and forgives them ("lor perdona," *Enr.* 27.93.5–6). He is depicted as a
perfectly restrained and courteous knight at 27.21–24 when a defeated Fausto
offers him a ransom for his life. Without hesitation, he "loses his scorn for one
worthy of his pity" ("frenò lo sdegno / c'avea contro colui di pietà degno," *Enr.*
27.22.7–8). Similarly, in a minor episode of the *Gerusalemme* (*GL* 20.140–42),
Goffredo both spared Altamoro, King of Samarkand, and refused his ransom.
These two details are notable because they suggest Goffredo's superiority over
the two most important heroes of classical epic: he is better than Achilles, who
accepted ransom from Priam for the body of Hector, and Aeneas, who refused
to spare the suppliants Magus and Turnus.[8] In the *Enrico,* Bonifazio's conduct
replicates that of Goffredo. He too behaves better than Achilles and Aeneas.
Bonifazio's actions are strikingly different from those of the crusader Giacinto,
who violently beheads one enemy (*Enr.* 27.26.8) and refuses to show mercy
to another ("chiusa ogni strada alla clemenza egli avea," "he had closed every
pathway to clemency," *Enr.* 27.29.5) even as the Greek begs for his life. Giacinto
is convinced that "it is a sin to show mercy" to his adversary ("l'usar teco
pietade è colpa grave," *Enr.* 27.29.1). But above all, Enrico is the hero portrayed
as the perfectly moderate captain. He displays his self-control throughout the
whole poem and, in particular, at the end. We see his tame heart in Canto 12
when "he becomes incensed with anger in front of this spectacle but reason
keeps his desire in check" ("a spettacolo tal s'infiamma d'ira, / ma raffrena il
desio ragion," 12.102.6–7). Victorious in Canto 24, he is celebrated for being
respectful of the dead and the living:

6. Ramusio 1604: 93; Madden 2007: 166.

7. Madden 2007: 173. Nicetas Choniates, whose account of the Crusade is normally hostile
to the Venetians, for once seems favorable to them; see Madden 2007: 173; Constanble 2008:
341.

8. Quint 2014: 203. The emphasis on the Venetian captains' restraint is indirectly commenting on Tasso's brutal representation of the conquest of Jerusalem at the end of the poem.
We know that Tasso was not satisfied with it and revised it in the publication of the *Gerusalemme Conquistata* (1593), which, as Garrison 1992 establishes, tries "to reassert the claim of
'arme pietose'" (186). About epic endings, see also Svensson 2011; for the editorial history of
Tasso's *Liberata* and *Conquistata* and an assessment of the latter, see Girardi 2002.

Benchè vittorioso e trionfante
Enrico fosse; nondimen doglioso
A l'ossa di color che 'l giorno innante
Guerreggiando perir, dona il riposo:
E perchè genti vede tante, e tante
Arse dal foco fervido, pietoso
Fa che i suoi di Sicena ai molli lidi
Traghettar molti, e pur son Greci infidi.
(*Enr.* 24.99)

Although Enrico was victorious and triumphant, sorrowful for the bones of those who had died fighting the day before, he granted them a tomb: and since he saw many people burnt by the blazing fire, filled with pity he commands his men to transport many of the untrustworthy Greeks to the gentle shores of Sicena.

Overall, Marinella describes the siege of Constantinople in negative terms, and the crusaders (the Italian and Frankish ranks mentioned in *Enr.* 24.53.2) are "greedy and without pity while they go through the high palaces and rich dwellings" ("senza pietà di preda avidi e d'oro / scorron gli alti palagi e i ricchi tetti," *Enr.* 24.54.1–2).[9] The siege is a cataclysm in which horror and fury prevail:

L'altezza guerriera avviene ch'apporte,
Piena d'orgoglio ancor contra il dovere,
Ferite, incendi e strazio, in ogni parte
Ferve e s'accende il furioso Marte.
(*Enr.* 24.53.5–8)

Full of pride and against duty, military success, as it happens, brings wounds, fire and devastation on every side. Furious Mars lights up and burns.

Similarly, a few lines later, we learn that "discord ... inflames people and hardens the hearts" ("e la Discordia ... le genti infiamma d'ira, inaspra i cori," *Enr.* 24.55.5 ... 7). Prayers are worth nothing ("prego ... non muove," *Enr.* 24.56.3), while old and young, rich and poor, noble and humble are victims of the mas-

---

9. In Marinella 2011: 528n7 Galli Stampino notes: "It is noteworthy that the entrance and conquest of Byzantium are not presented in a triumphal light; the ambivalence of M. towards the war emerges here as well, in the emphasis on losses and the pain inflicted by the crusaders to the city, defined as 'unhappy' (52.8), in contrast with the negative adjectives normally attributed to Byzantium in the poem" (my trans.).

sacre (*Enr.* 24.56). Some people commit suicide (*Enr.* 24.57.4), and a river of blood runs through the city (*Enr.* 24.58). Marinella represents the last hours of Constantinople, remembering Tasso's final canto in which—apart from Goffredo's merciful treatment of Altamoro—we see many atrocities inflicted by Christians on a defeated and unresisting enemy.[10] But in the madness of Canto 24, Dandolo, following Goffredo's example, remains pious and moderate.

Even when Bonifazio and Baldovino want to take advantage of the situation and punish Mirtillo, Enrico, "filled with pity and reasonable, sees the need of his beloved friends for food and rest . . . makes them stop fighting" ("pietoso e giusto / vede il bisogno degli amati amici / d'alimenti e di posa . . . fa che cessin da l'armi," *Enr.* 24.83.1–3 . . . 5). He is an exemplary leader meeting the needs of his own men and remaining gentle toward the enemy. Octaves 84 and 86 display his exemplary behavior:

Che sa che la clemenza e la pietade
Sono le gemme, onde il più bel diadema
Orna le sue ricchezze, nè beltade
Trovi tra l'ostro, se giustizia è scema;
Ei più non vuol che le latine spade,
Nè 'l vincitore il vinto insulti e prema.
(*Enr.* 24.84.1–6)

Who knows that clemency and pity are gems whose riches adorn the most beautiful diadem, (that) you cannot find beauty in purple without justice; he no longer wants for Latin swords nor for the winner to insult and oppress the defeated.

Il capitan, che scerne il tutto e vede,
E ch'ha rette le voglie e i pensier saggi,
Cui pietà dolce il nobil cor già siede,
Nè sia che cruda e fera voglia assaggi,
Vuol, che da le licenze e da le prede,
E da le uccisioni e da gli oltraggi
Cessino i suoi soldati, a suon di trombe
Fa che 'l suo pio voler suoni e rimbombe.
(*Enr.* 24.86)

The captain who sees and understands everything and has right desires and wise thoughts, in whose heart sweet pity resides already, lest he may taste

---

10. Stephens 1995: 301–2.

rough and cruel desire, wants his soldiers to stop from licentious behavior and pillaging and killing and other outrages, and so with the sound of the trumpet he makes his pious intentions ring and echo.[11]

Dandolo's virtue is highlighted again in Canto 26 when, before giving the signal for the final battle, he *reins in* ("raffrena") his soldiers "ferocious desires" ("l'empito feroce," *Enr.* 26.5.8). Finally, in Canto 27, he behaves like a wise ruler, sparing the entire populace that begs for life. Marinella admires this leader's control before, during, and after the siege. She does not feature him fighting in a *singolar tenzone* against an archenemy but rather granting mercy to the enemy on his knees, begging for pity:

> Già soggiogati sono e vinti e presi,
> Domate l'altezze, i fasti i vanti;
> Parte fuggiti e morti e parte stesi
> Chiedean venia per Dio, lassi e tremanti;
> Rotte le forti mura, i tetti accessi,
> Tutt'orror e terror cordoglio e pianti,
> Vinta d'Enrico al piè la Grecia giace,
> E se garrula resse, oppressa tace.
> (*Enr.* 27.90.1–8)

> *They were subjugated, vanquished, and captured, their haughtiness, their pomp, their boasts were put down. Some fled, some had died, and others on the ground asked for mercy, all tired and trembling. The strong walls were broken, buildings were set on fire, and everywhere there was horror, terror, fears and tears. Vanquished Greece lay at Enrico's feet, once garrulous in its rule, now it was silent in its oppression.*

> Deposto il cor superbo e 'l voler empio
> Piglian di servitù gravosa soma,
> Al capitano si danno, e cheggion fine
> A tanti morti, a l'ampie lor ruine.
> (*Enr.* 27.91.5–8)

They gave up their superb hearts and Godless will, and they took on themselves the heavy burden of servitude, giving themselves up to the cap-

---

11. The translations from Cantos 24 and 26 are mine because those Cantos do not appear in Galli Stampino's English edition.

tain [Enrico] and asking for an end to so many deaths and to their great devastation.

Ei ch'ha gli occhi de l'alma ne l'eterno
Principio fissi e sua bontà rimira,
Tenta a lui somigliarsi, e ne lo interno
Dolce pietà del cor placido spira;
Difende e accoglie con amor paterno,
(*Lor sventura fatal piange e sospira*)
L'altissime matrone e i giovinetti
Nobili saggi e tra maggiori eletti.
(*Enr.* 27.92)

He kept his soul's eyes on the eternal principle [God], admiring his goodness and trying to emulate Him. Inside his heart sweet mercy breathed, so he defended and welcomed the noble matrons and noble and wise young people, among the best in the land, and with a father's love *he cried and sighed over their fatal misfortunes.*

Il popol poi, che tra l'eccelse mura
Era de l'alta rocca umil si dona
A Bonifazio, in cui sede ha sicura
Soave amore, e di ciò vanto suona;
Non pur non li dà noia, ma procura
Qualch'agio a gl'infelici, e lor perdona,
Ah come bella splende tra l'orrore
De l'armi a gli occhi altrui pietà ed amore!
(*Enr.* 27.93)

Then the people inside the walls of that tall fortress humbly surrendered to Bonifazio. Inside him sweet love held firm sway, and this was his reason for boasting. Not only did he not bother them, but he gave some comfort to those unhappy people and he forgave them. How beautifully do mercy and love shine in one's eyes among horrible weapons!

The defeated people of Byzantium give themselves to Enrico and Bonifazio and beg for mercy, which is promptly bestowed upon them. Remarkably, Enrico cries with them. While history books remember the greediness and unspeakable acts of barbarism, Marinella memorializes the "dolce pietà" and "soave amore" of Enrico and Baldovino. This final depiction of succor illustrates Marinella's endorsement of pity. She wants to conclude her poem with the touching image of leaders who spare their enemy and Dandolo as a mourner of sorts. The emphasis on mercy sends a message about what, according to Marinella, deserves unending praise. "Among the horror of arms" ("tra l'orror de l'armi"), the "vanto" of great men (the reason for "boasting" *Enr.* 27.93.4) resides in having the strength to be merciful. This quality, Marinella realizes, is the only one worthy of being memorialized in epic.

Particularly important is the detail of Dandolo's tears in *Enrico* 27.92.6. In a 1999 article, Thomas Greene highlighted the literary epic's engagement with grief and its capacity to create a community of mourners. Greene argues convincingly that the *Iliad*'s primary concern is not so much with heroic achievement but with the affective cost of achievement.[12] He cites Priam's visit to the tent of his son's killer (*Iliad* 24.507–16) as proof, and claims that the supreme force of the encounter lies in the tears of Priam and Achilles, who mourn Hector and all the unnumbered dead.[13] What Greene calls "the epic telos of tears" (193) also occurs in Marinella's poem when the winner and loser cry together (*Enr.* 27.92.6). As in *Iliad* 24, compassion seems the most important qualification for a leader. Marinella's narrative agenda is revealed in this precise moment, when the hero who should be triumphantly celebrating his victory is instead crying with the defeated. Dandolo cries for and with his enemies, just as a few octaves earlier he had cried for the death of his beloved friend Venier. Marinella is not interested in the unqualified success of Venice: she is interested in the celebration of compassion and morally competent leaders.

Christine Perkell has recently elaborated Green's conclusions. She too interprets the *Iliad* as provocatively questioning traditional heroic values and identifies in Achilles the character who most openly (through his words and behavior) challenges the heroic code. In her interpretation, Achilles's pity for Priam, allowing for the return of Hector's body, "emerges as the true heroic act and high moral value of the poem."[14] Furthermore, in *Iliad* 24, in the women's lament over Hector's body, Hector's devotion to the gods and kindness toward women—*not* his ability as a warrior or his commitment to the fatherland—receives the most attention. Like Clelia and Areta lamenting their dead husbands and in that gesture reshaping their men's heroic identities, Hecuba, Helen, and Andromache at the end of the *Iliad* cry for Hector in public laments: in this act, they do not remember the man as he would like to

---

12. Greene 1999: 192.
13. Ibid., 191.
14. Perkell 2008: 96.

be remembered—so committed to heroic glory as to be ready to die for it—but first and foremost as a gentle and pious human being.[15]

That these lamentations come at the end of the poem requires reflection in determining the true nature and agenda of the *Iliad* as much as Enrico's tears at the end of Marinella's poem. As victory is obtained, Marinella makes us dwell on the image of Dandolo crying with the defeated and behaving like a good shepherd who "is above everyone in valor and rules over his warrior herd with justice and mercy" ("in virtù supera ogn'altro e regge / con giustizia e pietà guerriero gregge," *Enr.* 27.67.7–8). In a literary work, closure is achieved when it produces the sense of having reached a suitable endpoint. Effective closure reinforces the sense of finality, completion, and composure in a work of art; it should give unity and coherence to the reader's experience by providing a point from which all the former elements can be evaluated as parts of a significant design.[16] In Marinella's epic, this suitable stopping place is not the conquest of Constantinople but the mercy of Enrico.

---

15. Ibid., 101–4; Greene 1999: 189–203. For "textual mourning not dissimilar from Homeric praxis" in Tasso's *Conquistata,* see Brazeau 2014: 47*ff.*

16. Herrnstein Smith 1968: 36. On closure in Greek and Latin literature, see Roberts, Dunn, and Fowler 1997; Grewing, Acosta-Hughes, and Kirichenko 2013.

BIBLIOGRAPHY

Adlam, Carol, and David Shepherd (eds.) 2000. *The Annotated Bakhtin Bibliography*. London: Modern Humanities Research Association.

Adler, Eve. 2003. *Vergil's Empire: Political Thought in the Aeneid*. Lanham, MD: Rowman and Littlefield.

Ahl, Frederick, and Hanna M. Roisman. 1996. *The Odyssey Reformed*. Ithaca, NY: Cornell University Press.

Aiston, Sarah Jane. 2010. "Women, Education, and Agency, 1600–2000: An Historical Perspective." In Spence, Aiston, and Meikle (eds.) 2010: 1–9.

Alanen, Lilli, and Charlotte Witt (eds.) 2005. *Feminist Reflections on the History of Philosophy*. Dordrecht: Kluwer Academic.

Albis, Robert. 1996. *Poet and the Audience in the Argonautica of Apollonius*. Lanham, MD: Rowman and Littlefield.

Alexiou, Margaret. 1974. *The Ritual Lament in Greek Tradition*. Cambridge: Cambridge University Press.

Alighieri, Dante. 1986. *The Divine Comedy of Dante Alighieri. Paradise*. Trans. Allen Mandelbaum. New York: Bantam Classics.

Allaire, Gloria. 1994. "The Warrior Woman in Late Medieval Prose Epics." *Italian Culture* 13: 33–43.

Allen, Prudence. 2002. *The Concept of Woman: The Early Humanist Reformation, 1250–1500*. Volume II. Grand Rapids, MI: Eerdmans.

Almond, Philip. 1999. *Adam and Eve in Seventeenth Century Thought*. Cambridge: Cambridge University Press.

Alpers, Paul. 1996. *What Is Pastoral?* Chicago: University of Chicago Press.

Ambrosini, Federica. 2000. "Toward a Social History of Women in Venice: From the Renaissance to the Enlightenment." In Martin and Romano (eds.) 2002: 420–53.

Amussen, Susan D., and Adele Seef (eds.) 1998. *Attending to Early Modern Women*. Newark: University of Delaware Press.

Anderson, W. S. 1968. "*Pastor Aeneas*: on Pastoral Themes in the *Aeneid*." *Transactions of the American Philological Association* 99: 1–17.

Andrea, Alfred J. 2000. *Contemporary Sources for the Fourth Crusade*. Leiden: Brill.

Antonello, Pierpaolo and Simon A. Gilson (eds.) 2004. *Science and Literature in Italian Culture from Dante to Calvino. A Festschrift for Patrick Boyde*. Oxford: Humanities Research Center, University of Oxford.

Ardissino, Erminia. 1999. "La *Gerusalemme Liberata* ovvero l'epica tra storia e visione." *Chroniques italiennes* 58/59: 9–24.

———. 2001. *Il Barocco e il* sacro: *La predicazione del teatino Paolo Aresi tra letteratura, immagini e scienza*. Vatican City: Libreria Vaticana.

Ariosto, Ludovico. 1983. *Orlando Furioso*. Trans. Guido Waldman. Oxford: Oxford University Press.

———. 1999. *Orlando Furioso*. A cura di Cesare Segre. Milano: Mondadori.

Aristotle. 1894. *The Nicomachean Ethics*. Ed. Bywater and trans. H. Rackham. Loeb Classical Library.

Arrigoni, Giampiera. 1982. *Camilla Amazzone e sacerdotessa di Diana*. Milano: Cisalpina Goliardica.

Armstrong, Richard. 2014. "Homer, Translation." *Encyclopedia of Ancient Greek Language and Linguistics*. <http://referenceworks.brillonline.com/entries/encyclopedia-of-ancient-greek-language-and-linguistics/homer-translation-EAGLLCOM_00000390>

Ascoli, Russel Albert. 1987. *Ariosto's Bitter Harmony: Crisis and Evasion in the Italian Renaissance*. Princeton, NJ: Princeton University Press.

Asenso, Eugenio, and José V. de Pina Martins. 1982. *Luis de Camões: El humanismo en su obra poética Los Lusíadas y las rimas en la poesía española (1580–1640)*. Paris: Fundacáo Calouste Gulbenkian.

Baca, Albert R. 1969. "Ovid's Claim to Originality and *Heroides* 1." *Transactions of the American Philological Association* 100: 1–10.

Bacon, Helen H. 1986. "*The Aeneid* as a Drama of Election." *Transactions of the American Philological Association* 116: 305–34.

Badia, Janet, and Jennifer Phegley (eds.) 2005. *Reading Women: Literary Figures and Cultural Icons from the Victorian Age to the Present*. Toronto: University of Toronto Press.

Baker, R. J. 1968. "*Miles Annosus*: The Military Motif in Propertius." *Latomus* 27: 322–49.

Bakhtin, Mikhail. 1981. *The Dialogic Imagination: Four Essays*. Ed. Michael Holquist. University of Texas Press.

Bandera, Cesareo. 1981. "Sacrificial Levels in Virgil's *Aeneid*." *Arethusa* 14: 217–39.

Baranski, Zygmunt, and Shirley Vinall (eds.) 1991. *Women and Italy: Essays on Gender, Culture and History*. London: Macmillan.

Barbierato, Federico. 2012. *The Inquisitor in the Hat Shop: Inquisition, Forbidden Books and Unbelief in Early Modern Venice*. Farnham: Ashgate.

Barchiesi, Alessandro. 2001. *Speaking Woman: Narrative and Intertext in Ovid and Other Latin Poets*. London: Duckworth.

Bardazzi, Giovanni. 2001. "Le rime spirituali di Vittoria Colonna e Bernardino Ochino." *Italique. Poésie italienne de la Renaissance* 4: 63–101.

Bassi, Simonetta. 2004. "The Lunar Renaissance: Images of the Moon in Ludovico Ariosto and Giordano Bruno." In Antonello and Gilson (eds.) 2004: 136–53.

Basson, W. P. 1986. "Vergil's Camilla: A Paradoxical Character." *Acta Classica* 29: 57–68.

Bate, Marcus. 2004. "Tempestuous Poetry: Storms in Ovid's 'Metamorphoses,' 'Heroides' and 'Tristia.'" *Mnemosyne* 57.3: 295–310.

Bedani, Gino, Zygmunt Baranski, Anna Laura Lepschy, and Brian Richardson (eds.) 1997. *Sguardi sull'Italia: Miscellanea dedicata a Francesco Villari dalla Society for Italian Studies. Italian Studies Occasional Papers.* Leeds: Society for Italian Studies.

Beer, Marina. 1987. *Romanzi di Cavalleria: il "Furioso" e il romanzo italiano del primo Cinquecento.* Roma: Bulzoni.

Behr, Francesca D'Alessandro. 2014. "Thinking Anew about Lavinia." *Illinois Classical Studies* 39: 191–212.

Beissinger, Margaret, Jane Tylus, and Susan Wofford (eds.) 1999. *Epic Traditions in the Contemporary World: The Poetics of Community.* Berkeley: University of California Press.

Bellamy, Elizabeth. 1992. *Translations of Power: Narcissism and the Unconscious in Epic History.* Ithaca, NY: Cornell University Press.

———. 1994. "Alcina's Revenge: Reassessing Irony and Allegory in the *Orlando Furioso.*" *Annali d'italianistica* 12: 61–74.

Bellavitis, Anna, Nadia Maria Filippini, and Tiziana Plebani (eds.) 2012. *Spazi, poteri, diritti delle donne a Venezia in età moderna.* Verona: QuiEdit.

Belloni, Gino, and Riccardo Drusi (eds.) 2007. *Il rinascimento italiano e l'Europa: umanesimo ed educazione.* Vol II. Vicenza: Angelo Colla editore.

Benedetti, Laura. 1993. "La Sconfitta di Diana: note per una rilettura della *Gerusalemme Liberata.*" *MLN* 108.1: 31–58.

———. 1996. *La Sconfitta di Diana: un percorso per la Gerusalemme Liberata.* Ravenna: Longo.

———. 2008. "Le *Essortationi* di Lucrezia Marinella: l'ultimo messaggio di una misteriosa veneziana." *Italica* 85.4: 381–95.

Benedetti, Laura, Julia Hairston, and Silvia Ross (eds.) 1996. *Gendered Contexts: New Perspectives in Italian Cultural Studies.* New York: Peter Lang.

Bendinelli Predelli, Maria. 1994. "La donna guerriera nell'immaginario italiano del Tardomedioevo." *Italian Culture* 13: 13–32.

Benson, Pamela Joseph. 1992. *The Invention of the Renaissance Woman: The Challenge of Female Independence in the Literature and Thought of Italy and England.* University Park: Pennsylvania State University Press.

Benzoni, Gino. 1977. "Aspetti della cultura urbana nella società veneta del '500–'600: le accademie." *Archivio Veneto* 108: 87–159.

———. 1988. "L'accademia: appunti e spunti per un profilo." *Ateneo Veneto* 26: 37–58.

———. 1991. "La forma del dialogo." In Branca and Ossola (eds.) 1991: 23–42.

Bernard, John. 1989. *Ceremonies of Innocence: Pastoralism in the Poetry of Edmund Spenser.* Cambridge: Cambridge University Press.

———. 1999. "Ch'io nol lasci ne la penna": Ariosto's Discourses of Desire." *Italica* 76.3: 291–313.

Bernardo, Aldo S. 1962. *Petrarch, Scipio and the Africa.* Baltimore: The John Hopkins University Press.

Bernstein, Jane. 1998. *Music Printing in Renaissance Venice: The Scotto Press (1539–1572).* Oxford: Oxford University Press.

Biagioli, Mario. 1993. *Galileo, Courtier.* Chicago: University of Chicago Press.

Black, Robert. 2004. *Humanism and Education in Medieval and Renaissance Italy: Tradition and Innovation in Latin Schools from the Twelfth to the Fifteenth Century.* Cambridge: Cambridge University Press.

———. 2011. "Ovid in medieval Italy." In Clark, Coulson, and McKinley (eds.) 2011: 123–42.

Bloch, Howard R. 1991. *Medieval Misogyny and the Invention of Western Romantic Love.* Chicago: University of Chicago Press.

Block, E. 1982. "The Narrator Speaks: Apostrophe in Homer and Virgil." *Transactions of the American Philological Association* 112: 7–22.

Bloom, Harold (ed.) 2004. *The Italian Renaissance.* New York: Chelsea House.

Boas, George, and Joseph Campbell (eds.) 1967. *Myth, Religion, and Mother Right: Selected Writings of J. J. Bachofen.* Princeton, NJ: Princeton University Press.

Boccaccio, Giovanni. 1993. *The Decameron.* Trans. Guido Waldman. Oxford: Oxford University Press.

———. 2003. *Famous Women.* Trans. Virginia Brown. I Tatti Renaissance Library. Cambridge: Harvard University Press.

Bolzoni, Lina. 1981. "L'accademia veneziana: splendore e decadenza di un' utopia enciclopedica." *Annali dell'istituto storico italo-germanico* 9: 117–67.

———. 1989. "Campanella e le donne: fascino e negazione della differenza." *Annali d'Italianistica* 7: 193–225.

———. 1995. "Rendere visibile il sapere: l'accademia Veneziana tra modernità e utopia." In Chambers and Quiviger (eds.) 1995: 61–75.

Bond, Christopher. 2011. *Spenser, Milton, and the Redemption of the Epic Hero.* Newark: University of Delaware Press.

Borsetto, Luciana. 1990. *Il furto di Prometeo: imitazione, scrittura, riscrittura nel Rinascimento.* Alessandria: Edizioni dell'Orso.

Borsetto, Luisa. 1989. *L' "Eneida" tradotta: riscritture poetiche del testo di Virgilio nel XVI secolo.* Milano: Unicopli.

Bossier, Philip. 2010. "Female Writing and the Use of Literary Byways. Pastoral Drama by Maddalena Campiglia (1553–1595)." In Gilleir, Montoya, and Van Dijk (eds.) 2010: 115–35.

Botley, Paul. 2004. *Latin Translations in the Renaissance: The Theory and Practice of Leonardo Bruni, Giannozzo Manetti and Erasmus.* Cambridge: Cambridge University Press.

Bottoni, Luciano. 2002. *Leonardo e l'androgino: l'eros transessuale nella cultura, nella pittura e nel teatro del Rinascimento.* Milano: F. Angeli.

Booth, Wayne. 1961. *The Rhetoric of Fiction.* Chicago: University of Chicago Press.

Bowra, C. M. 1952. *Heroic Poetry.* London: Macmillan.

Bouwsma, William. 1968. *Venice and the Defense of Republican Liberty.* Berkeley: University of California Press.

———. 1990. *A Usable Past: Essays in European Cultural History.* Berkeley: University of California Press.

———. 2000. *The Waning of the Renaissance, 1550–1640.* New Haven, CT: Yale University Press.

Boyd, B. W. 1992. "Virgil's Camilla and the Traditions of Catalogue and Ecphrasis (*Aeneid* 7.803–17)." *American Journal of Philology* 113: 213–34.

Boyle, Anthony. 1986. *The Chaonian Dove: Studies in the Eclogues, Georgics, and Aeneid of Virgil.* Leiden: Brill.

———(ed.) 1995. *Roman Literature and Ideology: Ramus Essays for J. P. Sullivan.* Bendigo: Aureal Publications.

Branca, Vittorio, and Carlo Ossola (eds.) 1991. *Crisi e Rinnovamenti nell'autunno del Rinascimento a Venezia.* Firenze: Olschki.

Branca, Vittorio et al. (eds.) 1982. *Il Rinascimento: aspetti e problemi attuali. Atti del Congresso AISLLI, Belgrade 1979.* Firenze: Olschki.

Brand, C. P. 1965. *Torquato Tasso: A Study of the Poet and His Contribution to English Literature.* Cambridge: Cambridge University Press.

———. 1974. *The Writers of Italy 1: Ariosto.* Edinburgh: Edinburgh University Press.

Brazeau, Bryan. 2014. "Who Wants to Live Forever? Overcoming Poetic Immortality in Torquato Tasso's *Gerusalemme Conquistata.*" *Modern Language Notes* 129: 42–61.

Bridenthal, Renate, and Claudia Koonz (eds.) 1977. *Becoming Visible: Women in European History.* Boston: Houghton Mifflin.

Brockliss, W., P. Chaudhuri, A. Haimson Lushkov, and K. Wasdin (eds.) 2012. *Reception and the Classics: An Interdisciplinary Approach to the Classical Tradition.* Cambridge: Cambridge University Press.

Bronzini, Cristoforo. 1625. *Della dignità, e nobiltà delle donne.* Ed. Zanobi Piagnoni. Firenze.

Brooks, Robert. 1953. "*Discolor Aura*: Reflections on the Golden Bough." *American Journal of Philology* 74: 260–80.

Brown, Marshall. 1975. "In the Valley of the Ladies." *Italian Quarterly* 18: 33–52.

Brown, Robert. 1990. "The Homeric Background to a Vergilian Repetition (*Aeneid 1.744 = 3.516*)." *American Journal of Philology* 111: 182–86.

Brundin, Abigail. 2008. *Vittoria Colonna and the Spiritual Poetics of the Italian Reformation.* Aldershot: Ashgate.

Bruner, Jerome. 1996. *The Culture of Education.* Cambridge, MA: Harvard University Press.

Buchan, Mark. 2004. *The Limits of Heroism: Homer and the Ethics of Reading.* Ann Arbor: University of Michigan Press.

Bulckaert, Barbara. 2010. "Self-Tuition and the Intellectual Achievement of Early Modern Women: Anna Maria Van Shurman (1607–1678)." In Spence, Aiston, and Meikle (eds.) 2010: 9–27.

Burden, Michael (ed.) 1998. *A Woman Scorn'd: Responses to the Dido Myth.* London: Faber and Faber.

Burgess, Jonathan S. 2009. *The Death and Afterlife of Achilles.* Baltimore: Johns Hopkins University Press.

Burke, Peter. 2000. "Early Modern Venice as a Center of Information and Communication." In Martin and Romano (eds.) 2000: 389–419.

Burkhardt, Jacob. 1878. *The Civilization of the Renaissance in Italy: An Essay.* New York: American Library.

Burrow, Colin. 1993. *Epic Romance: Homer to Milton.* Oxford: Oxford University Press.

———. 1997. "Virgils, from Dante to Milton." In Martindale (ed.) 1997: 79–90.

Cabani, Cristina. 1995. *Gli amici amanti: coppie eroiche e sortite notturne nell'epica italiana.* Naples: Liguori.

Cahoon, L. 1988. "The Bed as a Battlefield: Erotic Conquest and Military Metaphor in Ovid's *Amores.*" *Transactions of the American Philological Association* 118: 293–307.

Calcagno, Mauro. 2006. "Censoring Eliogabalo in Seventeenth-Century Venice." *The Journal of Interdisciplinary History* 36.3: 355–77.

Campbell, David A. (ed.) 1982. *Greek Lyric: Sappho and Alceus, vol. 1.* Cambridge: Harvard University Press.

Campbell, Emma, and Robert Mills (eds.) 2012. *Rethinking Medieval Translation: Ethics, Politics, Theory.* Suffolk: Boydell and Brewer.

Campbell, Julie. 2006. *Literary Circles and Gender in Early Modern Europe: A Cross-Cultural Approach.* Aldershot: Ashgate.

———. 2011. "Stefano Guazzo's *Civil conversazione* and the *querelle des femmes.*" In Campbell and Stampino (eds.) 2011: 73–88.

Campbell, Julie, and Anne R. Larsen (eds.) 2009. *Early Modern Women and Transnational Communities of Letters.* Farnham: Ashgate.

Campbell, Julie, and Maria Galli Stampino (eds.) 2011. *In Dialogue with the Other Voice in Sixteenth-Century Italy: Literary and Social Context for Women Writings.* Toronto: Center for Reformation and Renaissance Studies.

Campiglia, Margherita. 2004. *Flori, A Pastoral Drama.* Ed. Lisa Sampson. Chicago: University of Chicago Press.

Capodivacca, Annalisa. 2007. *Curiosity and the Trials of Imagination in Early Modern Italy.* Ph.D. diss., University of California, Berkeley.

Caretti, Lanfranco. 2001. *Ariosto e Tasso.* Torino: Einaudi.

Carile, Antonio. 1967. "Note di cronachistica veneziana: Piero Giustinian e Nicolò Trevisan." *Studi Veneziani* 9: 103–25.

Carranza, Paul. 2002. "Philosophical Songs: The 'Song of Iopas' in the 'Aeneid' and the Francesca Episode in Inferno 5." *Dante Studies* 120: 45–51.

Carroll, Clare. 1997. *The Orlando Furioso: A Stoic Comedy.* Tempe, AZ: Medieval and Renaissance Texts and Studies.

Carroll, Linda. 2013. "Venetian Literature and Publishing." In Dursteler (ed.) 2013: 615–51.

Castiglione, Baldesar. 1965. *Il libro del Cortegiano,* a cura di Luigi Preti. Torino: Giulio Einaudi Editore.

———. 1967. *The Book of the Courtier.* Trans. George Bull. Penguin Classics.

Cavallo, Jo Ann. 1993. *Boiardo's Orlando Innamorato: An Ethics of Desire.* London: Associated University Presses.

———. 1999. "Tasso's Armida and the Victory of Romance." In Finucci (ed.) 1999: 77–111.

———. 2004. *The Romance Epics of Boiardo, Ariosto, Tasso: From Public Duty to Private Pleasure.* Toronto: University of Toronto Press.

Cavanagh, Sheila. 2006. "The Politics of Private Discourse: Familial Relations in Lady Mary Wroth's *Urania.*" In Miller and Yavneh (eds.) 2006: 104–16.

Cereta, Laura. 1997. *Collected Letters of a Renaissance Feminist.* Ed. and trans. Diana Robin. Chicago: University of Chicago Press.

Chambers, David S., and François Quiver (eds.) 1995. *Italian Academies of the Sixteenth Century.* London: Warburg Institute.

Chatman, Seymour.1978. *Story and Discourse: Narrative Structure in Fiction and Films*. Ithaca, NY: Cornell University Press.

Chemello, Adriana. 1983. "La donna, il modello, l'immaginario: Moderata Fonte e Lucrezia Marinella." In Zancan (ed.) 1983: 95–170.

Chiappelli, Fredi. 1981. *Il Conoscitore del caos: una* vis abdita *nel linguaggio tassesco*. Roma: Bulzoni.

Chojnacki, Stanley. 2000. "The Most Serious Duty": Motherhood, Gender, and Patrician Culture." In Chojnacki (ed.) 2000: 169–85.

———(ed.) 2000. *Women and Men in Renaissance Venice: Twelve Essays on Patrician Society*. Baltimore: Johns Hopkins University Press.

Ciccone, Nancy. 1997. "Ovid's and Ariosto's Abandoned Women." *Pacific Coast Philology* 32.1: 3–16.

Cicero. 2006. *De Re Publica, De Legibus, Cato Maior de Senectute, Laelius de Amicitia*. Ed. J. G. F. Powell. Oxford: Oxford University Press.

———.1884. *Scipio's Dream*. Ed. and trans. Andrew P. Peabody. Boston: Little, Brown and Company.

Cicogna, Emmanuele Antonio (ed.) 1828. *Delle iscrizioni veneziane raccolte ed illustrate*. Vol. II. Venezia: Picotti.

Clark, James G., Frank T. Coulson, and Kathryn L. McKinley (eds.) 2011. *Ovid in the Middle Ages*. Cambridge: Cambridge University Press.

Clausen, Wendell. 1966. "An Interpretation of the *Aeneid*." In Commager (ed.) 1966: 75–88.

Collina, Beatrice. 1989. "Moderata Fonte e *Il merito delle donne*." *Annali d'Italianistica* 7: 1142–64.

Comensoli, Vivian and Paul Stevens (ed.) 1998. *New Essays on Renaissance Literature and Criticism*. Toronto: University of Toronto Press.

Commager, Steele (ed.) 1964. *Virgil. A Collection of Critical Essays*. Englewood Cliffs, NJ: Prentice Hall.

Connolly, Kate. 2004. "Pope says sorry for Crusaders' rampage in 1204." *The Telegraph*. Telegraph Media group. <http://www.telegraph.co.uk/news/worldnews/europe/italy/1465857/Pope-says -sorry-for-crusaders-rampage-in-1204.html> (accessed November 7, 2013).

Constable, Giles. 2008. *Crusaders and Crusade in the Twelfth Century*. Farnham: Ashgate.

Conte, Gian Biagio. 1974. *Memoria dei poeti e sistema letterario*. Torino: Einaudi.

———. 1986. *The Rhetoric of Imitation: Genre and Poetic Memory in Virgil and Other Latin Poets*. Ithaca, NY: Cornell University Press.

———. 1994a. *Latin Literature: A History*. Baltimore: Johns Hopkins University Press.

———. 1994b. *Genre and Readers: Lucretius, Love Elegy, Pliny's Encyclopedia*. Baltimore: Johns Hopkins University Press.

Conti Odorisio, Ginevra. 1979. *Donna e società nel Seicento: Lucrezia Marinelli e Arcangela Tarabotti*. Roma: Bulzoni.

Copeland, Rita. 1991. *Rhetoric, Hermeneutics, and Translation in the Middle Ages: Academic Traditions and Vernacular Texts*. Cambridge: Cambridge University Press.

Correll, Barbara. 1990. "Malleable Material, Models of Power: Woman in Erasmus's 'Marriage Group' and Civility in Boys." *English Literary History* 57: 241–62.

Costa-Zalessow, Natalia. 1981. *Scrittrici italiane dal XIII al XX secolo*. Ravenna: Longo.

Cowan, Alexander. 2014. *Marriage, Manners and Mobility in Early Modern Venice*. Aldershot: Ashgate.

Cox, Virginia. 1995. "The Single Self: Feminist Thought and the Marriage Market in Early Modern Venice." *Renaissance Quarterly* 48.3: 513–81.

——. 1997. "Women as Readers and Writers of Chivalric Literature in Early Modern Italy." In Bedani, Baranski, Lepschy, and Richardson (eds.) 1997: 134–45.

——. 2000. "Fiction, 1560–1650." In Panizza and Wood (eds.) 2000: 37–52.

——. 2005. "Sixteenth-Century Women Petrarchists and the Legacy of Laura." *Journal of Medieval and Early Modern Studies* 35.3: 583–606.

——. 2006. "Attraverso lo specchio: le petrarchiste del cinquecento e l'eredità di Laura." In Finucci (ed.) 2006: 117–49.

——. 2008. *Women's Writings in Italy, 1400–1650*. Baltimore: Johns Hopkins University Press.

——. 2009. "Leonardo Bruni on Women and Rhetoric: *De Studiis et Litteris* Revisited." *Rhetorica: A Journal of the History of Rhetoric* 27.1: 47–75.

——. 2011. *The Prodigious Muse: Women's Writings in Counter-Reformation Italy*. Baltimore: Johns Hopkins University Press.

——. 2016. "Members, Muses, Mascots: Women and Italian Academies." In Everson et al. (eds.) 2016: 132–69.

Cox Brinton, Anna. 2002. *Maphaeus Vegius and his Thirteenth Book of the Aeneid: A Chapter on Virgil in the Renaissance*. London: Duckworth.

Cozzi, Gaetano. 1979. *Paolo Sarpi fra Venezia e l'Europa*. Torino: Einaudi.

Cracco, Giorgio, and Gherardo Ortalli (eds.) 1995. *Storia di Venezia: dalle origini alla caduta della Serenissima*, vol. II. Roma: Istituto Poligrafico e Zecca dello Stato.

Crouzet-Pavan, Elizabeth. 2002. *Venice Triumphant: The Horizons of a Myth*. Baltimore: Johns Hopkins University Press.

Culler, Jonathan. 1975. *Structuralist Poetics: Structuralism, Linguistics, and the Study of Literature*. Ithaca, NY: Cornell University Press.

Curtius, Ernst R. 1953. *European Literature and the Latin Middle Ages*. New York: Harper and Row.

Cusanus, Nicholas. 2007. *Of Learned Ignorance*. Eugene, OR: Wipf & Stock.

D'Amico, Jack. 2015. "The Dangers and Virtues of Theatricality in Ariosto's *Orlando Furioso*." *Modern Language Notes* 130.1: 42–62.

D'Aragona, Tullia. 1560. *Il Meschino altramente detto il Guerrino, fatto in ottava rima dalla signora Tullia d'Aragona*. Ed. G. Battista and M. Sessa. Venezia.

Davidson, Arnold. 2006. "Ethics as Ascetics: Foucault, the History of Ethics and Ancient Thought." In Gutting (ed.) 2006: 123–48.

Davis, P. J. 1999. "*Amores*: A Political Reading." *Classical Philology* 94.4: 431–49.

——. 2006. *Ovid & Augustus: A political reading of Ovid's erotic poems*. London: Duckworth.

De Caprio, Chiara. 2012. "Volgarizzare e tradurre i grandi poemi dell'antichità (XIV–XXI secoli)." In Scarpa (ed.) 2012: 56–73 (vol. 3).

Depew, Mary, and Dirk Obbink (eds.) 2000. *Matrices of Genre: Authors, Canons and Society*. Cambridge, MA: Harvard University Press.

De Sanctis, Francesco. 1950. *Storia della letteratura italiana*. Ed. N. Gallo. 2 vols. Torino: Einaudi.

Deslauriers, Marguerite. 2009. "Sexual difference in Aristotle's *Politics* and His Biology." *Classical World* 102.2: 215–31.

——. 2012. "Lucrezia Marinella." In Edward N. Zalta (ed.) *The Stanford Encyclopedia of Philosophy*. Winter 2012. <http://plato.stanford.edu/archives/win2012/entries/lucrezia-marinella/>

Desmond, Marilynn. 1994. *Reading Dido: Gender, Textuality, and Medieval Aeneid*. Minneapolis: University of Minnesota Press.

———. 2012. "On Not Knowing Greek: Leonzio Pilatus's Rendition of the *Iliad* and the *Translation of Mediterranean Identities*." In Campbell and Mills (eds.) 2012: 21–40.

De Vivo, Filippo. 2007. *Information & Communication in Venice: Rethinking Early Modern Politics*. Oxford: Oxford University Press.

DeWitt, N.-W. 1924–1925. "Vergil's Tragedy of Maidenhood." *Classical World* 18: 107–8.

Dialeti, Androniki. 2011. "Defending Women, Negotiating Masculinity in Early Modern Italy." *Historical Journal* 54.1: 1–23.

Dionisotti, Carlo. 1968. *Gli umanisti e il volgare fra Quattro e Cinquecento*. Firenze: Le Monnier.

Di Silvio, Patricia Foley 1979. *Orthographic Reform and the Questione della lingua in the Sixteenth Century*. Chapel Hill: University of North Carolina.

Dixon, Annette. 2002. *Women Who Ruled: Queens, Goddesses, Amazons in Renaissance and Baroque Art*. London: Merrell.

Dolce, Lodovico. 1527. *L'Achille et l'Enea di Messer Lodovico Dolce*. Ed. Giolito De' Ferrari. Venice.

Domenichi, Ludovico. 1557. *Vite de' Prencipi di Vinegia di Pietro Marcello tradotte in uolgare*. Venezia: Plinio Pietrasanta.

Donato, Eugenio. 1986. "'Per Selve e Boscherecci Labirinti': Desire and Narrative Structure." In Parker and Quint (eds) 1986: 33–62.

Dooley, Brendan. 1999. *The Social History of Skepticism: Experience and Doubt in Early Modern Culture*. Baltimore: Johns Hopkins University Press.

Dubois, Page. 1982. *History, Rhetorical Description and the Epic*. Cambridge: D. S. Brewer.

Dubrow, Heather. 1994. "The Term Early Modern." *PMLA*, Forum 109.5: 1025–27.

Dufallo, Basil. 2007. *The Ghosts of the Past: Latin Literature, the Dead, and Rome's Transition to the Principate*. Columbus: Ohio State University Press.

Duncan, Joseph E. 1972. *Milton's Earthly Paradise: A Historical Study of Eden*. Minneapolis: University of Minnesota Press.

Dursteler, Eric R. (ed.) 2013. *A Companion to Venetian History, 1400–1797*. Leiden: Brill.

Dyson, Julia. 1996. "Dido the Epicurean." *Classical Antiquity* 15: 203–21.

Edmundes, Lowell. 2001. *Intertextuality and the Reading of Roman Poetry*. Baltimore: The Johns Hopkins University Press.

Edmunds, Lowell. 2005. "Epic and Myth." In Foley (ed.) 2005: 31–45.

Einstein, Albert, et al. 1931. *Living Philosophies*. New York: Simon and Schuster.

Esmail, Aziz, and Abdou Filali-Ansary (eds.) 2012. *The Constructions of Belief: Reflections on the Thought of Mohamed Arkoun,* London: Saqui Books.

Everson, Jane. 2001. *The Italian Romance Epic in the Age of Humanism*. Oxford: Oxford University Press.

Everson, Jane, Denis Reidy, and Lisa Sampson (ed.) 2016. *The Italian Academies 1525–1700: Networks of Culture, Innovation and Dissent*. London and New York: Routledge.

Fahy, Conor. 2000. "Women in Italian Cinquecento Italian Academies." In Panizza (ed.) 2000: 438–52.

Fantham, Elaine. 1979. "The Metamorphosis of a Myth." *Phoinix* 33.4: 330–45.

——. 1999. "The Role of Lament in the Growth and Eclipse of Roman Epic." In Beissinger, Tylus, and Wofford (eds.) 1999: 221–35.

Farrell, Joseph. 1991. *Vergil's Georgics and the Traditions of Ancient Epic: The Art of Allusion in Literary History*. Oxford: Oxford University Press.

——. 1994. "Review of David Quint, *Epic and Empire: Politics and Generic Form from Virgil to Milton*." Bryn Mawr Classical Review. <http://bmcr.brynmawr.edu/1994/94.02.06.html>

——. 2014. "Philosophy in Vergil." In Garani and Konstan (eds.) 2014: 61–91.

Farron, Steven. 1980. "The Aeneas-Dido episode as an attack on Aeneas' mission and Rome." *Greece and Rome* 27.1: 34–47.

——. 1982. "The Abruptness of the End of the *Aeneid*." *Acta Classica* 25: 136–41.

Fear, Trevor. 2000. "Introduction. Through the Past Darkly: Elegy and the Problematics of Interpretation." *Arethusa* 33.2: 151–58.

Feeney, D. C. 1991. *The Gods in Epic: Poets and Critics of the Classical Tradition*. New York: Oxford University Press.

Fenlon, Iain. 1995. "Zarlino and the Accademia Veneziana." In Chambers and Quiviger (eds.) 1995: 79–89.

Fernandez-Cañadas De Greenwood, Pilar. 1983. *Pastoral Poetics: The Uses of Conventions in Renaissance Pastoral Romances: Arcadia, La Diana, La Galatea, L'Astrée*. Potomac, MD: Studia Humanitatis.

Ferraro, Joanne. 2001. *Marriage Wars in Late Renaissance Venice*. Oxford: Oxford University Press.

Fichter, Andrew. 1982. *Poets Historical: Dynastic Epic in the Renaissance*. New Haven, CT: Yale University Press.

Finucci, Valeria. 1992. *The Lady Vanishes: Subjectivity and Representation in Castiglione and Ariosto*. Stanford: Stanford University Press.

——. 1994. "La scrittura epico-cavalleresca al femminile: Moderata Fonte e Tredici canti del Floridoro." *Annali d'Italianistica* 12: 203–31.

——(ed.) 1999. *Renaissance Transactions: Ariosto and Tasso*. Durham: Duke University Press.

——. 2006. *Petrarca: canoni, esemplarità*. Roma: Bulzoni.

Foley, Helene P. 2005. "Women in Ancient Epic." In Foley (ed.) 2005: 105–18.

Fonte, Moderata. 1988. *Il Merito delle donne*. Ed. Adriana Chemello. Milano: Eidos.

——. 1995. *Tredici canti del Floridoro*. Ed. Valeria Finucci. Modena: Mucchi Editore.

——. 1997. *The Worth of Women. Wherein Is Clearly Revealed Their Nobility and Their* Superiority to Men. Ed. and trans. V. Cox. Chicago: University of Chicago Press.

——. 2002. *Das Verdienst der Frauen. Warum Frauen würdiger und volkommener sind als* Männer. Ed. and trans. D. Hacke. München: C. H. Beck.

——. 2006. Floridoro: A Chivalric Poem. Ed. V. Finucci and trans. Julia Kisacky. Chicago: University of Chicago Press.

Fortini-Brown, Patricia. 1996. *Venice and Antiquity*. New Haven, CT: Yale University Press.

Fragnito, Gigliola. 1983. "Contarini, Gasparo." *Dizionario Bibliografico degli Italiani* 28. <http://www.treccani.it/enciclopedia/gasparo-contarini_(Dizionario-Biografico)/>

Franchi, Piero L. 1987. "Le figure del silenzio: statuto retorico dei fenomeni ellittici." In Pecoraro (ed.) 1987: 439–55.

Franco, Cristiana. 2012. *Circe: variazioni sul mito, Omero, Ovidio, Plutarco, Machiavelli, Webster, Atwood*. Venezia: Marsilio.

Fränkel, Ferdinand. 1969. *Ovid: A poet Between Two Worlds*. Berkeley: University of California Press.

Franklin, Margaret. 2000. "Mantegna's *Dido*: Faithful Widow or Abandoned Lover?" *Artibus et Historiae* 21.41: 111–22.

———. 2014. "Vergil and the 'femina furens': Reading the 'Aeneid' in Renaissance 'cassone' paintings." *Vergilius* 60: 127–44.

Fratantuono, Lee. 2007. *Madness Unchained: A Reading of Vergil's Aeneid*. Lanham, MD: Lexington Books.

Freccero, John. 1966. "Dante's Prologue Scene." *Dante Studies* 84: 1–25.

Friedman, Alice. 1985. "The Influence of Humanism on the Education of Girls and Boys in Tudor England." *History of Education Quarterly* 25.1/2: 57–70.

Fubini, Riccardo. 2003. *Humanism and Secularization: From Petrarch to Valla*. Durham: Duke University Press.

Fulker, Jane (ed.) 2011. *The Oxford Handbook of the New Cultural History of Music*. Oxford: Oxford University Press.

Fulkerson, Laurel. 2005. *The Ovidian Heroine as Author: Reading, Writing, and the Community in the Heroides*. Cambridge: Cambridge University Press.

Fuqua, Charles. 1982. "Hector, Sychaeus, and Deiphobus: Three Mutilated Figures in *Aeneid* 1–6." *Classical Philology* 77.3: 235–40.

Furey, Constance. 2006. *Erasmus, Contarini, and the Religious Republic of Letters*. Cambridge: Cambridge University Press.

Gale, Monica. 2000. *Virgil on the Nature of Things: The Georgics, Lucretius and the Didactic Tradition*. Cambridge: Cambridge University Press.

Galinsky, Karl. 1988. "The Anger of Aeneas." *American Journal of Philology* 109: 321–48.

———. 1994. "How to be Philosophical about the End of the *Aeneid*." *Illinois Classical Studies* 19: 191–201.

———. 1997. "Damned if You Do, Damned if You Don't: Aeneas and the Passions." *Vergilius* 43: 89–100.

Galli Stampino, Maria. 2014. "The Woman Narrator's Voice: The Case of Lucrezia Marinella's *Enrico*." *Italian Studies* 69.1: 75–94.

Garani, Myrto, and David Konstan (eds.) 2014. *The Philosophizing Muse: The Influence of Greek Philosophy on Roman Poetry*. Newcastle upon Tyne: Cambridge Scholars Publishing.

Garber, Frederick. 1988. "Pastoral Spaces." *Texas Studies in Literature and Language* 30.3: 431–60.

Garin, Eugenio. 1949–1950. "Le traduzioni umanistiche di Aristotele nel secolo XV." *Atti e Memorie dell'Accademia fiorentina di scienze morali* 16: 55–104.

———. 1958. *Il pensiero pedagogico dell'umanesimo*. Florence: Coedizioni Giuntine Sansoni.

———. 1965. *Italian Humanism: Philosophy and Civic Life in the Renaissance*. New York: Harper and Row.

———(ed.) 1991. *Renaissance Character*. Trans. Lydia G. Cochrane. Chicago: University of Chicago Press.

———. 2008. *History of Italian Philosophy*. Vol. I. Amsterdam: Rodopi.

Garrison, James. 1987. *Pietas from Vergil to Dryden*. Detroit: Wayne State University.

Getto, Giovanni. 1977. *Nel mondo della "Gerusalemme."* Roma: Bonacci.

Giamatti, Bartlett A. 1966. *Earthly Paradise and the Renaissance Epic*. Princeton, NJ: Princeton University Press.

Gibson, Joan. 1989. "Education for Silence: Renaissance Women and the Language Arts." *Hypatia* 4.1: 9–27.

Gibson, Roy K. 1999. "Aeneas as *hospes* in Vergil, *Aeneid* 1 and 4." *Classical Quarterly* 49.1: 184–202.

Giesecke, Annette Lucia. 1999. "Lucretius and Virgil's Pastoral Dream." *Utopian Studies* 10.2: 1–15.

Gilardino, S. M. 1982. "Per una reinterpretazione dell'Olimpia Ariostesca: i contributi della filologia Germanica." In Branca et alii (eds.) 1982: 429–44.

Gilleir, Anke, Alicia Montoya, and Suzan Van Dijk (eds.) 2010. *Women Writing Back / Writing Women Back*. Leiden: Brill.

Girardi, Maria Teresa. 2002. *Tasso e la nuova "Gerusalemme": Studio sulla "Conquistata" e sul "Giudicio."* Napoli: ESI.

Gleason, Elisabeth. 1983. *Gasparo Contarini: Venice, Rome and Reform*. Berkeley: University of California Press.

Glenn, Cheryl. 1997. *Rhetoric Retold: Regendering the Tradition from Antiquity through the Renaissance*. Carbondale: Southern Illinois University.

Gold, Barbara K. (ed.) 2012. *Blackwell Companion to Roman Love Elegy*. Malden, MA: Wiley-Blackwell.

Gold, Barbara K., Paul Allen Miller, and Charles Platter (eds.) 1997. *Sex and Gender in Medieval and Renaissance Texts*. Albany: State University of New York Press.

Goldstein, Philip, and James Machor (eds.) 2008. *New Directions in American Reception Studies*. Oxford: Oxford University Press.

Gordon, Pamela. 2012. *The Invention and Gendering of Epicurus*. Ann Arbor: University of Michigan Press.

Gough, Melinda. 2001. "Tasso's Enchantresses, Tasso's Captive Women." *Renaissance Quarterly* 54.2: 523–52.

Gouwens, Kenneth. 1998. "Perceiving the Past: Renaissance Humanism after the Cognitive Turn." *American Historical Review* 103.1: 55–82.

Gowers, Emily. 2005. "Vergil's Sybil and the 'Many Mouths' Cliché (*Aen.* 6.625–7)." *Classical Quarterly* 55.1: 170–82.

Grafton, Anthony, and Lisa Jardine. 1986. *From Humanism to the Humanities: Education and the Liberal Arts in Fifteenth- and Sixteenth-Century Europe*. Cambridge, MA: Harvard University Press.

Grandsen, K. W. (ed.) 1991. *Virgil's Aeneid* 11. Cambridge: Cambridge University Press.

Gray, Hannah. 1963. "Renaissance Humanism: The Pursuit of Eloquence." *Journal of the History of Ideas* 24.4: 497–514.

Graziosi, Elisabetta. 1992. "Arcadia femminile: presenze e modelli." *Filologia e Critica* 17: 321–58.

Greene, Thomas M. 1979. *The Descent from Heaven: A Study in Epic Continuity*. New Haven, CT: Yale University Press.

———. 1982. *The Light in Troy: Imitation and Discovery in Renaissance Poetry*. New Haven, CT: Yale University Press.

———. 1999. "The Natural Tears of Epic." In Beissinger, Tylus, and Wofford (eds.) 1999: 189–203.

Greenblatt, Stephen. 1983. *Renaissance Self-Fashioning: From More to Shakespeare*. Chicago: The University of Chicago Press.

Greenblatt, Stephen, and Giles B. Gunn (eds.) 1992. *Redrawing the Boundaries: The Transformation of English and American Literary Studies*. New York: Modern Language Association of America.

Greene, Sally (ed.) 1999. *Virginia Woolf: Reading the Renaissance*. Athens: Ohio University Press.

Greg, W. W. 1906. *Pastoral Poetry and Pastoral Drama*. London: A. H. Bullen.

Grendler, Paul. 1977. *The Roman Inquisition and the Venetian Press, 1540–1605*. Princeton, NJ: Princeton University Press.

———. 1991. *Schooling in Renaissance Italy: Literacy and Learning, 1300–1600*. Baltimore: Johns Hopkins University Press.

———. 2002. *The Universities of the Italian Renaissance*. Baltimore: Johns Hopkins University Press.

———. 2013. "Education in the Republic of Venice." In Dursteler (ed.) 2013: 675–99.

Grewing, F., B. Acosta-Hughes, A. Kirchenko (eds.) 2013. *The Door Adjar: False Closures in Greek and Roman Literature and Art*. Heidelberg: Universitätverlag Winter.

Griffin, A. H. F. 1981. "The Ceyx Legend in Ovid, *Met.* 11." *Classical Quarterly* 31: 147–54.

Grilli, Alberto. 1953. *Il problema della vita contemplativa nel mondo Greco-romano*. Milano: Fratelli Bocca.

Guazzo, Stefano. 1589. *La civil conversatione del signor Stefano Guazzo, gentil'huomo del Casal di Monferrato divisa in quattro libri*. Ed. Domenico Imberti. Venezia.

———. 2008. "L'Arcadia sulla luna: un'inversione pastorale nell'*Orlando Furioso*." *Modern Language Notes* 123.1: 160–78.

Gullino, Giuseppe. 1993. "Erizzo, Nicolò." *Dizionario Biografico degli Italiani*—Volume 43. <http://www.treccani.it/enciclopedia/francesco-erizzo_(Dizionario-Biografico)/>

Günsberg, Maggie. 1987. "'Donna Liberata?' The Portrayal of Women in the Italian Renaissance Epic." *The Italianist* 7: 7–35.

———. 1998. *The Epic Rhetoric of Tasso: Theory and Practice*. Oxford: European Humanities Research Centre, University of Oxford.

Guthmüller, Bodo. 1991. *Ovidio Metamorphoseos Vulgare. Formen und Funktionen der volkssprachlichen Wiedergabe klassischer Dichtung in der italienischen Renaissance*. Boppard am Rhein: Boldt.

———. 1992. "'Non taceremo più a lungo': sul dialogo *Il merito delle donne* di Moderata Fonte." *Filologia e Critica* 17.2: 258–79.

———. 1997. *Mito, poesia, arte: saggi sulla tradizione Ovidiana nel Rinascimento*. Roma: Bulzoni.

Gutting, Gary (ed.) 2006. *The Cambridge Companion to Foucault*. Cambridge: Cambridge University Press.

Habinek, Thomas. 1989. "Science and Tradition in *Aeneid* 6." *Harvard Studies in Classical Philology* 92: 223–55.

Hagedorn, Susan. 2004. *Abandoned Women: Rewriting the Classics in Dante, Boccaccio, and Chaucer*. Ann Arbor: University of Michigan Press.

Hallett, Judith. "The Role of Women in Roman Elegy: Counter-Cultural Feminism," in John Peradotto and J. P. Sullivan (eds.), *Women in the Ancient World: The Arethusa Papers* (Albany 1984), 241–62. [First pub. *Arethusa* 6 (1973) 103–24].

Halliwell, Stephen. 1992. "Epilogue: The *Poetics* and its Interpreters." In Rorty (ed.) 1992: 409–25.

Hammer, Dean. 1998. "The politics of the *Iliad*." *Classical Journal* 94.1: 1–30.

Hampton, Timothy. 1990. *Writing from History: The Rhetoric of Exemplarity in Renaissance Literature*. Ithaca, NY: Cornell University Press.

Hankins, James. 1990. *Plato in the Italian Renaissance*. Leiden: Brill.

———. 2006. "Humanism and the Origins of Modern Political Thought." In Kraye (ed.) 2006: 118–41.

Hardie, Philip. 1986. *Virgil's Aeneid: Cosmos and Imperium*. Oxford: Clarendon Press.

———. 1993. *The Epic Successors of Virgil: A Study in the Dynamics of a Tradition*. Cambridge: Cambridge University Press.

———. 1997a. "Closure in Latin Epic." In Roberts, Dunn, and Fowler (eds.) 1997: 139–52.

———. 1997b. "Vergil and Tragedy." In Martindale (ed.) 1997: 312–27.

———. 1998. *Virgil*. Oxford: Oxford University Press.

——— (ed.) 1999. *Virgil: Critical Assessments of Classical Authors*. Vols. I–IV. London and New York: Routledge.

———. 2002. *Ovid's Poetics of Illusion*. Cambridge: Cambridge University Press.

———. 2009. *Lucretian Receptions: History, The Sublime, Knowledge*. Cambridge: Cambridge University Press.

———. 2014. *The Last Trojan Hero: A Cultural History of Virgil's Aeneid*. London: I.B. Tauris.

Harrington Becker, T. 1997. "Ambiguity and the Female Warrior: Vergil's Camilla." *Electronic Antiquity* 4.1.

Harrison, Robert Pogue. 2008. *Gardens: An Essay on the Human Condition*. Chicago: University of Chicago Press.

Harrison, S. J. 1990. "Some Views of the *Aeneid* in the Twentieth Century." In Harrison (ed.) 1990: 1–20.

——— (ed.) 1990. *Oxford Readings in Vergil's Aeneid*. Oxford: Oxford University Press.

——— (ed.) 2001. *Texts, Ideas, and the Classics: Scholarship, Theory, and Classical Literature*. Oxford: Oxford University Press.

Hauser, Gerald. 1999. "Aristotle on Epideictic: The Formation of Public Morality." *Rhetoric Society Quarterly* 29.1: 5–23.

Hawkes, Terence. 1977. *Structuralism and Semiotics*. Berkeley: University of California Press.

Heinze, Richard. 1993. *Virgil's Epic Technique*. Trans. H. D. Harvey and F. Robertson [1965]. Berkeley: University of California Press.

Heller, Wendy. 2003. *Emblems of Eloquence: Opera and Women's Voices in Seventeenth-Century Venice*. Berkeley: University of California Press.

Heninger, S. K. 1961. "The Renaissance Perversion of Pastoral." *Journal of the History of Ideas* 22.2: 254–62.

Herlihy, David. 1995. *Women, Family and Society in Medieval Europe: Historical Essays, 1978–1991*. Providence: Berghahn Books.

Herrnstein Smith, Barbara. 1968. *Poetic Closure: A Study of How Poems End*. Chicago: University of Chicago Press.

Hill, Timothy. 2004. Ambitiosa Mors: *Suicide and the Self in Roman Thought and Literature.* London and New York: Routledge.

Hinds, Stephen. 1998. *Allusion and Intertext: Dynamics of Appropriation in Roman Poetry.* Cambridge: Cambridge University Press.

———. 2000. "Essential Epic: Genre and Gender from Macer to Statius." In Depew and Obbink (eds.) 2000: 221–44.

Holst-Warhaft, Gail. 1992. *Dangerous Voices: Women's Laments and Greek Literature.* London and New York: Routledge.

Homer. 1919. *The Odyssey.* Trans. A. T. Murray. Cambridge, MA: Harvard University Press.

———. 2006a. *The Iliad.* Trans. Ian Johnston. Arlington, VA: Richer Resource Publications.

———. 2006b. *Odyssey.* Trans. A. Kline. <http://www.poetryintranslation.com/PITBR/Greek/Odhome.htm>

Horsfall, Nicholas. 1995. "Aeneid." In Horsfall (ed.) 1995: 101–216.

——— (ed.) 1995. *A Companion to the Study of Virgil.* Leiden: Brill.

Hubert, Jedin. 1953. *Contarini und Camaldoli.* Rome: Edizioni di Storia e Letteratura.

Hudson, Nancy. 2007. *Becoming God: The Doctrine of Theosis in Nicholas of Cusa.* Washington, DC: Catholic University of America Press.

Hunter, Richard. 1993. *The Argonautica of Apollonius. Literary Studies.* Cambridge: Cambridge University Press.

Hurlburt, Holly. 2007. "A Renaissance for Renaissance Women?" *Journal of Women's History* 19.2: 193–201.

Huxley, H. 1952. "Storms and Shipwreck in Roman Literature." *Greece and Rome* 21.53: 117–24.

Jacobs, Jason. 2013. "Galiziella's escape: Interconfessional Erotics and Love between Knights in the Aspremont Tradition." *California Italian Studies* 4.2: 1–23.

Jacobson, H. 1974. *Ovid's Heroides.* Princeton, NJ: Princeton University Press.

James, Sharon. 2003. *Learned Girls and Male Persuasion: Gender and Reading in Roman Elegy.* Berkeley: University of California Press.

Janan, Micaela. 2001. *The Politics of Desire: Propertius IV.* Berkeley: University of California Press.

Javitch, Daniel. 1984. "The *Orlando Furioso* and Ovid's Revision of the *Aeneid.*" *Modern Language Notes* 99: 1023–36.

———. 1991. *Proclaiming a Classic: The Canonization of the Orlando Furioso.* Princeton, NJ: Princeton University Press.

Jed, Stephanie H. 2011. *Wings for Our Courage: Gender, Erudition, and Republican Thought.* Berkeley: University of California Press.

Jenkins, Richard. 1989. "Virgil and Arcadia." *Journal of Roman Studies* 79: 26–39.

Johnson, W. R. 1965. "Aeneas and the Ironies of *Pietas.*" *Classical Journal* 60: 359–64.

———. 1970. "The Problem of the Counter-Classical Sensibility and its Critics." *California Studies in Classical Antiquity* 3: 123–51.

———. 1976. *Darkness Visible: A Study of Vergil's Aeneid.* Berkeley: University of California Press.

Jones, Ann Rosalind. 1990. *The Currency of Eros: Women's Love Lyric in Europe, 1540–1620.* Bloomington: Indiana University Press.

———. 1998. "Apostrophes to Cities: Urban Rhetorics in Isabella Whitney and Moderata Fonte." In Amussen and Seeff (eds.) 1998: 155–75.

Jones, Nancy J. 1997. "By Women Tears Redeemed: Female Lament in St. Augustine's *Confessions* and the Correspondence of Abelard and Heloise." In Gold, Miller, and Platter (eds.) 1997: 15–41.

Jordan, Constance. 1990. *Renaissance Feminism: Literary Texts and Political Models*. Ithaca, NY: Cornell University Press.

———. 1996. "Renaissance Women Defending Women: Arguments Against Patriarchy." In Marotti (ed.) 1996: 55–69.

———. 1999. "Writing Beyond the *Querelle*: Gender and History in *Orlando Furioso*." In Finucci (ed.) 199: 295–315.

Jurdjevic, Mark. 2007. "Hedgehogs and Foxes: The Present and the Future of Italian Renaissance Intellectual History." *Past & Present* 195: 241–68.

Kallendorf, Craig. 1985. "Boccaccio's Dido and the Rhetorical Criticism of Virgil's *Aeneid*." *Studies in Philology* 82: 401–15.

———. 1989. *In Praise of Aeneas: Virgil and Epideictic Rhetoric in the Early Italian Renaissance*. Hanover, NH: University Press of New England.

———. 1999a. "Historicizing the 'Harvard School': Pessimistic Readings of the *Aeneid* in Italian Renaissance Scholarship." *Harvard Studies in Classical Philology* 99: 391–403.

———. 1999b. *Virgil and the Myth of Venice: Books and Readers in the Italian Renaissance*. Oxford: Clarendon University Press.

———. 2007. *The Other Virgil: 'Pessimistic' Readings of the Aeneid in Early Modern Culture*. Oxford: Oxford University Press.

———. 2010. *Aldo Manuzio*. Oxford: Oxford University Press.

———. 2015. *The Protean Virgil: Material Form and the Reception of the Classics*. Oxford: Oxford University Press.

Kardulias, Dianna Rhyan. 2001. "Odysseus in Ino's Veil: Feminine Headdress and the Hero in 'Odyssey' 5." *Transactions of the American Philological Association* 131: 23–51.

Keenan, Siobhan. 2008. *Renaissance Literature*. Edinburgh: Edinburgh University Press.

Keith, Allison. 2000. *Engendering Rome: Women in Roman Epic*. Cambridge: Cambridge University Press.

Kelly, Joan. 1977. "Did Women have a Renaissance?" In Bridenthal and Koontz (eds.) 1977: 137–64.

———. 1982. "Early Feminist Theory and the 'Querelle des Femmes.'" *Signs* 8.1: 4–28.

Kelso, Ruth. 1956. *Doctrine for the Lady of the Renaissance*. Urbana: University of Illinois Press.

Kennedy, William. 1973. "Ariosto's Ironic Allegory." *Modern Language Notes* 88: 44–67.

Kermode, Frank. 1983. *The Classic: Literary Images of Permanence and Change*. Cambridge, MA: Harvard University Press.

Kieckhefer, Richard. 2000. *Magic in the Middle Ages*. Cambridge: Cambridge University Press.

King, Charles. 2003. "The Organization of Roman Religious Beliefs." *Classical Antiquity* 22.2: 275–312.

King, Margaret. 1980. "Book-Lined Cells: Women and Humanism in the Early Italian Renaissance." In Labalme (ed.) 1980: 66–90.

———. 1986. *Venetian Humanism in the Age of Patrician Dominance.* Princeton, NJ: Princeton University Press.

———. 1991a. "The Woman of the Renaissance." In Garin (ed.) 1991: 207–47.

———. 1991b. *Women of the Renaissance.* Chicago: University of Chicago Press.

———. 2003. *The Renaissance in Europe.* London: Laurence King Publishing

———. 2005. *Humanism, Venice, and Women: Essays on the Italian Renaissance.* Aldershot: Ashgate.

———. 2013. "The Venetian Intellectual World." In Dursteler (ed.) 2013: 571–615.

Kinsey, Thomas E. 1979. "The Song of Iopas." *Emerita* 47: 77–86.

Kisacky, Julia. 2002. "Siblings in Moderata Fonte's *Floridoro.*" Paper delivered at the AATI Conference, November 2002.

Klapisch-Zuber, Christiane. 1985. *Women, Family and Ritual in Renaissance Italy.* Chicago: University of Chicago Press.

Klosko, George. 2006. *Development of Plato's Political Theory.* Oxford: Oxford University Press.

Kolsky, Stephen. 1993. "Wells of Knowledge: Moderata Fonte's *Il Merito delle Donne.*" *The Italianist* 13: 57–96.

———. 1999. "Moderata Fonte's *Tredici canti del Floridoro*: Women in a Man's Genre." *Rivista di Studi Italiani* 17: 165–84.

———. 2001. "Moderata Fonte, Lucrezia Marinella, Giuseppe Passi: An Early Seventeenth- Century Feminist Controversy." *Modern Language Review* 96.4: 973–89.

———. 2003. *The Genealogy of Women: Studies in Boccaccio's De mulieribus claris.* New York: Peter Lang.

Konstan, David. 2006. *The Emotions of the Ancient Greeks: Studies in Aristotle and Classical Literature.* Toronto: University of Toronto Press.

———. 2008. "Aristotle on Love and Friendship." ΣΧΟΛΗ 2: 207–12.

Kraye, Jill (ed.) 2006. *The Cambridge Companion to Renaissance Humanism.* Cambridge: Cambridge University Press.

Kristeller, Paul O. 1961. *Renaissance Thought: The Classic, Scholastic, and Humanist Strains.* New York: Harper.

———. 1996a. "Aristotelismo e sincretismo nel pensiero di Pietro Pomponazzi." In Kristeller (ed.) 1996: 292–310.

——— (ed.) 1996b. *Studies in Renaissance Thought and Letters IV.* Roma: Edizioni di Storia e Letteratura.

———. 2004. "Humanism and Scholasticism in the Italian Renaissance." In Bloom (ed.) 2004: 117–51.

Kugel, James. 1990. *Poetry and Prophecy: The Beginnings of a Literary Tradition.* Ithaca, NY: Cornell University Press.

Kurz, Gebhard, Dietram Müller, and Walter Nicolai (eds.) 1981. *Gnomosyne. Menschliches Denken und Handeln in der frühgriechischen Literatur. Festschrift für Walter Marg zum 70. Geburtag.* Munich: Beck.

Labalme, Patricia. 1981. "Venetian Women on Women: Three Early Modern Feminists." *Archivio Veneto* 117: 81–109.

——— (ed.) 1980. *Beyond Their Sex: Learned Women of the European Past.* New York: New York University Press.

Landolfi, Luciano. 2001. *Scribentis imago: Eroine ovidiane e lamento epistolare*. Bologna: Patron.

Lane, Frederick. 1973. *Venice: A Maritime Republic*. Baltimore: Johns Hopkins University Press.

La Penna, Antonio. 1977. *L'integrazione difficile: un profilo di Properzio*. Torino: Einaudi.

Lattimore, Richard. 1951. *The Iliad of Homer*. Chicago: University of Chicago Press.

Lazzari, Laura. 2010. *Poesia epica e scrittura femminile nel Seicento: "L'Enrico" di Lucrezia Marinelli*. Leonforte: Insula.

——. 2012. "Forme di libertà nelle opere di Lucrezia Marinella." In Bellavitis, Filippini and Plebani (eds.) 2012: 205–12.

Leach, Eleanor Winsor. 1974. *Virgil's "Eclogues": Landscapes of Experience*. Ithaca, NY: Cornell University Press.

——. 1999. "Viewing the *Spectacula* of Aeneid 6." In Perkell (ed.) 1999: 11–27.

Lerner, Laurence. 1972. *The Uses of Nostalgia: Studies in Pastoral Poetry*. London: Chatto and Windus.

Levi Catellani, Enrico. 1879. "Venezia e le sue letterate nei secoli XV e XVI." *Rivista Europea* 15: 513–21.

Lindheim, Sara. 2008. *Mail and Female: Epistolary Narrative and Desire in Ovid's Heroides*. University of Wisconsin Press.

Lipking, Lawrence. 1989. *Abandoned Women and Poetic Tradition*. Chicago: University of Chicago Press.

Long, Kathleen P. (ed.) 2010. *Gender and Scientific Discourse in Early Modern Culture*. Farnham: Ashgate.

Looney, Dennis. 1996. *Compromising the Classic: Romance Epic Narrative in the Italian Renaissance*. Detroit: Wayne State University Press.

Loraux, Nicole. 1995. *The Experience of Tiresias: The Feminine and the Greek Man*. Princeton, NJ: Princeton University Press.

Lynn-George, Michael. 1988. *Epos: Word, Narrative and the Iliad*. Houndmill, UK.

Lyne, R. O. A. M. 1992. *Further Voices in Vergil's Aeneid*. Oxford: Oxford University Press.

——. 1998. "Love and Death: Laodamia and Protesilaus in Catullus, Propertius, and Others." *Classical Quarterly* 48.1: 200–212.

MacCarthy, Ita. 2004. "Alcina's Island from Imitation to Innovation in the *Orlando Furioso*." *Italica* 81.3: 325–50.

——. 2007. *Women and the Making of Poetry in Ariosto's Orlando Furioso*. Leicester: Troubador.

MacCormack, Sabine. 1998. *The Shadows of Poetry: Vergil in the Mind of Augustine*. Berkeley: University of California Press.

Macedo, Helder. 1990. "*The Lusiads*: Epic Celebration and Pastoral Regret." *Portuguese Studies* 6: 32–37.

Mack, Sara. 1988. *Ovid*. New Haven, CT: Yale University Press.

Maclean, Ian. 1980. *The Renaissance Notion of Woman: A Study in the Fortunes of Scholasticism and Medical Science in European Intellectual Life*. Cambridge: Cambridge University Press.

——. 2012. *Scholarship, Commerce, Religion: The Learned Book in the Age of Confessions, 1560–1630*. Cambridge, MA: Harvard University Press.

Madden, Thomas F. 1993. "Vows and Contracts in the Fourth Crusade: The Treaty of Zara and the Attack on Constantinople in 1204." *International History Review* 15.3: 441–68.

———. 1995. "Outside and Inside the Fourth Crusade." *International History Review* 17.4: 726–43.

———. 2007. *Enrico Dandolo and the Rise of Venice.* Baltimore: Johns Hopkins University Press.

———(ed.) 2008. *The Fourth Crusade: Event, Aftermath, and Perceptions.* Aldershot: Ashgate.

———. 2012. "The Venetian Memory of the Fourth Crusade: Memory and the Conquest of Constantinople in Medieval Venice." *Speculum* 87.2: 311–44.

Maggi, Armando (ed.) 2011. *De' Gesti eroici e della vita maravigliosa della serafica S. Caterina da Siena.* Ravenna: Longo.

Malpezzi Price, Paola. 1989. "A Woman's Discourse in the Italian Renaissance: Moderata Fonte's *Il merito delle donne.*" *Annali d'Italianistica* 7: 165–82.

———. 1994a. "Moderata Fonte, Lucrezia Marinella and their 'Feminist' Work." *Italian Culture* 12: 201–14.

———. 1994b. "Moderata Fonte 1555–1592." In *Italian Women Writers: A Bio-Bibliographical Sourcebook,* ed. Rinaldina Russel, 128–37. Westport, CT: Greenwood Press.

———. 2003. *Moderata Fonte: Women and Life in Sixteenth-Century Venice.* Madison, NJ: Fairleigh Dickinson University Press.

Malpezzi Price, Paola, and Christine Ristaino. 2008. *Lucrezia Marinella and the 'Querelle des Femmes' in Seventeenth-Century Italy.* Madison, NJ: Fairleigh Dickinson University Press.

Malusa, Luciano, and Olga Rossi Cassottana (eds.) 2011. *Le dimensioni dell'educare e il gusto della scoperta nella ricerca: studi in memoria di Duilio Gasparini.* Roma: Armando editore.

Marcus, Leah S. 1992. "Renaissance/Early Modern Studies." In Greenblatt and Gunn (eds.) 1992: 41–63.

Marenbon, John. 2015. *Pagan and Philosophers: The Problem of Paganism from Augustine to Leibniz.* Princeton, NJ: Princeton University Press.

Marin, Serban. 2000. "A Humanist Vision on the Fourth Crusade and on the State of the Assenides. The Chronicle of Paul Ramusio (Paulus Rhamnusius)." *Annuario. Istituto Romeno di cultura e ricerca umanistica di Venezia* 2: 51–120.

———. 2008. "Between Justification and Glory: The Venetian Chronicles' View of the Fourth Crusade." In Madden (ed.) 2008: 113–23.

———. 2010. "A Chanson de Geste in the 13th Century Venice: The Chronicle Written by Martino da Canal." *Medieval and Early Modern Studies for Central and Eastern Europe* 2: 71–121.

Marinella, Lucrezia. 1601. *La nobiltà et eccellenza delle donne, co' diffetti, e mancamenti de gli huomini.* Ed. G. B. Ciotti. Venezia. <https://archive.org/details/bub_gb_vdOMz7awxwQC>

———. 1621. *La nobiltà et eccellenza delle donne, co' diffetti, e mancamenti de gli huomini.* Ed. G. B. Combi. Venezia. <http://books.google.com/books/about/La_nobilta_et_l_eccellenza_delle_donne_c.html?id=dxnFeTdN1Y8C>

———. 1645. *Essortationi alle donne et a gli altri, se a loro saranno a grado.* Venezia: Ciotti.

———.1635. *L'Enrico, overo Bisantio acquistato.* Venezia: Ghirardo Imberti.

———. 1844. *L'Enrico ovvero Bisanzio acquistato.* Venezia: Giuseppe Antonelli Editore.

———. 1998. *Arcadia Felice.* Ed. Francoise Lavocat. Florence: Olschki.

———. 1999. *The Nobility an Excellence of Women, and the Defects and Vices of Men*. Ed. and trans. Ann Dunhill. Chicago: University of Chicago Press.

———. 2009. *Enrico; or, Byzantium Conquered*. Ed. and trans. M. Galli Stampino. Chicago: University of Chicago Press.

———. 2011. *L'Enrico, ovvero Bisanzio acquistato*. Ed. Maria Galli Stampino. Modena: Mucchi.

———. 2012. *Exhortations to Women and to Others If They Please*. Ed. and trans. Laura Benedetti. The Other Voice in Early Modern Europe: The Toronto Series, Volume 15. Toronto: Iter.

Marinelli, Peter. 1987. *Ariosto and Boiardo: The Origins of Orlando Furioso*. Columbia: University of Missouri Press.

Mariotti Masi, Maria Luisa. 1986. *Bianca Cappello: Una veneziana alla Corte dei Medici*. Milano: Mursia.

Markos, Louis. 2013. *Heaven and Hell: Visions of the Afterlife in the Western Poetic Tradition*. Eugene, OR: Cascade Books.

Marotti, Maria Ornella (ed.) 1996. *Italian Women Writers from the Renaissance*. State College: Pennsylvania State University Press.

Martelli, Daria. 2011. *Polifonie: le donne a Venezia nell' età di Moderata Fonte (seconda metà del secolo XVI)*. Padova: Coop. Libraria Editrice Università di Padova.

Martin, John. 1996. "Spiritual Journeys and the Fashioning of Religious Identity in Renaissance Venice." *Renaissance Studies* 10.3: 358–70.

———. 2004. *Myth of Renaissance Individualism*. Basingstoke and New York: Palgrave Macmillan.

Martin, John, and Dennis Romano. (eds.) 2002. *Venice Reconsidered: The History and Civilization of an Italian City-State, 1297–1797*. Baltimore: Johns Hopkins University Press.

Martin, Richard. 1989. *The Language of Heroes: Speech and Performance in the Iliad*. Ithaca, NY: Cornell University Press.

Martindale, Charles. 1993. *Redeeming the Text: Latin Poetry and the Hermeneutics of Reception*. Cambridge: Cambridge University Press.

———(ed.) 1997. *The Cambridge Companion to Virgil*. Cambridge: Cambridge University Press.

Maschietto, Francesco L. 2007. *Elena Lucrezia Cornaro Piscopia (1646–1684): The First Woman in the World to Earn a University Degree*. Philadelphia: St. Joseph University Press.

Mayhew, Robert. 2004. *The Female in Aristotle's Biology: Reason or Rationalization*. Chicago: University of Chicago Press.

Mazzacurati, Giancarlo.1965. *La questione della lingua dal Bembo all'Accademia fiorentina*. Napoli: Liguori.

Mazzetti, Mila. 1973. "La poesia come vocazione morale: Vittoria Colonna." *Rassegna della letteratura italiana* 77: 58–99.

McClure, George. 2013. *Parlour Games and the Public Life of Women in Renaissance*. Toronto: University of Toronto Press.

McCue Gill, Joy. 2009. *Vera Amicizia: Conjugal Friendship in the Italian Renaissance*. Ph.D. diss., University of California, Berkeley.

McGill, Scott. 2006. Review of Michael C. J. Putnam, Maffeo Vegio: Short Epics. *International Journal of the Classical Tradition* 12.2: 305–9.

McGushin, Edward. 2006. *Foucault's Askesis: An Introduction to the Philosophical Life*. Evanston, IL: Northwestern University Press.

McKinley, Kathryn L. 2001. *Reading the Ovidian Heroine: "Metamorphoses" Commentaries 1100–1618.* Leiden: Brill.

McKeown, James C. 1995. "*Militat Omnis Amans.*" *Classical Journal* 90.3: 295–304.

McLucas, John. 1988. "Amazon, Sorceress, and Queen: Women and War in the Aristocratic Literature of Sixteenth-Century Italy." *Italianist* 8: 33–55.

McNeill, William. 1974. *Venice: The Hinge of Europe, 1081–1797.* Chicago: University of Chicago Press.

McPhail, Eric. 2001. "Ariosto and the Prophetic Moment." *Modern Language Notes* 116.1: 30–53.

Medioli, Francesca. 2012. "Tarabotti fra omissioni e femminismo: il mistero della sua formazione." In Bellavitis, Filippini, and Plebani (eds.) 2012: 221–39.

Merisalo, Outi. 2015. "Translating the Classics into the Vernacular in Sixteenth-Century Italy." *Renaissance Studies* 29.1: 55–77.

Merklin, Harald. 1968. "Arethusa und Laodamia." *Hermes* 96: 461–94.

Meschini, Marco. 2008. "The 'Four Crusades' of 1204." In Madden (ed.) 2008: 32–37.

Miato, Monica. 1998. *L'accademia degli Incogniti di Giovan Francesco Loredan. Venezia (1630–1631).* Florence: Olschki.

Migiel, Marilyn. 1987. "Secrets of a Sorceress: Tasso's Armida." *Quaderni d'Italianistica* 8.2: 149–66.

———. 1993. *Gender and Genealogy in Tasso's Gerusalemme Liberata.* Lewiston, PA: Mellen.

———. 1995. "Olimpia's Secret Weapon: Gender, War and Hermeneutics in Ariosto's *Orlando Furioso.*" *Critical Matrix* 9.1: 22–44.

Migliorini, Bruno. 1961. *Storia della lingua italiana.* Firenze: Sansoni.

Milani, Raffaele. 2009. *The Art of the Landscape.* Montreal: McGill-Queen University Press.

Miles, Gary B. 1980. *Virgil's Georgics: A New Interpretation.* Berkeley: University of California Press.

Miles Foley, John (ed.). 2005. *A Companion to Ancient Epic.* Oxford: Blackwell.

Miller, Naomi, and Naomi Yavneh (eds.) 2006. *Sibling Relations and Gender in the Early Modern World.* Aldershot: Ashgate.

Miller, Paul Allen. 1994. *Lyric Texts and Lyric Consciousness: The Birth of a Genre from Archaic Greece to Augustan Rome.* London and New York: Routledge.

———. 2002. *Latin Erotic Elegy: An Anthology and a Reader.* London and New York: Routledge.

Miller, Paul Allen, and Charles Platter. 1999. "Introduction." *Classical World* 92.5 (1999) 403–7.

Modesto, Filippa. 2015. *Dante's Idea of Friendship: The Transformation of a Classical Concept.* Toronto: University of Toronto Press.

Muir, Edward. 1995. "The Italian Renaissance in America." *American Historical Review* 100.4: 1095–110.

———. 2006. "Why Venice? Venetian Society and the Success of Early Opera." *Journal of Interdisciplinary History* 36.3: 331–53.

———. 2011. "An Evening at the Opera in Seventeenth-Century Venice." In Fulcher (ed.) 2011: 335–53.

Moore, Clifford H. 1921. "Prophecy in the Ancient Epic." *Harvard Studies in Classical Philology* 32: 99–175.

Moore, Helen. 2000. "Elizabethan Fiction and Ovid's *Heroides.*" *Translation and Literature* 9: 40–64.

Murgatroyd, Paul. 1975. "*Militia Amoris* and the Roman Elegists." *Latomus* 34: 59–79.

Murnaghan, S. 1999. "The Poetics of Loss in Greek Epic." In Beissinger, Tylus, and Wofford (eds.) 1999: 203–20.

Murrrin, Michael. 1994. *History and Warfare in Renaissance Epic*. Chicago: University of Chicago Press.

Musiol, Maria. 2013. *Spurs and Reins: Vittoria Colonna, A Woman's Renaissance*. Berlin: Druck und Verlag.

Nagel, Alexander. 2011. *The Controversy of Renaissance Art*. Chicago: University of Chicago Press.

Nagy, Gregory. 1999. *The Best of the Achaeans: Concepts of the Hero in Archaic Greek Poetry*. Baltimore: Johns Hopkins University Press.

Nauert, C. 2006. *Humanism and the Culture of Renaissance Europe*. Cambridge: Cambridge University Press.

Newman, John K. 2003. *The Classical Epic Tradition*. University of Wisconsin Press.

Nicol, Donald. 1995. "La quarta Crociata." In Cracco and Ortalli (eds.) 1995: 155–83.

———. 1988. *Byzantium and Venice: A Study in Diplomatic and Cultural Relations*. Cambridge: Cambridge University Press.

Norton, Glyn P. (ed.) 1999. *The Cambridge History of Literary Criticism,* vol. 3, *The Renaissance*. Cambridge: Cambridge University Press.

———, and M. Cottino-Jones. 1999. "Theory of Prose Fiction and Poetics in Italy: *Novella* and *Romanzo* (1525–1596)." In Norton (ed.) 1999: 322–39.

Nussbaum, Martha. 2001. *Upheavals of Thought: The Intelligence of Emotions*. Cambridge: Cambridge University Press.

O'Hara, James. 1990. *Death and the Optimistic Prophecy in Virgil's Aeneid*. Princeton, NJ: Princeton University Press.

Öhrman, Magdalena. 2008. *Varying Virtue: Mythological Paragons of Wifely Virtues in Roman Elegy*. Lund: Centre for Languages and Literature, Lund University.

Olson, Kristina M. 2014. *Courtesy Lost: Dante, Boccaccio, and the Literature of History*. Toronto: University of Toronto Press.

Ong, Walter J. 2002. *Orality and Literacy: 30th Anniversary Edition*. London and New York: Routledge.

———. 2012. *Rhetoric, Romance, and Technology: Studies in the Interaction of Expression and Culture*. Ithaca, NY: Cornell University Press.

Otis, Brook. 1963. *Virgil: A Study in Civilized Poetry*. Oxford: Clarendon Press.

———. 1966. *Ovid as an Epic Poet*. London: Cambridge University Press.

Ovid. 1979. *Ovid's Amores I*. Ed. and trans. John Barsby. Bristol, UK: Bristol Classical Press.

———. *The Metamorphoses*. Trans. A. Kline. http://ovid.lib.virginia.edu/trans/Ovhome.htm

Ovidio, Publio Nasone. 1994. *Le Metamorfosi*. Ed. Rossella Corti. Milano: Rizzoli.

———. 2001. *Lettere di eroine*. Ed. Gianpiero Rosati. Milano: Rizzoli.

Panizza, Letizia (ed.) 2000. *Women in Italian Renaissance Culture and Society*. London and New York: Routledge.

Panizza, L. and S. Wood (eds.) 2000. *A History of Women's Writing in Italy*. Cambridge: Cambridge University Press.

Parker, Holt. 1997. "Latin and Greek Poetry by Five Renaissance Italian Women Humanists." In Gold, Miller, and Platter (eds.) 1997: 247–85.

———. 2012. "Renaissance Latin Elegy." In Gold (ed.) 2012: 476–90.

Parker, Patricia, and David Quint (eds.) 1986. *Literary Theory / Renaissance Texts*. Baltimore: Johns Hopkins University Press.

Parrett, Aaron. 2004. *The Translunar Narrative in the Western Tradition*. Aldershot: Ashgate.

Parry, Adam. 1963. "The Two Voices of Virgil's *Aeneid*." *Arion* 2: 66–80.

Passi, Giuseppe. 1618. *I donneschi difetti*. Venezia: Somascho.

Patanè Ceccantini, Rosaria. 1996. *Il motivo del locus amoenus nell'Orlando Furioso e nella Gerusalemme Liberata*. Lausanne: Université de Lausanne, Faculté des Lettres (Section d'italien).

Patterson, Annabel. 1984. *Censorship and Interpretation: The Conditions of Writing and Reading in Early Modern England*. Madison: University of Wisconsin Press.

———. 1997. *Pastoral Ideology: From Virgil to Valery*. Berkeley: University of California Press.

Paulicelli, Eugenia. 2014. *Writing Fashion in Early Modern Italy: From Sprezzatura to Satire*. Farnham: Ashgate.

Pavlock, Barbara. 1985. "Epic and Tragedy in Vergil's Nisus and Euryalus episode." *Transactions of the American Philological Association* 115: 207–24.

———. 1990. *Eros, Imitation and the Epic Tradition*. Ithaca, NY: Cornell University Press.

Pecoraro, Marco (ed.) 1987. *Studi in onore di V. Zaccaria in occasione del settantesimo compleanno*. Milano: Unicopli.

Pender, Patricia. 2012. *Early Modern Women's Writing and the Rhetoric of Modesty*. Basingstoke and New York: Palgrave MacMillan.

Perkell, Christine. 1999a. "*Aeneid* 1: An Epic Program." In Perkell (ed.) 1999: 29–49.

———. 1999b. *Reading Vergil's Aeneid: An Interpretative Guide*. Norman: University of Oklahoma Press.

———.1997. "The Lament of Juturna: Pathos and Interpretation in the *Aeneid*." *Transactions of the American Philological Association* 127: 257–86.

———. 2008. "Reading the Laments of *Iliad* 24." In Suter (ed.) 2008: 93–117.

Pertusi, Agostino. 1964. *Leonzio Pilato fra Petrarca e Boccaccio: le sue versioni omeriche negli autografi di Venezia e la cultura greca del primo umanesimo*. Venezia-Roma: Istituto per la collaborazione culturale.

Petrucci, Armando (ed.) 1980. *Libri, editori e pubblico nell'Europa moderna: guida storica e critica*. Bari: Laterza.

Pezzini, S. 2005. "Ideologia della conquista, ideologia dell'accoglienza: La Scanderbeide di Margherita Sarrocchi (1623)." *Modern Language Notes* 120.1: 190–222.

Phillippy, Patricia. 1992. "'Altera Dido': The Model of Ovid's *Heroides* in the Poetry of Gaspara Stampa and Veronica Franco." *Italica* 69.1: 1–18.

———. 1995. *Love's Remedies: Recantation and Renaissance Lyric Poetry*. London: Associated University Presses.

Picchio, Franco. 2007. *Ariosto e Bacco due: apocalisse e nuova religione nel Furioso*. Cosenza: Pellegrini Editore.

Pin, Corrado. 2006. "Una contesa tra Stato e Chiesa di risonanza europea: l'interdetto ecclesiastico del dominio Veneto del 1606–7." Bergamo 3 Maggio 2006: webdocument (www.comune .seriate.bg.it).

Plebani, Tiziana. 2003. "La civiltà della conversazione a Venezia (XVII–XVIII secolo)." In *Memorie di Lei. Corsi di storia delle donne* 2003: 38–52, Venezia: Commissione Pari Opportunità.

———. 2007. "Scritture di donne nel rinascimento italiano." In Belloni and Drusi (eds.) 2007: 243–63.

Podacataro, Alessandro. 1876. *Relatione de' successi di Famagosta dell'anno 1571.* Venezia: Cecchini.

Poggioli, Renato. 1975. *The Oaten Flute: Essays on Pastoral Poetry and the Pastoral Ideal.* Cambridge, MA: Harvard University Press.

Pöschl, Viktor. 1950. *Die Dichtkunst Virgils: Bild und symbol in der Aeneis.* Wiesbaden: Rohrer.

———. 1962. *The Art of Vergil: Image and Symbol in the* Aeneid. Ann Arbor: University of Michigan Press.

Prince, Gerald. 1982. *Narratology: The Form and Function of Narrative.* Berlin: Mouton.

Prosperi, Valentina. 2011. "*Enrico o Bisanzio acquistato*: poesia di genere/poesia di gender." *Nuova Rivista di Letteratura* 14.1–2: 25–37.

Pucci, Pietro. 1987. *Odysseus Polutropos: Intertextual Readings in the Odyssey and the Iliad.* Ithaca, NY: Cornell University Press.

Putnam, Michael. 1965. *The Poetry of the Aeneid: Four Studies in Imaginative Unity and Design.* Cambridge, MA: Harvard University Press.

———. 1970. *Virgil's Pastoral Art: Studies in the Eclogues.* Princeton, NJ: Princeton University Press.

———. 1999. "*Aeneid* 12: Unity in Closure." In Perkell (ed.) 1999: 210–30.

———. 2001. "Vergil's *Aeneid.* The Final Lines." In *Poets and Critics Read Vergil,* ed. Sarah Spence, 86–104. New Haven, CT: Yale University Press.

———. 2004. *Short Epics. Maffeo Vegio.* Ed. and trans. Michael C. J. Putnam, with James Hankins. Cambridge, MA: Harvard University Press.

———. 2011. *The Humanness of Heroes: Studies in the Conclusion of Virgil's Aeneid.* The Amsterdam Vergil Lectures 1. Amsterdam: Amsterdam University Press.

Queller, Donald E. 1997. *The Fourth Crusade: The Conquest of Constantinople, 1201–04.* Rev. 2nd ed. Philadelphia: University of Pennsylvania Press.

Queller, Donald E., and Irene B. Katele. 1982. "Attitudes towards the Venetians in the Fourth Crusade: The Western Sources." *International Review of History* 4.1: 1–36.

Quint, David. 1977. "Astolfo's Voyage to the Moon." *Yale Italian Studies* 1: 398–409.

———. 1993. *Epic and Empire: Politics and Generic Form from Virgil to Milton.* Princeton, NJ: Princeton University Press.

———. 2015. "Romance and History in Tasso's *Gerusalemme Liberata.*" In Whitman (ed.) 2015: 200–214.

Quaintance, Courtney. 2015. *Textual Masculinity and the Exchange of Women in Renaissance Venice.* Toronto: University of Toronto Press.

Quondam, Amedeo. 1980. "'Mercanzia d'onore' e 'Mercanzia d'utile': produzione libraria e lavoro intellettuale a Venezia nel Cinquecento." In Petrucci (ed.) 1980: 51–105.

Radway, Janice. 1984. *Reading the Romance: Women, Patriarchy and Popular Literature.* Chapel Hill: University of North Carolina Press.

Raja, Maria Elisa. 2003. *Le Muse in Giardino: il paesaggio ameno nelle opere di Giovanni Boccaccio.* Alessandria: Edizioni dell'Orso.

Ramsby, Theresa. 2015. Review of Thea S. Thorsen (ed.) 2013. *The Cambridge Companion to Latin Love Elegy. Cambridge Companions to Literature.* Cambridge: Cambridge University Press in *Bryn Mawr Classical Review* 2015.01.11.

Ramusio, Girolamo Paolo. 1604. *Della Guerra di Costantinopoli per la restitutione de gl'imperatori Comneni fatta da Sig. Ventiani et Francesi l'anno MCCIV. Libri sei.* Appresso Domenico Nicolini. Venezia.

Raaflaub, Kurt A. 2005. "Epic and History." In Foley (ed.) 2005: 55–70.

Raaflaub, Kurt A., and Mark Toher (eds.) 1993. *Between Republic and Empire: Interpretations of Augustus and His Principate.* Berkeley: University of California Press.

Ray, Meredith. 2009. *Writing Gender in Women's Letter Collections of the Italian Renaissance.* Toronto: University of Toronto Press.

———. 2015. *Daughters of Alchemy: Women and Scientific Culture in Early Modern Italy.* Cambridge, MA: Harvard University Press.

Redfield, James M. 1975. *Nature and Culture in the Iliad: The Tragedy of Hector.* Chicago: University of Chicago Press.

Richardson, Brian. 1999. *Printing, Writers and Readers in Renaissance Italy.* Cambridge: Cambridge University Press.

Richardson Lear, Gabriel. 2004. *Happy Lives and the Highest Good: An Essay on Aristotle's Nicomachean Ethics.* Princeton, NJ: Princeton University Press.

Rimmon-Kenan, Shlomith. 1983. *Narrative Fiction: Contemporary Poetics.* London: Methuen.

Rinon, Yoav. 2006. "'Mise an abyme' and Tragic Signification in the *Odyssey*: The Three Songs of Demodocus." *Mnemosyne* 59: 208–25.

Roberts, Deborah H., Francis M. Dunn, and Don Fowler (eds.) 1997. *Classical Closure: Reading the End in Greek and Latin Literature.* Princeton, NJ: Princeton University Press.

Robin, Diana. 1991. *Filelfo in Milan: Writings 1451–1477.* Princeton, NJ: Princeton University Press.

———. 1997. "Women, Space, and Renaissance Discourse." In Gold, Miller, and Platter (eds.) 1997: 165–87.

———. 2007. *Publishing Women: Salons, the Presses, and the Counter-Reformation in Sixteenth-Century Italy.* Chicago: University of Chicago Press.

Robinson, Lillian. 1985. *Monstrous Regiments: The Lady Knight in Sixteenth-Century Epic.* New York: Garland.

Robinson, Lorna. 2013. *Gabriel Marcia Marquez and Ovid: Magical and Monstrous Realities.* Woodbridge, VA: Tamesis Books.

Roche, Thomas P. 1988. "Ariosto's Marfisa: Or Camilla Domesticated." *Modern Language Notes* 103.1: 113–33.

Rodini, Robert. 1996. "Post-Petrarchism and Language(s) of Desire." In Benedetti, Hairston, and Ross (eds.) 1996: 69–77.

Rorty, Amélie O. 1978. "The Place of Contemplation in Aristotle's *Nicomachean Ethics.*" *Mind* 87: 343–58.

———. 1992. *Essays on Aristotle's Poetics.* Princeton, NJ: Princeton University Press.

Rosand, David. 2001. *Myths of Venice: The Figuration of a State.* Chapel Hill: University of North Carolina Press.

Rosand, Ellen. 2007. *Monteverdi's Last Operas: A Venetian Trilogy*. Berkeley: University of California Press.

———. 1992. "L'elegia al femminile: le *Heroides* di Ovidio (e altre heroides)." *Materiali e discussioni per l'analisi dei testi classici* 29: 71–94.

Rose, Gilbert. 1969. "The Unfriendly Phaeacians." *Transactions of the American Philological Association* 100: 387–406.

Rose, Peter. 1992. *Sons of Gods, Children of Earth: Ideology and Literary Form in Ancient Greece*. Ithaca, NY: Cornell University Press.

Rosenberg, Donald. 1981. *Oaten Reeds and Trumpets: Pastoral and Epic in Vergil, Spenser, and Milton*. East Brunswick, NJ: Associated Press.

Rosenmayer, Thomas. 1960. "Virgil and heroism: *Aeneid* 11." *Classical Journal* 55.4: 159–64.

Rosenthal, Margaret. 1992. *The Honest Courtesan: Veronica Franco, Citizen and Writer in Sixteenth-Century Venice*. Chicago: University of Chicago Press.

———. 1993. "Venetian Women Writers and Their Discontents." In Turner (ed.) 1993: 107–33.

Ross, Sarah Gwyneth. 2009. *The Birth of Feminism: Woman as Intellect in Renaissance Italy and England*. Cambridge, MA: Harvard University Press.

Rudd, Niall. 2008. "Ceyx and Alcyone: Ovid, *Metamorphoses* 11.410–748." *Greece and Rome* 55.1: 103–10.

Rundin, John. 2003. "The Epicurean Morality of Vergil's *Bucolics*." *Classical World* 96.2: 159–76.

Russell, Jeffrey B. 1998. *A History of Heaven*. Princeton, NJ: Princeton University Press.

Saccone, Eduardo. 1992. "Figures of Silence in *Orlando Furioso*." *Modern Language Notes* 107.1: 36–45.

———. 1997. "Wood, Garden, *Locus Amoenus* in Ariosto's *Orlando Furioso*." *Modern Language Notes* 112.1: 1–20.

Salvatore, Filippo, and Prudence Allen. 1992. "Lucrezia Marinelli and Woman's Identity in Late Italian Renaissance." *Renaissance and Reformation* 16.4: 5–39.

Sanson, Helena. 2010. "'Orsù, non più signora, [. . .] tornate a segno': Women, Language Games, and Debates in Cinquecento Italy." *Modern Language Review* 105.1: 103–21.

Santacroce, Maria Chiara. 1999–2000. *Aristotele misogino: la difesa delle donne negli scritti di L. Marinella*. Università di studi di Milano. Tesi di Laurea.

Savoretti, Moreno. 2001. *L'Eneide di Virgilio nelle traduzioni cinquecentesche in ottava rima di Aldobrando Cerretani, Lodovico Dolce e Ercole Udine*. Napoli: Loffredo Editore.

Sberlati, Francesco. 1997. "Dalla donna di palazzo alla donna di famiglia: pedagogia e cultura femminile tra Rinascimento e Controriforma." *I Tatti Studies in the Italian Renaissance* 7: 119–74.

Scaglione, Aldo. 1991. *Knights at Court: Courtliness, Chivalry and Courtesy from Ottonian Germany to the Italian Renaissance*. Berkeley: University of California Press.

———. 1997. "Petrarchan Love and the Pleasures of Frustration." *Journal of the History of Ideas* 58.4: 557–72.

Scarpa, Domenico (ed.) 2012. *Dal Rinascimento a oggi*. 3 vols. Torino: Einaudi.

Scarpati, C. 2004. "Le rime spirituali di Vittoria Colonna nel codice vaticano donato a Michelangelo." *Aevum* 78.3: 693–717.

Schachter, Marc D. 2010. "'Quanto concede la Guerra': Epic Masculinity and the Education of Desire in Tasso's *Gerusalemme Liberata*." In Tylus and Milligan (eds.) 2010: 215–41.

Schiesari, Juliana. 1991. "The Domestication of Woman in *Orlando Furioso* 42 and 43, or A Snake Is Being Beaten." *Stanford Italian Review* 10.1: 123–43.

———. 1992. *The Gendering of Melancholia: Feminism, Psychoanalysis, and the Symbolics of Loss in Renaissance Literature*. Ithaca, NY: Cornell University Press.

Schneider, Berndt. 1985. *Das Aeneissupplement des Maffeo Vegio*. Weinheim: Acta Humaniora— VCH Verlagsgesellschaft.

Schutte, Anne Jacobson. 2013. "Society and the Sexes in the Venetian Republic." In Dursteler (ed.) 2013: 372–74.

Schutte, Anne Jacobson, Thomas Kuehn, and Silvana Seidel Menchi (eds.) 2001. *Time, Space, and Women's Lives*. Kirksville, MO: Truman State University Press.

Sears, Olivia Erin. 1996. *Women Poets and War in the Italian Renaissance: Veronica Gambara, Vittoria Colonna, and the Petrarchiste of the 16th Century*. Ph.D. diss., Stanford University.

Seem, Lauren. 1990. "The Limits of Chivalry: Tasso and the End of the *Aeneid*." *Comparative Literature* 42: 116–25.

Segal, Charles. 1966. "*Aeternum per Saecula Nomen:* The Golden Bough and the Tragedy of History: Part II." *Arion* 5.1: 34–72.

———. 1971. "The Song of Iopas in the *Aeneid*." *Hermes* 99.3: 336–49.

———. 1996. "Kleos and Its Ironies." In Shein (ed.) 1996: 201–23.

Segre, Cesare. 1966. *Esperienze ariostesche*. Pisa: Nistri-Lischi.

Seider, Aaron M. 2012. "Competing Commemorations: Apostrophe of the Dead in the *Aeneid*." *American Journal of Philology* 133.2: 241–69.

Serpa, Franco. 1987. *Il punto su Virgilio*. Roma: Laterza.

Setton, Kenneth M. 1991. *Venice, Austria, and the Turks in the Seventeenth Century*. Philadelphia: The American Philosophical Society.

Shapiro, Lisa. 2005. "Some Thoughts on the Place of Women in Early Modern Philosophy." In Alanen and Witt (eds.) 2005: 219–38.

Sharon, James. 2003. *Learned Girls and Male Persuasion: Gender and Reading in Roman Elegy*. Berkeley: University of California Press.

Shein, Seth L. (ed.) 1996. *Reading the Odyssey: Selected Interpretive Essay*. Princeton, NJ: Princeton University Press.

Shemek, Deanna. 1989. "Of Women, Knights, Arms, and Love: The *Querelle des Femmes* in Ariosto's Poem." *Modern Language Notes* 104.1: 68–97.

———. 1998. *Ladies Errant: Wayward Women and Social Order in Early Modern Italy*. Durham, NC: Duke University Press.

Sider, Sandra. 2005. *Handbook to Life in Renaissance Europe*. Oxford: Oxford University Press.

Simon, Elliott M. 2010. "Pico, Paracelsus and Dee: The Magical Measure of Human Perfectibility." In Long (ed.) 2010: 13–41.

Simpson, Alicia. 2009. "Introduction: Niketas Choniates: The Historian." In Simpson and Efthymiadis (eds.) 2009: 13–34.

Simpson, Alicia, and Stephanos Efthymiadis (eds.) 2009. *Niketas Choniates: A Historian and a Writer*. Geneva: La Pomme d'Or.

Sitterson, Joseph. 1992. "Allusive and Elusive Meanings: Reading Ariosto's Vergilian Ending." *Renaissance Quarterly* 45: 1–17.

Sivelli, Sara. 2011. "L'androgino e il simbolo." *Itinera. Rivista di Filosofia e di teoria delle arti*. 1: 76–95.

Smarr, Janet. 2001. "Substituting for Laura: Objects of Desire for Renaissance Women Poets." *Comparative Literature Studies* 38.1: 1–31.

Smith, Rebekah. 1999. "Deception and Sacrifice in *Aeneid* 2.1–249." *American Journal of Philology* 120: 503–23.

Smith Pangle, Lorraine. 2008. *Aristotle and the Philosophy of Friendship*. Cambridge: Cambridge University Press.

Sowards, Jesse K. 1982. "Erasmus and the Education of Women." *Sixteenth Century Journal* 13.4: 77–89.

Sowerby, Robin. 1996. "The Homeric *Versio Latina*." *Illinois Classical Studies* 21: 161–202.

Spence, Jean, Sarah Jane Aiston, and Maureen M. Meikle (eds.) 2010. *Women, Education and Agency*. London and New York: Routledge.

Spence, Sarah. 1999. "*Varium et Mutabile*: Voices of Authority in *Aeneid* 4." In Perkell (ed.) 1999: 80–96.

———(ed.) 2001. *Poets and Critics Read Vergil*. New Haven, CT: Yale University Press.

Spentzou, Efrossini. 2003. *Readers and Writers in Ovid's Heroides: Transgression of Genre and Gender*. Oxford: Oxford University Press.

Sperling, Jutta. 1999. *Convents and the Body Politic in Late Renaissance Venice*. Chicago: University of Chicago Press.

Spini, Giorgio. 1983. *Ricerca dei libertini: La teoria dell'impostura delle religioni del Seicento italiano*. Firenze: La Nuova Italia.

Spongberg, Mary. 2002. *Writing Women's History since the Renaissance*. Basingstoke and New York: Palgrave Macmillan.

Spoth, Friedrich. 1992. *Ovids Heroides als Elegien*. Munich: Beck.

Stadler, Hubert. 1985. "Beobachtungen zu Ovids Erzählung von Ceyx und Alcyone. 'Met.' 11, 410–748." *Philologus* 129.2: 201–12.

Stahl, Hans-Peter. 1993. "The Death of Turnus: Augustan Vergil and the Political Rival." In Raaflaub and Toher (eds.) 1993: 174–211.

Starn, Randolph. 2007. "A Postmodern Renaissance." *Renaissance Quarterly* 60.1: 1–24.

Steegmann, Mary G. 1913. *Bianca Cappello*. London: Constable.

Stephens, Walter. 1995. "Reading Tasso Reading Vergil Reading Homer: An Archaeology of Andromache." *Comparative Literature Studies* 32.2: 296–319.

———. 1999. "Trickster, Textor, Architect, Thief: Craft and Comedy in *Gerusalemme Liberata*." In Finucci (ed.) 1999: 146–78.

Stephenson, Paul. 2009. *Constantine: Roman Emperor, Christian Victor*. New York: Overlook Press.

Stevenson, Jane. 2005. *Women Latin Poets: Language, Gender, and Authority from Antiquity to the Eighteenth Century*. Oxford: Oxford University Press.

Stoppino, Elena. 2012. *Genealogies of Fiction: Women Warriors and the Dynastic Imagination in the Orlando Furioso*. New York: Fordham University Press.

Subialka, Michael. 2011. "Heroic Sainthood: Marinella's Genealogy of the Medici Aristocracy and Saint Catherine's 'Gesti Eroici' as a Rewriting of the Gender of Virtue." In Maggi (ed.) 2011: 163–94.

Suter, Ann (ed.) 2008. *Lament: Studies in the Ancient Mediterranean and Beyond*. Oxford: Oxford University Press.

Suzuki, Mihoko. 1989. *Metamorphoses of Helen: Authority, Difference, and the Epic*. Ithaca, NY: Cornell University Press.

Svensson, Lars-Håkan 2011. "Remembering the Death of Turnus: Spenser's *Faeriae Queene* and the Ending of the *Aeneid*." *Renaissance Quarterly* 64.2: 430–71.

Tarabotti, Arcangela. 2012. *Letters Familiar and Formal by Arcangela Tarabotti*. Ed. Ray Meredith. Toronto: Centre for Reformation and Renaissance Studies.

Tarpley, Webster G. 2009. *Paolo Sarpi, His networks, Venice and the Coming of the Thirty Years' War*. Ph.D. diss., The Catholic University of America.

Tarrant, James. 1982. "Aeneas and the Gates of Sleep." *Classical Philology* 77.1: 51–55.

Tasso, Torquato. 1961. *Gerusalemme liberata*. Ed. A. M. Carini. Milano: Feltrinelli.

———. 1968. *La Gerusalemme liberata*. Milano: Scolastiche Mondadori.

———. 2000. *Jerusalem Delivered*. Ed. and trans. Anthony M. Esolen. Baltimore: Johns Hopkins University Press.

———.2009. *The Liberation of Jerusalem (Gerusalemme Liberata)*. Trans. Max Wickert. Oxford: Oxford University Press.

Taylor, Andrew (ed.) 2014. "The Translations of Renaissance Latin." *Canadian Review of Comparative Literatures* 41.4: 329–53.

Terpening, Ronnie. 1997. *Ludovico Dolce, Renaissance Man of Letters*. Toronto: University of Toronto Press.

Thesleff, H. 1981. "Man and *locus amoenus* in Early Greek poetry." In Kurz, Müller, and Nicolai (eds.) 1981: 31–45.

Thomas, Elizabeth. 1964. "Variations on a Military Theme in Ovid's *Amores*." *Greece & Rome* 11: 11–65.

Thomas, Richard. 1990. "Ideology, Influence, and Future Studies in the *Georgics*." *Vergilius* 36: 64–71.

———. 2001. *Virgil and the Augustan Reception*. Cambridge: Cambridge University Press.

Thorsen, Thea S. (ed.) 2013. *The Cambridge Companion to Latin Love Elegy. Cambridge Companions to literature*. Cambridge: Cambridge University Press.

Tigerstedt, E. N. 1968. "Observations on the Reception of the Aristotelian *Poetics* in the Latin West." *Studies in the Renaissance* 15: 7–24.

Tomalin, Margaret. 1982. *The Fortunes of the Warrior Heroine in Italian Literature*. Ravenna: Longo.

Torelli, Barbara. 2006. *Partenia: A Pastoral Play*. Ed. Lisa Sampson. Chicago: University of Chicago Press.

Traina, Alfonso (ed.) 1980a. *Poeti latini (e neolatini)*. Vol. 1. Bologna: Patron.

———. 1980b. "L'aiuola che ci fa tanto feroci: per la storia di un topos." In Traina (ed.) 1980: 305–35.

Turner, James G. (ed.) 1993. *Sexuality and Gender in Early Modern Europe.* Cambridge: Cambridge University Press.

Tylus, Jane, and Gerry Milligan (eds.) 2010. *The Poetics of Masculinity in Early Modern Italy and Spain.* Toronto: Centre for Reformation and Renaissance Studies.

Van Kessel, Elsje. 2010. "Staging Bianca Cappello: Painting and Theatricality in Sixteenth-Century Venice." *Art History* 33: 278–91.

Vegio, Maffeo. 2004. *Short Epics.* Ed. and trans. by Michael C. J. Putnam with James Hankins. Cambridge, MA: Harvard University Press.

Verducci, Florence. 1985. *Ovid's Toyshop of the Heart: Epistulae Heroidum.* Princeton, NJ: Princeton University Press.

Vergilius Maro, Publius. 1540. *I sei primi libri del Eneide di Virgilio, tradotti à piu illustre et honorate donne.* Ed. and trans. Ludovico Dolce. Venezia: Comin da Trino.

Veyne, Paul. 1988. *Roman Erotic Elegy: Love, Poetry and the West.* Chicago: University of Chicago Press.

Vice, Sue. 1997. *Introducing Bakhtin.* New York: Palgrave.

Viggiano, Alfredo. 2013. "Politics and Constitution." In Dursteler (ed.) 2013: 47–85.

Viparelli, Valeria. 2008. "Camilla: A Queen Undefeated, Even in Death." *Vergilius* 54: 9–23.

Virgil. 1981. *The Aeneid. Virgil.* Trans. Robert Fitzgerald. New York: Random House.

Virgil. *Georgics.* Trans. A. S. Kline. <http://www.poetryintranslation.com/PITBR/Latin/Virgilhome .htm>

Virgilio. 1990. *Eneide.* 6 Vols. Ed. E. Paratore and trans. L. Canali. Milano: Fondazione Lorenzo Valla, Arnoldo Mondadori Editore (II edizione).

Vitale, Maurizio. 1978. *La Questione della lingua.* Palermo: Palumbo.

Vivaldi, Vincenzo. 1983. *Sulle fonti della Gerusalemme Liberata.* Catanzaro: Officina Tipografica Caliò.

Von Albrecht, Michael.1999. *Roman Epic: An Interpretative Introduction.* Leiden: Brill.

Wallace-Hadrill, Andrew. 1982. "The Golden Age and Sin in Augustan Ideology." *Past and Present* 95: 19–36.

Warden, J. 2000. "*Ripae Ulterioris Amore*: Structure and Desire in *Aeneid* 6." *Classical Journal* 95: 349–61.

Warner, Christopher J. 2005. *The Augustinian Epic, Petrarch to Milton.* Ann Arbor: University of Michigan Press.

Warren, Rosanna. 2001. "The End of the *Aeneid.*" In Spence (ed.) 2001: 105–17.

Waswo, Richard. 1987. *Language and Meaning in the Renaissance.* Princeton, NJ: Princeton University Press.

Watkins, John. 1995. *The Specter of Dido: Spenser and Virgilian Epic.* New Haven, CT: Yale University Press.

Weaver, Elissa. 2006. *Arcangela Tarabotti: A Literary Nun in Baroque Venice.* Longo.

Weinberg, Bernard. 1961. *A History of Literary Criticism in the Italian Renaissance.* 2 vols. Chicago: University of Chicago Press.

West, G. S. 1985. "Chloreus and Camilla." *Vergilius* 31: 22–29.

Westwater, Lynn Lara. 2003. *The Disquieting Voice: Women's Writing and Antifeminism in Seventeenth-Century Venice*. Ph.D. diss., University of Chicago.

———. 2008. "Literary Culture and Women Writers in Seventeenth-Century Venice." In Bellavitis et al. (eds.) 2008: 1–23.

White, Paul. 2015. "Poetic Genres—*Heroides*." *Brill's Encyclopaedia of the Neo-Latin World*. Ed. Craig Kallendorf. Brill Online. <http://static.ribo.brill.semcs.net/entries/encyclopaedia-of-the-neo-latin-world/poetic-genres-heroides-B9789004271029_0108>

Whitman, Jon (ed.) 2015. *Romance and History: Imagining Time from the Medieval to the Early Modern Period*. Cambridge: Cambridge University Press.

Whittaker, Helen. 1999. "The Status of Arete in the Phaeacian Episode of the *Odyssey*." *Symbolae Osloenses* 74.1: 140–50.

Wild, Stefan. 2012. "Modern Discourses of Superiority: Muslims and Christians in Contact." In Esmail and Filali-Ansary (eds.) 2012: 75–93.

Williams, Gordon. 1993. *Techniques and Ideas in the Aeneid*. New Haven, CT: Yale University Press.

Williams, Raymond. 1973. *The Country and the City*. Oxford: Oxford University Press.

Wilson-Okamura, David S. 2010. *Virgil in the Renaissance*. Cambridge: Cambridge University Press.

Visser, Edzard (Basle). 2017. "Cassiphone." In *Brill's New Pauly: Encyclopedia for the Ancient World*. Ed. Hubert Cancik and Helmuth Schneider. <http://dx.doi.org/10.1163/1574-9347_bnp_e610200> (accessed on October 23, 2017).

Wlosok, Antonie. 1990. "Vergil in der neueren Forschung." In Wlosock, Heck, and Schmidt (eds.) 1990: 279–300.

Wlosock, Antonie, Eberhard Heck and Ernst A. Schmidt (eds.) 1990. *Res humanae—res divinae: Kleine Schriften*. Heidelberg: Carl Winter Universitätsverlag.

Wofford, Susan L. 1992. *The Choice of Achilles: The Ideology of Figure in the Epic*. Stanford: Stanford University Press.

———. 1999. "Epics and the Politics of the Original Tale: Vergil, Ovid, Spenser, and Native America Aetiology." In Beissinger, Tylus, and Wofford (eds.) 1999: 239–69.

Wollock, J. 2011. *Rethinking Chivalry and Courtly Love*. Santa Barbara, CA: Praeger.

Wood, Christopher S. 2012. "Reception and the Classics." In Brockliss, Chaudhuri, Haimson Lushkov, and Wasdin (eds.) 2012: 163–74.

Woodward, Harrison William. 1904. *Desiderius Erasmus, Concerning the Aim and Method of Education*. Cambridge: Cambridge University Press.

Wright, J. R. G. 1999. "Virgil's Pastoral Program." In Hardie (ed.) 1999: 1.116–72.

Wyke, Maria. 1995. "Taking the Woman's Part: Engendering Roman Love Elegy." In Boyle (ed.) 1995: 110–28.

Yarnall, Judith. 1994. *Transformations of Circe: The History of an Enchantress*. Urbana: University of Illinois Press.

Yates, Cristopher. 2010. "Stations of the Self: Aesthetics and Ascetics in Foucault's Conversion Narrative." *Foucault Studies* 8: 78–99.

Zabughin, Vladimiro. 1923. *Virgilio nel Rinascimento italiano da Dante a Torquato Tasso*. Vols. I and II. Bologna: Zanichelli.

Zanardi, Stefania. 2011. "La pedagogia dell'umanesimo nell'interpretazione di Eugenio Garin." In Malusa and Rossi Cassottana (eds.) 2011: 482–91.

Zancan, Marina (ed.) 1983. *Nel cerchio della luna: figure di donna in alcuni testi del XVI secolo.* Venezia: Marsilio editore.

Zanette, Emilio. 1953. "Bianca Cappello e la sua poetessa." *Nuova antologia* 68: 455–68.

Zanini-Cordi, Irene. 2007. "The seduction of Ariosto's Olimpia: Mythopoetic Rescue of an Abandoned Woman." *Pacific Coast Philology* 42.1: 37–53.

———. 2008. *Donne sciolte: abbandono e identità femminile nella letteratura italiana.* Ravenna: Angelo Longo editore.

Zanker, Graham. 1994. *The Heart of Achilles: Characterization and Personal Ethics in the Iliad.* Ann Arbor: University of Michigan Press.

Zarri, Gabriella. 2001. "The Third Status." In Schutte, Kuehn, and Seidel Menchi (eds.) 2001: 181–99.

Zatti, Sergio. 1983. *L'uniforme cristiano e il multiforme pagano: saggio sulla "Gerusalemme Liberata."* Milano: Saggiatore.

Zatti, Sergio. 1996. *L'ombra del Tasso: epica e romanzo nel Cinquecento.* Milano: Bruno Mondadori.

———. 2000. *Il modo epico.* Roma-Bari: Laterza.

———. 2006. *The Quest for Epic.* Toronto: University of Toronto Press.

Zetzel, James. 1989. "*Romane Memento:* Justice and Judgment in *Aeneid* 6." *Transactions of the American Philological Association* 119: 263–84.

Zika, Charles. 2002. "Images of Circe and Discourses of Witchcraft, 1480–1580." *Zeitenblicke* 1.1: 1–33.

———. 2007. *The Appearance of Witchcraft: Print and Visual Culture in Sixteenth-Century Europe.* London and New York: Routledge.

Zimmermann, Jens. 2012. *Humanism and Religion: A Call for the Renewal of Western Culture.* Oxford: Oxford University Press.

Zimmermann, Margarete. 1994. "Die Italianische 'Querelle des Femmes': Feministische Traktate von Moderata Fonte und Lucrezia Marinella." *Trierer Beiträge* 8: 5–61.

Zorzi, Niccolò. 2004/2005. "Niceta Coniata fonte dell'*Enrico, ovvero Bizanzio acquistato* (1635)." *Incontri Triestini di Filologia Classica* 4: 415–28.

INDEX

Achilles, 49, 54, 75, 91, 102n16, 154, 155, 213, 214, 237, 242; Agamemnon and, 154n7; Enrico and, 139; Hector and, 53n58; insight for, 156

Adriana, 94, 229, 230, 233–34

Aeneas, 8, 36, 49n36, 54n64, 101, 113, 119, 121, 124, 134, 153, 156, 177, 201–2, 217, 219, 237; behavior of, 9, 50, 51, 59; Dido and, 58, 60, 61, 109, 110, 111, 125, 168, 169n33, 170, 232; lamentation of, 11; Lausus and, 217–18; *pietas* of, 59, 110; Ruggiero and, 57, 90; Sibyl and, 24; storm and, 115n12; Turnus duel with, 35, 45, 45n32, 48, 51, 52, 52n51, 53, 53n56, 54, 55, 61, 77, 88n60

Aeneid (Virgil), 11, 23–24, 25, 28, 35, 74, 75, 77, 79, 80, 83, 85, 98, 100, 107, 108, 119, 120, 123, 124, 153, 156, 157, 168, 169, 171, 175, 195, 197, 213, 218, 234; Aeneas behavior in, 9, 50, 51, 59; Classical learning and, 8–10, 232; ending of, 36, 48, 50, 52, 53, 54, 54n64, 58, 73, 89, 94; influence of, 109, 110; Italian paraphrases of, 60; pastoral values and, 219; pessimism of, 29, 201, 202; reading of, 27, 59, 101; *Somnium* and, 201; storm in, 113, 114

Africa (Petrarch), 26, 197

Agamemnon, Achilles and, 154, 154n7

Alcina, 28, 156, 177, 179, 179n56, 235; Ruggiero and, 127n28, 178, 232

Alcyone, 23, 102, 112n7, 116, 119, 126–27, 131, 132; allusions to, 112–13; Clelia and, 113, 123

Alessio III, 136, 141n49

Alexius, 98, 237

Altamoro, 63, 64, 111n6, 237, 239

Altea, 102n16, 171, 172, 174, 173n39, 190

amazons, 34, 74, 84, 85, 87, 89, 90, 93, 94, 133, 165, 169, 233; death of, 80–81, 85; role of, 27, 74

Amores (Ovid), 104

Anchises, 11, 59, 201, 202, 203, 218

Andromache, 111n6, 136, 139, 232, 242; Hector and, 135, 137, 138

Angelica, 62, 100, 100n10, 177n48, 180, 232; Orlando and, 40, 40n23

Antigone, 144n55, 145

Apollonius of Rhodes, 174, 224n8

Aquinas, Thomas, 191n22, 192

Areta, 11, 27, 28, 99, 101, 102, 107, 141n49, 145, 154, 236, 242; Clelia and, 105, 142, 146, 147, 149, 150, 234; Corradino and, 135–44, 146

Argonautica (Apollonius of Rhodes), 174, 224n8

Ariosto, Ludovico, 26, 27, 28, 35, 41, 42, 48, 53, 65, 88, 105, 156, 177, 178, 179, 180, 203, 227, 233; categories of women and, 93, 93n69; Fonte and, 44, 71; influence of, 99, 101, 184; treatment of women by, 100; Virgil and, 50

Aristotle, 13, 13n42, 15, 28, 59n79, 90, 91n63, 92, 99n7, 101n15, 191n22, 211; cultural bias of, 7, 7n23; friendship and, 148, 149; influence of, 102, 147, 232, 234; *katamenia* and, 92n66; love and, 148; moral temperance and, 91; Ovid versus, 101–7

Armida, 28, 177, 180, 182, 183n65, 199; Rinaldo and, 181, 183, 183n66

Ars Amatoria (Ovid), 104

CLASSICAL MEMORIES/MODERN IDENTITIES
Paul Allen Miller and Richard H. Armstrong, Series Editors

Classical antiquity has bequeathed a body of values and a "cultural koine" that later Western cultures have appropriated and adapted as their own. However, the transmission of ancient culture was and remains a malleable and contested process. This series explores how the classical world has been variously interpreted, transformed, and appropriated to forge a usable past and a livable present. Books published in this series detail both the positive and negative aspects of classical reception and take an expansive view of the topic. Thus it includes works that examine the function of translations, adaptations, invocations, and classical scholarship in personal, cultural, national, sexual, and racial formations.

Made in the
USA
Middletown, DE

74815532R00175